Wm. A. Frosch

Drugs $\mathbf{I}$

Society and Drugs

A publication of the

INSTITUTE FOR THE STUDY OF HUMAN PROBLEMS

Stanford University

NEVITT SANFORD, Director

Drugs I

Social and Cultural Observations

Richard H. Blum & Associates

Jossey-Bass Inc., Publishers
615 Montgomery Street • San Francisco • 1970

Society and Drugs

SOCIETY AND DRUGS
Drugs I: Social and Cultural Observations

by Richard H. Blum and Associates

Copyright © 1969 by Jossey-Bass, Inc., Publishers

Copyright under Pan American and
Universal Copyright Conventions

Jossey-Bass, Inc., Publishers
615 Montgomery Street
San Francisco, California 94111

Library of Congress Catalog Card Number 73-75936

Standard Book Number SBN 87589-033-4

Manufactured in the United States of America
Printed by York Composition Company, Inc., York, Pennsylvania
Bound by Chas. H. Bohn & Co., Inc., New York
Jacket design by Willi Baum, San Francisco

FIRST EDITION

First printing: April 1969
Second printing: January 1970

Code 6903

PUBLISHED JOINTLY IN

THE JOSSEY-BASS BEHAVIORAL SCIENCE SERIES

General Editors

WILLIAM E. HENRY, *University of Chicago*

NEVITT SANFORD, *Wright Institute, Berkeley*

THE JOSSEY-BASS SERIES IN HIGHER EDUCATION

General Editors

JOSEPH AXELROD, *San Francisco State College*

MERVIN B. FREEDMAN, *San Francisco State College
and Wright Institute, Berkeley*

Preface

*D*rugs I, *Society and Drugs* and Drugs II, *Students and Drugs* provide information on the use of psychoactive drugs, including marijuana, LSD, heroin, alcohol, and the like. The work presented here, we hope, will help the reader to develop a perspective about these drugs, the conditions associated with their use, the kind of people most likely to use them, some of the results of their use, and the milieu—including attitudes, anxieties, and ideologies—in which drug use, especially social and personal drug use, is embedded. The need for additional information about drugs is apparent, for the United States and other Western nations are experiencing, especially among young people, dramatic changes in drug use habits. The information we have developed is by no means complete, nor does it assure an understanding of the rapidly changing drug scene; yet we trust that our observations—which embrace the history of drug use, cross-cultural comparisons, normal, hippie, and high school and college student use, along with data on drug effects, drug associations with crime, religion, educational status, and the like—will be useful.

Society and Drugs and *Students and Drugs* together represent an important portion of the investigations conducted by our psycho-pharmacology group at Stanford University and by our cooperating colleagues in other institutions. These drug endeavors began in 1960 with a cultural case study in Greece, reported in Drugs I, which was part of a larger program of investigation and innovation in public health and cultural medicine (see *Health and Healing in Rural Greece,* 1964). Beginning in 1962, our interests extended to a social-epidemio-logical study of LSD use and users (see *Utopiates,* 1964), went on to include an evaluation of treatment methods and problems for one group of drug disorders (see *Alcoholism: Modern Psychological Approaches to Treatment,* 1967), and embraced an appraisal of the re-lationship between drug use and crime, suicides, and accidents (see President's Commission on Law Enforcement and the Administration of Justice, *Task Force Report: Narcotics and Drug Abuse,* 1967, and *Task Force Report: Drunkenness,* 1967). The present two volumes represent further inquiries. These attend primarily to the social use of psychoactive drugs, the correlates, background, and short-term conse-quence of that use, and the cultural, attitudinal, and interpersonal milieu in which sentiments and conduct focused on drugs arise and are expressed.

In all of these endeavors we have been seeking to identify fac-tors associated with changing patterns of drug use, ones associated with observed constancies or similarities in use, outcomes, or associated beliefs, and to place the phenomena of individual drug use and re-actions into a broad perspective. Thus, over the years, we have sought to specify the variety and patterns of drug use by individuals, groups, or populations; to compare persons in similar settings; to compare common cultures; to examine similarities and differences among cul-tures in their drug use; and to inspect historical patterns associated with drug diffusion, acceptance, and social reactions. We have sought to consider treatment in something of the same fashion as we did in our *Alcoholism* book—that is, comparatively, in terms of the efficacy of methods, and contextually, by examining social, moral, and admin-istrative factors as well as clinical ones that affect treatment operation and outcomes. Throughout we have tried to maintain contact with individual cases and to link them—not forgetting the unique nature of the person, drug, group, or culture—to the larger context.

Even though the total number of individuals interviewed, observed, or completing questionnaires for the data reported here runs to about 20,000, and even though we have studied about 250 cultures as well as a variety of nations, historical events, and special groups, we are still in the frustrating position of having studied samples at moments in time rather than total populations continuously over time. Given such conditions, we must be cautious in generalizing, for our Western college students are not Midwestern rural ones, our hippies are in San Francisco and not in Boston, our cultural case study is of rural Greeks, not of Malayans or of people from Timbuktu, and our follow-up studies measure discrete rather than continuous events. Even so, we do generalize and imagine the reader will do the same, for in the absence of better data, one has to make do with the data at hand. As we trust that what we offer will open the door to greater understanding, so also do we trust that others will come through that open door with more and better information in the future.

Our study was made possible by grants from the National Institute of Mental Health (MH-12286) and was conducted in cooperation with the Pharmacology Service Center and the Center for Drug Abuse of NIMH. Coordinators from the Pharmacology Service Center were Mitchell Balter, Ph.D., and Jerome Levine, M.D., and from the Center of Drug Abuse, Roger Meyer, M.D. The coordinated study was directed by Richard Blum. In addition to support by NIMH, the project received on-campus financial support from the Urban Life Institute of the University of San Francisco, and the Office of the Dean of Humanities and Sciences at Stanford University.

RICHARD H. BLUM

Stanford, California
January 1969

Contents

Contents

The Associates

Anna Amera, B.A.; Ph.D. candidate in sociology, Fordham University

Mary Lou Funkhouser Balbaky, M.A.; graduate student in anthropology, Brandeis University

Eva M. Blum, Ph.D.; co-director, Psychopharmacology Project, Institute for the Study of Human Problems, Stanford University

Richard H. Blum, Ph.D.; director, Psychopharmacology Project, Institute for the Study of Human Problems, Stanford University

Lauraine Braunstein, M.A.; research assistant, Institute for the Study of Human Problems, Stanford University

Marguerite Crouse, M.A.; Community Development Program, City of Tucson

Joel Fort, M.D.; lecturer, School of Social Welfare, University of California, Berkeley; co-director, National Sex and Drug Forum, San Francisco

David Hoel, Ph.D.; Westinghouse Research Laboratory, Pittsburgh

Sophie Kallifatidou, B.S.; social worker, Athens, Greece

Alma Stone, M.S.; psychiatric social worker in private practice, Palo Alto, California

John H. Weakland, cultural anthropologist, Mental Research Institute, Palo Alto, California

Drugs **I**

Society and Drugs

A Background History of Drugs

Richard H. Blum

I

Our purpose is to set forth the major events which constitute the accessible history of those mind-altering drugs popularly used prior to our own time. We hope that such a history—one emphasizing social features of use whenever possible—will help create a perspective from which to view the contemporary phenomenon in our own society of widespread and expanding use of mind-altering drugs, which is often coupled with intense interest and emotion. In setting out to conduct this historical review, we expected to find certain principles operating —ones which would help us to understand how drugs come to be adopted for use, in what ways, and by what groups. We also looked for regularities from society to society or era to era in means or circumstances under which drug use would be reduced or constraints would be placed upon particular kinds of conduct emerging as drug effects. Concern with prohibitions leads to an assessment of social reactions to drugs and the judgments placed on drug effects and styles of drug use. In today's parlance this becomes a matter of drug abuse or of a society's having a drug problem.

In our purposes and expectations we have been disappointed—perhaps we should even say we have failed. Yet, in each instance we have also been pleased by small achievements which have been at least way stations on the road to a perspective. Our failures rest upon the limitations in ourselves and our enterprise. We shall be explicit about those of which we are aware.

The greatest limitation is the absence of artifacts, seeds, documents, and observations which constitute the subject matter of history or prehistory itself. Secondarily, with a few notable exceptions, there is an absence of historical studies as such. Up until the nineteenth century, not a great deal had been said about psychoactive drugs, either by those who had tried them or by those who had observed others using them. As for epidemiology, clinical reports, or social-problem analyses, these were not topics for even the most perceptive writers until after the Reformation and the subsequent advance in science had produced a social awareness which—with industrialization—gave rise to public-health endeavors (Dubos, 1959). Early medicine and pharmacology are exceptions to this rule of general disinterest, for the healers have long had an interest in drugs and their effects. In the first century A.D., Dioscorides, whose text was the leading one in pharmacology for sixteen centuries, wrote of the poppy both as a medication (". . . a pain easer, a sleep causer, a digester, helping coughes and coelicacall affections") and as a danger (". . . being drank too much ithorts, making men lethargicall and it kills"). But this only tells us that the poppy was employed in folk medicine—a popular utilization, to be sure; it does not tell us how widely the poppy was used or how many of which groups of patients were most likely to succumb to effects "lethargicall" or killing.

What are scarce data in the written literature are reduced to inference in prehistory. We know that early Anatolian beakers were constructed with a sieve at the bottom and straw-like tubes outside and that a more sophisticated version of a similar pot, seen in early dynastic Egyptian paintings, used real straws and a separate strainer. From these artifacts is deduced the presence of a yeasty, high-in-protein beer. When it was first introduced is unknown—possibly around the beginning of agricultural settlements qua villages, such as Beidha, Jarmo, Catal Hüyük, and similar centers—which would give dates within 7000 B.C. Some archaeological evidence to support such an early date for beer has been found (Mellaart, 1967) and the circumstances of life were such that these people could easily learn brewing.

Paleoethnobotanists (Helbaek, 1961) have found berry stones and seeds from a 2000 B.C. Alpine site—wine-making refuse probably, but some say human excrement instead. And when a cannabis seed is found in an ancient place, is it proof of hemp, bird feeding, ancient hashish, or nothing at all? Even eyes of observers disagree; what Kritikos and Papadaki (1963) describe as a poppy on a Minoan vase that proves the ritual use of opium, another may see as a pomegranate dispropor-tionately rendered.

Aside from the difficulties imposed by limited written sources and archaeological finds and by disputes over their interpretation (What was Homer's "nepenthe" after all?), this review suffers from a limited access to existing materials. In most instances, we have not in-spected primary sources, nor have we covered all the secondary sources, since we have been limited linguistically to French, English, German, and Greek; shortage of time has also restricted us to the most readily available sources. Too, in the interests of space and emphasis, we have been forced to be gross even when refinement was possible. For example, a great deal of work has been done on the recent history of one drug in one region: peyote diffusion among American Indians. Aberle (1966), La Barre (1964), and Slotkin (1956) have produced detailed studies but of necessity our reference to their important find-ings is brief.

A further limitation is not of sampling, as above, but of logic. We have sought sequences, patterns, unifying principles, chronologies, and geographies with the hope of making sense out of drug history, not only for its own sake but because we cannot yet make sense out of what we see in our own society's changing drug patterns. We wanted yesterday to inform us about the meaning of today. As a consequence, we have filled in bottomless pits in time, made parallels out of per-pendiculars, discounted incongruity, and elevated rare cases to exem-plary roles. No one intends to be illogical but, considering our purpose and limited data, we cannot but suspect ourselves of this fault for the tendency is to seek, out of understanding, an aesthetic structure, and such structures, while reducing uncertainty, do not always harmonize with the bits and pieces that are the data of the senses.

ASSUMPTIONS AND QUESTIONS

As one inspects the record of events comprising the introduc-tion, adoption, and/or resistance to psychoactive substances, certain features of man and his social and natural environments must be kept

in mind. In the first place, one assumes there will be no initiation into
any drug use until that substance is physically available. Drug availability is one key to use and that in turn leads to inquiries about agriculture, commerce, travel, and manufacture (for example, distillation).
That assumption, although generally correct, might lead one to ignore
magical substances whose pharmaceutical nature is inconsequential
(as long as it is inert) but whose symbolic presence is what matters.
An example is the placebo, which is found in the past as well as in
the present.

It is incorrect to assume that all inefficacious medication, as
judged by modern standards of pharmaceutical potency and physiological effect, was employed magically. Much in ancient medicine thought
to have healing properties because evaluative means were inadequate is
now known to be ineffective. In the ancient Middle East, for example,
opium faced stiff competition from such remedies as eunuch's fat,
virgin's urine, burnt frog, and crocodile dung. The Egyptians and some
peoples in the Fertile Crescent did try to determine dosage and toxicity by experimenting on slaves and prisoners (Thorwald, 1963) but,
as late as the sixteenth century in Europe, the "doctrine of signatures"
held sway. Accordingly, a plant with heart-shaped leaves was good for
heart trouble, one with kidney-shaped pods helped kidneys, and the
mandrake root, shaped like a whole man, was deemed a panacea
(Dawson, 1929; Gordon, 1949; Grenfel and Hunt, 1899; Haggard,
1929; LaWall, 1927). Modern America is, of course, usually considered advanced over such primitive notions, unless one takes into
account the use of tons of unproven home remedies and proprietary
over-the-counter nostrums each year. Many will remember the drug
industry's outcry against recent Food and Drug Administration proposals that drug efficacy be demonstrated scientifically before a product
be allowed on the market. They may also recall the rapid acceptance
by hippies in 1967 of banana peel as a euphoriant or their use of
other inert products (lactose disguised as LSD, for example), even
though more potent materials such as LSD and marijuana were available.

Once a substance is available, there must be an opportunity to
notice it and to ingest it and, for any kind of learning or repeated
dosage, to be able to identify it reliably. Identification leads to questions about environmental discriminations, as in folk medicine and
pharmacognosy, to publicity about substances which teaches potential

users about availability, identification, and techniques for administration, and to an analysis of the determinants of individual ingestion behavior. The assumption of identification and willful ingestion is again generally correct, but not comprehensive; it ignores use occurring without awareness or intent. An example of this probably occurred in early man's discovery of accidentally fermented products and in the fortuitous sniffing or tasting of active substances, such as may have happened with the Scythians and cannabis smoke, if Herodotus may be so interpreted, or as occurred—painfully—in the ergotism of St. Anthony's fire, or as happened in Basle in our century when Dr. Hoffman in casual tasting discovered the effects of LSD-25. Attention to ingestion—whether eating or sniffing—focuses on how ordinary behavior becomes a vehicle for drug administration; it excludes extraordinary behavior which requires that a technique be learned. Here one refers to learning how to smoke—a momentous development in the epidemiology of drug use—or how to inject—also an important event with widespread repercussions. Yet the assumption of intake of any kind—possibly even of absorption (Mexican peasants rub marijuana on their sore joints)—ignores noningestive use. Modern patients have been known to wear prescriptions as amulets (Blum, 1960). Psychoactive mandrake roots were handed down by generations as household ikons from Iceland to Egypt (Thompson, 1934); Great Plains Indians hung mescal beans about their necks as fetishes and Zuni priests applied peyote buttons to their eyes to bring rain (La Barre, 1964). Coca leaves were burned as sacrificial offerings by the Incas in pre-Columbian times (de Cieza, 1959) and ceremonial rites with cannabis or tobacco—without ingestion—occurred in Africa (Laufer, Hambly, and Linton, 1930). Today, in San Francisco, one may see hippies wearing marijuana in their lapels or LSD cultists offering that drug as a sacrament.

Repeated ingestion and conduct instrumental to that ingestion lead most observers to speak of motives and purposes of such behavior. These are inferences by the observer even if the observer himself is also the doer. These are the common explanations given by men to account for what they do and, as such—no matter how suspicious one may be of either self-awareness or motivation theory—should not be ignored. Anyone interested in drug taking is soon confronted with human intentions as well as with these aims redefined as effects. Thus, one finds over the centuries men seeking—and drugs offering—health, relief of pain, security, mystical revelations, eternal life, the approval of the gods, relaxation, joy, sexuality, restraint, blunting of the senses, escape, ecstasy, stimulation, freedom from fatigue, sleep, fertility, the approval of others, clarity of thought, emotional intensity, self-understanding, self-improvement, power, wealth, degradation, a life philosophy, exploitation of others, enjoyment of others, value enhancement, and one's own or another's death. Drugs have been employed as tools for achieving perhaps an endless catalogue of motives. One suspects that the statement of intentions is at least an expression of the view of any one man, or of men in any era, of what man is and ought to be and, teleologically, why he busies himself as he does. The catalogue also suggests that what men say they seek with drugs is also what they say they seek without them.

To attend to motives must not lead the observer to ignore either the uses or consequences of drugs which can hardly be attributed to intentions. Jellinek (1960), for example, describes the syndrome of delta alcoholism as a surprise consequence of drinking over a long period of time even if no apparent psychological factors—such as escape or anxiety reduction—are present. The French child who drinks wine regularly from age four or five on because his parents believe water unsafe may discover when he grows up—after the fifteen-or-so years necessary for "incubation" of alcoholism—that he is an alcoholic. Iatrogenic morphine dependency can be similar. A patient is given that drug to relieve pain or he may be given it or a sedative or a strong tranquilizer without choice or the knowledge of what it is—and only when he stops his use does he discover his discomfort. He may also discover, as Lindesmith (1965) once suggested, that others instruct him in the fact that he is now an addict. The history of the discovery of opiate dependency itself reveals how frail the link between intentions and outcome when outcomes themselves are unknown. It was not until the 1700's that we have reports of withdrawal phenomena (Sonnedecker, 1958)' and not until the nineteenth century that physicians were aware of opium's potential for producing physical dependency. Consequently, in a motivational analysis, care must be taken not to confuse specific drug effects with what the user intended, provided he had any effect-related intentions at all. In this regard, one curious but little noted feature is the frequency with which initial ill effects, quite specific to the drug, do not discourage continued experimentation. The first experience with tobacco, alcohol, opiates, peyote, and LSD is often unpleasant, producing nausea or dysphoria or—as is often the case in marijuana smoking—nothing at all. Apparently, specific drug effects may play but a small part, at least initially, in the establishment of patterns of use. This paradox is of interest to the pharmacologist as much as to the epidemiological historian.

In a different vein, Aberle (1966) describes how motives can multiply once drug use begins. Among Navajos the simple reason of curing an ailment accounts for most Indians' initial use of peyote. Afterwards, when the investiture in the cult has taken place, peyote becomes, as Aberle says, "polyvalent": ". . . once people have entered the cult . . . its meaning becomes much more differentiated for them, and its appeals diverse (p. 187)." In such circumstances, the appeals of the cult and of the drug are not easily distinguished. But a similar and more specific drug finding is reported by Horn (1967) with regard to cigarette smoking. Those tobacco smokers who report several positive satisfactions from smoking find it harder to give up than those with only one. We (Blum and Associates, 1964) have found a like pattern in our studies of users of LSD-25; those who experimented and stopped reported fewer different satisfactions from the drug than those who continued. Whether continuing private or social use of drugs is interpreted as involvement, learning, multiple gratification, or multiple rationalization, the observer needs to consider the import of multiple motivations as a critical feature for such use. If this be so, the historian will wish to ask how much opportunity a given culture provides for variety in individual drug use. The more restraint and the greater the sanctions limiting time and place and behavior, the more likely that variety in gratification will be restricted, and neither widespread secular use nor individual drug dependency and commitment will emerge. This expectation is not new. We (Blum and Associates) have seen the phenomenon in comparing institutional (externally controlled) use of LSD-25 with noninstitutional (private, social) use. The same phenomenon seems to be apparent when one compares medical controls on morphine and relative infrequence of emerging dependency with the uncontrolled use characteristic of informal slum initiation into taking heroin. This argument, of course, is restricted, since individuals who engage in acceptable institutional practices are already likely to be "adjusted," and societies capable of massively ordering behavior in institutionalized ways are already nonsecular and presumably without serious problems of deviancy. Child, Bacon, and Barry (1965) have shown this fact nicely in their cross-cultural alcohol studies; where drinking is customary or integrated—a matter of acceptable institutional use—there are no problems with drunkenness, no matter how much drinking or drunkenness occurs, for it is approved and part of that larger life pattern which is deemed acceptable.

In considering motives, we must keep two other things in mind, neither of them derived from historical studies. One is the probability of a kind of simplicity in fact, as proposed by Cofer and Appley (1964), in which the underlying psychophysiology is viewed as an anticipation-invigoration mechanism that not only becomes shaped or channeled by experiences but is accompanied by some selective sensitization (sensitization-arousal) which is discriminating of environmental events. (See also Pribram's [1967] new neurology of emotion.) Thus, a catalogue of motives is not necessary to account for behavior. Learning does occur, shifts and channeling do take place; as a result, that which was diffuse becomes specific, and intentions do play a part in enhancing, invigorating, or driving action once there are sensitivity and arousal. The other feature is that individual behavior in reference to drugs need not be consistent, especially in regard to the determinants operating at various stages in drug use or in what sociologists might call a "career." The presence of esteemed individuals offering a marijuana cigarette may be sufficient, in deferential or subordinate persons, to trigger experimental use. But continual use may be derived from a chain of habit arising from that social group's repetitive behavior, and specific intentions come into play when the person learns what the drug does for him, such as relieving his tension. The same shift in determinants along the chain from the point of initiation to continued use and even, perhaps, to augmented use and dependency—or to use termination—is observed with many different drugs and persons.

This contemporary observation leads one in a historical inquiry to focus on the opportunities within a given society or era for persons to alter the circumstances of their drug taking and to change the amounts of dosage or kinds of drugs, as well as the means and frequency of administration. Rephrased, the question can be one of individual freedom of access to drugs and differing social environments; in turn, these include the opportunities for social mobility, for travel, for exposure to knowledge about individuals with different backgrounds and outlooks, for escape from institutional restraints—including those inculcated as beliefs or knowledge—and, perhaps, for the expression of individuality as such.

As social complexity increases (whether defined in terms of social organization, stratification, and the diffusion of authority within a society or as a sense of awareness of differences and complexity that comes with cultural diffusion, travel, and knowledge per se), one expects variation will increase in individual behavior—even if within sanctioned roles. One also expects on intellectual as well as technological grounds that more products will become available—including drugs. Consequently, one expects the record of events to show that kinds of drug use within a society or era vary with that society's complexity. As a corollary, the more complex the society, the more one anticipates internal variety in drug use and in views about drug use. It is at this stage, when heterogeneity is introduced, that ideological as well as political and social conflict is expected; if so, such conflict might include conflicting evaluations of drug behavior. When social heterogeneity is accompanied by increasing individuality as well—that is, by variability in conduct not prescribed by traditional institutional roles— one would anticipate not only disputes about *what* is desirable but also increasing disagreement about *who* is desirable. Perhaps, under these circumstances, the notion of drug abuse in its pejorative sense will be found—that is, bad people doing bad things. On the other hand, the concern with abuse simply as an observation of specific ill effects of pharmaceuticals—pain, mental disturbance, lethargy, and death— does not imply any conflict in values about conduct but only a concern with the health and welfare of individuals as such. Presumably, this concern is as old as man's nature as a social animal; however, its documented expression might require that concern on the part of families or tribes be elevated to the status of an acknowledged value, as was indeed the case in ancient Greece, where preoccupation with health as a virtue as well as an immediate satisfaction was evident. These become questions for the epidemiologist-historian.

We shall see that awareness as to individually painful or disastrous outcomes from drug employment is not sufficient to arouse either social concern or a conclusion as to abuse; we shall also see that social concerns and the label of "abuse," or its equivalent, do not require that any ill effects from drugs be demonstrated. For example, in the Moslem Eastern Mediterranean region, seventeenth-century rules strictly forbade the drinking of coffee. The death penalty was pro-

vided for owning or even visiting a coffee house. Behind this severity
lay a threat unconnected with an evaluation of caffeine, for the coffee
house had become a meeting place for leisured political malcontents
who were thought to be secretly hatching plots against established political and religious authority (El Mahi, 1962a).

Reactions against tobacco were just as severe and these occurred before any evidence related heart disease and lung cancer to
smoking. In Germany, Persia, Russia, and Turkey, it was at one time
death for the smoker—but by hangman rather than from carcinoma or
infarction (Kolb, 1962). King James of England, in 1604, raged in
righteous indignation over "the filthy, stinking weede, tobacco." His
reaction, however, seemed a matter of national pride, for Englishmen,
he thought, ought not to emulate the savages—that is, the American
Indians who introduced the habit (Corti, 1932; Laufer, 1924a). Nevertheless, by 1614, over 300,000 pounds sterling "had gone up in
smoke in one single year." Then, as now, economic considerations
played no small part in public policy regarding drugs. The first Chinese imperial edicts banning opium were issued in 1729 and frequently
thereafter. Initially, they appear to have been protests against a disastrous drain of silver from the empire. An element of chauvinism was
present, too, since the Chinese at that time were forbidden contact with
"barbarians"—that is, with Europeans and their products, since most
opium was being brought in by English, Dutch, and Portuguese merchants.

On the other hand, we know from early Egyptian manuscripts
and later from classical Greek and Roman texts that there were governmental reactions to the specific disabling effects of drugs; in each
of these lands—in particular places and at particular points in time—
various efforts toward control were made. These aimed to reduce
drunkenness, crimes committed on drunken persons, or the public lia-
bilities to which drunkenness led, as in a drunken army's losing a
battle. Ill effects from opium were also acknowledged early. Dioscorides provides us with the earliest report but, later, Turks and Persians
(Sonnedecker, 1958) were alert to opiate disabilities. Reports of dire
effects from cannabis first came from Crusaders, whereas problems
arising from other hallucinogens—for example, fly agaric—were not
reported until recent centuries. What is striking is the inconsistency
about judgments of ill effects from various mind-altering drugs over
time and from place to place. If the range of specific drug effects is

presumably constant—even though particular kinds of outcomes become more probable under various settings and with particular populations and styles of use—at least part of the explanation for differing social evaluations of drug behavior must be found in the times themselves and not in the pharmacological action.

PREHISTORY: ARCHAEOLOGICAL FINDINGS

For mankind before writing existed, archaeological findings are our only source for data on drugs. As an alternative or supplement, we may also examine contemporary nonliterate societies, assuming that their hunting and gathering, pastoral, or simple farming economics are fair parallels to our preurbanized ancestors. Even now, many societies remain prehistoric in the sense of not being literate. The fact that their neighbors do know how to write has not meant that life in these societies has been adequately described—a point strongly made in our chapter on cross-cultural drug use. In other words, at any particular time, up to and including today, there is much left unsaid about how human beings use drugs. Indeed, no society exists, however modern, for which an adequate social and epidemiological assessment of drug use is available. One would have expected differently, that so interesting a matter as what kind of pharmacology men practice on their minds would be widely inquired after, but it has not been so.

On the basis of archaeological data, there is one psychoactive substance, in several forms, which can be identified as having been used in prehistory. The date of discovery is unknown. The substance is alcohol. Tentative evidence from Catal Hüyük (Mellaart, 1967) in Anatolia of hackleberry wine and of beer dates from about 6400 B.C.

Predynastic Egyptain farmers, in about 4500 B.C., had learned to maximize fermentation and alcoholic content by malting their grain, or sprouting it before grinding (Linton, 1955), and all Southwestern Asian cultures had beer as a liquid staple. Hammurabi's laws, again a written document but nevertheless an archaeological one, set forth how much and what kind of beer workmen on different jobs were to receive. That beer, yeasty and full of proteins and vitamins, was an important food. (Certain South American Indian cultures also used beer as food, and when missionaries inhibited Indian consumption, dietary deficiency and illness increased [Linton, 1955].) Confirmatory evidence of ritual beer drinking, the subject of stylized art themes, came from Egypt and Babylon between 2400 B.C. and 2800 B.C.

(Childe, n.d.) and from Sumer circa 3500 B.C. (Hoffman, 1956). A pitcher suitable for straining thick residue in early beer and termed a "beer jug" by its excavators has been found in Asia Minor; its date is circa 3000 B.C. (Schmidt, 1931). Other Anatolian finds include pithoi with sieves dated circa 3500 B.C. (Mellaart, 1963), Anatolian sieve-spouted jars from 3000–2000 B.C. (Ozguc, 1963), and wine decanters circa 900 B.C. from Urartu (Burney, 1966). These dates are no longer prehistory. During this same Old Kingdom period, Egypt was engaged in a considerable commerce in which wine as well as beer was extensively traded in the Eastern Mediterranean region and possibly deeper into Asia as well. Evidence for this comes from written material —including the Old Testament—as well as amphorae (Wilson, 1951). In the Old Kingdom, beer was widely used but wine seems to have been limited to the upper class, whose tastes were already sophisticated, for wines were marked by grade of excellence (*Encyclopaedia Britannica*, 1965). An early date for wine must be presumed since its commerce implies considerable human experience in production and shipment, as well as a widespread and established consumer market. The Egyptian evidence of wine enjoyment as limited to the upper class may be interpreted—in the light of findings on other drugs which we shall discuss later—as very tentative evidence of a more recent introductory date, since the general pattern, as we judge it, seems to be that both ritual use (religious, medical, festival) and high-status secular use occur in earlier phases of a society's adoption of a drug. Beer in Egypt was used both ritually and secularly and by all classes; wine was restricted. In Europe, archaeological evidence for wine (Helbaek, 1961) is available for Alpine peoples of what is now Northern Italy; themselves without writing, they had discovered wine making from grapes, blackberries, raspberries, elderberries, bittersweet nightshade, and the Cornelian cherry. The Beaker Folk of Europe, an early merchant people identified by their characteristic tumbler-like beakers, are thought to have traded heavily in beer—the beakers representing the vehicle of their stock in trade circa 2000 B.C. (Bibby, 1956; Childe, 1956; Linton, 1955; Piggott, 1965). Their distribution over Europe was rapid and their culture was present in the British Isles about 1800 B.C. A little later, beginning in 1300 B.C., another group of artifacts was focused on drinking; Central European beaten-bronze vessels identified with the Urnfield cultures were found by archaeologists from the Caspian to Denmark (Piggott). These vessels include a handled cup, a bucket, and a cup-shaped strainer, since wine was mixed with other materials even as it is now in Greece mixed with resin. Such vessels are presumed to have been filled with wine produced in the Mediterranean, perhaps Southern Europe. In Central Europe, wine drinking was also a class phenomenon, since importation was expensive and, thus, in all likelihood the expensive bronze vessels were also an upper-class drinking utensil. (Piggott compares them with the tea sets imported to England from China along with the first tea imports.) Archaeological finds in Central Europe continued to show the importance of wine; for example, in France and Germany of the Hallstatt period, circa 750 B.C., imported Greek gold, bronze, and pottery amphorae were found. Later, the development of Celtic art in the fifth century B.C. was also linked to the wine trade, for nonrepresentational Greek designs were transformed into Celtic forms and became adornments for that warrior aristocracy which Piggott so well describes. The archaeological data remain consistent, showing continued trading in wine and its implements from south to north along the great rivers and passes. By the third century B.C., Italy began to produce wine and, within a few hundred years, production in Italy was 660 million gallons annually, according to Piggott's estimate. The amphorae of the first century were found from Marseilles to England; Belgic tombs revealed that the buried lord was allowed three amphorae for his afterdeath feast, each one holding about 5 gallons. Written materials cited by Piggott (Ammaianus, Pliny, Tacitus, Posidonius, Diodorus, and Pytheas) indicate that the Celts were considered intemperate, for they were the first to be noticed to use wine not mixed with water. The Roman historian Ammaianus Marcellinus described them as "a race greedy for wine, devising numerous drinks similar to wine and among them some people of the baser sort, with wits dulled by continual drunkenness . . . rush about in aimless revels." They also used mead and beer made from barley or wheat.

With regard to psychoactive drugs other than alcohol, we shall see in our discussions of opium that archaeological evidence from Cyprus, Crete, and Greece shows that opium was known and probably used ritually about 2000 B.C. (Kritikos and Papadaki, 1963; Merrillees, 1962, 1963). Writing was known at this time in nearby cultures (disregarding untranslated Cretan linear *A*) and disputed suggestions indicate that earlier than 1500 B.C. (see Sonnedecker, 1958) Egyptians were using opium medically; later texts, Assyrian seventh-century ones, describe its cultivation.

We have come across suggestions pertaining to archaeological finds of cannabis in early Central European cultures, but although we pursued these through correspondence with paleoethnobotanists (Helbaek, 1965), we have been unable to verify them. The earliest acceptable archaeological evidence appears to be from the Pazarik excavations of the Altai Scythian group dated circa 430 B.C. (Rudenko, 1953; see discussion by Rice, 1957). The burial objects included the tent, cauldron, stones, and hemp seeds exactly as described by Herodotus in the *Histories* prior to 450 B.C. As for other psychoactive substances, some scholars (Wasson and Wasson, 1957; Wasson, 1963, 1967) have claimed widespread early use for the mushroom *Amanita muscaria* primarily on the basis of philological-ethnographic evidence. Gordon Wasson (1963) suggests that "the adoration of the fly agaric was at a high level of sophistication 3500 years ago among the Indo-Europeans (p. 413)." Another claim for very early drug use is advanced by Willey (1966) and cited by Wassén (1967), who proposes that chewing lime or ashes with a narcotic—such as betel nut and coca leaf and perhaps even the premastication per se of kava or grains to produce fermented drinks—in being both an Old World and New World practice is a Paleolithic survival. This is, of course, only speculation. Archaeological evidence of tobacco smoking among Southwestern American Indians yields dates of 200 A.D. and for Eastern Coastal Indians about 800 A.D. We have been unable to uncover sound archaeological evidence for other psychoactive substances in our own prehistory—that is, before 4000 B.C.

Another approach to prehistory is to assume that contemporary nonliterate societies represent styles of life extant before any society became literate. Specifically, the assumption is that generalizations can be made from the isolated hunting and gathering societies which apply to our ancestral groups prior to their agricultural settlement and later urbanization. What is stated is essentially a theory of cultural evolution, diffusion, and implied limited diversity. Thus, it is argued that isolated hunting, fishing, fowling, and gathering folk of today, as well as some pastoral herders, have characteristics that are much like those of prehistoric—and specifically preagricultural—peoples. Clark (in Kroeber, 1953a) has discussed the problems and merits in such an assumption; Steward's commentary (in Kroeber, 1953a) is also relevant. As long as one is cautious, and recognizes the need to match ecology as well as life style as closely as possible, the comparative method based on that assumption is useful. Clark cites in particular the value of contemporary folk usage in interpreting archaeological data. We (Blum and Blum, 1968) would add, on the basis of our work, that such survivals are also invaluable in interpreting early history. In either case, the comparative method based on study of survivals offers optimism—but not proof—for a comparative method based on parallels and general evolutionary assumptions.

Since in all likelihood there has always been a multiplicity of human societies (Coon, 1962; Linton, 1955; Steward, 1953), it would be most unwise to assume that any particular technique or usage, at least with regard to drugs, was common to them all. Today, given tremendous opportunities for cultural diffusion over thousands of years, the pattern is still one of diversity of drug use among nonliterate and literate societies (Schultes, 1967a); among today's disappearing hunters and gatherers, diversity is also the rule. Nor can any statements be made which assume a fixed and inevitable course of cultural evolution, although regularities are again observed (Adams, 1966; Linton, 1955). Adams, for example, concludes that when cultural evolution occurs there is

> A common core of regularly occurring features . . . that social behavior conforms not merely to laws but to a limited number of laws, which perhaps has always been taken for granted in the case of cultural systems . . . and among "primitives" (p. 175).

Simply knowing what drug-use patterns exist at a given level of social development does *not* allow one to anticipate exactly what forms of use will follow, but there should be similarities in invention as well as in practice—for example, the development of beer drinking after grain production has begun, the invention of distilling after fermentation is discovered, the increase in complexity of drinking equipment (beakers, strainers, and so on) as commerce and technology expand, the production of manufactured pharmaceuticals after technical chemistry is introduced, the spread of application of a manner of drug preparation or administration from one drug to another after the method has been introduced, and the increasing diversity of drug uses and effects as societies grow secular, larger, and more heterogeneous. What cannot be assumed is that a given society, especially an isolated hunting and gathering one, will inevitably proceed to a more complicated development or that use of a drug once inaugurated will be maintained.[1] Which will occur, for example, upon exposure to a more complex colonizing power, resistance to or adoption of its drugs? If the latter, will there be accommodation with social control or will there be, as has been so often the case, the development of individual and community-wide alcohol problems? For example, Child *et al.* (1965) found that problem drinking most often occurs in those societies where new drinking patterns have been introduced after contact with a more modern society.

In Chapter Eight we report on our cross-cultural study of drug use. Within the dubious limits of accuracy of these primarily contemporary observations on nonliterate societies, our conclusion is that alcohol is the most commonly used substance and that widespread use of alcohol is consistent with the relative ease of discovering fermentation in the normal course of storing foods—a practice of hunting and gathering peoples as well as agricultural folk. Hunting and gathering societies are capable, as Helbaek's Alpine evidence shows, of such production although it is impossible to know whether the Alpine tribes in question discovered it, since they could have developed berry wine after the diffusion of knowledge of fruit or grape wines from elsewhere. Loeb (1943) cites Beals and Cooper to the effect that modern use of intoxicating beverages is generally limited to agriculturists, such folk as the Australian, Tierra del Fuegian, or California Indian hunters. Loeb argues that the discovery of fermentation and the development of drinking practices were likely to have occurred in many places at any time after the development of agricultural practices. (These include harvesting wild cereals as well as cultivation per se.) His arguments as to the context in which drinking then occurred are based on ethnographic descriptions. We shall return to these, but we shall first point to a limitation of inference from ethnographic accounts and then to a summary of cross-cultural data on drug use by hunting and gathering peoples, whose known acceptance of drugs from other societies —including Western colonizers—was minimal.

In our cross-cultural study we found that tobacco ranked second among the psychoactive substances used. Among nonagricultural

[1] For example, Wassén (1967) describes how varied forms of snuff use have been lost to South and Central American Indians.

peoples it is commonly found. Reasoning backward, one would assume that by Neolithic times some Old World peoples at least would have smoked it. This would be in error, for all species of the plant, with an Australian exception, are native to the Americas. Tobacco use throughout Asia and Africa followed the introduction of American Indians' smoking techniques into Europe in the late 1500's. In a later chapter we present the history of tobacco's diffusion. We have the warning: what appears to be an indigenous practice may well have been borrowed.

Looking at hunting and gathering societies about which we have data, ninety-two in number, we find the distribution in Table 1 of reported (and by no means do we assume this is actual) drug use.

Table 1

DRUGS REPORTED USED IN CONTEMPORARILY OBSERVED
HUNTING AND GATHERING SOCIETIES

Drug	Reported Use
Alcohol	52
Tobacco	57
Stimulants	15
Hallucinogens	40
Opium	3
Cannabis	7
Coca-cocaine	1

We might reasonably expect that at least some of these societies discovered their own drugs rather than having been introduced to them, however indirectly, from more sophisticated sources, such as pastoral, agricultural, or urban people. After all, Western societies learned tobacco use from American Indians, are now learning about exotic hallucinogens from isolated South American groups (for example, Wassén, 1967; Wassén and Holmstedt, 1963; Schultes, 1967b), learned about coca-cocaine from the highland Indians of the Andes, discovered mushroom eaters after anthropological observations in Siberia or Mexico (Wasson, 1958; Wasson and Wasson, 1957), heard about peyote from North American Indians, and so on. Consequently, it is possible that some of these discoveries were early enough to qualify as prehistoric when the history under discussion is that of Western civilization—that is, before 4000 B.C. (excluding alcohol, which we assume may have been fermented by the time of early agricultural settlements)'. The possibility exists, then, that those hunting and gathering tribes in Paleolithic, Mesolithic, and Neolithic times did use mind-altering drugs. However, we know of no proof on either side of the question.

If they used drugs, how did they do so? Again, our estimates must be based on the inferences from archaeology as to life styles and on contemporary observations of groups similar to some Stone Age man. Early man lived in small groups, the size of which was controlled by food supply and other variables such as disease and predators. His religion and ritual developed early, probably, as James (1957)' contends, 100,000 years ago (and perhaps 500,000 years ago if Peking man was the death-feasting cannibal James proposes)'. Whether or not the earlier dates are accepted, the archaeological evidence from paintings, burials, and steles (see Anati, 1964, for an example of interpretive method)' certainly for the upper Paleolithic (40,000–8500 B.C. following Piggott's dating rather than Zeuner's)' is very strong indeed for a system of beliefs that imply attempts to control nature through ritual and magical means as well as by simply physical means. It is very likely that medicaments were also developed early. Food gatherers must have engaged in pharmacognosy to learn to identify safe and edible plants. During these sometimes perilous trials, they discovered plants with other qualities, including those leading to changes in physical function or in feeling. Flannery (1965)', in discussing preagricultural subsistence in the Near East, emphasizes the intensive collection of plants, based on paleobotanical evidence, and cites data indicating that such collection precedes agriculture for a long period. He notes that an immense variety of plants were available and suggests that from 40,000 to 10,000 B.C. man developed the exploitation of plant resources.[2]

Both religious and medical practices are limited to particular

[2] The written record of prescriptions is almost as early as writing itself. LaWall (1927) dates the original of a later transcribed Egyptian papyrus containing a prescription at 3700 B.C. The Ebers Papyrus, circa 1550 B.C., contained remedies listing wine, beer, oil, onion, vinegar, yeast, turpentine, castor oil, myrrh, wormwood, cumin, fennel, juniper berries, henbane, gentian, mandragor, and others. There are also early Biblical and Babylonian apothecary's guides. In Indian medicine, Rig-Veda medicinal uses of plants are claimed (Chopra cited in Krieg, 1964) before 1600 B.C. and drug therapies described about 1000 B.C. in the Sushruta Samhita.

settings, are usually supervised by some type of authority, and, when magically elaborated, include rituals which are, if current practice is any guide, *compulsive* or not allowing of variation. Given the early documented use of mind-altering drugs in medicine and religion—certainly by 2000 B.C. in the Eastern Mediterranean and Western Asia —it is likely that earlier undocumented use was along the same lines.[3]

In addition to specific ritual and the necessarily controlled use of psychoactive drugs in religion and healing, there is early evidence for using at least alcohol as food. In later periods (see McKinlay, 1949; Piggott, 1965), drugs were also used for social purposes such as ceremonial occasions or for informal, spontaneous, and noninstitutionalized gatherings like parties. Long before the time of Christ, descriptions were written of private or individual-centered drug use, as, for example, in drinking without regard for social circumstances that resulted in stupor, euphoria, and other comparable states. Opium and perhaps cannabis are also implicated by that date. Drug use that is without ritual or ceremonial significance we term as "secular." This approximates culturally the unintegrated drug use referred to by Child *et al.* (1965).

On the basis of observations in contemporary nonliterate societies, where most behavior is self- and other-controlled and is therefore carefully role-prescribed, we assume that drug use in prehistory was likewise integrated and, even though social and individual components in setting and intent were likely to have been present, was not secular. Ford's (1967) description of kava drinking in Fiji is a good example of how a variety of behaviors can be connected with drug use without its ever becoming private, individualistic, or escapist. Indeed,

[3] Loeb (1943) has proposed that in the case of alcohol the initial focus was always religious and that drunkenness at sacred feasting thus became an obligatory communion. The Catholic use of wine in communion would then be interpreted as a vestigial practice; the drunkenness of the Guatemalan Indian in order to communicate with ancestral spirits (Blum and Blum, 1965; Bunzel, 1940) would be a contemporary demonstration. Outside of the sacrament, "deviant" drinking would not be allowed. Indeed, Bunzel notes that under the Aztec law nonworshipful drinking was punishable by death, except for persons over seventy. Loeb notes that the Moi of Indo-China put to death any who failed to get drunk at religious ceremonials. According to Loeb, only with increased production and storage facilities does secular drinking become possible, at which time extreme sanctions are no longer appropriate. He does not account for anthropological evidence showing secular drinking among societies with limited facilities for alcohol production and storage.

the very notion of "individual" or "private" is inconsistent with life in little communities (Redfield, 1960) for it implies an autonomy and self-centering not known until the end of the Middle Ages (Ullmann, 1966). This, of course, does not rule out the function of drugs to grease the skids of social interaction or to enhance shared euphoria.

In Table 2 we present observations from contemporary hunting and gathering societies made prior to culture change under Western impact and showing the settings and intentions for psychoactive drug use as reported by observers.

Table 2

SETTING AND INTENTIONS FOR PSYCHOACTIVE DRUG USE IN
CONTEMPORARY HUNTING AND GATHERING CULTURES

SETTING-INTENT All Psychoactive Drugs	Number of Societies (N = 144)
Social	49
Social/mind-modifying/escape	3
Social/religious-magical	21
Mind-modifying	7
Social/mind-modifying	16
Mind-modifying/religious-magical	10
Escape only	0
Escape/social	1
Escape/mind-modifying	1
Religious-magical	6
Social/mind-modifying/escape/religious- magical	4
Social/mind-modifying/religious-magical	26

As expected, individualistic drug use for escape is least frequent, although its presence at all is inconsistent with a theoretical picture of the group-centered little community. Similarly, mind modification outside of religious-magical settings is also individualistic but present in hunting-gathering societies. Social settings-intentions do not imply a secular pattern, but they are a step removed from the religious and healing ceremonial uses implied by Loeb and others as primary to psychoactive substances. Table 2, then, suggests the conclusion that— at least among the hunting-gathering societies which constitute our limited sample—religious-magical functions for drugs are *less* common than social uses and no more common than individualistic functions. We further conclude that expectations of more frequent and more elaborate religious-magical drug functions represent observer romanticism and that if prehistoric societies did use psychoactive drugs as hunting-gathering societies use them now, they used them primarily for simple social facilitation and shared personal pleasures. Magical superstructures supported or elaborated by drugs would have been less common, if our backwards-in-time extrapolation holds, and no more common than individualistic and indeed private (although rarely escapist) functions for drugs. Such a conclusion implies that primitive man resembled modern man in the uses to which he put psychoactive substances and that there will be little justification for those generalized romantic abstractions that moderns build to house their images of strange and far-away peoples.

A History of Alcohol

Richard H. Blum

II

*I*n our discussion of archaeological and cross-cultural findings, we
have already discussed the evidence for the religious, medical, nutritional, and social use of alcoholic beverages in early Mesopotamia and
Egypt. The possibility of a Paleolithic discovery and use of alcohol is
advanced by many writers (Hoffman, 1956; Roueché, 1963; Smith
and Helwig, 1940; Westermarck, 1912), but we have noted that the
evidence does not confirm the speculation. Neolithic evidence for beer
and berry wine about 6400 B.C. tells us that these beverages were
known to the early settled agriculturists; we can expect earlier dates
as excavations continue. Grape wine did not appear before the fourth
or third millennium. An important commerce in alcohol and its apparatus apparently followed shortly after evidence for its presence in
each region, and social distinctions in alcohol use also appeared very
early. By 2500 B.C., evidence also indicates trouble associated with
drinking. Crothers (1903), in an early report without adequate cita-
tions, describes how the distribution of beer and wine on feast days at
temples was terminated because of thieves' exploitation of the drink-

ing masses. He also reports that the regimes of the pharaohs sometimes suppressed drinking, especially when it took place in temple "houses of beer and wine" (as at Memphis) where altar offerings were drunk by worshippers who talked politics of a sort leading to plots and intrigues against the regime.[1]

By 2000 B.C., one has reason to suspect, according to Crothers, that military disasters occurred because the soldiers were drunk before battle. Regulations prohibiting Egyptian soldiers from drinking were promulgated. Egyptian efforts to suppress drinking—to which deaths were attributed in early "public-health" concern—included restrictions on public wine sales, fines, and property confiscation. Later, by 1500 according to McKinlay (1959d), heavy drinking was accepted and drunkenness among Egyptian women as well as men was commonplace. By the time of Rameses III (1198 B.C.), soldiers received a strong, daily wine ration, and priests, too, were apparently given wine by the state.

During the same centuries wine, of course, received the attention of the Hebrews, who memorialized its early role in shame and sin and in stirring up family troubles when Noah (as described in Genesis 9:20–29, written probably about 1700 B.C.) fell drunk and was seen naked by Ham, father of Canaan, for which Canaan was cursed for generations. Nearby in Babylon, Hammurabi (circa 1800–1760 B.C.) in his code detailed restrictions on wine sales, on the company in wine houses (if outlaws were found, they and the wine seller were to be executed), priestesses were forbidden entry to wine shops, and wine prices were controlled (Harper, 1904).

To the west in the Indus Basin, the evidence for alcohol's use

---

[1] We shall see during the course of history that "Establishment" suppression of one or another drug was often political—for example, when the innovators gathering together to try a new drug also engaged in antistate activities as another aspect of their change orientation, the holders of power responded violently to that new drug use, which was symbolic, for all concerned, of rebellion, separatism, or other dissatisfaction with the status quo. Government opposition to traditional drugs may also occur on political grounds, as, for example, when occupying or colonial powers sensed a traditional or ceremonial drug use as a unifying symbol of the old ways, which might help subject peoples resist imposed changes. Contrariwise, when changes in styles of use of a traditional drug—or subsequent behavior—were identified with new groups which threatened established power, the elite sought to curb such changes by regulating either the drug or the behavior of power-aspiring or otherwise convention-challenging groups.

is later. By inference the stemmed cups, termed "champagne" or "brandy" pots by excavators, may have been used for drinking. These date about 1700 B.C. (Wheeler, 1966). Only by the sixth century in the Indus Basin is there proof of at least knowledge of drinking—this from Greek objects and later, in the first century, from Greek wine jars. Lucia (1963) cites a mention of wine in the fifth century B.C. in India in which discriminations were made by sex and class as to who might drink; wives could not, mistresses could, and higher castes were forbidden wine, although it was associated with the worship of the gods and with healing—an inconsistency suggesting an inadequacy in the sources available to us.

Northwest of the Indus, in the plains of Central Asia, the first descriptions of alcohol use come from Herodotus describing the Scythians. There, wine was used in manly martial ritual. Once a year, the king gave a banquet and only those who had slain a man in battle could drink the wine; slayers of many men were given *two* cups of wine to drink. The Scythians also used wine in swearing oaths, for they mixed it with blood and drank the brew. Sacrificial use is also described; human victims had their throats cut, after which a libation of wine was poured over their heads; the mixed blood and wine after flowing to a bowl below were then put on faggots and a scimitar. Herodotus also describes the Persians' use of wine. When drinking, they were not allowed to get sick or urinate in the presence of others, but they did discuss the most important matters. Decisions made when drunk were re-examined when they were sober. If the same, action was taken. Likewise, decisions made when sober were re-examined when they were drunk before there was a commitment to action. One of the earliest reports of the use of alcohol in warfare comes from the time of Cyaxares (624–584 B.C.), who, Herodotus tells us, regained Persia from the occupying Scythians by inviting them to a feast, making them drunk, and then slaughtering them. These same Persians had, by a later date, apparently come to imbibe too much themselves, for the Roman historian Ammaianus Marcellinus describes a fourth-century A.D. penal code requiring that heavy drinkers be led by a cord strung through their nose; persistent offenders were tied with a nose cord to a stake in the public square (MacKinlay, 1959b).

As for China, the early tales are legendary and cautionary. Prior to written records, two royal astronomers were said to have been put to death for being drunk and missing an eclipse (Smith and Hel-

wig, 1940), and another tale claims that the man who invented rice
wine was banished (Moore, in McCarthy, 1959). By the time of the
Shang (Yin) Dynasty (1766–1123 B.C.), drunkenness was not only
known but railed against (Waley, 1958) and wine was used as an
everyday beverage. During the later Chou Dynasty (1122–256 B.C.),
the religious use of wine was emphasized in documents—as, for example, mixing red wine with blood and bone marrow for sacrifice and
ceremonial drinking (Waley; Moore in McCarthy, 1959). Waley
(1954), in his translation of *The Book of Songs,* presents several
eighth- and ninth-century B.C. poems, all mentioning the ceremonial
importance of wine, which was offered to ancestors, at harvest time,
and at social ceremonies. It is also clear that ceremonial controls were
by no means always effective, as these lines show:

> When guests are drunk, they howl and bawl . . . cut capers, lilt
> and lurch. . . . It is always the same when wine is drunk, some
> are tipsy, some are not . . . (p. 266).

Further Chinese realism during the same period is cited by Roueché
(1963), quoting, "Men will not do without beer, to prohibit it and
secure total abstinence from it is beyond the power even of sages"
(p. 170). Confucius (551–479) counseled against boisterous drinking,
consistent with his general counsel for ethics, order, and ceremony in
an age of social and political upheavals. In Japan both the orderly
ethic of Confucius and the Buddhist creed, which was introduced later
(about 550 A.D.), led to stringent regulations on drinking. One tenet
of the latter is never to take strong drink. Prohibition was declared by
a number of emperors from 646 through 777 (Yamamuro in Mc-
Carthy, 1959). On the other hand, an eighth-century A.D. poet,
Ohtomo, praised sake and a merry drunkenness in this world as opposed to reincarnated uncertainty in the next. In China, in the seventh
century A.D., one emperer, Tai Tsung, undertook what appears to be
the first formal educational effort in how to drink by circulating a
pamphlet to teach wine-drinking propriety (Moore, 1959). In Japan
the temperance decrees continued for centuries, apparently in competition with drinking extravaganzas. Sake sales were prohibited again
in 1252 after the Mongol invasion, and tea drinking was promulgated
as a substitute activity by Eisai, the Zen Buddhist. Later, however,
popular Buddhism was more relaxed and total abstinence was no
longer required (Yamamuro, 1959). In China, by the early fourteenth

century, decrees were passed against the manufacture, sale, and consumption of wine, with penalties including confiscation of property,
slavery, and death. The purpose of these is said to have been to conserve grains rather than to counter inebriety; in any event, Chinese
prohibition vs. Chinese drinking had a see-saw history, since the prohibition laws were repealed and then passed again on dozens of occasions over the years. During the seventeenth and eighteenth centuries,
"heroic" drinking was praised in novels but no adverse social effects
were implied (Weakland, 1968). Contemporary data on Chinese
drinking are absent. Moore (1959) states that moderation is the rule
and that any problems with drunkenness are quite rare. In 1967, police statistics from Hongkong supported that contention, since, in a
city of over three million, practically no cases of problem drunkenness
(drunk and disorderly and so forth) were reported. Such drunkenness
as does occur is among family or friends and neither involves public
exposure on the street nor constitutes an issue for concern.

Let us return now to the history of drinking in the Near East. The
many therapeutic uses of wine are set forth by Lucia (1963b), beginning with Mesopotamian culture. During early Greek medicine, wine
was much employed, as it was later in Rome. For details about the
uses of wine in modern medicine, the reader is referred to Leake and
Silverman (1966).

Herodotus introduces a familiar hedonism plus a warning in
his description of the Egyptian custom whereby at rich men's banquets
a wooden corpse in a coffin "painted exactly to look like a real corpse"
was carried about and shown to each of the company. The bearer
said, "Look upon this and drink and be merry: for thou shalt die and
such shalt thou be." A little later, writing in Luke (12:19) and in
Ecclesiastes (8:15), the Hebrews reaffirmed the Egyptian advice. Coexistent were Hebrew injunctions against drunkenness and, in later
writings, recommendations for the medicinal use of wine. Consider
Timothy (5:23): "Drink no longer water, but use a little wine for
thy stomach's sake. . . ." Binkley (in McCarthy, 1959) correctly
notes the ambiguity and inconsistency in Hebrew-Christian writings
concerning drinking. For example, the New Testament (Gal. 5:21)
warned, "They which do such things [drunkenness, revelings] shall not
inherit the kingdom of God," as well as, ". . . make not provision for
the flesh, to fulfill the lusts thereof (Rom. 13:14)." And finally in
Romans 14:21–23:

It is good neither to eat flesh, nor to drink wine, nor any thing
whereby thy brother stumbleth, or is offended, or is made weak.
. . . Happy is he that condemneth not himself in that thing which
he alloweth. And he that doubteth is damned if he eat, because he
eateth not of faith; for whatsoever is not of faith is sin.

Here, of course, is expressed that Gospel foundation for abstinence
which Comber (1964) points out continues to divide the Western
community in its beliefs on the propriety of using any euphoria-pro-
ducing drugs.

History after Herodotus is full of tales demonstrating how alcohol was used to manipulate and destroy enemies. Judith charmed the
Assyrian Holofernes, who, drinking too much, lost his head to her.
During a fourth-century war, Illyrians left poisoned wine for the enemy
to drink (Gremek, 1950). During the Gallic Wars, the Romans would
wait for the Gauls to drink themselves into a stupor and would then
attack—a device the Romans themselves fell victim to during Rome's
own civil wars (McKinlay, 1959e). During the First Punic War, a
Roman general blamed a defeat upon his soldiers' being drunk; another general, to prevent a similar outcome, banned liquor sales in
camp. Conversely, when, during a Byzantine siege, defending soldiers
were deserting their posts, one commander is said to have set up wine
sellers' booths on the defending ramparts. At a later date, Babur, the
Mogul emperor, described the widespread alcoholism in his army and
court (and in himself) and how he, fearing defeat in battle because
of that drunkenness, prohibited wine in Mogul India (Lamb, 1961).
In Mohammed's day the penalty for drinking was forty lashes.

Much attention has been paid to drinking in early Greece and
Rome because of the wealth of documentation and because our own
cultural roots are there. Greek wine use, as recorded by the time of
Homer and Hesiod (eighth century B.C.), involved several distinct
functions, including magical-religious invocations and appeasements
of the dead, offerings to the gods, hospitality rituals, manly displays,
formal banquets and informal feasts, healing and pain relief, and as a
food. We have taken a special interest in the cultural context of drinking in both ancient and modern Greece (see Chapter Nine). We suggest a long-standing ideal of temperance contrasted with tendencies
toward outbursts of passion and for ecstatic (Dionysian) experience—
a conception which implies polarity. McKinlay (1953) might agree,
at least in denying consistent temperance as a quality of the Homeric

Greek warrior. Certainly wine's capabilities for debauching a man and unstringing an enemy were known, for, as McKinlay observes, Odysseus overcame Cyclops by getting him drunk and then boring out his eye. Several centuries after Homeric times, a recognized antisocial hazard in drinking was reflected in a Mytilene law that doubled the penalties for offenses committed while drunk (McKinlay, 1949). In Lesbos at the same time, McKinlay describes drinking rampant enough to deserve suppression by Cleomis.

In early Rome, Pliny contended that wine was scarce and costly. Beer never became popular. Wine remained scarce through the fourth century when it was still used in worship, but by the time of the Republic wine was easily available and debauchery was often described (McKinlay, 1959e). Temperate men were singled out for praise. By the second century, women were allowed to drink; earlier Roman law, albeit legendary, provided the death penalty for drinking or adultery (McKinlay, 1959f). In early Rome children, men under thirty, and servants were also forbidden wine, although soldiers received a limited ration. In Sparta and Carthage soldiers were restricted in the amount they could consume, although in Sparta McKinlay (1959a) says drunkenness itself was unknown; generally, Greece was more moderate than Rome (Rolleston, 1927). Indeed, as feasting became fashionable in Rome, it was the practice to eat as well as to drink too much—and to vomit voluntarily so that consumption could be continued. Feasting was necessarily limited to either the wealthy or to those—like the soldiery—who were in a position to seize supplies or to be issued them. By the first century B.C., alcoholism as such was recognized in Rome and reached its zenith by 100 A.D. (McKinlay, 1959e) when it was apparently common among wealthier folk. The Greek philosophers of the fifth and fourth centuries considered intoxication as debasing (McKinlay, 1959a)—a view still prevalent in Greece; Plato recommended wine be prohibited to children, slaves, judges, and councilors. It was his view that drinking parties should be regulated, demonstrating that in Athens intemperate drinking was common. Critias' description of the disabling effects of such a party is recounted by McKinlay, who notes that, given the Greek practice of watering wine, it took a great amount to produce intoxication.

As earlier indicated, Roman viticulture expanded immensely from the fourth to second centuries and the international wine trade became of great importance. Rome imported from Greece and Spain and in turn exported throughout the Mediterranean. To protect her trade she restricted vine planting in Gaul—a restriction not lifted until 280 A.D. (McKinlay, 1959d). The prestige of Rome is held to have led its subject peoples to emulate its practices—one reason to expect a considerable expansion in wine drinking throughout the Roman world. A modern parallel is in the adoption of the use of spirits throughout Asian and African urban society in the nineteenth and twentieth centuries with the spread of colonialism and of admired industrialism. In 90 A.D., Domitian was worried about the devotion of land to grapes rather than to food products and decreed a decrease in viticulture both in Italy and abroad. The edict was most unpopular and was enforced only in parts of Gaul and Spain. It was repealed by about 280 A.D. on the grounds of its being unenforceable. A modern parallel here is found in the unsuccessful Moroccan endeavor to prevent cannabis production without providing an adequate economic substitute for farmers. Modern failures in Asia to control opium planting are also analogous. Before the end of the Western Empire, vine culture had spread through Gaul and was the beginning of the fine vineyards of France and the Rhineland.

The introduction of spirits—that is, the discovery of distillation—is of uncertain date and subject to considerable dispute but was independent in many areas of the world. China, India, and Central Asia sometimes are credited with the discovery of fermentation before the time of Christ, whereas mead from honey appeared in Britain about 500 A.D., brandy from grapes appeared in Italy about 1000 A.D., and whiskey in Scotland appeared not before 1500 A.D. (*Encyclopaedia Britannica,* 1965). Poznanski (in McCarthy, 1959) proposes that it was the Arabian physician Rhazes whose distillation led to European spirit production in the tenth century. Leake and Silverman (1966) and Roueché (1960), on the other hand, credit the Arabian Jabir Ign Hayyan about 800 A.D. They note that the invisible essence of the wine when distilled was called the "finely divided spirit" or "alcohol" in Arabic. As with many other potent newly discovered psychoactive agents, initial dramatic claims for spirits were broadcast —at least in Europe—hailing the value of various preparations in medicine and in magic. Spirits were held to be an antidote to senility— thus, "aqua vitae" and the same meaning in the Gaelic "usequebaugh" from which "whiskey" derives (Poznanski, 1959). Almost all human ailments were claimed curable with one or another distilled preparation. During medieval times, various prescriptions against hang-overs and alcoholic disability were offered, as were means for producing abstinence, such as drowning an eel in one's wine (Eis, 1961). Medieval and pre-Reformation drinking and drunkenness were widespread in Europe; monks, the clergy, and the nobility were well chronicled in their cups.

In eleventh-century Russia, the church accepted moderate drinking, and in Russia under Ivan IV the central government closed private taverns and opened drinking places as a state monopoly. Operators of these had to render increasing profits to the government, which led government and sellers to encourage drinking. That policy was also said to encourage robbery of patrons by tavern operators. According to Efron (1955), this was the beginning of the long-standing Russian pattern: state monopoly on sales and widespread public drunkenness.

By the sixteenth century, European alcoholism was widespread across social classes (Blanke, 1953). Luther, Zwingli, and Calvin pleaded for moderation without success, so it was from the extreme dissentist movements such as the Baptists that the demand for total abstinence emerged. In England, James I (1603–1625) decreed drastic punishment for drunkenness—also without effect—and Charles I tried quite as ineffectually to suppress it, so that during the Cromwell reign (1649–1660) England was known as the land of the drunkards (Smith and Helwig, 1940).

A Dutch physician in the mid-1600's distilled alcohol in the presence of the juniper berry to produce a diuretic, thus inventing gin. British soldiers, returning from continental wars, brought back the taste for gin, which was soon heavily imported (*Encyclopaedia Britannica*, 1965). Queen Anne gave home distillation a boost by raising import duties and lowering home excise in the early 1700's, so that by 1715 spirits were retailed cheaply and indiscriminately. "Drunk for a penny, dead drunk for two pence, clean straw for nothing" read the inn advertisements (George, 1965).

It was during this same period, 1700–1800, that England began undergoing massive socioeconomic changes. Overseas discovery, colonization, and expanding international trade thrived, while the process of industrialization was effecting changes at home. The first invention revolutionizing the textile industry was the flying shuttle in

1733, a process which gave England the world's industrial leadership. A decline in the death rate increased the population by 50 per cent in one century. As a consequence of land enclosure and reduced farming, urbanization increased, bringing mercantile-industrial development and, of course, population expansion. Each of these developments contributed to the growth of the urban poor, a mass whose misery was not much reduced by employment in jobs with a thirteen-hour working day, low wages, residence in slum tenements, and slavery to the machine. Many others were without work, so that in this century the city saw for the first time chronic mass unemployment.

By the Mutiny Act of 1720, retailers who were distillers were exempted from having to quarter soldiers—a fact that led to massive installation of stills. In 1729, an act was passed to control retail sales by requiring an excise license and paid duty on spirits. In this period the crude death rate was one in twenty, much of it attributed to alcohol-related disease (MacGregor, 1948). The act was repealed in 1733 after protests, but in 1736 a new law prohibited retailing of spirits. This in turn led first to bootleg sales, then to rioting—the famous "gin riots" in which the liquor-loving mob's pressure defeated the government bills (George, 1965). Again, in 1743, an act to control gin shops was passed which also increased the price of gin; licenses were granted only to alehouse license holders, and distillers were forbidden to retail. This act is said to have reduced consumption but in 1747 distillers petitioned Parliament for the right to sell, and this, being allowed, reportedly led again to increased consumption and public drunkenness. A general protest against debauchery took place in 1751 (see Hogarth's "Gin Lane" drawings and read Fielding's "Reasons for the Late Increase of Robbers"), and a new act strengthened retail controls. This act, enforced, is said to have been a turning point in the social history of London in that it led to considerably reduced public drunkenness. Nevertheless, Britain imported ten million gallons of Dutch gin in 1792. Gin had been the drink of the poor, of workhouse inmates, and beggars, so that as its price went up, consumption by poor people necessarily was reduced. Artisans apparently never became gin tipplers; they limited themselves to beer and reportedly suffered neither from disability nor from abstinence.

AN ETHER INTERLUDE

Later in the history of the British Isles, an experiment in prohibition occurred which led to a remarkable chapter in the epidemi-

ology of psychoactive substances—the history of which is well chronicled by Connell (1965). In the early 1800's, ether had been mar-
keted as an industrial solvent and as a pharmaceutical. Social use of
ether soon followed and expanded, first as its anesthetic use brought its
properties to public attention and later as both increased publicity and
decreased production costs made it more easily available. English
physicians at conventions, American young people at dances, and depressed ladies on the continent explored its pleasures but abandoned
it because of certain difficulties in its administration and retention and
because it had a telltale odor. According to Connell, the daring moved
on to newer drugs (morphine at the end of the 1800's), whereas their
ether pioneering was adopted by persons lower in the social scale—a
common-enough sequence in the history of psychoactive substances.
European peasants, faced with high alcohol costs due to taxes, took
to ether, although never in large numbers except in Ulster, the scene
of Connell's remarkable account where an eighth of the population in
one area became "etheromaniacs" in the 1890's.

Connell accounts for the phenomenon in terms of a number
of factors. The Irish, already accustomed to hard liquor in large quantities, were faced with an initial poverty which became nearly intolerable as alcohol prices went up under taxation, as temperance campaigns fought the use of spirits, and as the constabulary's enforcement
of tax laws reduced the widespread home-brew distilling of poteen—
an enforcement made easier as malt and grain used in home-brew became harder to get due to changes in farming and merchandising.
Looking for a substitute, the Irishmen were first taught of ether by re-
turnees from Glasgow, who had learned its use there as a preventive
and remedy against cholera and who touted it as a folk remedy. This
lesson was expanded by fierce temperance campaigners, for their leaders undertook to bundle off any reformed drinker to cooperative physicians who in turn sold him ether. That manly fellow soon enjoyed the
"hot-all-the-way-down" sensation, the triumphant, trumpeting flatus
which followed, and in ten minutes an intoxication achievable repeatedly during the day without hang-over. Soon, druggists, grocers,
hawkers, bakers, and others were selling ether, although tavern-keep-
ers were reluctant to do so because its low cost brought little profit.

In response to the "epidemic," a reaction built up against its
use. Church and government cried "abuse" and gave instances of terrible things that happened to users, although physicians on the scene
reported few untoward consequences (except the one which tragically

came to those who unwarily lit a pipe while taking ether). Alarmists
won out, and restrictive legislation controlled importation of the stuff,
which, coming from England, was easily monitored. Clerical denunci-
ations aided the reform, but paramount to the Irish change of heart
were, as Connell (1965) reports, rising incomes, which lessened the
need for ether intoxication since more attractive drugs could be purchased. In retrospect, Connell holds that ether was maligned; neither
crime nor illness was attributable to it although there were risks from
an overdose, fire, and possible suffocation when the vapor escaped from
a broken bottle.

We deem Connell's history to be the classical epidemiological
case. It shows how a potent psychoactive substance spreads from small
to large groups and from informed and wealthy innovators to poorer
and less informed folk. One sees how there are initial claims for dramatic medical virtue—some of which may be substantiated over time
—how folk medical application leads to widespread self-dispensing,
and how use depends upon publicity and, economically, upon low cost
and high availability. Spread of use depends upon a self-diagnosed
need—in this case the clear desire among a heavy-drinking population for an immediate substitute after being deprived of their traditional intoxicant. Further, the substitute must bear a resemblance to
the original; with ether, its fiery sensation was akin to the home-brew
itself and appealed to the same image of the drinker as a "he-man."
Necessary, of course, is the effect, and ether provided a most satisfactory intoxication. Its limitations, on the other hand, aided in its aban-
donment—nausea, flatus, the strong smell, and the awkward nose-
holding administration. Fundamental to its control were these factors:
government ability to enforce controls over distribution; an alliance of
moral and state authority in its denunciation; the failure of ether to
enlist an overt lobby or covert activists in its behalf; and, in the turn
of the wheel, a change in economic conditions, which resulted once
again in the production of a better-tasting, more-prestigeful, and traditional brew, whiskey. Thus, the population did not need to suffer
abstinence and deprivation and could return to prized old ways.

ALCOHOL IN AMERICA

In Colonial America there was, according to Bay (1968),
widespread acceptance of beer, wine, and cider as well as rum. The
Puritans, contrary to some notions, were not anti-alcohol (Beard and

Beard, 1947)̄ but did punish drunkenness. However, the first stirrings of condemnation were in the early colonial days when Increase and Cotton Mather both inveighed against "demon rum." While the colonies were importing rum but making cider, Franciscan priests in California in the mid-1700's were planting vineyards to establish a pattern of wine production and drinking which continues in that state to the present. By 1774, physicians were writing about the harmful effects of spirits (Keller, 1966), and the first political-social problem over liquor in the United States was the Whiskey Insurrection in Western Pennsylvania in 1794, which took place when the federal government tried to enforce the excise law of 1791. Revenue officers were tarred and feathered, and a militia was sent to subdue the folk in this first test of the power of the Congress and the central government to enforce law within the states. Earlier, a different "social problem" had been evident, but one which did not evoke great sympathy from the colonial Americans; it was the plight of the Northeastern Indian tribes who, upon exposure to the white man's ways, suffered social and physical disintegration, some part of which was attributable to alcohol (Horton in McCarthy, 1959). By the early 1800's, the debate over the effect of alcohol—on Americans—was great enough to agitate Congress as it considered the whiskey ration of the military—a ration abolished for the Army in 1830 and for the Navy in 1862 (Keller, 1944). It was during this period that the Reverend Beecher described alcohol use as a disease, the American Temperance Society was formed in 1827 (Binkley in McCarthy, 1959; McPeek, 1945), and the first prohibition law came into effect in Maine in 1851. By 1855, thirteen states had such laws, but by 1863 eight had repealed them and four others had modified them (McCarthy and Douglass in McCarthy, 1959). In the 1880's, a second wave of prohibitory laws was passed and again, by 1904, most states had repealed the enactments. In the 1890's, Carrie Nation, after an unhappy marriage to an alcoholic, took to the "hatchetation" of saloons (and to lecturing at carnivals and burlesque shows). A third prohibition wave hit the United States and, under the pressure of Protestant churches, by 1919 the Eighteenth Amendment and the Volstead Act were passed. In that same year lobbies against prohibition were formed and by 1933, after an epoch of speak-easies and organized crime, the Twenty-first Amendment repealing the Eighteenth was passed (the only Constitutional Amendment ever to be repealed). In an appropriate historical juxtaposition, Alcoholics Anonymous was founded in 1934.

Over the years American drinking patterns have changed. As Leake and Silverman (1966) and Bay (in Sanford, 1968) observe, drinking in Colonial America was nearly universal and not a problem. It was not until the Westward movement that a concern over excessive drinking grew and drinking as a "social problem" came to be defined. These were the result of a combination of events, including at least (1) the social disorganization and lawlessness of the frontier, (2) industrialization, urbanization, and heavy immigration from abroad to the new cities, (3) possibly growing individual behavioral excesses in the East with the increasing availability of rum, and (4) the production of corn "likker" for rural drinkers and Western frontiersmen who required a strong, cheap, and portable liquor. The campaign against drinking was based on moral grounds and began with temperance but came to call for total prohibition. As far as the drinker was concerned, it vilified him and called for criminal penalties, although the notion of reform implied individual regeneration. The prohibition banner was buttressed by concern for public health, by the growing industrial ethic of individual efficiency, and by the exercise of political muscle on the part of middle-class mid-America—the small-town, Anglo-Saxon mentality directed against the foreign immigrant, the Eastern elites, and the Western frontier rowdy.

Observers claim that after the 1850's American drinking became extremist. People were either abstinent or were heavy consumers of spirits.[2] By the end of World War II, moderate drinking had increased and the consumption of milder beer and wine surpassed that

---

[2] This is not to say that all Americans were teetotalers or drunkards but, rather, that extreme drinking behavior and rigid moral positions were prominent. On the other hand, in that same period, among cultivated men very different perspectives on alcohol were possible. Among these the position of William James is outstanding. In *The Varieties of Religious Experience* (1902), he wrote of the potential of alcohol for producing mystical experiences. "The sway of alcohol over mankind is unquestionably due to its power to stimulate the mystical faculties. . . . To the poor and the unlettered it stands in the place of symphony concerts and of literature. . . . The drunken consciousness is one bit of the mystic consciousness, and our total opinion of it must find its place in our opinion of that larger whole" (pp. 377–378). James' emphasis on the pharmacological production of religious experience bears profoundly on today's debates about mystical experience as producible by LSD, peyote, and mescaline, among others.

of spirits. Cisin and Cahalan's 1966 national survey shows that 68 per cent of all adults consumed some alcoholic beverages. Heavy drinkers are not necessarily alcoholic, but those who become heavy drinkers from among deprived minority groups, the big-city poor, religious older males, and especially persons who drink to escape and are unhappy and badly adjusted do suffer a high risk of having alcohol-related problems. Heavy drinkers who, on the other hand, are among the elite—better-off, well-adjusted young males—are better able to drink without disability (Knupfer, Rink, Clark, and Goffman, 1963).

A number of writers, including Leake and Silverman (1966), Plaut (1967), and Blum and Blum (1967), reviewing the literature agree that the differences among groups generating high numbers of problem drinkers as opposed to those generating proportionately low numbers are strong indications for cultural, social, psychological, and physiological determinants of risk. Groups with a low risk of generating alcoholism are those in which drinking is learned at an early age in a context of complex social and ceremonial activity supervised by respected authorities who themselves drink safely. In such groups drinking is of milder beverages accompanied by food and is not an emotional release linked to escapist, rebellious, self-proving, personal tension-reducing, or solely hedonistic functions. As well, safe and acceptable behavior with alcohol is explicitly communicated by a cohesive group norm. Risk is not linked to per-capita alcohol consumption, to the occurrence of approved intoxication (as in ceremonials), or to the existence of blanket prohibitions in the law. It does seem likely to be reduced by educational endeavors, by socioeconomic reforms which reduce misery, deprivation, and anxiety, by child-rearing procedures which foster mental health, by nutritional and hygienic regimens fostering good physical health, and by social controls which limit drinking settings and the variety of behavior allowed under the influence of alcohol.

SUMMARY

The available evidence suggests that alcoholic beverages were the first psychoactive substances to be discovered by man and, upon discovery, rapidly diffused so that they remain, with tobacco, a paramount drug. Dates of discovery and initial routes for diffusion are unknown, but alcoholic beverages appeared shortly after agricultural settlement in Mesopotamia and Asia Minor and shortly thereafter in

Egypt. Different beverages were used in different ways in early civilizations, depending upon cost and availability and, apparently, on taste and nutritive value. Early archaeological findings and documents suggest that within the same culture alcohol would be used in religious-magical ceremonials, in healing, in social ceremonials, and in feasting. Evidence exists for differences in styles of use depending upon the social status of persons; age, sex, social class, and religious roles appear early as determinants of who employed what beverage in what settings. Evidence also exists from contemporary nonliterate societies which, if extrapolated backwards in time, would imply a diversity of uses for alcohol in prehistorical societies prior to agriculture, settlement, and civilization. These uses are also social and occasionally personal (private, secular) as well as—secondarily—religious and magical.

In early civilizations there was recognition of the disabling effects of alcohol, including ill-health and death, predatory exploitation of the intoxicated through crime, war, or politics, personal foolishness or disgrace, and the impairment of group solidarity or competence. Early methods to control alcoholic excess included regulations governing production and distribution, taxation, punishment, and, of course, group norms and individual ideals and controls dictating safe and acceptable behavior. We see no reason to posit a "golden age" in urban civilizations whereby alcohol problems would have been unknown; nevertheless, among urbanized societies in pre-Christian times, as well as among preurban peoples, marked differences existed in the extent to which disapproved or damaging behavior occurred as related to alcohol use. This is a function, of course, of the standards of judgment as well as of drinking styles and variability of behavior within a population. Among primitive groups the inferred frequency of disapproved behavior in association with alcohol is taken to be very low.

Documents reveal considerable differences within a society—over time from one era to another and within an era among classes and individuals—in the extent of alcohol problems. There is also a record of considerable differences in the effectiveness of efforts to control alcohol production, distribution, or alcohol-associated behavior. Retrospectively, it is an uncertain exercise to attempt to identify factors within societies which increase or decrease the risk of alcohol abuse's being defined and the extent of its occurring once defined. Various authorities have linked extensive alcoholism to rapid social change, to nonaccommodating culture contact, to urbanization, to strain, social disorganization, and the like. These may well be valuable notions; certainly Horton (in McCarthy, 1959) and Child, Bacon, and Barry (1965) have shown that economic-agricultural and socio-psychological factors can be linked to the prevalence of alcohol problems in nonliterate societies. Nevertheless, in an examination of complex societies, which are necessarily heterogeneous and often changing, such global yardsticks are difficult to apply reliably. We have, at the moment, no better conceptions or variables to propose as determinants of extensive alcohol problems in complex societies. We would agree, after this cursory historical review, that rapid social change leading to inferred group disorganization and personal hopelessness, uncertainty, misery, and anxiety when occurring in situations where alcohol is cheaply available appear linked to some rampant alcohol problems. However, the data are insufficient for identifying such factors in, let us say, ancient Egyptian "abuse." It is equally important to note that Asian societies with apparently similar troubles—if not much greater ones—have avoided serious alcohol problems for several thousand years. If some of them are now coming to alcohol troubles—as is said to be occurring in some Asian urban centers—it is reportedly among Westernized, wealthier persons rather than among the traditional poor. This suggests that an additional necessary component for actual abuse is compatibility of a drug's image as well as its effects with acceptable, if not prestige, values within a group (Carstairs, 1954; Lolli, Serianni, Golder, and Luzzato-Fegiz, 1958; Sadoun, Lolli, and Silverman, 1965).

On the other hand, quite different features also appear linked to alcoholic excesses—for example, prizing manly drinking and the warrior code appears repeatedly as a component of heavy drinking in the armies of Rome and ancient Gaul, in the Viking raiders, and among the contemporary Irish. Valuing the free and passionate spirit, the mystical embrace, and the plumbing of the depths reflects itself also in a pattern discernible from time to time whether in Dostoevsky or William James. One sees alcohol-inspired intensity in association with the Dionysian ethic (Benedict, 1950), religious frenzy, as in the Bacchae, or in communion with the dead, a modern practice in Guatemala (Bunzel in McCarthy, 1959; also Blum and Blum, personal observation, 1966). In any event, these are not matters of strain or anxiety; they are matters of life style and a way of seeking experience. Whether or not the accompanying drunkenness constitutes abuse depends upon whether or not there are observers who do not adhere to the warrior, mystical, or ecstatic creed. In any case, a moral may be drawn from Ulster, which is that the authoritative cry of "abuse" may have the same irrational, if not self-serving, roots. Whether or not a pattern of heavy, continuing alcohol intake as a life style leads, as in Jellinek's delta syndrome, to dependency is another matter—one probably involving nutrition, manner of intake, and individual personality and life stress.

As a final comment, we would note that from its beginnings alcohol appears to have been a favored drug and, in its competition with other psychoactive substances, is maintaining its preferential position. It continues to be employed in religion, in healing, and in ceremonies, but nowadays these functions are secondary to secular ones. Although alcohol is the drug most widely abused, it is, nevertheless, used safely and acceptably by the majority of those employing it (Blum, 1967). This suggests that with it, as with most other drugs in widespread use, human beings generally can handle mind-altering experiences rather well. There are, of course, those who cannot—upwards of 7 per cent in our own society. For them, the ancient regulatory methods of control over distribution and intake, along with the modern methods of rehabilitation (Blum and Blum, 1967), are clearly necessary.

A History of
Opium

Richard H. Blum

III

*T*here is dispute about the dates and correct interpretations of Western Asian and Eastern Mediterranean steles, papyri, tablets, pictographs, paintings, and the like which are cited as proof of early opium use. Some writers (Lewin, 1924; Terry and Pellens, 1928) have accepted 4000 B.C. as a date for Sumerian use, about 3500 B.C. for Egyptian use. Taylor (1963) sets 200 B.C. for opium use by Swiss lakeside dwellers. We have not been in a position to evaluate the primary sources cited, but it does seem clear that such early dates are subject to contest. By way of illustration, Dawson (1929), from his examination of Egyptian papyri, says it is unlikely that the Egyptians used opium medically before the first century A.D. Kritikos and Papadaki (1963) would disagree, as would Merrillees (1962); all of them present convincing evidence. Kritikos and Papadaki propose that opium was known in Crete, Cyprus, Greece, and the Aegean Islands—the Cretan finds, along with the Mycenian ones, being dated by Kritikos at 2000 B.C. They (citing Kramer and Levy, 1954) accept dates of 3000 B.C. for its presence in Sumer. They propose that it was used in religious ritual—the production of ecstatic states—since it was found in association with cult objects and divinities and in medicine. It was used in oracular divination and in the Asclepia. Merrillees, studying Cypriot finds, dates an active trade in liquid opium between Cyprus, as the producing country, and Egypt, as the importing one in the sixteenth century. He suggests that Egypt began cultivation about 1300 B.C. It was used in Cyprus in religious rituals circa 1700 B.C., while Fort (1965a) gives a date of about 850 B.C. for its mention in Persian annals. Its production for medical use in seventh-century Assyria is discussed by Sonnedecker (1958). Kritikos and Papadaki, in their review, note the medical use for myconeum—a tea made from whole-plant infusion—as a beverage for eyewash, and for plasters. They state that opium itself was sucked as a lozenge, taken in liquid form, sniffed, eaten, and used in suppositories; they even propose that smoke from burning resin was inhaled. Used as a hypnotic and analgesic when mixed with hemlock, opium was employed to kill. Its medical uses in Greece were systematized by 400 B.C., as the work of Hippocrates suggests. It was not, however, a paramount drug, for we see in Dioscorides that it was but one from among many plant remedies—some of the others of which were much more highly touted. Kolb (1962) cites a reference (which we have not seen) to the effect that in the fifth and third centuries B.C. Greek physicians were recommending avoidance of opium. Pliny and Celsus repeated the information of Dioscorides in the first century. Had it been of first-rank importance in the biblical world at that time, perhaps the wise men would have brought it as a gift to the infant Jesus along with frankincense and myrrh, which were then used as medicines, fumigants, and preservatives.

Despite its early use in religious rituals and medicine, opium was not quickly spread to other areas nor dare we assume its use was widespread even in locations where some employed it.[1] There is no evidence, as Sonnedecker points out, of any widespread concern with its effects or of any awareness of its dependency-producing potentials. Nor by medieval times does such mention occur, according to Sonne-

---

[1] In folklore research on a Greek island (Blum and Blum, 1965), we found that some islanders used the juice from the pod as a hypnotic and analgesic for infants, whereas other villagers, not more than a kilometer away, were not employing it in this manner; still others were ignorant of the practice. There was no evidence of folk medical use among adults or of any adult self-administration of any kind.

decker, although the Arabs used it widely. The general thesis is that Arab use increased as a substitute for alcohol following the prohibitions on the latter by Mohammed.

The history of opium in India is well described by Chopra and Chopra (1965). It was first mentioned by Barbosa in 1511, and its cultivation appears in the same century. During the Mogul (Timerud) period, opium trade with China was of great importance and was a state monopoly; in 1757, the monopoly passed into the hands of the East India Company and from there to, first, the British and then to the Indian governments. During the time of the Moguls, beginning with Babur and continuing with Akbar, opium taking was popular among all classes. The nobility drank "charburgha," which was a mixture of hemp, opium, wine, and kuknar; opium was also taken with water or in pill form. In 1893, the Royal Commission issued its voluminous report on opium (and one on cannabis), which concluded that opium smoking was rare but adult drinking and pill use were common and that it was used to treat ailing infants or given to them when their mothers left them to work. Generally, dosages were small and use was irregular; chronic opium eating was limited to older persons. Its folk medical use was paralleled by and probably derived from its employment in traditional Ayurvedic and Unani (Tibbi) medicine, probably being adopted in these systems in the fourteenth and fifteenth centuries. It continues to be used in Indian traditional medicine and in folk medicine (only occasionally including dosing infants) and is now eaten and smoked by what is reportedly a very small sector of the lower classes, where Chopra and Chopra state it is a group rather than an individual activity. Opium smoking was also practiced in social ceremonies—for example, at marriages and funerals and some Hindu religious rituals—but these practices are said to have disappeared. At no time has India been described as having an opium problem in the sense that China did, in spite of the fact that India has been and is an opium-producing country and one in which access to and use of the drug have been widespread. Official reports may well be suspect in terms of accuracy, but we do take them to reflect at least the level of concern if not of use, assuming the accuracy of observer accounts. A considerable mystery remains as to why the Chinese instead of the Indians came either to decide abuse was present and/or to suffer more adverse effects in fact. Poverty, nutritional deficit, and social disorganization cannot be differentially invoked as explanatory concepts. As will be seen, the role of local merchants, local government, and trading nations did differ. In India, merchandising locally was directed to traditional medical and folk medical use and, secularly, to organized social or group use; licit distribution was limited to forms suitable for eating rather than for smoking. International trading was directed toward China (and now Persia and the United States illicitly) rather than internally. Nowadays, opium for eating is still legal, but the sale of opium for smoking and the existence of smoking dens are prohibited. Only registered addicts may smoke legally. What accounts for the Indian/Chinese differences? Was it the Indian advertising and merchandising patterns, coupled with government restrictions on kinds of preparations legally available and kinds of settings tolerated for use, plus official Indian government support for production and sales (and implicit use)', as contrasted to official Chinese disapproval on economic-political-attitudinal grounds? This remains an open and interesting historical question.

It was certainly not in India that opium was first labeled a dangerous drug or a source of trouble. When that judgment was first rendered is difficult to ascertain. That remarkable traveler and writer Richard Burton observed in 1858, and wrote a year later about, the work disability and ill health present among Muslims and natives of East and Central Africa, commenting that locally their ailments and failings were attributed to their opium use. Regardless of whether or not the Arabs first recognized opium-induced disabilities, they certainly were the major early traders in the stuff and responsible for its diffusion throughout Asia and Africa. They are credited with introducing opium into China about the seventh century (Lewin, 1924; Williams, 1923), where the most flamboyant events in the political history of any drug later occurred. The Chinese themselves had no name for opium. Their term as well as ours is Arabic and that in turn is derived from the Greek for "vegetable juice." Sonnedecker (1958), citing Merrillees (and Terry and Pellens, 1928, as well as Williams, 1923), says there is no trace of intoxication mentioned in China and that its use was medical for nearly a thousand years. Only in the seventeenth century when, despite Ming prohibition, tobacco smoking had become well established, after being introduced by the Portuguese, did recreational use of opium smoking become popular. Although it was first mixed with tobacco ostensibly for folk medical use, later the proportion of opium was increased. In the 1840's, there were an estimated million users (Kolb, 1962), and after the 1850's, purportedly many millions smoked. The activity spread to all social levels; among the affluent it was a formal social ritual—for example, a ceremonial pipe smoking preceded business dealings. Doctors smoked while in consultation, diplomats and mandarins smoked at the conference table. Coolies enjoyed a pipe after the day's work. Some of the constabulary demanded a pipeful as a treat, prepayment, or bribe from the victim before investigating his complaint of a crime (Doolittle, 1867).

Within a short time, the setting for opium smoking among the working classes was institutionalized. Dens, divans, and clubs appeared. Although most opium taking was social in the sense that it was done in the company of others and was taught by one person to another (or imitated), its use by the lower classes did not seem to have facilitated social intercourse. Descriptions by contemporary observers (Fort, 1965a, b; Hess, 1965) emphasize dulling effects. On the other hand, even contemporary use by the wretched poor—the case in Hong Kong today—seems to have a self-medicating component; it is considered a cure for disease, a means for overcoming fatigue, and an aphrodisiac. Hess reports that today the majority of arrested Hong Kong addicts cite medical needs; about one third speak of it as a social experience—taken with other people for euphoric effects.

The assessment of ill-effects from opium smoking created controversy from the beginning. Not only merchants but physicians argued it did little harm—no more than tobacco or alcohol. When class and personality variables are considered, it is evident that the argument is not yet over. Testimony before the Philippine Opium Commission in 1905 cited moderate and nondamaging use by the Chinese, especially among better-off persons with established patterns of self-control and social adjustment and the need to buy opium so that withdrawal will never occur. A Formosan study in 1935 (Tu, cited by Kolb, 1962) showed most users then to be working in good jobs and without bad effects. The Hong Kong user, to the contrary, is poor and sick, according to Hess. Today, evidence shows successful maintenance of addicts (Schur, 1962), provided those addicts are initially nondelinquent and motivated toward the conventional world. On the other hand, most "susceptibles" to personal and social use do not appear to be so fortunate in birth and rearing.

There was a general consensus among observers through the years that the poor, once they took to the pipe—with the choice between opium and food—became more undernourished and ill than ever. Moderate use, however, did occur among those with intact minds, healthy bodies, and the means to afford both opium and food. Admittedly a small per cent of Chinese society, they nevertheless corresponded to those Americans who before the Harrison Act (our 1914 narcotic-control endeavor) used medicines containing opium or morphine[2] without observable personal decline—at least until the opium was withdrawn.

China, the importing nation with its millions of poor addicts, is to be compared with India, the exporting country. Once opium smoking began, Chinese use was personal or social—that is, unregulated, informal, and nontraditional rather than medicinal as such. In India, on the other hand, medicinal use was paramount after opium's introduction by the Moslems, and opium remains an important feature

[2] United States, Philippines Commission, *Report of the Committee to Investigate the Use of Opium in the Far East,* 59th Congress, First Session, 1905, Govt. Document #265 (Washington, D.C.: Government Printing Office, 1905). This is important because it is largely at variance with most published work on the so-called opium problem in nineteenth-century Asia. This collection of testimony points to the fact that the tide of reformism in the Western world coincided with the American victory in the Spanish-American War (1898). This left the United States with jurisdiction over many areas in the Pacific where opium-smoking Chinese minorities resided.

A vocal minority of the missionaries testifying before the committee admitted that most Chinese used opium moderately and that its effects were less destructive than those of alcohol. Insurance executives admitted asking whether Chinese applicants for insurance smoked opium, but stated they would insure moderate smokers. The United States Consul at Nanking, Mr. W. Martin, stated that men of wealth used opium for a lifetime without ill effects of any kind. Reverend Timothy Richards, in China for thirty-three years, testified that many Chinese use opium as moderately as people in the United States do tea or coffee. Doctors and businessmen generally agreed in their testimony that moderate use was frequent and abuse, both in quantity and quality, was no greater than abuse of alcohol in America and Europe.

Te-Duc-Luat (1925), an Indo-Chinese medical doctor, further questions the thesis that opium is an unadulterated vice and evil. At age seventy-four he made daily rounds, on foot, to some twenty patients, was the father of twenty-two healthy children (opiates are generally supposed to have anaphrodisiac effects, and heroin use is frequently associated with virtual sterility by researchers today), and since puberty he claims to have smoked "thirty pipes of opium daily . . ." Luat's conclusions are that the Chinese "moral" war against opium was economically motivated. Unable to grow their own opium in sufficient quantity or to stop the drain of silver from the country, he believes they enlisted the aid of the Puritan ethic and the Western reform movement to cast opium in the role of the ultimate evil.

of Ayurvedic medicine (Dwarakanath, 1965). There are Indian references to its use to keep political enemies out of circulation (doping
them up) or indeed to keep profligate sons from gambling and wench-
ing (P. N. Chopra, 1955) by sedating them. But most applications
seemed to have been for insomnia, nervousness, upset stomach, diar-
rhoea, rheumatic pains, and the like. Infants left by their mothers were
(and are) given opium to lull them. It was advertised as a prolonger
of sexual intercourse and for refreshing the weary. India, with this
traditional orientation, never attempted country-wide bans. It has
sought to reduce its use and availability. R. N. Chopra (1933, 1934,
1935) has described those who suffer ill effects as coming from lower
economic brackets, especially those undergoing the abstinence syndrome. As with many other descriptions of untoward effects, those of
withdrawal are said to be far more noticeable than those of sustained
use.[3] In any event, at the same point in time, two nations with an immense population of poor responded quite differently to opium; in one
it was smoked and became a problem; in the other, use remained, for
the most part, traditional and no problem or problem orientation appeared.

By the 1850's, millions of Chinese men—but very few women
—had become opium smokers and were reported to be drug addicts.
Agreement on addiction was by no means unanimous, for although
opium's withdrawal effects had been described by 1701 and compulsive
use by large numbers of Asians (Turks and Persians) had been described later in that same century, it was not until late in the 1850's
that there was agreement about opium's "addicting" potentials. Sonnedecker's (1958) review of the development of the concept of addiction
provides an interesting commentary. In China itself opium was advertised as having an exhilarating effect and as being an aphrodisiac.
Since its effects are more pronounced when it is smoked (it is absorbed
through the lungs) than when eaten, the change in method of use
provided an impetus for the rapid increase in its popularity—even if
neither of the prime claims for it were found to be its major immediate
effects or its long-term actual effects.

Commerce in the drug was of major international importance
and no spread of use would have been possible unless adequate supplies

[3] Withdrawal distress, of course, cannot occur unless there has been
sustained use, so that initiation and use remain problem areas even if acute
symptomatology is associated only with the absence of the drug.

existed. The Portuguese, Dutch, and Indians offered that supply in its early phases, but because opium was cultivated primarily in India, British trading interests in the eighteenth century gained a near monopoly, although American "China Clippers"—many of which would more accurately have been called "Opium Clippers"—also did a lively trade. In China, total prohibition alternated with heavily taxed legal importation. The former spawned a number of smugglers— "scuttling crabs and fast dragons"—plying rivers and coast, while the latter came under the jurisdiction of frequently corrupt officials whom the government designated as wholesalers. The first edict against opium was that of the emperor in 1729; as the boom developed, nevertheless, the emperors were made more aware of its cost in terms of a disastrous revival in the balance of payments, which, due to tea and silk exports, had favored China. The official imprecations—"a devilish foreign substance"—no more discouraged traffic in the mid-1800's than had the first imperial prohibitions. Laws continued to be passed by the Chinese as control efforts, but did not affect opium consumption or importation. What happened was comparable to prohibition in the United States with the added fillip that the Chinese were quietly encouraging opium-poppy production internally, but their morphine content remained inferior to the Indian variety. Chinese resistance to imported opium led to the two Opium Wars with England in 1842 and 1858, which enabled English merchants to continue their profitable trade.

As the nineteenth century grew older, a shift occurred and the worm began to turn. What had been pressure for importing opium to China—the Opium Wars as a supreme example—and grounds for arguing that opium was a comfort and benefit were reversed as opium, and the Chinese, appeared in the West. The shift was due in part to the literary endeavors which told of the risks—real and fancied—of opium; De Quincey led the field, beginning in 1821. The growing resistance to opium was also due to a public response to official Chinese sentiments. The Emperor Yung-Cheng, unable to control public demand, official corruption, or merchant smuggling at home, appealed instead to the English conscience. By mid-nineteenth century, opium had become, for the first time anywhere, a *moral* issue with the Christian church, ladies' aid societies, and some journalists as advocates. There were other important events as well. Physicians were becoming more scientific and observant, morphine was isolated, and, in 1853, the hypodermic needle was invented. When the Crimean, American

Civil, and Franco-Prussian Wars occurred (1854–1856, 1861–1865, 1870–1871), the wounded were given morphine, increasingly by means of injection. Wounded veterans became a visible habituated population. Coolie labor was simultaneously being imported into the United States, Canada, Europe, and Oceania, and with the laborers came their pipes. The "Yellow Peril"—those strangers who represented competitive labor with odd ways and opium—became Western-world inhabitants. Opium came to San Francisco in 1851.

The response to the Chinese neighbor and to opium was negative. The reform and the missionary saving of heathens at a distance were popular enough, but "heathen" habits at home were frightful. Tracts and broadsides, lurid articles, and pious "eye-witness" accounts of degenerate, drug-sodden, sex-crazed dope fiends fascinated and horrified the public. Most were interested in the reportage, not the drug, but a few citizens became interested in the latter and, for the first time in the West, not just for medical reasons. Artists looking for new experiences, distraught widows (so it is said) for whom alcohol was taboo, gamblers, miners, prostitutes, and soldiers of fortune took morphine, relied on "soothing syrups" loaded with opiates, or picked up the pipe. The literate continued to entertain with their terrible experiences, even as they do now (Burroughs in Ebin, 1961; Cocteau, 1957)'. Lobbies were formed, physicians identified addiction as such, and temperance (meaning abstinence) societies took to the field.

The first narcotics-control act was passed in San Francisco in 1875 to suppress opium smoking (Kolb in United States Public Health Report, 1964). Between 1897 and 1922, every state except one had regulated opiate distribution. After the report of the Philippine Opium Commission in 1905, the United States in 1909 prohibited the importation of smoking opium; international action had begun with the Shanghai Conference in 1901 and with the 1912 Hague Conference. International cooperation in control of opium trade had begun and continues today under the auspices of the United Nations Narcotics Bureau. With law came criminals: users who would not stop, merchants who would not quit. The drug market went underground and, in the Western world, the narcotics underworld was born.

Enter heroin!

Some expected morphine to cure the dependent opium eater. It did not. Heroin, expected to be the "heroic" cure for morphine dependency and so named, came on the scene in 1898. Requiring no pipe, easily administered, light to carry, and much more powerful than opium, it gave quick relief for anyone suffering withdrawal distress. As a cure for opium smoking, it was too late. Control of imports in China had reduced opium smoking in that country by the turn of the century; only older wealthier folk continued, as did the Southern hill tribesmen, who continued to grow their own. Kolb (1962) states that by 1917 China was nearly free of opium use; however, if so, a latent demand must have remained because cultivation was resumed and opium, now supplemented by heroin and morphine, was back in use by the 1930's. On the other hand, Fort (1965a) estimates eight million users in the same years. By 1937, one estimate was of fifteen million Chinese opium smokers, although Fort estimates ten million. Some of this use was social; opium parties akin to cocktail parties were held. In spite of local controversy as to ill effects, the Chinese government instituted the death penalty for addicts who failed to be cured, and many were executed. There are no data on modern China; the government claims no more use, although it is evident that hill tribesmen are still smoking and exporting opium.

In the Western world the social and private use of opiates had not expanded remarkably except by those frontiersmen and delinquents who took them up in their small societies (see Stevenson, 1956, for a superb study of its diffusion in Vancouver, British Columbia). Opium importation and distribution controls led to changes in the content of remedies; Lydia Pinkham's alcohol replaced Dover's Powders and Sydenham's Syrup on the chemists' shelves. For a short and remarkable period in history, ladies rather than gentlemen appear to have been the predominant sex using a mind-altering substance (see Brown in O'Donnell and Ball, 1966)—a trend which continues today since women predominate in the use of tranquilizers. For this brief period, the females were seeking opium out, not simply receiving it from doctors—or so the reports tell us. If that be so, it was the only period in history in which female drug use in informal settings (albeit self-medicating and, in that sense, traditional folk-medical) was greater than male use. As to how many Americans used opium in pre-Harrison Act days, we shall never know. Use varied by locality, and statistics varied by case-finding method. The range of rates of use seems to have been from 1/1000 to 16/100 (O'Donnell and Ball; also Terry and Pellens, 1928).

Heroin was another story. Easily smuggled, easily hidden, it met the demand of the delinquent, unstable poor, or adventuresome public (Chein, Gerard, Lee, and Rosenfeld, 1964; Wakefield, 1964; Chein, 1956; Freedman, 1963; Finestone, 1960)—a public still involved in illicit-drug activities. It remains popular with these groups whose using numbers although small—an estimated maximum of 200,000 in the United States (see Blum, 1967c)—nevertheless remain an object of great public concern. Elsewhere in the world, opium smoking is on the decline but where it has been outlawed in Asia (O'Donnell and Ball; also Radji, 1959), heroin has become a more dangerous substitute. Opium itself is still in use in Southeast Asia and among some now old-fashioned Chinese elsewhere. In Asia, as in the Western world, the urban dweller using opiates tends to rely on heroin or sometimes on heroin-cocaine combinations. It may be injected or inhaled as in "chasing the dragon." (See Hess, 1965.)

Aside from the urban poor—especially the disorganized, male, minority poor in the United States—there are particular groups who risk opiate use. One group is immense and uses it almost without any difficulty. These are patients receiving opiates or their synthetic analogues in supervised medical treatment. In the United States, for example, it is estimated (Blum, 1967c) that in 1963 over a billion doses of these true narcotics were administered or prescribed. Few, if any, cases of dependency were reported. On the other hand, those who did the prescribing—physicians—get in trouble at a rate much greater than any other group. The presumption is not of any economic privation and related social distress. The obvious feature is their unsupervised access to the drug. Other features, according to Modlin and Montes (1964), are a point of vocational and life crisis, neurotic fatigue, and a background of alcoholic fathers and childhood illness. Inferred but not yet demonstrated must be an unusual reaction to opiates as well, for Beecher (1959) reports that most well persons who are given morphine do not enjoy its effects.

There is recent evidence of an increase in heroin use among populations with whom it has been unpopular before. In Western Canada, for example (Stevenson, 1956), the number of users has tripled over a thirty-year period (whereas Canada on the whole has showed a decline); similarly, in England, which has long enjoyed very little opiate use, there has been a recent dramatic increase (Bewley, 1965, 1966; Chapple, 1965)—from about 20 new cases of heroin dependency in 1959 to 270 cases in 1965 and to over 500 cases in 1966.

The new population of users in England are young, some are female; occasionally, upper as well as middle and lower classes are represented; and nearly all users have had prior experience with a variety of other drugs without medical supervision. After heroin use they continue with other drugs as well. Sources are said to be overprescription by physicians, which in turn allows proselytization by users with a supply among their own social groups. In the United States, as our student data in the companion volume (Blum and Associates, 1969) show, there is also experimentation with heroin by some middle- and upper-class high school and college students—a pattern which seems to parallel the English phenomenon and is not explicable on the grounds either of easy access or social deprivation but which, rather, emerges as part of a willingness to experiment with a variety of mind-altering substances regardless of legal restraint or Establishment warnings of the undesirability of drug-oriented life styles.

As for the contemporary means of diffusion of heroin, opium, and other illicit drugs, these are through criminal channels. The study of these operations is outside the scope of this chapter. In brief, however, it may be said that for any drug in demand there has never been a shortage of persons willing to engage in traffic for gain (see Walker, 1960). Economic gain is obviously not a sufficient motive for criminal commerce, since most citizens do not engage themselves in it. What social, psychological, economic, and political circumstances account for the emergence of criminals trafficking in drugs is a subject of continuing interest. In terms of the world-wide scene, it is clear that the levels of criminal organization, sophistication, and culturally defined criminality vary markedly and are intimately related to other features of both the drug trafficker's aim in life and to the setting in which he lives.

SUMMARY

Probably used medically and in religious ceremonies in Western Asia and the Eastern Mediterranean before 2000 B.C., opium has continued in systematic use in folk cultures throughout Asia. Its ritual religious use disappeared before being described in any literature, although its potential for producing mental states interpreted as mystical or religious is occasionally affirmed today by individuals. Distributed to Eastern Asia by Arabs, it remained in medical use in China and India until tobacco smoking was taught (in the 1600's). The Chinese became the first nation with a drug-abuse problem when opium was mixed with tobacco and the social and personal, as well as the medically sanctioned, use of opium became widespread. Ill effects were associated mostly with poverty, especially since withdrawal symptoms were more likely to be seen in those who could not afford to maintain themselves on the drug. In those countries where traditional folk medical patterns were stable, neither a problem nor a social reaction occurred.

The concept of physical dependency was slow to develop, as was the concern with the social aspects of opium use; both appeared in the 1800's, and by 1900 opium was considered medically to be a danger, socially to be a menace, and morally to be a vice. These developments were associated with sociopolitical, economic, and reformist changes in the Western world. Campaigns invoking morality and criminal law developed with the subsequent and partial control of drug traffic. This control was made more difficult by the discovery of heroin, which is more easily smuggled and is more potent than opium. Its use—now primarily by means of injection following discovery of the hypodermic syringe—is still considered a major social, criminal, and moral threat, even though in the Western world only a relatively few persons are involved and most of them are already members of deprived and disaffected groups. Heroin use is centered among male urban dwellers, apparently young more often than old (although our statistics may play us false) and more often (in the United States) minority members. Data from other countries are scarce, except for rare studies such as that of Hess (1965) in Hong Kong.

When supplies are controlled, administration is supervised, personal expectations are limited and defined by those in authority, and recipients are healthy and well adjusted, dependency, a deviant label, or untoward consequences are unlikely to appear in those to whom opium, its derivatives, or synthetic analogues are administered. However, when these conditions are not met, the risk of a troublesome outcome is increased. Who will fall victim to what risk is still but poorly understood; situational crises, psychological deficiencies, learning in a peer group, the presence of pain and anxiety, disaffection from controlling norms of virtue, lack of ordinary gratifications from life and work, nutritional deficiency, special "autonomic" learning—all have been implicated. To these complex and interacting variables the following must also be added: reasonably straightforward pharmacological considerations such as potency of substance, frequency of use, manner of administration, and condition of the person receiving the drug. What risks we are talking about is another matter. Physical dependency, compulsive use, associated illness and malnutrition, correlated membership in deviant groups, accidental death, mental clouding, criminal involvement, arrest and imprisonment, failure of treatment—each is a kind of risk. There is no reason to lump them together or to expect that the determinants of one are determinants of another. These considerations of effects are beyond our immediate concern, but an awareness that there are differing kinds of risks, each with considerable argument associated with it, cannot be divorced from an epidemiological history. The reason is that both sanctions for use and reactions against use affect patterns of use and that sanctions of either kind, positive or negative, rest upon either an appraisal of effects or an inference as to their correlates.

A History of
Cannabis

Richard H. Blum

IV

"Marijuana," "pot," "grass," "bhang," "hashish," "charis," "ganja," and "kif" are among the names given to the plant *Cannabis sativa* or to preparations made from it.[1] Growing wild in a great variety of soils and climates, it is also especially cultivated as a cash crop in India, Nepal, Ceylon, Afghanistan, Mexico, and parts of Africa. It is also illicitly cultivated in the United States and elsewhere.

There is a tendency for writers to accept very early dates for the use of psychoactive substances—opium, cannabis, amanita mushrooms, and, as we have seen earlier, alcohol. One often reads that cannabis was known in ancient China, as, for example, "the liberator of sin" in the Emperor Shen Nung's 2737 B.C. pharmacopeia. Unfortunately, Shen Nung is only a legend and few Chinese dates before 1000 B.C. can be accepted with confidence (*Encyclopaedia Britannica*, 1962; also Sullivan, 1967). There is archaeological evidence for Chi-

---

[1] For other names, and some botanical confusion, see World Health Organization, Expert Committee on Addiction Producing Drugs, *The Question of Cannabis: Cannabis Bibliography*, 1965 (Mimeographed).

nese hemp cultivation at an early date, perhaps 3000 B.C. (Kwang-Chih-Chang, 1963), and Bretschneider (1895) reviews references to hemp during the early period, but whether it was ever used in ancient China as a psychoactive substance is an open question.

There is a similar uncertainty about the earliest dates for cannabis in India, although there is general agreement upon knowledge of its potency prior to the time of Christ. Spellman (1967) states that "bhanga appears in the Atharva Veda in the sense of cannabis about 1300 B.C."—a date in agreement with Grierson writing in the *Indian Hemp Commission Report* (1893–1894), although he suggests that no mention of its intoxicating qualities appears until the tenth century A.D. Ingalls (1967) comments that "bhanga" does appear meaning "cannabis" in the *Sus'ruta* at a date somewhat before Christ. Rosevear (1967) claims dates between 2000 and 1400 B.C. for the Indian mention of cannabis and claims that its use was taught to Indian priests by Iranians. His proposal that early yogis smoked it is dubious in view of the very recent dates for smoking of any sort except in the Western hemisphere.

A verified mid-Asian date for cannabis is based on both written and archaeological evidence. Herodotus in his *Histories,* published circa 430 B.C., describes how the Scythians used wild hemp ("kannabis" is Greek for hemp) in a purification rite which followed the elaborate ceremonies upon burial of a king. Hot stones were placed in a cauldron within a tent, seeds were thrown on the stones, and the bathing Scythians (it is likely water was added to the stone-heated cauldron in a practice not unlike the Finnish sauna of today) inhaled the vapor and "howled for joy."[2] Rice (1957) describes an archaeological find at Pazrik (Rudenko, 1953) confirming Herodotus' writing; a cauldron of stones and hemp seeds was found along with tent poles. Rice doubts whether inhalation was purificatory; she proposes relaxation instead but offers no evidence. It is likely that the Scythians were using cannabis before Herodotus, perhaps even before their settlement circa 700 B.C. in South Russia. These dates for mid-Asian use of cannabis conform to those which ascribed its use to Persia circa 700–600 B.C. (inferred from the *Zendavesta*) and to Ashurbanipal's Assyrian reign (669–626 B.C.) based on cuneiform-tablet interpretation. It has also been proposed that cannabis was the grass that Nebuchadnezzar ate when he

[2] Whether or not cannabis has any mind-altering effects is another matter.

was described as being mad—a tenuous deduction but amusing in view of today's slang, "grass" for marijuana. Fort (1965a) gives a date of 800 B.C. for its introduction into India; however, Dwarakanath (1965) gives its earliest Indian date as circa 400 B.C.

Early Indian use seems to have been religious; it was not until the twelfth century A.D. that medical applications were set forth. Cannabis was a holy plant to some Hindus, with early legends (Fort) indicating that the angel of mankind lived in its leaves. Its later Indian use included traditional medical, religious, and social components; in recent times it has been smoked (in the form of ganja and charas), sometimes mixed with tobacco, datura, or opium, according to Fort, chewed (as bhang), or eaten as a confectionery. In the 1830's, its Indian use was incorporated into modern medicine. The importance of cannabis in religious practice in modern India is not to be overlooked. According to the Indian Hemp Commission (1893–1894) and Chopra and Chopra (1965), it is taken at Hindu and Sikh temples and Mohammedan shrines; bhang from a common bowl is one way it is used. When Mohammedan fakirs congregate they may be joined by other cannabis users; among fakirs, bhang is viewed as the giver of long life and a means of communion with the divine spirit. Ascetics and religious mendicants (sadus) also use cannabis to overcome hunger and thirst, as well as to aid in meditation. High-caste Hindus not allowed alcohol are allowed bhang at religious ceremonials; bhang can also be used at marriage ceremonies and family festivals. In Nepal it is distributed at temples to all Shiva followers on certain feast days. According to Sharma (1967), certain Buddhist priests in Nepal also use bhang, and there are Shiva sadus, now being studied by Sharma, who use bhang chronically several times a day. Nepalese use (whether bhang or charas)—either by sadus or more intermittently among the poor, and occasionally among the "urban set" socially—is not seen as a social problem nor are there yet reports of adverse medical effects (Sharma).

By the tenth century A.D., cannabis was well known throughout the Mediterranean and Arab worlds. It is of interest that its use was not prohibited by Mohammed (570–632 A.D.) while that of alcohol was. Even so, some African Moslems have outlawed it on religious grounds whereas most of Islam has not; legal restraints, in the sense of laws promulgated by political authority, have been recent (nineteenth and twentieth centuries), so that in nearly all Moslem countries except Morocco cannabis is not prohibited.

Cannabis was one of the first psychoactive drugs to develop a bad reputation of the sensational sort. The story comes in many versions, the earliest attributed to Marco Polo. Generally agreed is that just prior to the First Crusade, about 1090 A.D., a fanatical Moslem group led by Hasan-i-Sabba, the "Old Man of the Mountains," settled near Baghdad and spread from there through Persia and parts of Iraq and Syria, remaining powerful until the last part of the thirteenth century. Descendants of the group are the contemporary Ismaeli sect (now led by Karim Aga Khan). Hasan (from whose name both "hashish" and "assassin" are often said to be derived, comes both from the Arab word for a dry herb or hay—thence the dry leaves of hemp—with "assassin" coming from hashish eater) had vowed to rid the world of false prophets. The legend has it he enlisted young followers to kill those of whom the "old man" disapproved. There is controversy over whether these fanatics killed (1) because they were under the influence of hashish, or (2) because they were promised a reward of paradise induced by hashish (perhaps that vision supplemented by material flesh and pleasantries), or (3) because they were simply a violent and politically dangerous group who came to the attention of the West, including the Crusaders, and who were subject to romantic speculation in the sense that a drug they may well have taken (but which was new to the Westerner) was given a causal role for political behavior not unusual in those (or our own) times in the Middle East, or (4) because they were simply a revolutionary group and were tarred with the hashish label by their conservative rivals (Hodgson, 1955). It has even been suggested (Mandel, 1966) that opium may have been the drug in question. In any event, the importance of the assassins from a social-historical point of view is that they mark the first instance of a widespread attribution of dangerous behavior arising from intentional manipulation of drug effects for a whole group. It is a clear-cut example of drug "abuse" as popularly defined—that is, the damage occurs not so much to the user as to those around him. It is also an early case of a legend publicly accepted without attention's being paid to complicating uncertainties. For example, what was the assassins' behavior when they were not using drugs? According to their political kindred, what other effects did the hashish have? Had a first-hand observer seen the events which were later incorporated into the story?

Although the assassins were the first group said to have killed because of hashish, they were by no means the last for whom some relationship between that drug and violence was set forth. Walton (1938) notes that some believed Genghis Khan induced the fury of his Mongols, the Golden Horde, by encouraging hashish use. Although the nomad hordes did drink alcohol heavily, the hashish devil need not be invoked to account for the periodic fierce sweeps of Mongol nomads west and south. One of these has given us an autobiography in which hemp use is indeed described, but nowhere mentioned as the cause of his violence. Babur, the first of the Moguls (Lamb, 1961) and a descendant both of Tamerlane and Genghis Khan, described how he would sometimes mix tincture of hemp and opium, too (beginning in his mid-twenties, the date about 1505 A.D.). He also ate hemp sweetmeats and, when taking hemp, abjured alcohol. He reports no ill or violent effects from either hemp or opium, but was sorely distressed by wine—his "death-in-life."

The route of introduction is not known. Given its use in the Scythian and South Russian area, it may have moved through Eastern Europe or, equally possible, it could have been introduced via the Balkans or Spain during the expansion of Islam or the later Ottoman Empire. Moreau (1845), author of one of the first works on cannabis, believes that hemp itself was introduced via Russian Asia but that its adoption by Europeans as a psychoactive substance was subsequent to European contact in the eighteenth and nineteenth centuries with the Arabs. Ibn al-Baitar (1197–1248), cited by Laufer, Hambly, and Linton (1930), was an earlier Moslem traveler to Egypt. A botanist, he discussed the cultivation of hemp and its use—either eaten or drunk in tincture—primarily by religious mendicants, the Mohammedan fakirs. Their use, al-Baitar said, led to excitement, hilarity, and fits of folly.

Ibn Battuta was another Moslem botanist and merchant who traveled from Persia to East Africa and provided detailed descriptions of custom and trade in much of the Arab world. In *Travels A.D. 1325–1354* (published in 1959), he describes alcoholism as a serious condition among the upper classes (compare Babur). He notes that the betel nut was a more esteemed gift than gold or silver in South Arabia, being symbolic of friendship and valued as an aphrodisiac, and he describes hashish (dry grass) as being made *either* of hemp or henbane.

The latter contains hyoscyamine and scopolamine, both of which have strong effects on the central nervous system.[3] Battuta says that the henbane hashish was common in Turkey, Persia, and India and was also known as bhang (an Indian term now reserved for cannabis). Battuta does not describe any traditional ritual use of hashish (religious—as in al-Baitar's fakirs—medical, or sociopolitical) but does speak of its being widely eaten. Mosques were one of the public places where it was taken, but he offers no indication about special motivation for its use there.

Information on the spread of cannabis to Africa and to Europe is meager. It is indigenous in locales on both continents, but there is no evidence that simply because a plant is native or even cultivated as hemp for fiber that there will be knowledge of its psychoactive properties. It is likely that Africans in contact with the Arab world learned of cannabis use during the spread of Islam (ninth through eleventh centuries) and its resultant conversions, acculturation, and trade (including the slave trade). It did not appear to reach South Africa until the Dutch brought it in 1852 (Laufer et al., 1930; Walton, 1938, gives a later date). As for its introduction to Europe, it is not possible to date the plant origins. Helbaek (1965) on paleoethnobotanical grounds does not believe it was introduced into Europe until after the fall of Rome (circa 450 A.D.). It is reported (Reininger in Andrews, 1967) that Busse opened a fifth-century B.C. tomb in Germany in which a funerary urn containing cannabis-plant remnants was found. Its documented use as a psychoactive is a considerably later phenomenon.

The most important event in the next stage of the cannabis sequence was, curiously, unrelated to cannabis itself. It was the introduction of tobacco and the technique of tobacco smoking into Europe. We shall present that history separately. Suffice it to say here that the plant was introduced to England in 1565 and by 1614 it was in widespread use there. The technique of smoking dried materials spread rapidly throughout the world, and it was this technique which, once learned, provided a new method for ingesting cannabis. Subsequent to this, cannabis use changed and spread and is, in fact, still spreading.

As with tobacco, the new method for ingesting cannabis was without tradition and was not absorbed into any traditional or ritual usage in any area where it was introduced with smoking. Thus, there

---

[3] One wonders to what extent the various hashish effects—as, for example, in the assassin stories—reflect the variety of ingredients in that stuff.

is no evidence of any initial religious employment of the smoking method, although we shall see that for some groups a religious mystique —almost always in conjunction with symbolic sociopolitical group activities—later emerged. As with tobacco, there were some initial claims for medical utility, although once smoking was introduced, the private and social uses have predominated over folk-medical applications. What this has meant, depending on class and culture, has been that secular use has not infrequently been associated with sudden and dramatic increases in individual or group use of cannabis. With this nontraditional drug use have come considerable variations in settings and intentions and, subsequently, in drug effects as well. These instances of rapid cannabis adoption—usually by individuals acting as such even though identifiable as members of particular subgroups—have occurred repeatedly since the 1600's. We shall later give some illustrations.

Cannabis smoking was, according to Walton (1938), introduced into South America by the Spaniards in 1545. Its spread in the New World occurred partly through Spanish activities, but also seems to have been introduced—again, always in conjunction with smoking and substitution for tobacco—by the slave trade. West Coast Africans who had first traded slaves among themselves, then with the Arabs, and finally ironically were themselves traded, appear to have introduced it into Brazil and possibly into the West Indies. The events are difficult to disentangle and dates are tenuous. For example, it is also possible that cannabis was not brought into the West Indies until the late eighteenth century with the Asian Indian migration; in Jamaica, for instance, the word for cannabis is "ganja," which is Indian.

The adoption of cannabis by Europeans has been limited, the reasons for which—given their remarkable acceptance of tobacco— remain a question of great interest to an epidemiologist. Moreau (1845), a French psychiatrist, was one of the first to write a book on cannabis. It contains many important observations, including ones on drug diffusion. In that regard, he dates French interest in the drug around the mid-to-late 1700's and early 1800's. Noting the much earlier presence of hemp in Europe (the great botanist Linnaeus named it *Cannabis sativa* in 1753), he expresses the view that personal experimentation with the drug depended upon (his) contemporary European travelers—writers and scientists—learning its use from Arabs and returning to be the link for its distribution to others with artistic or scientific curiosity. He describes his own observations on its effects and on his endeavors to induce his colleagues at Bicêtre to try it as a personal experience. The medical community was not receptive but artists and writers were. So it was that Moreau himself introduced its use to Theophile Gautier about the turn of the century, and Gautier in turn organized the Club des Haschischins, whose members included Victor Hugo, Charles Baudelaire, and Honore de Balzac—all of them Romantics dedicated to art for art's sake, individual freedom, and the overthrow of tyranny, patriotic (egalitarian) nationalism, and a sense or rebirth of mankind based on optimism following the French Revolution (and ignoring its terror and chaos). Importantly, the hashish consumed by the Bohemian elite ("Bohemian" based in the fifteenth century on the French assumption that gypsies came from Bohemia) in Paris was not smoked but was eaten as a sweetmeat ("Dawamesc"), just as Arabs had eaten it for hundreds of years. Interesting, too, in terms of drug-use learning is that Baudelaire, who had prior personal difficulties due to wine and opium (laudanum, a mixture of wine and opium—another Asiatic beverage), had been to India where he had not learned hashish use, we surmise, because he had no contact with traditional medical or religious use there, but had learned it among his fellow artists in Paris. His hashish use was short lived and replaced by opium. For descriptions of the hashish experience by both writers see their reprinted articles in Ebin (1961). Both accounts emphasize personal experiences (aesthetic, mystical, euphoric, hallucinatory, frightening, psychotic-like, and erotic) and so, necessarily, the exaltation of inner states. We might paraphrase Baudelaire's remark that "the true hero finds his entertainment by himself" as "finds his entertainment *in* himself."

Moreau himself did more than initiate cannabis use among an artistic, optimistic avant-garde—thereby setting off a chain of events which continues to this day. He also was one of the first psychiatrists to experiment with psychoactive drugs in the treatment of mental illness, applying datura (homeopathically) to fight hallucinations with hallucinations. He must be regarded as one founder of pharmacology as a science. He also wrote knowledgeably of drug effects, emphasizing hashish variations due to personality, physical condition, motivation and self-control, dosage, settings, admixture with other drugs,[4] expec-

---

[4] Moreau describes how the Arabs mixed hashish with opium, datura,

tations, and the like—in short, an almost complete description of variables now known to be associated with psychoactive-drug outcomes. Moreau's experimentation with drugs on mental patients and his theories about mental states and drug therapy constitute a scientific landmark in psychiatric care, the subject of which is beyond the scope of this chapter.

Writers were also important in introducing knowledge of cannabis into the United States. The extremely popular writer Bayard Taylor (excerpted in Ebin, 1961) tried hashish first in Egypt and then in Damascus. Taylor, too, ate his hashish as was the Damascene custom. His book included his hashish experiences and appeared in 1855. Another American, Fitzhugh Ludlow, took cannabis, not in the mystic East but in his home town of Poughkeepsie, procuring it shortly after his local pharmacist had imported the resin for use in treating lockjaw. Ludlow, a college junior at the time, says his curiosity stemmed from his having read Taylor's work a few months before. Ludlow's own laudatory article followed two years later, in 1857, proclaiming emotional, mystical, and aesthetic merit for the experience. On the other hand, Ludlow soon abandoned hashish eating, this time on the grounds he had read something which was a counterinfluence. That something was the first of the popular "I-was-an-addict" type of article published anonymously in *Scribner's* magazine in 1856. In it, an American and former Damascus resident and hashish user reports how—when he was shipped a box at his American home and persuaded by his fiancée and a doctor friend to take it—he had the fantasy that he killed his fiancée and afterwards felt that he was indeed close to that act. Ludlow himself, although abandoning drugs, maintained his interest in the problems of addiction and rehabilitation.

It was some years after Ludlow and Taylor that cannabis use as an identifiable social phenomenon occurred among North Americans. Merchant seamen were said to have introduced it to Costa Rica and, by 1916, first Puerto Rican soldiers and then American soldiers in the Panama Canal Zone were using it—a matter which became subject to official inquiry (Siler, Sheep, Bates, Clark, Cook, and Smith, 1933).[5] American soldiers had also learned its use when fighting Pancho

---

or Spanish fly (cantharides, a kind of beetle, ingestion of which causes gastroenteritis and priapism, used by Arabs as an aphrodisiac).

[5] The military report found marijuana to be a mild intoxicant used to alleviate monotony by primarily moronic and psychopathic soldiers, most of

Villa about 1916 along the Mexican border. Mexican use in turn is difficult to date; Walton (1938)' states the first reference in Mexico is 1886 and that by 1898 smoking had spread rapidly. By 1920, it was known in New Orleans, where a newspaper account said it was being sold to school children by vicious elements. Investigations termed it a tempest in a teapot, but journalistic coverage continued. These events of the 1920's appear to be the first widespread sensationalism over the drug and the first in which the exploitation of the innocent (a still-popular view of children)' in America was a theme. We are unable to learn how that sensationalism took hold—perhaps it was aided by the foreign (Mexican)' image of the drug (compare the reaction with opium when brought in by Chinese laborers)' and perhaps, too, by earlier accounts (Ludlow, Baudelaire, and De Quincey on opium)' of licentious, drug-using Bohemians. Perhaps, too, the general reform agitation against opium during the preceding years had set the stage for an antidrug reaction which would include marijuana.

We consider none of these as sufficient explanations for the focus—which has continued to this day—of public concern about the exploitation of childish innocence and the emphasis on murderous and sexually aberrant behavior under drug influence. We do not imply that impulses are not released under drug influence; we simply remark on early journalistic preoccupation with these ill-documented possibilities. Becker (1963), facing the same question, attributes American preoccupation with drug control (including the Prohibition experiment)' to three values: the Protestant ethic demanding self-control, hard work, and future-oriented planning; pragmatism and utilitarianism, which disapprove of ecstasy or withdrawal from the material world; and humanitarianism, which encourages moral crusades for reform. In *Utopiates* (1964)' and in Chapter Twelve, we discuss some other possible features underlying this national interest in drug dangers.

In any event, we find, beginning in the mid-1800's in the United States, the start of the public debate about cannabis and by 1920 we find use increasing, primarily among a few soldiers exposed to other cultures and by some citizens (probably lower-class)' in port cities. By the late 1930's, use had spread to Northern urban centers

whom preferred tobacco to marijuana and none of whom misbehaved because of marijuana.

but was confined (New York City Mayor's Committee on Marihuana, sometimes called the La Guardia Report, 1940) almost entirely to Negro and Latin-American slum dwellers. At that time, there was little use by children or adolescents, no association with crime or sexual excess, and no evidence of the "stair-step" chain of marijuana to heroin. Its use was social and friendly and mild euphoria was the stated reason for use. During that same ten-year period, there occurred widespread journalistic interest and public anxiety, the development of what appear to be important and strongly held myths about marijuana's dangerous nature, and a sustained campaign for punitive control, which led, in 1936, to the Marihuana Tax Act. Ironically, the negative reports as to dangers (the Mayor's Committee, the Panama investigations, and the earlier report of the British Indian Hemp Commission in 1894) did not relieve anxiety or produce lack of interest but merely became part of an expanding public interest, which even as early as 1931 had been decried by a Treasury Department report (Becker, 1963) as encouraging the spread of cannabis through publicity. A similar interest in the effects of publicity was voiced by the Mayor's Committee, which offered the opinion that European restraint in marijuana use was attributable to the acceptance by Europeans of the reports (Baudelaire, De Quincey, *et al.*) by their artistic and literary elite as to the frightening effects of toxic doses. What kind of publicity produces what kind of public interest has yet to be determined; similarly, what kind of educational endeavor leads to what changes in drug interest or drug taking is not established. It does seem clear that public information plays a role in shaping interest, curiosity, and willingness to take cannabis as well as other drugs.

Since the *La Guardia Report* of 1940, there has been an exaggeration in the trends of each of these: use, punitive legislation, public concern with effects, journalistic interest, and other publicity, including claims of inner revelations not unlike the early "kingdom of dreams" of Ludlow. Our history cannot accurately take us to the moment but we offer some American trends. Elsewhere (Blum and Associates, 1964, 1969), we describe expanding interest by the upper and middle class in the smoking of cannabis (and in Alice B. Toklas' recipes for Arab-style marijuana cookies). Among adolescents the slum poor, mostly male, can be heavily involved (Blumer, 1967; Chein, Lee, Gerard, Rosenfeld, 1964) whereas preadolescent use appears learned either from older peers or from parents and, at the moment, seems to be an upper-income phenomenon.

Although there is still no evidence of any causal "stair-step" effect such as that marijuana use leads to heroin, evidence does indicate (Blum and Associates, 1964) that an initial interest in drugs, which is necessarily expressed in taking one of many possible illicit-exotic substances, can lead to expanding drug interests and commitment to a life style in which drugs play a predominant role. A recent California report (1967) shows that one out of eight juveniles initially arrested for marijuana use were arrested for heroin use within the next five years. On the other hand, the majority of juveniles originally arrested for marijuana offenses remained free of any further arrest record during the five-year period. Arrest figures do show a dramatic rise for juvenile marijuana offenses.

Unlike the United States, there have been no reports from continental Europe of expanding marijuana use. As we shall see, there have been dramatic Scandinavian increases in the use of stimulants. Only in England does a parallel to our own situation appear to exist, and it is on a small scale indeed—at least at the date of this writing. Nevertheless, it has been striking enough to require convening of a Royal Commission, to bring about changes in British methods of drug distribution (including heroin) and, as a result, to worry the body politic. Our data are from Chapple (1964, 1965; Joyce, 1964, 1965) and personal interviews and observation. Most English pot smokers are in their twenties, begin adolescent experimentation with easily available amphetamine-barbiturate combinations ("purple hearts"), and then discover marijuana. Ideologically, many are pacifistic, left wing, and anti-Establishment. Chapple contends that some have an admiration for an image of a fully alive black Jamaican—the fantasy of the white Negro of Mailer—as a cannabis user, although actual incidence of Jamaican use in England is very low. Supply has been from Pakistan, Nigeria, and possibly Jamaica. The initiation pattern is both within peer groups and within families; most have histories of multiple-drug use and what we would call a drug orientation. As yet, no epidemiological studies show actual distribution of experimentation in the population; certainly it occurs among children of the elite as well as among middle- and lower-class youths. It is likely that the future will bring both more data and more illicit-exotic drug use in England.

Elsewhere, the last hundred years have seen great changes in patterns of cannabis use; these have been particularly noteworthy in Africa. We have already indicated that African exposure to traditional hashish followed Islam in the north and was introduced by colonial powers in the south beginning in the 1950's. The technique of smoking was simultaneously a colonial introduction. From the beginning (early 1600's), tobacco was immensely popular and cannabis popularity also developed. Almost immediately, damaging effects of cannabis were described among Africans in Madagascar (Flacourt, cited by Laufer *et al.*, 1930). These effects are attributed in part to the manner of use, which requires the smoker to inhale as deeply and as swiftly as possible (for either hemp or tobacco) with the apparent intent of producing rapid intoxication or a comatose state. Later, water pipes were introduced, which may be a technique to modify effects. According to Laufer, it was the smoking itself which was the paramount pursuit and either tobacco or hemp was equally popular; it was availablity which was the key. In some places datura was also smoked. When a drug was in short supply, wood chips were mixed in as a supplement; when no drug was available, a hot coal might be smoked to provide substitute gratification. Sociocultural factors did provide limitations; for example, among more puritanical groups, such as the Wahabis of Arabia and the Senussis of Libya, no smoking of any kind was tolerated nor was even coffee accepted. In some places smoking was resisted by governmental authorities as in Morocco, but even with imprisonment of smokers the habit was not controlled. In North Africa, social rank also dictated use, with aristocratic Moors scorning smoking of either hemp or tobacco and preferring, as compatible with high status, to eat opium instead.

Sigg (1960)', who has written a comprehensive (Marxist-oriented) monograph on cannabis, underdevelopment, and capitalism, concurs in the ill effects of cannabis use among Africans as first noted by Flacourt. He adds Indians to the vulnerable group suffering widespread ill effects (contradicting the Indian Hemp Commission and the descriptions of Chopra, 1935, which we will discuss later). He cites Warnock's 1895 findings in Cairo that reported about a sixth of his mental-hospital admissions were due to cannabis psychosis and another sixth to combined cannabis-alcohol ingestion. Benabud is cited as reporting a 1956 admission incidence where 49 per cent suffered from disorders due to cannabis and 27 per cent from cannabis psychosis per se. Sigg's own hospital data yielded 30 per cent cannabis-psychosis admissions. He attributes this picture immediately to nutritional deficiency, ill-health (tuberculosis primarily), and poor hygiene, but poverty conditions in turn are said to be due to colonial-capitalistic exploitation. Cannabis in Morocco—smoking kif (hemp and tobacco) or eating hemp macaroons or the more exotic "mahjoun," which contains datura and belladonna as well as butter, honey, almonds, and gum arabic—is centered among young urban males who are poor, illiterate, single, unemployed, badly housed, and without resources. He considers the Moroccan phenomenon to illustrate the general plight of the poor in underdeveloped countries and offers the thesis that it is in these countries that cannabis use is expanding, citing African, Middle Eastern, Southeast Asian, and Latin American nations as cases. As a countercase, he proposes that Cuba under Batista had a high rate of use of marijuana but now, under Castro, is free of such practices. Sigg considers the concept of alienation originated by Hegel and emphasized by Marx as a sense of estrangement or dispossession, of not being able to enjoy the essence of human work. When man has no work or his work does not belong to him, Sigg proposes that he is alienated generally—from family and community and from strong interpersonal ties of any kind. What is left is only imaginary—the world of dreams —and cannabis is part of that world.

Sigg describes the impotent history of law-making to suppress cannabis in North Africa and elsewhere; in 1956, a million users (population then eight million) spent 4 per cent of the national income on cannabis. A private monopoly has been allowed to grow cannabis since 1906 but pressure in 1951 was directed toward restricting the sale of kif. In 1947, cannabis was ordered destroyed and an epidemic in cocaine use threatened. The monopoly agreed to prohibition and, in 1955, an educational campaign was begun by the government to reduce use. When cultivation was prohibited in 1956 and 1960, whole growing regions suffered potential economic disaster, so that the government first had to buy the crop and second had to give up control endeavors. In nearby Tunisia and Algeria, cannabis suppression was more effective as vineyards replaced hemp fields; there alcohol consumption replaced cannabis use, so Sigg reports, with no improvement in public health. Sigg's thesis follows that control-repression cannot work where populations are in the habit of using mass intoxicants which are nonaddictive (he cites coca as another example). Addictive drugs such as opiates can be controlled. Treatment efforts are likewise hopeless for the intoxicants, he claims, and (Marxist) socioeconomic development provides the only solution for what he sees to be a massive problem of drug abuse.

There are many inconsistencies and contradictions in Sigg's argument. We present it as a thesis bearing on one trend in modern drug use, which is the visible symptoms of individual disability among the urban poor exposed to intoxicants and using one or another of them in apparently increasing amounts. The data from Africa— Nigeria particularly—offered by Asuni (1964), Benabud (1957), Halbach (1959), Lambo (1965), and Sotiroff (1965) point to the problem without the limitations of Sigg's doctrinaire thesis. In West and North Africa since World War II, there has been a rapid increase in cannabis use in regions where it was unknown. Elsewhere in Central Africa (not Nigeria), ritual use has occurred. In tribal areas there are certain secret societies with cannabis components and some ritual-orgiastic or warrior-cult use—prior to battle, for example. These appear to be relatively recent themselves but, nevertheless, have been integrated into tribal custom. The new pattern is urban use among persons who have abandoned tribal life. Among students, migrant workers, underworld groups, and, more recently, professional persons as well as marginal people, cannabis use is growing popular. The users include women as well as men. Soldiers apparently brought it into some areas following travel to North Africa in World War II; in other regions it was introduced by travelers and migratory transportation workers. In West Africa, smoking is the only manner in which hemp is employed. As new urban centers develop without traditional social structures and when work opportunities are not available, a variety of unstable behaviors develop. Among them, Lambo proposes that the stress of deprivation finds some relief in stimulants and intoxicants (alcohol is also widely used by the same persons, and amphetamine use is also increasing when available). Direct spread is from one user to another in their social groups—whether these groups are formed in housing areas, work places, or prison.

As cannabis use increases, so does the illicit apparatus of supply and economic gain. By 1964, a pound of hashish was selling for more than $150. Furthermore, with development of cultivation, an export market in Britain was opened with much higher prices there. In the West African "rootless proletariat," the rates of ill effects are not as high as those offered by Sigg; although in five years in Nigeria over 7,000 were hospitalized, Benabud estimates an admissions rate of 5/1,000.

H. B. M. Murphy (1963) in a wide-ranging review attempts to draw together the data from various regions undergoing transition in patterns of cannabis use. He recognizes that cultural features may dictate who may or may not use it and that use ordinarily conforms to other demands of role behavior or interpersonal action. As far as abuse is concerned—taken as chronic heavy use with possible insomnia, memory deterioration, intestinal disturbance, acute intoxication, and possible, but rare, psychosis—it seems limited to males under thirty-five who are poor, unstable, deprived, and without strong relations to others. Psychological inadequacy determined by environmental economics and family deficiencies appears implicated in compulsive heavy use. There are also instances of occupational risk, for the most part associated with religious mendicants—either monks of India or fakirs of North Africa who use the drug apparently to produce religious excitement but possibly also to enhance their special religious roles before those laymen from whom they seek alms. Some of these become compulsive users suffering ill effects.

Murphy joins with Carstairs (1954) and Benabud (1957) in suggesting that a limiting feature of cannabis expansion is the cultural requirement for action. When a culture fosters action and aggressiveness, then cannabis, which appears to have as its most probable specific (pharmacological) effect the production of passivity, will be renounced and alcohol (or nowadays amphetamines) accepted. When a culture values calm, impersonal inaction, cannabis in controlled or ritual use may be incorporated into acceptable conduct. Fort (1965b) also emphasizes cultural features as he describes the failure of various Western (or sometimes local) campaigns to restrict cannabis among populations employing it. If there are traditions of medical and holy use, if the behavior engendered is socially acceptable and even desired, if the personal experiences are compatible with cultural values and expectations, if there may, in fact, be personal gains in terms of euphoria or relief of fatigue (and possible medical utility), and if, further, there is an economic apparatus for production and distribution upon which persons depend for their livelihood, then control endeavors will be faced with massive resistance, for use itself will be widespread (Chopra, 1935). This will be the greater (Sotiroff, 1965) if the elements of control, the local police, themselves share the values of their society and do not readily accept the injunctions, transmitted only incompletely at best through educational and technological development, which originate in the morals—or the myths—of Western societies. As for ill effects, since the person with visible symptoms of abuse is most likely to be a poor, sick, alienated man who also uses other drugs and has many reasons to be miserable, it is not possible to evaluate what cannabis has done to him as opposed to what life in general has done to him—or he has done to himself. The same is true for opium and many other substances. The evidence for drug as demon is slim; the evidence for people in trouble using drugs so that they exaggerate their difficulties—in spite of what can be their immediate intent of assuaging these troubles—is considerable. One's own difficulties are, of course, easily made difficulties for others. These are the matters which concern us as we watch the spread of cannabis among the miserable of this earth.

In our discussion of the spread of cannabis, we should not ignore reductions in its use, for these too have been reported. Ordinarily, reductions in individual use occur when (1) supplies are restricted—either because the drug is no longer available or the means to purchase it are missing—when (2) individuals have reacted to their drug experiences with distress, when (3) they have been taught to fear an untoward effect (Ludlow quoted in Ebin, 1961), when (4) the drug is not satisfying and some other or stronger mind-altering substance need be employed (compare Baudelaire, also quoted in Ebin), when (5) the individual embraces a new group which frowns on the use of the drug, or, occasionally, when (6) group (including national) values, practices, or laws shift so that what was acceptable conduct now becomes unacceptable. In addition, a major limiting factor appears to be aging among those predominant contemporary groups and persons where use is casual, social, or otherwise not traditional. Most observers are agreed that marijuana smoking is concentrated among persons under age thirty-five. We cannot now ascertain whether this reflects our times, during which a new wave of young people around the world have started to use marijuana and will continue to do so, but somehow are all under thirty-five just now (and that "now" has been for the last ten years!), or whether it reflects the greater visibility of younger people so that observers have seen them—perhaps on admission to a hospital or in social situations—and not their older counterparts. There may even be a real shift in drug use (perhaps akin to the "maturing out" of opiate users proposed by Winick, 1962), which reflects older people's loss of interest in either hemp effects or membership in hemp-using groups. It is an intriguing question for future investigators.

Sigg (1960) has argued that a Marxist revolution by itself brings reduction of cannabis use as it betters the plight of the poor. He offers a Cuban example but, unfortunately, the Cubans have offered no one else any statistics to prove the point. Acting slowly under laws to control cultivation and distribution, but not outlawing use, India has reported slow reductions in use. Chopra (1935) and Chopra and Chopra (1939) suggest that reduction has actually occurred in response to gradual government intervention, so that a previously estimated 10/1,000 rate of use—Chopra says marijuana is used more widely among the poor—is now going down. In 1939 that reduction, say Chopra and Chopra, was being followed by a rising incidence of alcohol use. In many other countries where cultivation and use have been outlawed in the twentieth century (Greece and Egypt, for example), the assumption is usually made that use has declined, although Sigg again, without statistics, argues an increase instead. Fort (1965b), who has made recent on-the-spot observations, doubts the effectiveness of most legal interventions as practiced in Asia. He notes the total absence of reliable statistics on use as such (and there is much uncertainty in reports of arrests or hospitalization as well), but, calling attention to what appears to be increasing illicit traffic (opium included), he wonders whether there is any reduction in intoxicant use based simply on casually applied legal intervention. Walker (1960) in describing smuggling patterns makes no mention of changes in traffic, although clearly these have occurred since Egypt is no longer supplied from Greece. He appears to assume that amounts of smuggled cannabis are not decreasing remarkably. Were he to attend to smuggling increases— as between the United States and Mexico or Nigeria and Great Britain —a different conclusion would emerge.

There is one form of cannabis use—one associated with increased consumption—which has yet to be discussed and which is of great interest, not only in terms of past history but because of its modern parallels with symbolic uses of other drugs. We speak of the use of cannabis as a unifying symbol in connection with some group activity other than traditional healing or religious mysticism or ecstasy. If the assassins *had* used hemp, for example, theirs would have been a symbolic use, for it was instrumental in facilitating group activities (albeit murder) and a focus for group goals (paradise). Another instance is based on the brief allusions to cannabis use in Central African rituals —preparation for and use in battle, the most recent of which occurred during the 1964 Congo fighting when Simba warriors were said to use hemp and alcohol to rouse themselves for battle and magically guarantee their immunity from harm. These are both illustrations of the drug's role as a magical ingredient in a warrior cult. Von Wissman, Wolf, Francois, and von Mueller (1891) offer an eye-witness account of the adoption of cannabis into the ritual life of a tribe and into its warrior cult. Their observations were conducted on the Baluba of the Kassai (Congo) region in 1883–1885.

Kalamba-Mukengge had just come to power and as a leader saw the potential for firearms, which were new on the Congo scene. He adopted a chief of another tribe who was in a position to trade for guns. The elders resisted Kalamba's gun acquisitions and in the resulting civil war the elders were subjugated along with neighboring tribes (the guns worked!). Kalamba decided that his wild and undisciplined tribe needed to be organized. Shortly before, cannabis smoking had been introduced by a neighboring tribe which believed its use led to a migration of the soul. As a result, Wissman himself was greeted as an earlier chief returned from the dead. Kalamba began to see how cannabis might be the center of a new state religion. First, he ordered all fetishes and old magic destroyed; "riamba" (cannabis) was the new fetish, with Kalamba's sister as cult priestess. Riamba was heralded as the universal magic, sole protection, and holy symbol of peace and friendship. Riamba smoking became a ritual duty of the new "sons of hemp." It was to carry them into war as well. All festivals were celebrated with riamba smoking; it was also used to punish some criminals, who were made to smoke it until losing consciousness. A riamba dance was developed for war expeditions, festivals, and amusement, and to demonstrate religious zeal (for example, at the full moon to help plants grow). Blood brotherhoods were sealed with riamba, replacing the blood-and-water potion previously used.

Wissman and his colleagues attribute all of these ritual innovations—including the implicit psychological effects on individual warriors or religious celebrants—to the conscious plan of the gifted King Kalamba. They make no comment on why the tribe was ready to acquiesce or as to how the changing times may have provided a crisis to be utilized constructively. For example, guns were being introduced, as well as cannabis and some apparently new religious notions, and the colonial powers were competing for possession of territory; too, the Congo Free State of Belgium was established in 1884, the slave trade was eradicated, and, if Wissman is correct, the Baluba were suffering seriously from tuberculosis and other ailments. Whatever else may have been happening besides, the Wissman account suggests the potentials that existed for the use of cannabis as a symbolic rallying point for a disorganized and ailing people. The account also shows how such use can be associated with an increased organization and social coherence—presumably by elaborating existing structures—in contrast to the disorganization obtaining among the displaced tribal migrants to African cities for whom no pre-existing social structure exists.

Another example of hemp's symbolic use as social cement and as a pennant advertising belief is found among the Ras Tafarians of Jamaica (Norris, 1962; Simpson, 1955; Smith, Augier, and Nettleford, 1960; also Blum and Blum, 1965). The Ras Tafarians are Negro poor centered in urban Jamaica[6]—an outgrowth of black national sentiment which itself goes back to the 1920's and Marcus Garvey's back-to-Africa movement (and is currently found in Black Muslim, Afro-American, and Black Power movements, as well as in the Nyabingi Order in Abyssinia and the Congo). In the 1940's, the founder Howell gathered 600 followers, who lived together raising yams and hemp for ganja. Sect self-identification developed during this period—hair was never cut, the African heritage was emphasized, the belief that ganja was sanctified by God was promulgated, ties with the Ethiopian Orthodox Church were developed, the back-to-Africa dream was enunciated, and Haile Selassie was proclaimed as the living God. (The emperor's name before coronation was Ras Tafar.) Other beliefs are that a spiritual tie exists with Islam, that Christ and God are black, and that Haile Selassie is invincible; there is also the acceptance as fact of a world-wide, military-espionage network headquartered in Addis Ababa as a basis for war on the white man. The movement itself is

----

[6] Although racial discrimination ended legally in 1938, Norris (1962) found a color bias still operating. High positive correlation exists between darkness of skin color and poverty, illiteracy, disease, and superstition. This remains in spite of the fact that as an independent nation its government and police are primarily black. Historians argue that black and white are attitudes, not skin colors.

nativistic, antiwhite, messianic, and democratic internally. The Ras Tafarians consider Jamaican police and preachers as their enemies and their own situation in Jamaica as hopeless; too, they refuse to participate in local politics, will not work for others, and refuse charity. Some foresee revenge upon the white man as a sweet moment, and Abyssinia as the final heaven and hope of men is the common dream. Ganja is the "wisdom weed" and is used as a sacrament.

Police opposition formalized in 1954 when the Howell settlement was broken up. Ras Tafarians were encouraged to migrate to England; for some the trip to Africa was paid for—but these migrants returned when West African leaders gave them a hostile reception. In 1959, another leader, Repairer-of-the-Breach Henry, was arrested, following the discovery of a weapons cache and letters to Castro asking for his help. Followers took to the hills and a guerrilla movement which threatened was broken up, but not before several police were killed. During this same period, Jamaican citizens became frightened not only by the political overtones but by the fierce appearance of these "dreadlocks" or locksmen whom they considered dangerous criminals. Early criminal statistics, except for the violence of the short-lived guerrilla action, did not support the public view; the most common arrest was for growing ganja, a practice which continues beyond the capability of the police to prevent. More recently, the group itself has become better disciplined and the actual gentleness and religiosity of members have been noted. Rebellious teenagers and other marginal persons have been attracted to their nonviolent conduct.

With growth and publicity, membership (and hangers-on) becomes more complex. The unemployed, older persons, idlers, and ganja enthusiasts have also joined, as have advocates of violence. Membership in 1940 was about 1,600; by 1960, it was 15,000. In addition to members or participants, others have come to masquerade or exploit. Criminals have grown long hair and taken to costume without accepting dictates of membership or nonviolence. These "beardmen" engage in hoodlum acts and crime. Marxist revolutionaries, Jamaican black-nationalist revolutionaries, ganja traffickers, and predators on the group have also been attracted. A further feature, not one so much of membership but of the spread of values, has been the subscription to Ras Tafarian notions—especially ganja and revolution—by middle-class black youth and unemployed intelligentsia. Thus, while maintaining a deep chasm between itself and most of conventional Jamaica, some of the most disadvantaged citizenry are attracted to the group or have been influenced by its exported beliefs.

The role of ganja is central to group activity for the members hold that in smoking the sacred herb they are united with God. Nevertheless, some brethren have argued against ganja on the grounds that it leads to a disadvantageous conflict with the police. Some have accused the police themselves of being suppliers. Recently (1967), public arguments have favored legalization of ganja; police administrators have argued in favor of legalization but without success. Obviously, some citizens believe the drug itself to be undesirable in spite of the fact that ganja itself has long been used on the island—either smoked or taken in liquid form, including mild infusions. It is employed folk-medically and is generally considered a good drug; the medical use and the name both stem from East Indian rather than African origins; smoking is probably an African or Spanish import.

SUMMARY

Mid-Asian use of cannabis is documented about 500 B.C. and use there appears to have been part of religious-purificatory rituals. Early Indian use, circa 400 B.C., was religious but by the twelfth century A.D. was medical as well. By 1100 A.D., hemp had earned a bad reputation in association with the assassins—a legend incapable of verification. Claims that it leads to dangerous behavior have continued to present times, although the evidence now as then is slim indeed. Many reports of Arabian use in the Middle Ages exist; a few link it to individual ill effects—for example, folly and excitement. On the whole, during the Arab period of widespread hashish eating and drinking, it was not implicated as damaging by first-hand observers of either self or others, whereas alcohol was.

The most dramatic change in cannabis-use patterns occurred throughout the world with the diffusion of tobacco smoking, which was learned in the Americas in the 1500's. Cannabis smoking followed and was soon widespread in Africa, and later was common in the Americas. Smoking of cannabis did not occur in Europe, although during the same period French intellectual and artistic elites did experiment with it in limited medical and more general personal use. The great French Romantics reported their experiences—aesthetic, mystical, emotional—but neither they nor their countrymen continued or spread the drug. It appears to have been in the United States, first

in the 1850's and then in the 1920's, that sensational reports of danger
or vice were associated with hemp. There followed a rise in interest,
public concern, punitive legislation, claims, and actual use, which continue to this day.

Some patterns of American use, as with hippies or other "pot-
head" groups, bear remote relations to its symbolic use elsewhere.
Characteristic of that use is a group focus on the drug as but one of
many shared values. In each case, the group's existence is explicable on
the grounds of other social forces, most of which may be seen as individually damaging or unpleasant, so that group formation and euphoric drug use may have a restorative, defensive, or quietly revolutionary function. Although the symbolic group involvement in cannabis
has elsewhere been associated with either nonliterate tribal or economically deprived status, its use in the United States and England has
been by the children of the elite as well as by some urban poor. There
have been two visible patterns in underdeveloped countries. One involves fairly stable and probably widespread use without reports of
individual or social difficulties. Thus, in India, Pakistan, Afghanistan,
Nepal, and other mid-Asian areas, traditional religious and medical
use occurs along with limited social and perhaps private use—the latter
secular in our sense but nevertheless unassociated with abuse. The other
pattern is of apparently dramatic increase in use in Africa. Although
African tribal use has been accommodated to existing cultural patterns
and rituals, its use in the cities is by male urban migrants and the rootless proletariat; this use is seen as symptomatic of major economic,
social, and individual health problems. There are reports of adverse
effects in association with chronic use, including occasional psychosis,
but these outcomes cannot be divorced from other defects in persons
and their environments.

Cannabis diffusion has been by long traditional routes of commerce, war, and travel, and ordinarily diffusion is in a personal social
group except where use is traditional and thus initiated by authorities.
Traditional use has rarely been associated with either public concern
or private despair—except in the case of culture conflict when primarily Western-derived morals have confronted Asian traditional use
(as in Jamaica) or integrated folk use (as in Mexico). Efforts at legal
control usually have been unsuccessful whenever folk use or cultivation has been extensive, unless substitute crops and substitute drugs
have been made available—for example, alcohol or cocaine. Ordi-

narily, substitute drugs are available, since the primary pattern of cannabis ingestion over the centuries has been one of mixing it with other substances, at the time of smoking (combining it with tobacco, datura, opium)', or drinking (combining with wine, opium), or eating (opium, henbane, belladonna, and so on). For an individual to have used only cannabis is most unusual. Certain factors limit use; these appear to include cultural ethos, class or caste snobbery, availability and price, sex (females have been infrequent users except in recent urban expansion —African or American), and possibly age. Generally, cannabis has not been an integral part of the lives of older, stable, conventional, better-off persons except in medicine and ritual use. A number of important questions are unanswered, including the nature of limiting factors, indiffusion, the identification of factors in persons subject to genuine untoward reactions (psychosis), and the reasons for the persistence—in Western society—of the myth of the demon in hemp.

A History of Tobacco

Richard H. Blum

V

*T*he earliest date for tobacco use is 200 A.D. with evidence of pipe smoking among Arizona Indians. The archaeological findings are interpreted as suggesting that tobacco was magico-religious in nature, possibly in connection with rain-making rituals. Indians on the east coast of North America were pipe smoking by 800 A.D. As with so much of our archaeological evidence on drug use, dates are subject to constant revision as new finds push further back the frontiers of time. Since tobacco is native to the Americas, and one species to Australia, it is unlikely that evidence for tobacco use per se will be found elsewhere than these continents for earlier dates; however, it may be that evidence of smoking will be uncovered for earlier dates in other areas. One find leads in that direction. Sassoon and Yellen (1966) have discovered stone bowls in Tanzania which they date at 400 to 800 B.C. and describe as "pipe bowls." No smoking material was uncovered but the excavators deduced that some sort of smoking occurred. If these interpretations are substantiated, they will introduce a new dimension into the history of smoking.

The burning of incense and fumigants as such has been known from at least 3000 B.C. (Corti, 1932). In the temples of Karnak and Jerusalem and possibly later at Delphi, the inhalation of substances dedicated to the gods was a priestly function. Coca leaves are said to have been burned and the smoke either inhaled or, alternatively, its wind drift used for omen interpretation by Inca priests (de Cieza, reprint, 1959). Among Romans the medicinal benefits of drawing smoke through a reed were recommended for coughs (Pliny) and, as noted in the chapter on cannabis, Herodotus described the Scythians' inhalation of fumes from burning cannabis seeds. In all likelihood, other smoking or inhalation practices have occurred elsewhere and are either as yet undiscovered or simply unknown to us. In any event, the practice of inhaling burning substances other than tobacco seems never to have been popular, and such inhalation of fumes as did occur seems to have been limited to medical and religious intentions. The oracular trances of the Delphic oracle are an exception in that these were politically important, although the pythoness was a priestess of Apollo and all oracles were delivered as though received from the god. Whether or not any psychoactive inhalation ever occurred at Delphi is quite another question; in spite of references to volcanic or sulphuric vapors, laurel leaves, and what-have-you, no one has established mind altering in connection with the Delphic oracle. The political wisdom of her utterances was such that no reduction in astuteness or rationality through drugs could have occurred.

A most interesting but little known shamanistic practice which involves inhalation and oracles in a magical-religious setting still occurs in the mountains of Central Asia. Friedl (1965) has described shamanism in the region, and von Snoy (1960) has taken movies showing Farphu shamans inhaling smoke from mulberry leaves, going into a trance, and then delivering prophecies. In the same Gilgit areas, other shamans use the burning leaves of the mountain juniper to achieve trance and prophecy (Blum and Blum, 1967). One wonders about the historical links between these inhalation practices that occurred in some of the most isolated mountain regions of Asia (Gilgit, Hunza, Chitral, Dir) and those of the Scythians and Greeks of pre-Christian times.

The sniffing of nonburning substances—snuffs—is a practice in limited locales. South American Indians, especially those in North Central parts of the continent, engage in various forms of inhalation of hallucinogens and tobacco. Wassén (1965, 1967) describes these in detail. The dates of origin are unknown; it is assumed that sniffing of drugs other than tobacco preceded tobacco sniffing (Zerries, cited in Wassén). Such activities are social in the sense that they are done in company; indeed, one form of sniffing uses an X-shaped blowing tube in which two persons blow substances into each other's nostrils. The function and intent of such sniffing—which may find tobacco combined with a hallucinogen—is magical-religious (communing with and controlling the spirits, comparable with Guatemalan Indian spirit communion by means of alcohol) and medical.

It is the combination of the technique of smoking with the tobacco plant that demands our attention as an event of the greatest epidemiological interest, for only subsequent to the diffusion of that practice from the Americas to Europe did the smoking of other psychoactive drugs take place. Thus, the spread of tobacco smoking, opium and cannabis smoking, and the less common smoking of datura—or, as nowadays, aspirin among "teenyboppers" and hollyhock stems among farm youngsters—depended entirely upon the technique itself and the exceptional pharmacological potency and immediacy of drug effects that resulted. We have already seen a parallel in the importance of technique of use when we considered the rapid spread of intravenous heroin use after the discovery of the hypodermic syringe—an event in its turn leading to the injection nowadays of other substances, such as DMT, LSD, and, very importantly, methedrine and other amphetamines.

The first European observation of tobacco was reportedly in Brazil in 1555 (Laufer, 1924a). In 1564, Frenchmen in Florida were claiming its virtues, taught them by local Indians, for averting hunger and thirst—an important use for explorers and adventurers. In 1565, John Hawkins brought the plant to England but no use occurred; but in 1573, when Sir Francis Drake brought tobacco to England, smoking became a fad. The drug itself was in short supply so that henbane (*Hyoscyamus*)' was used as a substitute. Cultivation in England was reported in 1576 and pipe smoking, learned from sailors who had visited the Americas, was reportedly fashionable. By 1614, seven thousand shops in London purveyed the substance—"ale houses, grosers, apothecaries, chaundlers." Medical value was attributed to the plant, and during this period the medical profession attempted to limit its use (Consumers Union, 1963) and to employ it for its pre-

sumed enormous curative worth. (It was also deemed a floral decora-
tion and was in demand as a display plant.) Nevertheless, secular use
expanded remarkably so that English expenditures in 1614 were over
three hundred thousand pounds sterling. King James in 1604 had already reacted against the drug even before so much money began "going up in smoke," but his "Counterblaste" admonishing the English
not to act like savages had little effect. Failing to prevent use, the
crown turned frustration to capital and began to tax tobacco heavily.

By 1586, tobacco cultivation had begun on the European continent. English sailors, students, merchants, and soldiers carried it and
their pipes on their travels, but a traveling Italian cardinal carried it
back from England to Italy with him in 1610. It had spread to Turkey
by 1605 and was banned under penalty of death in 1623 because of
fires in Constantinople due to smokers falling asleep with pipes in
their mouths. By 1655, the Sultan had abandoned efforts at control,
and water pipes as well as clay pipes were in widespread use.

The Thirty Years War was important in the diffusion of tobacco, for English and Spanish soldiers carried it to Central Europe,
so that by 1650 all the Central European peasantry were said to be
lighting up. Other armies carried the habit to the Balkans (Corti,
1932). Poland received the plant in 1590 via its ambassador to Turkey; from Poland and also via English travelers it went to Russia. By
1634, it was forbidden in Russia, reportedly because it was preferred
by the poor over bread and because it led to "stinking and infectuous
breath." Russian use was unlike other European use; there, smokers
inhaled as deeply and as rapidly as possible so that combined hyper-
ventilation and intoxication produced unconsciousness—a prospect
not altogether heartening to conventional authority. The Russian
proscription, of course, failed.

Japanese use was first reported in 1615 (Laufer, 1924b) when
the Japanese emperor prohibited it because Japanese men, women,
and children were "besotted in that herb not ten years since its introduction." (It was probably introduced by the Portuguese.)[1] In China,
about the same time, it was heralded as a medicament for colds, ma-
laria, and cholera, but use quickly became social and personal; soldiers
were the first group to take it up, but soon all ages and classes were

---

[1] In Japan it appears to have been taken in tincture and not smoked—
perhaps an example of carry-over of older opium-taking methods; considering
its toxicity upon ingestion, one wonders about the effects.

smoking when tobacco was available. The imperial response was an edict of decapitation for smokers in 1638, which proved unenforceable as illicit use continued and expanded. One religious sect continued to forbid it, but—according to one herbal—it was popularly used for intoxication, as an antagonist for wine, and to reduce hunger and aid digestion. In India, use began in 1605 when, according to the records, a king took it on advice of a traveler who claimed that, since the Europeans would do nothing foolish, smoking must be the correct thing to do. The king's physician demurred but the image of the wise European carried the day. Elsewhere in Asia, its spread was rapid and among some peoples it was incorporated into rituals. Among the Ainu, for example, it was said that a "tobacco ordeal" was used as a trial for accused women; those not vomiting a mixture of water and tobacco ash were declared innocent. Laufer states that by the twentieth century only one Asian group was not using it—the Yami on an island near Formosa, who are also alcohol prohibitionists. How they managed their resistance would be well worth knowing. An interesting point made by Laufer is that tobacco chewing was adopted in Asia only by groups already given to betel chewing. Although he is not quite correct, the tendency for one drug to be substituted for another, once a method of administration has become popular, is emphasized by the betel- and tobacco-chewing correspondence.

The spread of tobacco in Africa followed the same pattern as elsewhere—a wildfire adoption (Laufer, Hambly, and Linton, 1930). By 1607, it was planted widely in West Africa with men, women, and children growing and using considerable quantities. Traded in return for slaves by the Portuguese, it was so popular that its purchase took priority over any other commodity. Women took it in trade for their bodies, men for a day's labor, and—it is said (LaLoubere, cited in Laufer et al.)—the Hottentot peoples accepted rather than resisted Dutch colonists simply because the latter carried tobacco. In some places the Russian manner of use was popular—deep and rapid inhalation to produce intoxication and coma. In parts of Africa, as we have noted in the chapter on cannabis, smoking per se was of great importance, so that if no tobacco—or substitute such as hashish—was available, a hot coal would be smoked instead "for solace." If one man had tobacco and another none, others would stand close to inhale the smoke. To make the supply last longer, tobacco would be "cut" with wood chips. In Dahomey, female warriors considered it an

honor to manufacture smoking equipment for chiefs, and on state occasions a man's smoking apparatus was carried behind him to signify
his rank. During ceremonial speeches the king's head smoker moved
among the guests, blowing smoke in their faces as a sign of royal favor.
A reverse-status association occurred among aristocratic Moors, who
considered it lowly to smoke tobacco—or hemp. A religious stricture
among the Senussis of Libya and the Moslem Wahabis of Arabia
prohibited the use of tobacco. There was also more general Moslem
resistance in Morocco to its adoption, but use nevertheless developed.
A delayed-reaction constraint was introduced by law in 1887, with
smokers being put in prison. But this was to no avail.

In the Americas its use was already widespread among Indians
so that no reintroduction needed to occur. Colonists, of course, used it
and newcomers brought the habit they learned in Europe with them,
rather than learning it directly from the dwindling indigenous folk. In
Mexico, in 1575, the first "American" edict against use was issued, a
Catholic council enjoining its use in any church. A year later, it was
necessary to order priests to forbid smoking while performing the
Mass. Elsewhere in Europe and among Europeans in America, there
was resistance on grounds of taste—the noxious smell, cost, or the implied depravity of emulating the heathen savages of the New World.
As we have seen—except among a few isolated religions or culturally
insulated groups—state or religious prohibitions or restrictions by taxation or medical control were rarely successful anywhere in reducing
the prevalence of smoking.

Scholars present many factors to account for the tobacco "epidemic." Laufer (1924a) argues that there was no prior resistance anywhere on grounds of convention, religion, morality, or law simply because neither the substance nor the technique was known. Both were
completely new and there were no direct arguments against innovation. In Europe, furthermore, it was an era of exploration and discovery and popular heroes—men like Sir Francis Drake—were copied
as they brought back the wondrous treasures of new worlds. Laufer
argues further than the smoke itself suggested fire, dragons, and devil-
try, making it a status symbol in the post-Reformation era. Generally, diffusion proceeded from those with prestige to those with less
prestige; in other words, the people copied smoking from those they
admired. Smoking's initial "carriers" or "vectors" were necessarily
those who moved about—whether ambassadors or fleet admirals or

simply merchants and sailors. The plant was cheap and the technique easy to copy; exposure to a smoker allowed the onlooker to learn easily.

There is contemporary evidence for the same learning process, whether the drug be alcohol, LSD, tobacco, or any other. McArthur, Waldron, and Dickinson (1958) clearly show that whether or not a man smokes or does not seems to be determined by whether or not he has been oriented to the habit as a result of his social milieu. That milieu includes the smoking habits and correlated attitudes of family, peers, and socioeconomic-class associates. Salber and her colleagues in a number of studies (Salber and MacMahon, 1961; Salber, Mac-Mahon and Harrison, 1963; Salber, Reed, Harrison, and Green, 1963) have shown that the likelihood of smoking increases as a function of parental smoking, older-sibling smoking, and age-mate associate smoking. What contemporary studies and historical data both indicate is that exposure to others who use tobacco, especially exposure to admired or prestigeful persons (parents, older siblings, or—as in seventeenth-century England—folk heroes), is one set of factors leading to a smoking habit. Modern data show that moral and drug factors, as well as attitudinal and personality (and physiological) factors, also play an important role. For example, nonsmokers are also more likely not to drink alcohol or coffee (McArthur et al., 1958); heavy smokers are generally more tense, constricted, and maladjusted. Significantly, infant oral experience and inferred gratification differ, for as McArthur and his colleagues show, nonsmokers were weaned at an average of 8 months, heavy smokers able to stop were weaned at an average of 6.8 months, heavy smokers who didn't try to stop were weaned at 5 months, and heavy smokers who tried and could not stop (are addicted) were weaned at 4.7 months. Looking at the rapidity with which the tobacco habit spread over the world, we assume that its attractiveness must be related to the oral satisfaction of sucking as well as to the pharmacological effects which, although diversely described introspectively, are apparently related to felt tension reduction.

To illustrate that diversity in stated reasons for using tobacco, Corti (1932) quotes a perplexed English observer in 1667:

Some drink their tobacco, some eat it, others sniff it, but other methods I have seen practiced from prince, to bishop, to barber and each can explain how it benefits him. One smokes because it enables him to see better, another because it disperses water in the

brain, a third to ease his toothache, a fourth to stop the singing in
his ears, a fifth will tell you that it makes him sleep, a sixth that it
quenches his thirst, a seventh that it neutralizes the bad effects of
too much water-drinking, an eighth that it expels evil humours, a
ninth smokes to pass the time and a tenth because he doesn't wish
to be unsociable.

The observer adequately portrays the multiplicity of personal functions,
such as social-recreational, self-medicating, magical, and mood-alter-
ing, which a drug in popular use is said to serve. Studies show—not
with tobacco but with peyote (Aberle, 1966) and with LSD (Blum
and Associates, 1964)—that a correspondence exists between the extent of an individual's use of a given drug and the variety of different functions which the individual says that drug accomplishes for
him. Whether or not an observer would concur is another matter; what
is implied—and what we would expect to hold true for tobacco or
alcohol or any other popularly employed psychoactive substance—is
that a correlation exists between the extent an individual uses a drug
and the variety of needs, interests, or aims which he believes the drug
to meet, fulfill, or facilitate for himself. There is also the expectation
that as the ritual, or traditional, institutionally controlled use of a drug
is reduced and secularization occurs that—depending upon the heterogeneity of myths, ills, interests, and values within a society—an increasing diversity of individual functions or intentions served by the drug
will be reported. In the case of tobacco, where both substance and
method of administration were novel, no controlling rituals or proscriptions existed to limit the variety of intentions or settings which
surrounded the initial use of the drug. Consequently, a diversity of
reasons offered for its use was to be expected—each an interpretation
of what was obviously a gratifying drug experience and simultaneously
a gratifying method of administration.

In retrospect, it seems clear that the spread of tobacco use,
especially of tobacco smoking, was the most dramatic "epidemic" of
drug use in the observed history of mankind. The spread of the practice was itself dependent upon the historical era itself—an age of exploration, expanding commerce, and openness to new ideas—which
brought Europeans to the Americas and allowed their folk heroes to
return to the Continent with the "foule weede" and in turn to spread
it outward to Asia and Africa as they voyaged, traded, and made war.
The adoption of tobacco by a tremendous variety of nonliterate so-

cieties and literate cultures with immense differences among them tends to rule out cultural and social features as facilitators or determinants of tobacco-use innovation. Similarly, in almost all instances, the failure of prohibitions adopted on the grounds of taste, health, religion, or criminal penalty to prevent adoption emphasizes the frailty of social controls when a society is faced with an attractive substance, even if that substance serves no primary physiological need or traditional interpersonal function. What remains a question of great interest, as we also noted earlier, is what circumstances allowed a society such as the Formosan Yami or the Libyan Senussi to resist successfully a drug whose initiation and continued use were so compelling for most other societies.

Given the dramatic nature of the epidemic of tobacco use and the evidence for smokers' immediate substitution of other psychoactive substances in its place (opium, cannabis, henbane, datura, for example), the spread of use of these latter drugs (especially opium and cannabis) appears far less sensational. The principle that emerges is that if new techniques of ingestion are developed, people with an interest in psychoactive drugs—and that includes most human beings in most societies—will try a variety of drugs with that technique. If it happens that the technique itself is psychologically gratifying in a special way, as smoking seems to be, then the method of administration takes on considerable independent importance. If it also happens that the method allows the use of a psychoactive substance which has powerful pharmacological effects that are rewarding in the sense that people repeat the experience and which is easily made available (we must not forget that the epidemic of tobacco use could not have occurred if the tobacco plant had not been so hardy, so adaptable to new climates, so easily transported to places it does not grow, and so cheap to process), then we must expect epidemics. An "epidemic" implies a bad thing and, specifically, a disease. Since tobacco use is not a disease in itself, we have put "epidemic" in quotes. That it is causally associated with disease now seems agreed upon, although it is only one of several correlated causative factors. Whether or not the term "epidemic" is deservedly applied to any marked increase in drug use per se or of a particular drug—especially when a good deal of such use has no demonstrable ill-effects and may, in fact, be an effective self-medication or oil for the social machinery—is a matter for the reader to decide.

SUMMARY

Although likely to have been employed quite early for magico-religious use by American Indians, tobacco by the time of its discovery by New World colonizers was used by Indians for medical purposes, including self-medication to allay hunger and for ceremonial occasions. Its use was thus controlled and ritualistic. Europeans responded quickly once they learned about Indian tobacco smoking in about 1550. Although initial claims for medical benefits were made, private and social use soon predominated. Carried by envoys, sailors, and soldiers throughout Europe, tobacco also spread rapidly throughout Asia and Africa, so that by the early sixteenth century its distribution was world-wide with only few societies resisting its introduction. Numerous control efforts were initiated by medical, political, religious, or simply conventional authorities, but in no case did control or prohibition attempts reduce use once it had become popular. In most cases, European governments turned prohibition failure to advantage by heavily taxing sales—a practice carried on today.

A number of factors appear to have accounted for this first major epidemic of drug use. Tobacco itself was easily produced and transported so that availability was no problem; it was also ingestible in many ways—drunk as tincture, sniffed, chewed, or smoked. However, smoking became the paramount means of administration. It seems likely that smoking provided oral satisfactions independent of drug effects, which may account in part for the popularity of that method. On the other hand, the pharmacological efficacy of that administration and the widespread positive response of users to the effects of the drug itself are obviously of critical importance. As with any drug popularly employed, a great variety of reasons are offered for its use, including tobacco's being self-medicating, tension-relieving, magical, mood-changing, and helpful in facilitating social intercourse. Ritualistic and ceremonial use still occurs in nonliterate societies, not only for medical and magico-religious purposes but especially in conjunction with status demonstrations.

The reasons for beginning use—a phenomenon dependent upon exposure to those who have prestige and smoke—need not be the same as reasons for continuing or increasing use. Heavy use appears associated with particular psychological and social features, especially with tension and maladjustment and also with early infant oral gratification. The longer that heavy use has occurred, the more difficult it is for a smoker to stop (McArthur *et al.,* 1958). Although the tobacco habit in some societies does divert scarce funds from necessities to drug purchases, is compulsive and as such gives evidence of dependency (complete with withdrawal symptoms for some), and is now causally linked to disease, its use is rarely termed "drug abuse." Indeed, the initial reactions of political and religious authorities in the sixteenth century were much more intolerant of use than are modern responses by authorities, in spite of the fact that it is the modern evidence which indicates the physical danger arising from use. Psychological dangers are not often claimed, although in cultures where smoking is done by fast and deep inhalation intoxication and unconsciousness are said to result.

The introduction of smoking as a method of drug administration stands as one of the major discoveries in terms of popularizing drug use. The common practice of substituting one drug for another by any known means of ingestion has led to the smoking of cannabis, opium, datura, henbane, and other substances. One must anticipate that new drugs which are combustible, available in large supply, and enhanced in potency by smoking will be smoked as they become available.

A History of
Stimulants

Richard H. Blum

VI

*U*ntil now, our discussion has been focused on particular substances identifiable either as a particular plant or a particular chemical. In the following two chapters we deal with classes of substances—the classes unsatisfactorily defined in terms of probable pharmacological effects and conventionally called stimulants and hallucinogens. Within these classes particular substances will be identified and a brief historical commentary offered. More extensive histories will be found in Lewin (reissue, 1964) and de Ropp (1957).

NATURAL STIMULANTS

Among the naturally occurring stimulants that we discuss (either plants ingested directly or products derived from plants and processed for consumption without elaborate chemical preparation) are coffee, tea, betel, kola nut, kava, and khat. We also classify coca as a stimulant although it has analgesic properties.

Tea. Tea was first known in China, according to legend, about 2700 B.C. but verifiably only in A.D. 350. Its cultivation was encouraged by Buddhist priests, according to Ukers (1965), in order to combat wine intemperance in China. Tea taxation began in 780 as cultivation spread. Diffusion outside of Asia did not occur until the age of exploration and colonial commerce. The Dutch brought the first tea to Europe in 1610; the first English advertisement for tea appeared in 1658. Claims for its efficacy were in terms of health and mood. The English maintained monopolistic control over its Indian production (when it was indigenous) for several hundred years (1600–1858)—a factor in the American Revolution since the Tea Act of 1773 was followed by the Boston Tea Party. According to Ukers, Americans shifted from tea to coffee following this period of protest and lack of supply during the Revolutionary War. We see that political sentiment, taxation, and, ultimately, availability influenced that shift. Americans now, according to Ukers, drink twenty-five times as much coffee as tea. In England the trend was the reverse; the English, beginning as coffee drinkers, shifted to tea as a consequence of the advertisement and subsequent production and availability provided by the East India Company. In part, English use also copied the practices of its leaders. Queen Catherine had begun tea drinking by the 1660's, and the Duchess of Bedford introduced the afternoon tea to counteract her "sinking feeling"—a testimonial to tea's stimulating effects. Tea drinking as a social ritual without magical overtones is still to be found in the English tea ceremonial and in the more elaborate Japanese tea ceremony.

   Coffee. Coffee was probably indigenous to Abyssinia but was first placed under cultivation in Arabia in the 1300's (Wilson, 1965). It was initially employed, according to Wilson, during religious ceremonials (by dervishes in particular, says Lewin, 1964)—a practice resisted by the conservative priesthood, who argued that it was intoxicating and therefore religiously prohibited by the Koran. The use of coffee together with khat developed in the Arab world, the belief being that the two had a mutually enhancing (potentiating) effect. Both substances became disapproved, especially as the coffee house itself developed. Throughout the Arab Near East, these coffee centers became institutionalized as places where men with leisure time congregated. In urban areas these centers became places not only for political discussion but, in the eyes of religious and political authorities, places in which rebellion and opposition were fomented (El Mahi, 1962a, 1962b)'. Thus, both coffee-house frequenters and coffee-house owners became subject to criminal penalties, including death. In spite of prohibition of an extreme sort, coffee drinking spread in the Arab world. (See also Lewin, reissue 1964.)

Introduced in Europe in the 1500's, coffee was claimed to have medical and religious virtues. European introduction was not without resistance, however. Lewin reports that some German princes decreed physical punishment to users; others limited use to the aristocracy while prohibiting it to middle classes and peasantry. Frederick II of Prussia instituted a high tax and also proposed that beer rather than coffee be drunk since he had been reared on beer. Medical advice too claimed dangers, but physicians were not in agreement. Lewin notes that use in France also began with the aristocrats and that the lower classes copied the upper classes in drinking it.

The coffee house became a London institution beginning in 1652 with the much-written-about establishment in St. Michael's Alley. In England the coffee house became a social center where politics, intellectual exchange, and business were transacted but the English, unlike the Arab rulers, did not view the public meetings as a threat to the realm. Advertisements appeared at the same time with claims for medical and mood-elevating properties. By the end of the 1600's, coffee houses had spread through Europe; in the United States in the early 1700's, they also became meeting places for men of the world. As demand increased, cultivation was expanded to Java, Ceylon, and, later, to the Americas and Hawaii. Wilson states that introduction to America was by a French naval officer who in 1723 obtained a plant from Louis XV's hothouse, where they were guarded as plants of great value.

Coca and Cocaine. Coca has been intensively cultivated in Peru since 1000 A.D., perhaps earlier (Mortimer, 1901), and slightly cultivated over a broader region of the entire continent. Among the Incas, who grew and used it, coca was an integral part of religious ceremonies. It was regarded as a sacred emblem of strength, endurance, and fertility; offerings of it were made on all important occasions. Legend indicates that its early use was confined to the court and nobility of the Inca kingdom, but by the time of the Spanish conquest its use was almost universal. Aside from its religious significance, it played an important role in allaying hunger, fatigue, and cold; storehouses containing coca were placed along the roads for use by messengers and troops.

At first, after Pizarro's conquest in 1532, the conquistadores paid off their Indian slave labor with the coca plant.[1] However, beginning about 1560, both political and Catholic Church authorities set about to eradicate coca use on religious, medical, and humanistic grounds. "The plant is only idolatry and the work of the devil . . . it shortens the life of many Indians . . . they should therefore not be compelled to labour and their health and lives should be preserved" (cited in Lewin, 1964, p. 76). Nevertheless, the prohibition was to no avail and coca became a monopoly of the government and, later, of private entrepreneurs. It continued to be the currency of wages to near-slave laborers. The Indians themselves also used it as money, at least shortly after the conquest (de Cieza, 1553). The Pope (Leo XIII) himself approved after using coca "to support his ascetic retirement."

The active element, cocaine, was isolated from coca by Neimann in 1858. Taylor (1963) credits Gaedecke in 1855; Jones (1953) says 1859. It was soon used as a local anesthetic and Germans opened plantations and factories in Peru, an enterprise defeated by competition from the Dutch, whose Java-grown coca proved superior. After its medical introduction into Europe, it was heralded by Freud in 1884 as a cure for morphinism. It was, for many morphine addicts, a very satisfactory "cure," for its use as a euphoriant expanded rapidly; according to Lewin cocainists were concentrated among physicians, writers, and other well-placed persons. This would be expected since their access to physicians and to knowledge of the drug would be easier, proceeding along lines of acquaintance within a social class. By 1886, cocaine addiction was a matter of considerable alarm in Germany, where use had occurred among lower- as well as upper-class persons. In America the famous surgeon Halsted discovered its use in nerve blocking but, in the process, himself became dependent on it. Freud (Jones, 1953) was slow to assess the risk of cocainism, at first blaming the hypodermic injection method which he in 1885 had recommended (his own professor, Scholz, having perfected the syringe).

The use of cocaine continued to spread; the initial pattern was one in which its introduction was by and into wealthier groups. In Egypt (de Monfried, 1930), it was preferred by the upper class over the unfashionable hashish. In the United States it was introduced into

[1] The practice of paying laborers with drugs in lieu of cash also occurs in Guatemala, where alcohol was used to pay Indian laborers (Bunzel, 1940); in Scotland, where bottlers paid laborers in spirits (Phillipson, 1964); in Egypt, where they were paid in hashish, and in Ethiopia, where they were paid in khat.

popular life by means of commercial folk medicine. Dr. Pemberton's "French Wine of Coca, the Ideal Tonic" was offered in Georgia with the opening of the first soda fountain in a drugstore as such (Wilson, 1959)—an institution which quickly became part of American life. Coca as an ingredient in home remedies and in soft drinks developed until early in the twentieth century when the Pure Food and Drug Laws were passed (1906). In India it was introduced in 1880 and spread along main routes of commerce from one urban center to the next (Chopra, 1935). Since it is chewed as a quid, its use spread primarily among persons already accustomed to chewing psychoactive substances; in India these are the betel chewers.

We have few accurate data on its use in advanced societies at this time. There are reports (Bewley, 1966) of an increase in cocaine consumption among English young people interested in illicit-exotic drugs; there it is obtained by prescription and then redistributed among social acquaintances. Heroin users enjoy its employment in sequence with heroin; other users prefer cocaine for itself. Considering the potentials of the drug for producing euphoria (and later irritability, excitement, and delusional states), it is quite likely that the drug-oriented young people in Western countries will show an interest in cocaine, and since many are now familiar with hypodermic injection methods, some will begin to use the substance. We do not regard this as a happy prospect. In South America, where among Indians coca and not cocaine is employed, use has remained extensive among the high Andean folk in Bolivia, Peru, and Colombia—especially among males. In Bolivia miners are still paid in coca leaf (Sotiroff, 1965). Given the hunger, cold, and pain of Alti Plano life, given the awful taste of frozen potatoes, which are the dietary mainstay, given, in high altitudes, the fatigue of workers whose average age at death is between thirty and thirty-five, it is not surprising that a feeling-suppressant, analgesic, and stimulating drug is required. Coca is not sufficient as a mood alterer; consequently, the Indians also use alcohol when they can afford it. When Indians leave the Alti Plano to venture to the lowland cities, Sotiroff reports that their coca chewing is reduced dramatically. Considering the reported capacity for interrupting the practice and the ugliness of upland life, it is understandable why some argue that coca is in no sense a dangerous drug. Others (for example, Granier-Doyeux, 1962), including those who have proposed programs for the suppression of coca use, have considered it addicting and have attributed to the drug some of the worse features of Indian life. Similarly, some (among them Bejarano, 1961) of those critical of coca use have emphasized it as a necessary and, subsequently, an undesirable element in the exploitation of Indian labor.

Kava. This substance, *Piper methysticum,* appears at one time to have been widely consumed in Oceania. It was used ritually in similar ways throughout Polynesia (Lester, 1941, 1942) wherever available. There is reason to believe that migrating groups used to kava drinking continued rituals focused on the drug even when their migrations carried them to places where the plant did not grow. In Fiji kava drinking was restricted to men of the priestly or ruling class. Observations in 1750 showed it to be a religious ceremonial of great importance; however, in 1829, a warrior chief, Ratu Tanoa, killed the last of the Fiji priests and, having thus obtained rather than ascribed status (to use the jargon), he desired to keep the ritual while eliminating its religious symbolism, which reflected to the glory of the priests. He turned it into a political ceremony to honor the head of the state, himself, rather than the priest-god. Its drinking spread to other ritual political occasions, so that installation ceremonies for all chiefs came to include kava drinking. Indeed, without such a proper installation, islanders did not acknowledge a chief—a fact which suggests that the transfer of the ritual from religious to political realms did not eliminate the interpersonal style of relationship between follower and leader, regardless of whether the leader was priest or chief. Ratu Tanoa, a clever man, had no doubt anticipated that ritual, awe, and magic would remain even if objects of authority shifted. By the late 1930's, women had come to drink kava, a practice which suggests secularization coincident with European occupation and a change in Fiji life styles.

Lewin notes that in other islands its use was individual as well as ceremonial, although primary employment was magical-medical. The kava plantation itself was consecrated in part to the dangerous gods, a part to the gods of sleep, and a part to the family using the substance. By Lewin's time the portion of the gods had been, in most islands, discarded. Festival use continued as did use on sociopolitical occasions, in entertaining guests, and in medical care. In some places, Lewin says that it was consumed as a daily beverage. Kava drinking eventually began among European settlers although it was class-linked; at first it was more respectable to abstain since only "inferior whites" drank it. (This brings to mind the tobacco edicts in England enjoining one against acting like a savage.) Interisland diversity was observable in its use by some along with singing, elsewhere not; in some places ceremonial use was abandoned and private use only remained; elsewhere, rituals continued; in some islands (Samoa) women as well as men participated, elsewhere not. For the most part, missionaries opposed kava drinking, the Presbyterians more than Anglicans. When alcohol was available, kava drinking tended to decline. Whether or not the resulting individual disorder and cultural disruption can be ascribed wholly to alcohol or, as is more likely, to the general response to the West—which brought disease, technology, Christianity, clothing, colonialism, and other blessings—is not certain.

A welcome collection of articles on kava has appeared recently (Efron, Holmstedt, and Kline, 1967). Holmes (in Efron) describes the function of kava in Samoa. In earlier days warriors consumed it prior to battle; today, as well as in the past, its use is related to religious, social, and political practices. Some healing properties have also been ascribed to the drug. Holmes suggests that kava drinking fits into the Polynesian veneration for village and social organization; kava etiquette dramatizes the system of rank and prestige. Quite possibly such traditions have stabilized the culture and aided it in resisting Western impact. Gajdusek (in Efron et al.) describes the use of kava on an island in the New Hebrides, an island where it had not been used before. Elsewhere in these islands, kava drinking has been associated with the cargo-cult response to wartime technology and, symbolically, as part of a resistance campaign against missionary dictates —some directed against kava itself. The drinking that Gajdusek describes on this particular island is associated with clannishness and a withdrawal from outside contacts, including mission work or local government. Nevertheless, these islanders continue to attend church and do not use kava as a direct protest. Without ceremony and informally, adult males use it each evening; females do not employ it. Use does not seem to enhance sociability, but rather it is taken in private houses in such a way that individuals can achieve solitary stupor. Ford's description (in Efron et al.) emphasizes how use does differ even on islands close together. He notes that in Melanesia it may be given as a libation to the gods but not drunk by islanders. Ford's Fiji observations record its earlier religious importance, which, as Lester found, had shifted to a political employment. He describes contemporary use as highly integrated with other activities; the drug itself is pleasant, but integrated with dancing, feasting, gift giving, and social ceremonials— marriage, birth, death, and hospitality—it enhances social activities and interpersonal ties, providing symbolic as well as social and—perhaps secondarily only—mind-altering gratifications. Ford observes that the preparation of kava, by chewing the root, is widely found in Asia as a way of producing fermented rice, maize, or cassava. He further notes that premastication of food by mothers for infants is so widespread that any culture might have discovered a fermented beverage by generalizing the technique. In any event, kava preparation gives further evidence of the importance of generalization on techniques of preparation and use, by means of which a variety of psychoactive substances come to be discovered and employed in diverse cultures. Kava use is also a good example of how, within the same culture area, rather considerable differences can exist in the styles and significance of use of one drug— differences not attributable on the basis of present evidence to gross institutional, ethnic, or socioeconomic variations.

Betel. The areca nut, or betel, and the betel leaf, which is chewed as a quid, are given earliest notice, according to Lewin, by Theophrastus in 340 B.C. Use was widespread in Persia by 600 A.D. for, by that time, over 30,000 betel-selling shops were described by the historian Ferishta (cited by Lewin) in one town. Indians by the tenth century used it as a "national custom" and it is assumed that Arabian travelers, so important for drug diffusion during medieval times, brought it to their countries and to Africa from India. Contemporary use extends from points on the west coast of Africa through India to Southeast Asia and parts of Oceania. It is a commercial product used by men and women but it may be turned to particular interests; for example, Lewin says that Burmese monks used it to inspire self-reflection. A mild substance ordinarily producing a pleasant sensation in the mouth (for those used to it) as well as stimulation, it is nevertheless said to be the focus of compulsive use; Lewin is of the opinion that its use is helpful digestively in Far Eastern diet.

Our observations indicate that mixing several psychoactive materials together is a world-wide practice, as is taking such different substances in one or another sequence. In the case of betel, in Thailand it is chewed with *Mitragyna speciosa,* which according to Schultes (in Efron *et al.,* 1967) has narcotic properties. Ford (also in Efron *et al.*) calls attention to the similarity between kava and betel in terms of effects—betel being chewed by people west of kava-drinking regions. Betel chewing can also be social, for sharing the mixture, Ford says, is important in establishing friendships, in courtship, and in marriage. Far less involved with ceremony and etiquette than kava, betel use, nevertheless, is a social as well as an individual activity.

Khat. In Ethiopia and East Africa, khat was eaten before 1200 A.D. but initial dates of its use are unknown (El Mahi, 1962a). Lewin gives a date of 1332 for its first mention in Ethiopia. Its eating was and is an individual rather than a ritual activity, although it was favored by mystics and, early, by intellectuals. Khat has also been employed in folk medicine; khat spittle, for example, was placed on the female genitalia to assuage labor pain. Ascetics used it as an aid in austerity. El Mahi says its use as a social facilitator is valued to promote good feeling and exchange in social intercourse. As so often occurs with drugs, the khat user may employ other substances either in sequence or simultaneously—particularly coffee and tobacco and, perhaps, hashish. Opposition to khat use has been based on religious grounds, some Moslems contending it is an intoxicant and therefore forbidden; on pragmatic grounds it has been opposed since some chronic users display irritability and depression; it has been opposed on medical grounds—by Lewin, for example—because of cardiac disturbance, loss of appetite, loss of sexual interest, and other distress when it has been used excessively. On other grounds it is argued that khat cultivation occurs instead of much-needed food cultivation in the agriculturally unproductive Arab areas, that its leisure enjoyment displaces time that might be spent in work, and that poor individuals spend money on khat that would be better spent on food and self-care. Recently there have been governmental expressions of opposition to khat reflecting these arguments.

SYNTHETIC STIMULANTS

Synthetic stimulants, of which the amphetamines are the most important in terms of nonmedical use, are a twentieth-century product and thus without a history in the conventional sense. Nevertheless, their use is so widespread and such an interesting epidemiological phenomenon that the pharmaceutical class should not be ignored. Since they were initially employed by physicians for treatment of depression, fatigue, and overweight, a market in proprietary remedies soon developed, especially for inhalers and other anti-allergy devices. The euphoriant capability was soon noted and benzedrine-containing inhalers came to be used by young people in the United States in the late 1930's without any self-medicating intent. Actual self-medication may have occurred in the sense that, according to some reports, amphetamines actually suppress certain kinds of agitated, juvenile, "psychopathic" behavior (Eisenberg, 1963; Pasamanick, 1951). State laws followed prohibiting benzedrine in over-the-counter remedies.

A related development occurred in Sweden following the introduction into medical practice of phenacetin, an analgesic with stimulating properties, in 1918 (Grimlund, 1963). First used to reduce muscle spasms and initially available without prescription, phenacetin was used on a daily basis by workers in several Swedish towns to increase work output, relieve headache, and so on. Near-ritual use developed morning and evening and, by the time of the study in the 1950's, considerable overdose use was widespread in the various worker groups. Inquiries revealed that use had begun either in response to social suggestion when no discomfort was present or was self-initiated when pains occurred. Continued use was attributed to the desire to maintain high work pace and because a habit had presumably set in. Because of the serious renal damage it caused, insuring health authorities placed the drug under prescription control; workers then substituted a new and less harmful (to kidney function) over-the-counter preparation. Retrospective analysis of the reasons for the popularity of the drug suggests that rapid technological change was a stress for workers who felt more was required of them; the medicine stimulated them and, psychologically, made them feel more secure. Workers who were satisfied with themselves and their jobs did not take phenacetin; those who were anxious about their work, who were afraid of being fired, or who had poor interpersonal relations did use it.

A later Swedish increase in nonmedical stimulant use is described by Bejerot (1966). Beginning with oral amphetamine consumption by Bohemian artists, writers, and actors in Stockholm in the 1940's, it spread downward in terms of status so that asocial and criminal groups adopted it by the 1950's. In 1958, an increased illicit supply, brought in from Spain, allowed increasing nonmedical use, at which time other urban centers became involved and younger people became interested. One out of ten persons arrested in Stockholm in 1965 was taking phenmetrazine intravenously, concentration of use being in the twenty-to-thirty age group and among males; a few were also alcoholics. Important in each case was that an experienced user had taught a novitiate the method of injection, drug preparation, and, presumably, the source of supply. Beyond delinquents, rootless youngsters have become involved, as well as an increasing number of females (our inference from the data).

Bejerot comments that the syringe itself is an object of considerable interest to users; to employ it is a status device, but beyond that there is a ritualistic preoccupation. One is reminded of the preoccupation with the needle on the part of "dope fiends" in the United States —a feature suggestive of the independent importance of the means of injection regardless of what is injected. One may interpret this either on psychoanalytic grounds by proposing a considerable mutilative or sexual significance to injection or on the grounds of a conditioning process whereby the instrument leading to reward (the drug effect) takes on reward value itself. In either case, the correspondence between oral satisfactions derived from smoking and preoccupation with the hypodermic apparatus and act is not to be overlooked. Given a commitment to a method, the substitution of drugs with it takes on more than simple replacement function, becoming a part of "play" or a compulsive focus on the method of administration itself. If such is the case, then further substitution of drugs—once the intravenous technique has been learned—is to be expected in any population in which injection has taken on importance. Such a phenomenon is visible in hippie groups' substitution of methedrine for DMT, LSD for methedrine, and who-knows-what as a next step.

At about the same time that the Swedish were experiencing the spread of amphetamine use, so were the Japanese (Masaki, 1956). Use was attributed to availability after the war of large military supplies of amphetamines and to marked changes in social life following defeat in war and democratization of government. Young people, in fact, began to use amphetamines in such numbers that a survey in one city in the early 1950's showed 5 per cent of those sixteen to twenty-five had used them; among these nonmedical users, about one fourth of the group was considered dependent on the drugs or suffering ill effects. By 1954, over half a million users were estimated, with half suffering dependency; a later report suggested one and a half million users, almost all of whom were young people. No users over the age of forty were reported. There was a particularly high concentration of use among delinquents; one third of one sample of reformatory inmates had experience with the drug. More recent reports (Ministry of Health and Welfare, Japan, 1964) show use to be high among show-business people, artists, and waitresses, as well as among wilder youngsters. Lambo (1965) reports that in Nigeria nonmedical amphetamine use is increasing among students (urbanized Western-trained population) along with an increase in the use of barbiturates, alcohol, and cannabis. He attributes such social use to migration and subsequent cultural instability as newcomers under stress try to adapt to city life. In contrast, in India, where widespread wake-amine experience among wealthier urban young people is also encountered (Banerjee, 1963), use of amphetamines is restricted to combat fatigue for studying and work. (These same differences by setting, in the intent and associated frequency and pattern of amphetamine use, are to be seen between different colleges in student drug-use data reported in the companion volume.)

England has also been experiencing an increase in nonmedical and disapproved amphetamine use among young people. Bewley (1966) describes how initial postwar use was of nasal-inhaler contents. Later, pills and tablets were taken, especially in combination with barbiturates ("purple hearts"). Localized in Soho, a swinging recreational area of London, the drugs were stolen and resold in cafes and bars. Scott and Willcox (1965) indicate that most use was occasional and festive without delinquent involvement; chronic users were youngsters with personality disorders who came from unfavorable family backgrounds. In response to public concern generated in part by newspapers, a Drug Misuse Act was passed in 1964, making it an offense to possess amphetamines without medical authority. However, medical prescription hardly guarantees limited use, for a study by Kiloh and Brandon (1962) shows that 500 persons in an English town of 250,000 had become dependent on amphetamines in consequence of medical prescription. Most of these were middle-aged women. An extrapolated estimate gives a rate of 1/1000 or 2/1000 in England for such iatrogenic dependency. As for illicit use, Bewley estimates that it, too, is about 1/1000 to 2/1000. Further data on risks and sources of the drug are to be found in Kalant (1966).

The pattern in the United States appears quite similar to that in England, Japan, and Sweden, although adequate data are lacking. Our own pilot study of a normal population (Chapter Eleven) and the student data in the companion book show that quite a number of

younger citizens have had experience with illicitly obtained amphetamines. Production figures for the United States for 1962 (Blum and
Funkhouser-Balbaky, 1965) show four and a half billion tablets produced, or twenty-five tablets per citizen. The Food and Drug Administration estimates indicate half of these were consumed without a
medical prescription. Popular reports and the few available studies
suggest that unsanctioned use is concentrated among show-business and
communication-media people, delinquents, drug-experimenting high
school and college youth, rootless hippies, and probably a little-known
sample of females originally receiving the drug from physicians. Although social and psychological factors must play a partial role in accounting for amphetamine dependency, the self-medicating aspects—as
in treating depression—must not be overlooked, nor should the fact that
continued ingestion by itself can lead to a habit which, in the case of
many drugs, is reinforced by physiological as well as psychological distress upon withdrawal.

SUMMARY

None of the natural stimulants has been shown to be damaging
to the majority of the population of users, although, as with any psychoactive drug, heavy ingestion can lead to distress; even so, strictures
against use have been imposed either during the period of introduction
—as group codes form within a society where the substance is used—
or when a new authority has been imposed on an existing culture. An
example of the first is the reaction against coffee by political leaders
when it was introduced in the Moslem world and Germany. An example of the second is the anticoffee morality of such religious groups
as Mormons or Adventists. An example of the third kind of opposition is found in missionary disapproval of kava drinking in Polynesia
or in Spanish edicts against coca in Peru. Sociopolitical perspectives,
economic conditions, religious and moral values regarding stimulation
and pleasure, and snobbery based on racial, cultural, or status features
can all influence views of whether a drug is good, bad, or indifferent.

Ordinarily, natural stimulants have been introduced into a
society by conventional routes of commerce; the rapid expansion of
commerce and associated readiness to receive new goods have occurred
about the same time—in the 1600's and 1700's in the Western world
—at which time acceptance of coffee, tea, cocoa, and tobacco came
into use. Popular acceptance is facilitated when that which is new and

rare is first tried or owned by those of wealth and high status. Generally, people who can afford a very new product are in touch with travelers and merchants and are, perhaps, less bound by convention. They in turn are copied by people lower on the prestige ladder. High-prestige people—whether bishops, kings, artists, or intellectuals—are also in a good position to advertise a product. In Western countries initial acceptance has been followed by rapid commercial exploitation. As with any international commerce, the subsequent history of drug availability and price has been affected by political events.

Not all stimulants are accepted. Coca never became popular in Europe, perhaps because of initial Spanish disapproval and its reputation as an aid in exploiting Indian labor, perhaps because of bulk and the graceless quid chewing and subsequent saliva-dripping consequence, and quite possibly because its pharmaceutical effects were—and are—unnecessary for the ordinary Westerner.

In regard to the natural stimulants, two different historical patterns of use suggest themselves. One shows development of use in advanced societies (China, India, Europe) with no real evidence for ceremonial practices, either religious or medical, except as incidental to popular noninstitutionalized use. The use of tea or cocaine in medicine, of tea by priests or in aesthetic social rituals, or khat or coffee by dervishes is as such a secondary ritual. Tea, coffee, cocaine, betel, khat—as well as cocoa and kola nut, maté, and so on—are in the category of popular or casual drugs. Coca and kava are different, for originally in native cultures their use was only in association with magico-religious practices conducted by authorities. These substances were also status symbols in the sense that authorities controlled access and employment. With both drugs, as societies changed diffusion occurred, so that use became more popular and uncontrolled and no longer ritual—that is, the process of secularization took place. It is interesting that conquering colonials—whether represented by missionaries or conquistadores—opposed these drugs. We wonder whether the opposition was as symbolic as the use. May not opposition to a drug practice occur simply because the drug is seen as expressive of an older way of life and as a symbol that vests power in the political-religious institutions which are disapproved? In both of the above instances, we must consider that there was no continuing opposition to drugs per se; missionaries were tolerant (perhaps we should say they looked the other way) of the potent drug alcohol when it was introduced in Polynesia, where they fought the milder kava. The Spanish opposed coca chewing until they realized not only that it could not be eliminated under conditions of life as they were—and are—in the Alti Plano, but that coca chewing could be of use to them in ways compatible with their own colonial institutions, which were designed to keep laborers at work in the mines and fields. What we are suggesting is that colonial opposition was itself symbolic, since unified, "occupying-power" opposition to a mild stimulant occurred only—as far as we can see—when the stimulant represented ceremonials integral to the native culture's religious and political authority, rather than when the stimulant was much more widely used but not in ways sacred to that local authority. Insofar as that opposition did destroy remaining institutions of native authority, it was, of course, functional as well. One sees something of the same thing in the Moslem mullah-sultan decrees against coffee; there the drug was—according to El Mahi (1962a)—a convenient focus when the attack was actually against those groups with feared political potential whose members drank coffee. Lewin disagrees and suggests that opposition was merely based on misinformation which indicated that coffee was intoxicating. It need not be an either/or situation; quite likely, misinformation is necessary to justify an attack which also has latent—or at least unstated—sociopolitical implications. It is of interest that in each instance the attack finally failed; coffee use expanded, while coca and kava use continued. We stress that much better data are needed about all of the hazy sociopolitical aspects of drug use.

As far as the synthetic stimulants are concerned—and cocaine as a manufactured derivative is functionally one of these in social if not pharmacological perspective—cocaine was isolated by a medical scientist and within a few short years was proclaimed medically efficacious as a mood elevator, painkiller, local anesthetic, and cure for morphinism. Within a short time after its medical use began, some people commenced to try it on themselves without medical supervision. At first, these were physicians, men with access to supplies; later, they were intellectuals and professionals who knew physicians or had other access. Somewhat later, public supplies appeared and use was taken up by criminal groups. During this same short period, the discovery of cocaine dependency and toxicity was made. Public knowledge of that discovery probably played some part in inhibiting further spread of cocaine use; professional application of that knowledge in limiting distribution of it probably played a larger role. Nevertheless, some illicit popular use of cocaine continues to this day.

The popular use of the amphetamines is a different story; widespread use has arisen subsequent to widespread over-the-counter or by-prescription sales. Prodigious quantities have been manufactured. "Epidemics" of use center among the fifteen-to-thirty age group in Japan, Sweden, England, and the United States—four of the most technically advanced nations. There is no evidence that use itself— whether by entertainers, drivers, studying students, partying youth, or delinquents—leads to ill effects; some who take amphetamines in excessive doses do suffer toxic reactions, while others taking them on a chronic basis show dependency. Current limited evidence suggests that excessive and chronic use is increasing and that among drug-oriented groups intravenous injection has replaced oral administration. With that, new public-health problems arise (such as hepatitis and abscesses), along with presumption that methedrine users (the drug mainly so employed) will also experiment with injection of other drugs which can further complicate their health and adjustment to life. Fascination with the needle, the up-down drug cycle (heroin-cocaine-heroin, amphetamine-barbiturate[2]-amphetamine, LSD-thorazine-LSD, and so on), and the cultural-pharmacological significance of being "high" for young people are facets of amphetamine use which merit much attention.

[2] We have not prepared a separate section on barbiturates. Their history is modern, their use widespread, their ill effects well documented. Their epidemiology has yet to be written. An interested reader is referred to Fort (1964b), Brooke and Glatt (1964), and Blum (1967c).

A History of
Hallucinogens

Richard H. Blum

VII

*E*lsewhere, we (Blum and Funkhouser-Balbaky, 1965) have discussed the inadequacy of nomenclature which categorizes drugs on the basis of one aspect of the outcome of use. Such a nomenclature is obviously not chemical nor pharmacological; it is at best a convenience and at worst a source of confusion and unnecessary argument. The hallucinogens constitute such a category. A wide variety of manufactured (derived) and plant materials conventionally are included in this class: LSD, DMT, mescaline, peyote, psilocybin, datura, fly agaric (a mushroom), pituri, parica (cohaba), ololiuqui, teonanactl, caapi, mandrake, and henbane. For material on specific substances see de Ropp, 1957), Efron, Holmstedt, and Kline (1967), Lewin (reissue, 1964), Schultes (1963a, 1963b), and Wassén and Holmstedt (1963). The history of many of these substances lacks documentation; for others there is a dispute over plant sources and effects, as well as for early dates for use and patterns of diffusion. In this section we shall restrict ourselves to a presentation of limited historical-epidemiological data on just a few of the hallucinogens.

Schultes (1963a, 1963b, 1967) finds a much greater variety of mind-altering, naturally occurring (plant-derived) hallucinogens in the New World than in the Old—forty known species in the former as opposed to about six in the latter. Along with this variety in the Americas are a much wider natural distribution and a greater number of tribal peoples availing themselves of these substances. In the New World, use is almost entirely ritual in association with magico-religious ceremonials.

Mushrooms. The most enthusiastic chroniclers of the hallucinogens are Gordon Wasson and his wife, who have set forth both a history and a theory of mushroom use. Wasson (1957, 1958, 1963) and Wasson and Wasson (1957) contend that in prehistory a proto-religion evolved from hallucinogenic mushroom experiences. It is their thesis that man perceived a deity and subsequently a need for a deity as a consequence of eating hallucinogenic plants. Much of this religion is assumed to have been lost as peoples migrated, but elements or folk memories remain in language, in the presence of mushroom-loving or mushroom-fearing attitudes among peoples (the Russians as the former, Anglo-Saxons as the latter), and in the scattered tribes who at least until recent times continued ritual use of these plants. The Wassons describe these practices in the Siberian Samoyed, Yenisei-Osyaks, Yakuts and Yakhaghirs, Tungas, Chuckchee, Koryhaks and Kamchadales, and the Oaxaca Indians of Mexico. An eighth group, the Mt. Hagan people of New Guinea, are also said to be mushroom religionists but no adequate descriptions of them are available. The Borneo Dyaks are also cited (Wasson and Wasson, 1957). The Wassons describe mushroom stones with phallic significance dating to 1000 B.C. in Central America (an earlier date is given in Wasson, 1963). They propose that other early findings may be expected in China and Africa. They ask whether the Greeks used mushrooms in the Eleusinian mysteries, whether the Delphic oracle employed them, and whether the Sanskrit soma might not be the same. Wasson offers detailed descriptions of contemporary magico-religious use of mushrooms based on his and his wife's own participant observation in Mexico. There, the intentions are sacred and involve healing, divination, and mystical experiences.

Cautious readers will be dubious of the claimed early dates, ubiquitousness, and religious etiology of the mushroom cult as proposed by the Wassons. For example, no evidence supports the link to Greek religious practices nor is their thesis of an early wet period in the Fertile Crescent conducive to mushroom growth supported by geological-archaeological evidence. On the other hand, there are references (Sullivan, 1967) in connection with the literature of cooking, immortality, and visions in Taoist (third century B.C.) Chinese texts; there are European (Swiss) practices linking mushrooms to religious festivals (Christmas); and there is no reason to exclude the likelihood of early discovery of the hallucinogenic properties of fungi by at least some tribal people, which would be expected to lead to the incorporation of the fungi into religious, healing, and other ceremonial rites. But that the hallucinogenic experience was responsible for developing a religious sense—rather than simply expanding or enriching it—does seem unlikely. Certainly the dates for evidence of religious practices (James, 1957) are earlier, by many thousands of years, than are the dates for mushroom-eating cults.

Another disputable proposition for the use of fungi is offered by Fabing (1957)—following Odman and Schubeler (cited by Fabing)—who contends that the Berserkers, wild Scandinavian warriors (named for using bear skin, or "ber sark," instead of armor) drew their fury from the *Amanita muscaria* mushroom. The practice of berserk-going was outlawed in the eleventh and twelfth centuries; anyone who went berserk was to be banished and any companion who failed to tie up the berserk-goer was also subject to banishment. Other descriptions of the berserkers agree on their fury but do not provide evidence of fungi use. Walter Scott (reissue, 1902), for example, in a very liberal translation of an Icelandic saga argues for their heavy use of wine, mead, and ale. He proposes that they lost their supernatural strength upon assuming the Christian faith (as opposed to their abandoning fungi use under penalty of the newly passed Christian laws of Jarl, Thorlaks, and Ketil (see Fabing). Beckett (1915) describes the berserkers as a class of Viking warriors organized into a special fighting corps known for their bloodthirsty nature. This "warlike frenzy, stimulated by large portions of strong drink," was reduced, according to Beckett, when Triggvason forcibly Christianized Norway. We gather it was force rather than sudden virtue which calmed the berserkers. Obviously, a consensus on those warriors has yet to be reached. That a hallucinogen must be invoked to account for their performance may be gilding the lily, for violence subsequent to alcohol imbibing amongst a warrior class is part of an old tradition.

Several scholars have written of mushroom use by Aztecs and later Indians. Safford (1915) believes that teonanactl was actually peyote, an erroneous identification. He calls attention to initial opposition to teonanactl by the Catholic clergy because of its connections with pagan rites which they were trying to eliminate. These rites, described by a number of observers (cited by Safford; also by del Pozo, 1967, and Schultes, 1940a)', included religious divination through communion, human sacrifice, and also suicide during the period of intoxication, as well as religious-political rituals such as those used in the coronation of Montezuma, and possibly individualistically in political murder, for Thompson (cited by Schultes) says Tozon may have been killed when a very poisonous variety was substituted for the ritual mushroom. Johnson (1939) describes the later (1930's) use of teonanactl among the Mazatecs, at which time use was still part of strictly shamanistic rituals devoted to divination, healing, and interpersonal black magic—that is, harming one another. This latter use was integrated by the 1930's with the notion of the evil eye, which is a Mediterranean belief brought into Mexico by the Spaniards. Johnson cites Sagahun to the effect that the early diffusion of mushroom eating through Mexico and Central America was accomplished as part of Aztec merchant travel and commerce. As far as the earliest dates are concerned, Schultes (1940a) appears to concur in the Wassén interpretation of stones and art suggesting mushroom religious relevance as far back as 1000 to 500 B.C. In actual use there were a number of highly individualistic reactions, according to Schultes, even though the setting for use was ceremonial. Thus, individual aspirations and fears were reflected in the visions, as were behaviors of singing, dancing, weeping, and meditation. Schultes describes the geography of recent teonanactl use—an admittedly difficult task since use is a secret rather than a public activity. Contemporary ritual use—at least as described by observers (see also Wasson, 1958, 1957, 1963)—although ritualistic and traditional, is geared to individual needs, such as healing, finding lost objects, and interpersonal witchcraft. What this means is that traditional uses need not be communal ceremonies—and most often are not—but instead can be ceremonials conducted by "curanderas" or healers[1] upon request of persons or families—a practice wide-

---

[1] There is no good word in English—"witch" has much too medieval a connotation.

spread through Mexico and Central America with or without the use of mind-altering substances.

Other on-the-spot descriptions of mushroom eating for mind-altering purposes are to be found in writings by travelers to Siberia, where fly agaric was consumed in certain regions. Kennon wrote in 1870, Lansdell in 1883, Jochelson in 1908, and Bogoras in 1909 (observations were made in 1900). Contradictions abound in descriptions of practices of the Koryak and Chuckchee. Kennon found the settled Koryaks (in contrast to the nomadic ones) a reprehensible breed and attributes their degradation and brutalization to the "toadstool habit." His implication is of compulsive individualistic use by a group of licentious thieves who were, additionally, rum drinkers. At least part of their misbehavior he attributes to contact with the Russians. Because fly agaric was so rare, the Koryak paid high prices for it and, to conserve effects, the urine of the first eater thereof was drunk by another, his urine by a third, and so forth. Lansdell, a minister, found this practice abhorrent but is less harsh on the Koryaks, even though he agrees they were debased. Bogoras points out that fly-agaric use was more common among those with easiest access to it but notes that Christianized former users abandoned the practice out of shame, while others were abstinent even though it grew near them and they traded it. Male hunters were most prone to employ it. Use led mushroom eaters to see visions of spirits who resembled the mushroom; the spirits were jokesters whose "visit" was followed by acute intoxication ("lunacy") and then by sleep. The urine-conservation drinking method was so valued that Bogoras, reporting for the Jessup expedition, notes that others' urine was consumed even when no mushrooms had been eaten.[2] He also describes the intensive use by Siberian tribes of tobacco and alcohol—some people smoking, chewing, and sniffing tobacco all at once, consuming 95 per cent alcohol in as large a quantity as could be found, and, commonly, drinking forty cups of black tea a day besides.

Jochelson discusses addiction to fly agaric among the Koryak, saying that only the old men ate mushrooms and that the youngsters

[2] One again is reminded of the conditioning process, an important form of secondary reinforcement, whereby the instrumental action or discriminated prior stimulus takes on the value of a reward and in the absence of a reward (that is, a drug) may still be engaged in. Morphine-dependent rats can be trained to follow much the same pattern, favoring the liquid given before morphine over another discriminated liquid followed by no morphine.

gave it to them as a mark of deference. He also found that shamans used mushrooms during divination ceremonies, during funeral rituals, for healing by spirit communion, and for other magical communion with spirits, as well as for euphoric purposes in gatherings. Jochelson reports that the mushroom spirit was said to kill those who overindulged by taking more than the three to ten mushrooms which constitute a normal dose (high doses can be fatal since the mushroom is toxic). During carousing, men remained intoxicated for several days at a time. Some would drink their own urine to prolong the effect. Interestingly, the Koryak would also drink their own urine after alcohol imbibing for the same reason—another example of the generalization of a drug-taking method from one to another substance. On the other hand, alcohol was not taken at the same time as fly agaric since the two were felt to be antagonists. Alcohol drinking was also confined, according to Jochelson, to older men among the Koryak.

The disagreement among observers as to who among the Koryak used fly agaric and under what settings and intentions allows few conclusions—all but one tentative. The strong conclusion is that observers can see remarkably different reasons, practices, and effects even when they are all presumably watching the same people at about the same point in time. This should give us pause as we consider ethnographers' reports, single-purpose historians, or the morals drawn for us by watchers on the contemporary scene. As for the Koryak and fly agaric, we tend to accept Jochelson, who ascribes both traditional magico-religious and magico-healing settings (the distinction is modern and Western, since magic, religion, and healing are all part of the same ceremonial cloth for many around the world) to its use, as well as more individualistic and sometimes gaudy performances. Whether the latter represents the end stage of a process of secularization after culture impact with the West (Russia), as we suspect, or whether both practices evolved simultaneously is not known.

Datura, Jimson weed, or thorn apple (containing hyoscyamine, scopolamine, and atropine as psychoactive compounds). This substance is another hallucinogen for which some historical-epidemiological data are available. Schultes (1963a) says it was early used by the Incas and Chibchas of South America and that it was reintroduced into Andean regions more recently. The expectation of spirit visitations accompanies use, although it is said to be given to misbehaving children so that the spirits will admonish them. Among the ancient

Chibchas it was given to slaves and women who were to be buried alive during the funerals of their masters; that ritual use would seem to have had a fear-deadening intention.

Lewin (reissue, 1964) believes that *Datura stramonium* was the plant which Marc Antony's troops accidentally ate on their retreat from Parthia in 38 A.D. and which produced stupor or, in larger doses, insanity and death. Blakeslee, Avery, Satina, and Rietsema (1959) state that its earliest specific mention was by the Arab physician Avicenna in the eleventh century; he was aware of its intoxicating as well as medical potentials. These authors, like Lewin, identify Aztec *ololiuhqui* as *Datura meteloides*—an identification which others, including de Ropp (1957) and Schultes (1963a) would dispute. Blakeslee *et al.* state that Aztec use of datura was for healing and by priests for spirit communion. For the Aztecs it was a sacred plant which was the object of offerings. Lewin describes its use in East Africa, where it is smoked, and in Bengal, where it is smoked with cannabis or taken as a tincture in wine; in Japan, Lewin says, it is smoked with tobacco. Regarding its Indian use, Blakeslee *et al.* say it has been used by the thugs ("Thuggee," a criminal tribe whose methods were highly stylized) to stupefy their victims. Smartt (1956) states that South African criminals also used it for the same purpose. Since there are many Indians in South Africa, it is possible that thuggee practices were an import. Smartt also says it is smoked there in conjunction with cannabis to produce individual intoxication. We presume that Central European use is implied by Lewin when he speaks of the devil's herb used "by religious fanatics, clairvoyants, miracle workers, magicians, priests and imposters" to invoke hallucinations and deceptions as part of demonology. He also describes Amerindian use of one or another datura variety for divination, for spirit communion, in ritual healing by shamans, in ceremonial preparation for warfare, and in puberty rites of passage. To this list Blakeslee *et al.* add its use in funeral ceremonies and state they have observed a wide variety of effects dependent in part upon dosage. We would add the other environmental and personal variables which influence drug reactions—for example, Blakeslee describes Indians as seeing visions, dancing, laughing, weeping, or sleeping.

Kroeber (1953b) describes the Jimson weed (*Datura*) or toloache cult of the California Indians, who used the substance for puberty rites lasting for several months. It was also used as a painkiller. Some

California tribes gave it to small children in pursuit of visions of a personal spirit who would become the protector of the individual. Others used it prior to endurance trials. Kroeber remarks upon the variety of use aside from puberty initiations; he also points out that not all Indians knowledgeable as to its effects used it in ceremonial or cult fashion.

European use of datura is rarely reported. Beverley (reissue, 1947) describes how the "James-Town Weed" was gathered for salad by some early soldier settlers. They were said to have become "natural fools" for some days, "sitting naked in the corner like monkeys and making mows" (faces) and wallowing in their own excrement unless constrained. No more recent use of datura has come to our attention, except for some few reports of experimental intoxication by modern California youngsters—including Big Sur hippies.

Mandrake.   A history of mandrake (*Mandragora,* a solanaceous plant also containing hyoscyamine, scopolamine, and hyoscine) is presented by C. J. S. Thompson (1934). Since the mandrake root resembles a man, or can be perceived as such, it has long been believed to have magical properties. Mentioned in Genesis as a fertility inducer (Rachel and Leah), in the Song of Solomon, it also figured in Egyptian medicine. Assyrian reference is dated circa 700 b.c. (R. C. Thompson, cited in C. J. S. Thompson), and Hippocrates speaks of it as a reliever of depression and anxiety when taken in wine. By Hellenistic times more elaborate magical notions were developing. Theophrastus observed that it must be uprooted in a ritual way; such ritual harvesting of the plants survives into modern Greece (Blum and Blum, 1968), and the witchcraft of mandrake has likewise continued through medieval times in Europe. Dioscorides describes its healing value, whereas others have proposed that during the Roman occupation of Israel, Sanhedrin women gave the drug to those crucified so that they might appear dead. Crucified persons were taken from the cross, and afterwards they revived. Thompson (1934) comments that some scholars have speculated that Christ's rising—that is, living after death—might be so attributed. Its military use was ascribed to Hannibal, who is said to have simulated a retreat in Africa and, leaving in his camp wine jars spiked with mandragora, returned after his enemies had "captured" his camp, drunk the wine, and fallen asleep. Caesar is said to have repeated the strategy against Sicilian pirates. It was also used as an aphrodisiac, at least symbolically, and was a common ingredient in love philters. Thompson reports on the mandrake legend transplanted to China—where the plant was unknown—in the ginseng and Shang beliefs about these plants with human-shaped roots. Believed by Europeans and Chinese to be most efficacious when sprung from the urine or semen of a hanged criminal (a European notion specifically), mandrake became sufficiently in demand for the Chinese to traffic in counterfeit roots.

The Arabs used the plant medically and against maladies caused by demons so that magico-healing as well as empirical Arab medicine knew its use. Thompson proposes a date of about 1000–1050 for its introduction into England, where it was sold for magical properties. Another highly valued, man-shaped root plant (Briony)', an imposter, was sold in counterfeit. Mandrake talismans came to be worn, embellished with "hair" on their heads and genitals that grew from planting barley in the wet plant. Mandrake mysticism, says Thompson, was at its height in the twelfth to sixteenth centuries through Europe and the Near East, during which time the little men were clothed, fed, and counted on to perform miracles medical and otherwise. The Franciscans in the 1400's sought to stamp out the magical practices but to no avail. Before that date its actual medical use vied with its symbolic magical value; after that date, magic took precedence. In later centuries its importance diminished, although in Europe and America it can still be purchased from some herbalists.

Peyote. The cactus *Lophophora Williamsii*, or peyote, has been the subject of a number of excellent recent studies focusing on the circumstances of its adoption by increasing numbers of American Indians. J. S. Slotkin (1955, 1956), an anthropologist, has provided an excellent source book, as has La Barre (1960, 1964). Slotkin was an official in the (Indian) Native American Church, where the drug is ritually employed. A comprehensive hypothesis testing study of its use among the Navajo has been offered by Aberle (1966). Slotkin makes the important point that "peyote" was a generic term covering many hallucinogenic Mexican plants; this explains much of the contradiction and confusion, especially the citation by several historians of the same early observation, with each historian disagreeing as to how the drug was actually employed.

According to Schultes (1940b)', the Aztecs used peyote as a specific for rheumatism; other Indians used it for a wide variety of healing purposes. Among some athletes observed by early Spaniards, it was used as a stimulant, whereas others used it prior to battle to give courage. The Chichimecas (described in 1575, discussed by Safford, 1921) so employed it, but also used it because it was magical and would protect them from all danger.[3] They further used it to ward off hunger and thirst. Among other Amerindians it served as a stimulant before ceremonial dances. When Catholic missionaries came to Mexico, Safford says that they opposed peyote use—a pattern of Christian opposition which we have seen before directed toward other substances (coca, mushrooms, and other hallucinogens) in the Americas and elsewhere (kava in Polynesia; opium in China; and cannabis, tobacco, and alcohol [by Fundamentalists] in the United States). In Mexico, peyote use was sometimes in conjunction with alcohol; thus, "mescal liquor" became the term for alcohol and "mescal buttons" for peyote. These are all early uses prior to the remarkable spread of the peyote cult itself. Schultes says it is the most important Indian medicine, as well as being the focus now for religion. It is also important to remark that Aberle's data show that most Navajos initially took peyote only in (ceremonial) healing endeavors and then became cult members using the drug more diversely. As with most folk cultures, healing-religious-magical ceremonials are linked.

Contemporary Indians continue to use the drug for healing. Schultes says Plains Indians use it as freely as Caucasians use aspirin, that rural Mexicans employ it as a household analgesic. It has also been used as a cure for drug dependency or toxic reactions—for example, in the treatment of opium dependency,[4] alcohol hang-overs, and alcoholism. Safford cites the claim of peyote cultists that cult members lose all interest in alcohol once initiated. Aberle observes that there is an antialcohol morality which is part of the peyote religion; as a result, many teetotalers are found among the cultists.

The recent history of the peyote cult (Aberle, 1966; La Barre, 1960, 1964; Slotkin, 1955, 1956; see also Barber, 1941) is supplemented by a number of studies of particular tribes (for example, Aberle, 1966; Petrullo, 1934; Spindler, 1955, 1952; and Zingg, 1938). Briefly, the cult beginnings appear to have been in the 1860's with ritual and cult practices established by 1885. The cult departed from

[3] One is reminded of the similar use by modern Congo warriors of cannabis or cannabis plus alcohol as a magical drug to ward off danger in battle.

[4] We had hoped to find an account of Indian adoption of opium but could not do so.

healing, trance, power seeking, or divination intentions by stressing pan-Indian nativistic features. Christian elements were incorporated by the 1890's. By 1899, sixteen tribes had adopted the cult; by 1955, sixty-six more had done so. The appeals of the cult are well described by modern anthropological observers, who view it as an accommodation to white domination—one which provides a sense of identity and solidarity in the face of discrimination and threat of cultural extermination. The spread of the peyote cult followed the demise of the more strongly antiwhite Ghost Dance movement, which had itself evolved as intertribal contacts increased, for these contacts served as a means of communication by which the peyote cult could be transmitted. This transmission was, and is, by no means easy since resistance to the cult exists among missionaries (Petrullo) and both traditional and modern Indians (Aberle). Among the Navajos, for example, the majority of people oppose the peyote cult. Each set of opponents claim dire effects from peyote use—intoxication, sexual immorality, laziness, mental disease, malformed infants, death, and addiction, to name a few. These claims are not substantiated by any careful observers of the Indian peyote users and thus constitute an example of notions of drug abuse which reflect at least an incorrect understanding of drug effects; more fundamentally, as Aberle shows, they reflect a negative reaction to the cult itself, which its opponents view as a threat to their values, systems, and self-interest (for example, they see the cult as foreign, nontraditional, and uncontrollable). Aberle offers the important finding that neutralism about the peyote cult is rare among Navajos; those who view it neutrally are most often among the highly educated. Many Navajo opponents believe peyote to lead to unbridled sexuality and loss of self-control. Aberle proposes that a deeper but unstated concern is that it threatens conventional Navajo ways, is not compatible with the ideals or goals which most Indians have for tribal development, and generates deep anxiety associated with concern about any mind-medicine and its potential harm to health and sanity.

Aberle carefully examines the function of peyote for those who do adopt it, pointing to how its ideology does allow an adjustment to or compensation for degraded status vis-à-vis the white, an ethical code relevant to socioeconomic circumstances, and a source of varied individual satisfactions, which include access to power, miracle cures, transcendental knowledge, divination, self-guidance, protection from witches and ghosts, and a release from guilt. The cult itself safely expresses antiwhite sentiment and provides a sustaining social group.

Aberle's data are most instructive about those Navajos who become peyotists as contrasted to those who do not. Early use is best predicted by access or the closeness to supplies. Later use (by region) is best predicted by prior use and inversely with acculturation. Communities most likely to be upset by peyotism and to charge drug abuse are those where there is peyote use and where the community suffers from those features which are, in fact, most likely to be associated with further peyote-cult development. Specifically, these are places where Navajos with previously large livestock holdings have lost them during the government-sponsored, livestock-reduction campaigns or where large numbers of persons reported bad dreams connected with illness and death (the latter we take to be a measure of anxiety and the combination of which, economics and anxiety, Aberle calls deprivation and disturbance). For these people peyotism is a redemptive movement offering compensation rather than restitution; "blessed are the poor and the weak," it would say. For the peyote cultists, the drug takes on greater and more differentiated importance once interest develops. Although the mind altering is an experience which they feel they cannot communicate to outsiders, group interaction among cult members tangibly increases and contact with other Indians diminishes; an ethnocentric spirit arises which makes both conventional Indians and white society outsiders (see Becker, 1963).

With the expansion of the peyote cult among American Indians, there has been a simultaneous development of tribal law and state and federal laws either prohibiting use or setting forth limited acceptable circumstances for use, such as in religious ceremonies by bona fide church members instead of by unorganized individuals. This latter feature affects non-Indian users, small groups of whom have been described among Oklahoma Negroes (Smith, 1934) geographically close to peyote and to Indian users. A large group of Caucasians have experimented with peyote. At first, these were anthropologists and students with interests in the cult, but with the advent of broader interests in drugs—what we (Blum and Associates, 1964) have elsewhere termed the "Drug Movement"—other professionals, artists, intellectuals, and students began to experiment with peyote, ordering it from Southwestern supply houses. Although this traffic has apparently been reduced in some states because of legal controls and increased law-enforcement effort, there are now a number of younger people, hippies,

drug-curious individuals, and the like who have at least experimented
with peyote. On the basis of reports made to us, its unpleasant effects
limit its attractiveness to casual users.[5]

LSD. This drug has no history; history requires time for careful documentation and perspective over decades. A manufactured pharmaceutical, its popularity is a subject of profound public interest and
concern—an interest which reflects the fascination-repugnance so often
seen (Blum and Blum, 1967) when considering the emotions associated
with mind-altering drugs. From its discovery in Switzerland, its use
spread first to experimental subjects under medical care and in labora-
tories, next through physicians and research workers to their families
and friends, then downward to university students and from there to
high school students, and now, occasionally, to elementary school children as well. There has also been a diffusion by class. Initially an up-
per-middle-class phenomenon associated with healing (alcoholic treatment, psychotherapy, distress relief)', religious states (particularly
mystical experience and aesthetics), and euphoria such as results from
felt relief of anxiety and depression, extension of use to lower-class
groups has altered settings and intentions compatible with the new
surroundings and people. As a consequence, use by young people for
kicks and by delinquents to harm others has been reported. We (Blum
and Associates, 1964)' have elsewhere described early patterns of LSD
diffusion which suggest that the variability of behavior observed and experience reported is highly dependent upon prior expectations, the degree of control in the setting of use, and the homogeneity of belief among
companions in the post-LSD experience. Personality differences among
continuing users as contrasted to those who discontinue use or are nonusers have also been proposed by McGlothlin, Cohen, and McGlothlin,
in a 1966 study (see also McGlothlin and Cohen, 1965). They found
that prior information as well as life-style orientations influenced decisions whether or not to use the drug; more important, perhaps, the relationship of the potential initiate to the initiator in terms of prestige and
the desire to continue in his favor loomed large. Continued use was

[5] Users of alcohol, opium, heroin, tobacco, LSD, cannabis, and other
mind-altering drugs often experience distress on the first occasion; anxiety and
nausea are generally common. Peyote differs in that many features of use are
difficult—the taste is bitter, anxiety and depression can be severe, the nausea is
unpleasant—and these do not disappear as tolerance develops by continued use
as occurs with toxic reactions to moderate doses of the other substances,

associated not only with expectation and personality but apparently also with the quality of the initial experience and with the development or nondevelopment of membership in drug-interested social groups. When such groups did develop, they became ethnocentric, developed sensitivity to "square" opposition to their drug interests, became critical of the square world, and frequently engaged in further use of a number of mind-altering substances, some of which were illegal. As LSD use expanded and anxiety grew about its effects and social significance (the latter rarely stated), legislation was enacted at federal levels and, more punitively, at state levels. Licit sources were dried up, and illegal manufacture and traffic became widespread; some of these same traffic sources engaged in the distribution of other illicit products, primarily marijuana. At the time of writing, trends in LSD use cannot be divorced from the general interest in exotic-illicit drugs expressed by special sectors of the population—primarily young people but also professionals, artists, mass-media writers, and so on. The hippie community, once centered in San Francisco but now widespread, continues to arouse both sympathy and hostility—feelings which can occur simultaneously within any one individual as well as be polarized in official attitudes. Our student data in the companion book indicate that, while the LSD experience itself is not widespread in the colleges sampled, the basic phenomenon of widespread interest in and experience with one or several illicit-exotic drugs is. For these nonconventional substances the present pattern seems to be one in which only a small number of persons engage in chronic use. Nevertheless, both the experimental and chronic users are increasing in number in urban American centers, and there is now in England an interest among drug-curious young people in taking LSD. As more articulate enthusiasts become involved with LSD or other hallucinogens and as citizens regard the several arguments surrounding use—ranging from Constitutional questions of law to biochemical questions as to effects—the likelihood is both for continued controversy and for further expansion of use in urban centers. An increasing effort in research and communication about drug effects is also occurring, not only for LSD but for its strongly symbolic (in American-youth culture) companion drug, marijuana, and for other substances as well. Happily, these endeavors apply to the conventional drugs of known toxicity and pathogenic power, alcohol and tobacco, as well as to the less well-known, illicit-exotic substances. Cisin and his coworkers' research endeavor which seeks to describe patterns of multiple-drug use for the nation as a whole should be most enlightening when it is completed.

SUMMARY

Characteristically, the use of hallucinogens by groups within Western society has involved intense emotionality and has revealed, as attitudes polarize around use, many of the social issues, personal hopes and stresses, and value systems of the antagonists. Were one to include cannabis among the hallucinogens (easily done since these categories of probable effects are flexible), it would be clear that at least in the United States and England considerable legal, political, social, psychological, and pharmacological significance figures in the debates about expanding use.

The most frequent pattern of hallucinogen use, cannabis excluded, appears to have been ritualistic in magico-religious-healing settings among nonliterate societies. Emphasis on these same intentions is found in the claims accompanying the introduction of many of these substances—LSD, peyote, and so on—into use by Caucasian Americans. In a secular society these claims—and the controls required for traditional use by authorities, whether these be physicians or religious leaders—must vie with others. In urban societies generally and in contemporary societies particularly, casual social or individual use outside of authority-controlled settings has proven more popular. In more homogeneous tribal societies where traditional controls have not broken down, it has been possible to introduce new drugs without producing widespread behavior variability or destructive private use—as witness the peyote cult. Even so, it has been impossible to accomplish that introduction into religious-social ritual without some persons fearing that damaging individual and social effects were in fact occurring.

There is a remarkable similarity between the expressed fears of the Navajo traditionalists and modernists opposing peyote and those of Caucasian Americans worrying about marijuana or LSD. One hears very similar definitions of drug "abuse" in cases where the empirical evidence as to physical or disruptive social ill effects is absent (peyote), where it is unclear (marijuana), where some such evidence is present (LSD, fly agaric), and where such evidence is strongly present (as with datura). We take it as obvious that scientific knowledge is itself not a prerequisite for damning a drug, although scientific ignorance provides a welcome for some of the contestants in the battle. There are parallels between the Navajo and secular American cultures in the conflict between imposed legal and conventional religious restrictions and enthusiastic users. Missionaries in Mexico and the United States did not eliminate hallucinogen use mong tribal folk; laws and clerical pronouncements have not eliminated production, commerce in, or use of similar substances by Caucasian Americans.

Actual use of hallucinogens is determined by a number of features; an individual's knowledge of laws and his morals are only part of the fabric, easily isolated from the rest. Knowledge of actual drug effects cannot be discounted—it appears that datura is unpopular because it is unpleasant and dangerous; many avoid LSD for the same reason. Availability of the drug is a paramount feature, as is the opportunity to learn to procure and administer the substance with appropriate expectations as to its desirable effects. Economics, geography, politics, technology, and laws do affect availability. A supporting-group structure for drug use must also exist, whether that be a band of youthful pot heads or a profound tribal tradition. In this regard, the symbolic value of the substance to the group and the person is of foremost importance; it is perhaps one of the keys to the attractiveness of hallucinogens that the induced experience lends itself to elaborations of symbolic functions. We propose that conceptions of magical power are a substrate for these elaborations (magic or magical thinking is by no means limited to tribal folk; among them magic is simply more respectable). The greater the number of symbolic benefits and satisfactions felt to be derived from the drug, the greater the likelihood of a commitment to the substance. Thus, Aberle's Navajos found peyote polyvalent—that is, it did many things for them. Professionals enthusiastic about LSD were those reporting several satisfactions derived from it; those who reported no solutions or rewards in the drug experience or any gains in the group experiences which form the environment for symbolic drug use were much less likely to continue with LSD. Aberle explains this partly in terms of personal significance, the meanings attached to what is experienced. Meanings of course are not derived just culturally or through groups; they are also individually salient and are formed in the context of psychodynamic features. Consequently, the meaning attached to the drug reaction—as, for example, the reaction to anxiety—or the meaning attached to the mind-altered state of consciousness itself is affected by personality. Nor can individual differences in regard to drug effects as biochemical processes be ignored.

Some people do have good experiences, some have bad ones; some become psychotic and others do not. Dosage, potency of the substance, manner and frequency of administration, concurrent physiological status, the presence of others who may be antagonistic or favorable to the drug, and possibly genetically linked biochemical-reaction variability must also be counted upon to determine individual behavior and postdrug evaluations, which in turn bear upon continued use.

We are sure that we have by no means set forth even the major possible influences on the spread, adoption, and evolving use pattern by persons and groups either of hallucinogens or other mind-altering substances. Certainly, the pattern of hallucinogen use of any group is not to be divorced from behaviors involving other drugs, from, perhaps, attitudes toward ingestion per se, from morality, and from the personal and social consequences of membership in that drug-oriented group. Because hallucinogens do involve profound personal and social experiences for large numbers of users, as well as profound worries on the part of others who observe them, they provide—along with other substances which take on strong symbolic functions, such as cannabis—an opportunity not just for epidemiological study but, through that study, an insight into the cleavage of values and personal stresses in any society where their abuse is argued.

A Cross-Cultural
Study

Richard H. Blum

VIII

*T*his chapter describes some aspects of the use of several mind-altering drugs in those nonliterate societies for which data are available. It also identifies relationships between styles of drug use and certain culture characteristics. It describes cross-culturally consistent relationships among several different aspects of drug use and presents the results of a test of relationship between one style of use for one drug and certain characteristics of nation-states. Given the limitations of data and method, the study should be considered exploratory rather than definitive.

The thrust of the work reported is consistent with earlier cross-cultural investigations on alcohol as initiated by Horton (1943)', supplemented by Field (in Pittman and Snyder, 1962), and recently extended by Bacon, Barry, and Child (1966). These cross-cultural studies are, in turn, related to a number of single culture investigations which describe or account for drug-use styles in terms of other cultural or social characteristics. Illustrations from the field of alcohol studies include Bunzel (1940), Lolli, Serianni, Golder, and Luzzatto-Fegiz

(1958), Blum and Blum (1964), Connell (1965), and Sadoun, Lolli, and Silverman (1965). Extending beyond investigations of whole cultures or normal samples drawn from such cultures, a considerable number of studies link styles of drug use in particular groups within a given society to other aspects of the person and his environment. Given the consistent findings which show that drug use is a social and psychological phenomenon, as well as a pharmacological and physiological one, one might expect that a systematic analysis of cross-cultural data would reveal certain regularities in the use of drugs other than alcohol, and between drug use and other characteristics of societies. It is that premise upon which our work is based.

METHOD OF APPROACH

Initially, a search was made for descriptions of drug use in cultures of varying complexity. Therefore, we originally included nation-states as well as nonliterate societies. This proved unsatisfactory since, for the most part, drug use in nation-states appears to vary considerably, depending upon the ethnic, class, generational, and status membership. (See Cisin and Cahalan [1966] for an illustration with reference to alcohol.) Thus, descriptions of the use of the lesser studied drugs (cannabis, stimulants, hallucinogens, medical opiates) threatened to be unreliable when reported for nation-states as a whole. For that reason, with one exception, we restricted our work to a description of mind-altering drug use in nonliterate societies. That exception is the use of drug "abuse" data for nation-states. For both the nonliterate societies and nation-states, we tested for relationships between styles of drug use and other characteristics of societies. As a source of characteristics of nonliterate culture, we relied on Textor (1967), and for nation-state characteristics on Banks and Textor (1963).

With reference to nonliterate societies, we sought data on alcohol, tobacco, natural hallucinogens (such as peyote, fly agaric, datura, and parica), natural stimulants (betel, kola, khat, kava, and so on), cannabis, opium, and coca-cocaine. No attempt was made to describe the use of medically employed synthetic pharmaceuticals. Our primary data sources were the Human Relations Area Files (HRAF) at Yale and (in limited number) at Stanford and supplemental reading conducted as part of our other work in social and epidemiological psychopharmacology (see Blum in Joyce, 1967). The appendix contains the list of nonliterate cultures used.

Using standard coding sheets, raters recorded styles of drug use as follows: (1) extent of drug use; (2) changes in use over time; (3) availability; (4) how the drug was introduced; (5) primary present source; (6) presence of abuse as defined by within-culture elements; (7) presence of abuse as defined by nonnative observers; (8) circumstances of use; (9) settings and inferred intents in use; (10) attitudes (supports and restraints) surrounding use; (11) differences between the sexes in use; (12) differences in age groups in use; and (13) status differences in use. Toward the end of our data gathering, the monograph by Child, Bacon, and Barry (1965) was published. In those instances in which their data were more complete than ours, we incorporated their findings into our descriptive categories, provided no conflict existed between their sources (when these were evident for ratings) and ours. We obtained a final sample of 247 nonliterate societies for each of which at least one aspect of use of one mind-altering drug was described.

RELIABILITY OF DATA

A constant problem was that of reliability. Frequently, different observers of a culture offer contradictory observations. Two different raters reading the same material may disagree on their coding. Further, the same rater reading the same source on different occasions may sometimes be inconsistent. In addition, clerical unreliability may occur when codes are transferred to Balgol sheets, and to cards for computer processing. Table 3 illustrates the problem of contradictory observations since conflicting reports occurred in 29 out of the 172 (17 per cent) cultures about which any alcohol data were available. This per cent is not an estimate of proportionate total unreliability, for it is derived only from cultures where two observers disagreed. When only one culture description is available, there can be no test of reliability (unless of an internal-consistency sort), and when there were three or more different reports on one culture, our procedure called for recording the majority description—rather than recording a "conflicting-information" entry, which we treated as a "no-information" entry and did not include in our analysis. As a test of agreement among raters on the same material, some of the HRAF material at Stanford and Yale was independently coded by two different persons. Using a measure of agreement between raters based on information-bearing codes alone (excluding the "no-data" entry), one obtains an interrater reliability

Table 3*

How Introduced
(N = 247)

	Alcohol	Tobacco	1-Hallucinogen	2-Hallucinogen	3-Hallucinogen
Indigenous	71	34	26	14	2
From others first	41	50	26	0	0
Both indigenous, others	16	7	2	1	0
No information	109	148	192	232	245
Conflicting information	10	8	1	0	0

	1-Stim.	2-Stim.	Cannabis	Opium	Coca-Cocaine
Indigenous	15	1	7	2	5
From others first	16	3	20	17	0
Both indigenous, others	1	0	1	2	0
No information	213	241	219	224	242
Conflicting information	2	2	0	2	0

* In this and later tables, there are three columns for hallucinogens and two for stimulants. This occurs because some societies use two or three different hallucinogens and up to two stimulants. Thus, all entries in the second hallucinogen column are for societies using a hallucinogen already recorded in the first column.

of .82. Including the "no-data" codes, interrater agreement rises to .96. In the cases when one of our raters reported differently for cultural observations on two occasions (occurring 8 per cent of the time in a test run of 712 coding operations), our procedure was to compare it with codes entered by a second rater and choose the most commonly selected code; thus, we have not excluded such cases by placing them in the "conflicting-information" category. As a second-step check, one showing 73 per cent agreement, two raters compared three sets of original code entries on those cultures where three different sources or ratings occurred (one set derived when one rater repeated ratings a second time). In another comparison, we examined our descriptive entries for forty-nine cultures against the data from Child *et al.* For 405 coding operations, there is full agreement between ours and the Child data on only 109 items (34 per cent) and complete disagreement on 91 items (22 per cent). For 84 items, Child *et al.* reported no entries where our sources gave data. For 67, Child has data where our sources provided no information (16 per cent). Additionally, for 91 items the Child report displays internal conflict.

The foregoing illustrates reliability problems arising from a series of tests of the data. Although disagreement between raters and inconsistency in repeat observations by the same rater are apparent, the largest source of error seems to come from disagreement in reports by observers of a society, as is shown in our "conflicting-information" entries, in Child *et al.* inconsistency reports from several sources, and in the disparity between our sources and the Child material (presumably arising from other than HRAF since interrater reliability using the File sources is high). Our confrontation with the reliability problem has not led us to solutions other than the procedural ones noted (majority judgments when possible, not using culture data when conflicts are not reconcilable by majority judgment). We must assume that the unreliability of sources and, secondarily, of ratings contributes to an unknown, but probably considerable, error in the cross-cultural method as we employ it here.

Our interest in learning whether cross-cultural inquiry would yield variables related to similar styles of drug use for *several* drugs, or variables related to particular drug use (in addition to those identified for alcohol), required measures of correlation—or association—between drug use styles and culture characteristics. We proceeded by selecting, on a priori grounds, 67 culture characteristics from among the

480 available culture "classifications" in Textor (1967). Our selection emphasized variables relating to environment, social complexity, child-rearing methods, and cultural themes. Each of these variables was tested against selected aspects (styles) of drug use for the 247 nonliterate societies. The statistic employed for these operations was the Yates correction of Chi Square (two-tailed). By testing with this "shotgun" computer approach (each variable against each drug-use style for all cultures), one would ordinarily expect 5 per cent of all tests to prove significant (when alpha = .05) by chance. The limiting factor here was that the majority of tests run were not completed because of insufficient data; out of more than 6,000 tests run, an estimated two thirds had multiple-cell entries in the 0 to 5 range; most others had but small numbers in each cell, so, as a result, the likelihood of achieving significant results was greatly diminished. We face, therefore, the loss of statistical power because of a paucity of original data, as well as an uncertain proportion of our significant findings being simply chance phenomena. For these reasons, beyond the demonstration of trends and general principles, our study is intended as a device for deriving hypotheses and generating theories, not as a test of theory or of particular relationships.

In the second portion of the study, the analysis of drug-abuse data and nation-state characteristics, our selection of twenty-one polity characteristics was also made on a priori grounds, the variables being selected from the fifty-seven polity characteristics in Banks and Textor (1963). Information on nation-state drug abuse was obtained from UN documents (1963) for 102 reporting nations. Drug-abuse ratings (a rating of 1 for one or more addicts per 1,000 population, 2 for one addict per 1,000 to 5,000 inhabitants, and 3 for less than one addict per 5,000 inhabitants) were treated in 2 × 3 contingency tables, and the statistic employed for tests of association (two-tailed) was the Wilcoxin two-sample test. It is important to note that the UN drug-abuse data exclude alcohol and are not derived from what would be considered adequate sources or research. Were alcohol included one would anticipate a quite diverse set of findings from those obtained.

In advance of presentation of tabular data, we again call attention to the paucity of observations on drug use in nonliterate societies. Lack of attention by ethnographers, travelers, and other observers to drug behavior is coupled with the already-noted unreliability among them where there has been observer interest. In consequence, there is *no* drug for which adequate descriptions exist for the majority of societies in our sample. Furthermore, the culture characteristics (Textor's classifications) are often absent, so that, for some of our cultures, few if any descriptors are available (the Aleut, for example)'. These lacks constitute a severe deficiency for investigators seeking to identify determinants or correlates of drug use on a cross-cultural basis. This unreliability of observation calls attention to inadequacies in ethnographic methods—a matter we (Blum and Blum, 1964)' discuss more fully elsewhere.

FINDINGS

Descriptions of styles of use.   We begin by presenting the data showing the distribution of aspects of drug use for the several drugs of interest among the cultures in our sample. The tables reflect simple counts based on descriptions by observers as transcribed by our raters into categories of style of use.

Drug introduction: initial source.   Drugs may be introduced into a culture from outsiders, as through commerce or war, or they may grow indigenously. Sometimes a native plant may be exploited only after its properties have been taught by outsiders and sometimes a society may be introduced to a substance from both indigenous and external sources. According to Table 3, there is no communality across drug classes. For most societies where there are data, alcohol, some hallucinogens, and coca-cocaine are indigenous, whereas tobacco, some hallucinogens, most stimulants, cannabis, and opium are not native but have been brought in by outsiders. It is unusual for a drug to be of mixed (indigenous and outside)' origin. Observations are insufficient in number and are in conflict.

Present source.   Table 4 presents data on the present sources of drugs in use, whether indigenous or outside. For all drugs, except some hallucinogens, the most frequent pattern is that the primary drug sources are indigenous. Given the greater frequency of outside origins for drugs at the time of introduction, the implication is that over time production of drugs becomes localized and reliance on outside sources is diminished. As with other descriptions, data are available only for a few of the societies observed.

Availability.   The most common case, as seen in Table 5, is for drugs to be plentiful. That holds for alcohol, many hallucinogens,

Table 4

PRESENT SOURCE
(N = 247)

	Alcohol	Tobacco	1-Hallucinogen	2-Hallucinogen	3-Hallucinogen
Indigenous	31	39	15	11	2
From others first	5	10	25	0	0
Both indigenous, others	10	5	3	0	0
No information	200	192	204	236	245
Conflicting information	1	1	0	0	0

	1-Stim.	2-Stim.	Cannabis	Opium	Coca-Cocaine
Indigenous	16	7	21	9	4
From others first	0	0	1	4	0
Both indigenous, others	0	0	3	4	0
No information	231	240	219	229	243
Conflicting information	0	0	3	1	0

Table 5

Availability
(N = 247)

	Alcohol	Tobacco	1-Hallucinogen	2-Hallucinogen	3-Hallucinogen
Plentiful	79	30	14	5	2
Some limit	29	27	15	2	0
Scarce	4	8	16	0	0
No information	118	174	199	239	245
Conflicting information	17	8	3	1	0

	1-Stim.	2-Stim.	Cannabis	Opium	Coca-Cocaine
Plentiful	26	4	18	14	3
Some limit	11	2	4	3	0
Scarce	5	2	0	1	0
No information	204	238	222	228	244
Conflicting information	1	1	3	1	0

143

stimulants, cannabis, opium, and coca-cocaine. Scarcity is an unusual circumstance, but occurs most frequently with respect to some hallucinogens. For the majority of societies and for all drugs except alcohol, observers have generally failed to note availability.

Extent of use. Table 6 summarizes observations on the extent of use of drugs among the cultures.

The tables indicate that high or excessive use characterizes behavior regarding alcohol, tobacco, some stimulants, opium, and coca-cocaine for the majority of all nonliterate societies where observations have been made. The most common pattern of use for all hallucinogens and some stimulants is more moderate.

It is apparent in Table 6 that for the majority of cultures the observer has failed to record whether or not the use of the drug of interest occurs. The exceptions are alcohol, where there is information in about two thirds of the cases, and tobacco, where information exists for about three fifths of the cases. The presence of conflicting reports by observers are also most often in regard to alcohol among all the drugs. From Table 6 two inferences may be drawn: one is that, with the exception of the hallucinogens, the most frequent pattern of mind-altering drug use in nonliterate societies is for high or excessive use rather than for moderate or low use and, secondly, that observers have generally been inattentive to drug use other than alcohol and tobacco. What accounts for observer inattentiveness is not known; it is possible that high or excessive use of a drug—the most common observation in Table 6—is what attracts attention. If that were the case, then the large number of societies for which data are missing would be assumed to be in the low- or moderate-use categories. There is, at present, no evidence either to support or to negate such an assumption.

Changes in extent of use. Available data provide little information on changes in patterns or amounts of drug use for most societies. We see from Table 7 that when changes are noted, the most frequent development is an increase in use.[1] Some stimulants are an exception. We conclude tentatively that increased drug use is the most commonly observed phenomenon.

Abuse assessed by within-culture elements. "Abuse" implies undesirable behavioral or physiological outcomes as a result of indi-

---

[1] The dates of the observations on societies in our sample range from 1520 (Inca, Maya) to the present. A total of fifteen reports are prior to 1850, so we cannot say that all changes in extent are recent ones.

Table 6

Extent of Use
(N = 247)

	Alcohol	Tobacco	1-Hallucinogen	2-Hallucinogen	3-Hallucinogen
Mere mention	29	37	21	4	2
High or excessive	65	70	1	1	1
Moderate	29	20	33	7	1
Low	9	5	4	4	0
Totals:	132	132	59	16	4
No extent, high individual use	0	0	2	0	0
No use	11	5	5	1	0
No information	75	109	178	229	243
Conflicting information	29	1	3	1	0

	1-Stim.	2-Stim.	Cannabis	Opium	Coca-Cocaine
Mere mention	9	2	11	3	4
High or excessive	26	1	5	7	4
Moderate	16	5	10	2	0
Low	2	0	0	4	0
Totals:	53	8	26	16	8
No extent, high individual use	0	0	3	2	0
No use	11	4	6	2	0
No information	182	235	210	222	239
Conflicting information	1	0	2	5	0

Table 7

Change in Extent of Use
(N = 247)

	Alcohol	Tobacco	1-Hallucinogen	2-Hallucinogen	3-Hallucinogen
Increase	12	39	9	0	0
Decrease	2	0	6	5	0
No information	232	207	232	242	247
Conflicting information	1	1	0	0	0

	1-Stim.	2-Stim.	Cannabis	Opium	Coca-Cocaine
Increase	3	0	6	3	0
Decrease	5	2	3	3	0
No information	239	245	238	241	247
Conflicting information	0	0	0	0	0

146

vidual drug use; the evaluative response of "undesirable" in turn rests upon religious, hygienic, normative, legal, or other value sources. When some persons within a culture view with alarm the drug-use habits or drug-response behavior of others (or themselves)', a problem of drug abuse may be said to occur. When this occurs, the presence of extreme individual differences or of group heterogeneity may also be implied. Table 8 presents findings as to the presence and degree of such drug abuse as reported by within-culture members (natives)'. When information on abuse judgments is present—and that is the unusual case—the estimation of "considerable" abuse applies to alcohol, hallucinogens, and opium. "Minor" abuse, reported on the basis of judgment by persons within the culture (natives)', occurs infrequently with reference to alcohol. In the case of the stimulants, and of opium in one case, people within the culture specifically deny any abuse. We draw two tentative conclusions: first, most observers have rarely attended to how persons within a society view use within that society and, second, when such observations are made, the more common within-culture response is concern—that is, disapproval is expressed. This, of course, may be a biasing factor in the sense that such concern may account for an observer's recording. No stimulants are said to be perceived as abused.

Abuse assessed by outsiders.   Table 9 presents the frequency data on judgments of drug abuse as rendered by the observer whose report constitutes the description of the culture. It is apparent that observers from the outside (nonnatives)' have been quicker to report their own reactions to drug use than to report the judgments of people within a society. Thus, we have observer assessments more often set forth than indigenous ones for all the drugs. Alcohol has drawn the most frequent judgments of abuse by observers and the most frequent conflicts among observers. Absence of abuse is noted in most cases of stimulant and hallucinogen use. For the majority of societies, the abuse of alcohol, cannabis, tobacco, and opium is described where problem use has been considered. Our conclusion from Tables 8 and 9 is that observers have been more sensitive to their own than to indigenous views of drug use within cultures. When there is alertness to abuse, both indigenous people and observers are likely to find it considerable for alcohol, opium, and occasional hallucinogens. Observers, but not indigenous people, find considerable abuse of tobacco and cannabis.

Table 8

ABUSE (AS DEFINED BY PERSONS WITHIN THE CULTURE)
(N = 247)

	Alcohol	Tobacco	1-Hallucinogen	2-Hallucinogen	3-Hallucinogen
No mention	67	12	24	4	0
None	0	0	0	0	0
Considerable	14	0	1	0	0
Minor	2	0	0	0	0
No information	164	235	222	243	247
Conflicting information	0	0	0	0	0

	1-Stim.	2-Stim.	Cannabis	Opium	Coca-Cocaine
No mention	10	3	12	11	0
None	2	3	0	1	0
Considerable	0	0	0	1	0
Minor	0	0	0	0	0
No information	235	240	235	234	245
Conflicting information	0	1	0	0	2

148

Table 9

ABUSE (BY OBSERVER)
(N = 247)

	Alcohol	Tobacco	1-Hallucinogen	2-Hallucinogen	3-Hallucinogen
No mention	1	1	0	0	0
None	5	3	23	1	0
Considerable	45	3	1	0	0
Minor	32	6	1	2	0
No information	153	234	221	243	247
Conflicting information	11	0	1	1	0

	1-Stim.	2-Stim.	Cannabis	Opium	Coca-Cocaine
No mention	0	0	0	0	0
None	10	6	1	3	0
Considerable	0	0	5	10	0
Minor	2	0	6	1	0
No information	234	240	234	233	245
Conflicting information	1	1	1	0	2

149

The use of stimulants is but rarely characterized as abusive by either outsiders or insiders.

It is of interest to examine the frequency of drug abuse, as cited by observers, as a proportion of drug use per se. Taking the drug-using cultures of Table 3 (excluding "no use," "no information," and "conflicting information") and the abuse data in Table 9 (combining "minor" and "considerable," excluding "conflicting information"), one obtains the following distribution of drug-using cultures reported to have abuse (in percentages):

Alcohol	Tobacco	1-Hallu-cinogen	2-Hallu-cinogen	3-Hallucinogen
61%	5%	3%	12%	0%

Stimulant-1	Stimulant-2	Cannabis	Opium	Coca-Cocaine
4%	0%	42%	61%	0%

It is apparent that alcohol and opium are equally ranked as drugs abused in the majority of nonliterate cultures in which they are employed. Cannabis ranks third, with problems of abuse noted in about two fifths of the using cultures. For the other drugs, abuse is rare or subject to conflicting opinion.

Social vs. individual use. Observer reports were reviewed to determine when drug use took place primarily as a group activity (integrated use), as an individual (private) one, or as both. Table 10 presents the meager data; there is almost no clear explication of the social circumstances of use defined in these terms. For the few cultures described, one sees a predominance of individual use as opposed to group use.

Conditions of use: setting and motivation. Another way to approach the style of use is to examine institutional settings, ritualistic content, or—translated into an inference about individual expectations—motives for use. These may also be inferred functions for drug use. Observer data were categorized in terms of these setting-motive conditions as follows: social (including interpersonal, other-oriented, used in eating, and festivals), mind-modifying (including private, self-oriented, and introspective), escape (including private, anxiety-reducing, and personal-problem dampening), religious-magical (traditional, ritualistic, and institutionalized, including folk medical). Table 11 shows the distribution of these styles of use and the combinations that were reported. Conditions of setting-inferred intent are fairly often described

Table 10
WHEN USED
(N = 247)

	Alcohol	Tobacco	1-Hallucinogen	2-Hallucinogen	3-Hallucinogen
Group only	0	0	7	1	0
Group, personal	1	0	5	2	0
Personal only	1	0	6	4	1
No information	245	247	229	240	246
Conflicting information	0	0	0	0	0

	1-Stim.	2-Stim.	Cannabis	Opium	Coca-Cocaine
Group only	0	0	0	0	0
Group, personal	0	0	3	1	1
Personal only	0	0	5	5	0
No information	246	247	239	241	246
Conflicting information	1	0	0	0	0

151

Table 11
SETTING-MOTIVATION

	Alcohol	Tobacco	1st Hall.	2nd Hall.	3rd Hall.	1st Stim.	2nd Stim.	Cannabis	Opium	Coca	Total N
Social only	55	58	2	0	1	34	3	12	8	3 =	176
Soc./mind-mod./escape	9	3	2	1	0	0	0	0	0	0 =	15
Social/relig.-mag.	15	11	5	4	0	7	4	1	1	3 =	51
Mind-mod. only	6	2	3	0	0	0	0	0	0	0 =	11
Social/mind-mod.	8	10	1	0	0	0	0	3	1	0 =	23
Mind-mod./Relig.-mag.	0	0	12	1	0	0	0	0	0	0 =	13
Escape only	0	0	0	0	0	0	0	0	0	0 =	0
Relig.-mag. only	1	0	0	0	0	0	0	0	3	1 =	5
Escape/social	2	0	0	0	0	0	0	0	1	0 =	3
Escape/mind-mod.	4	3	2	2	0	0	0	0	0	0 =	11
Soc./mind-mod./escape/ Relig.-mag.	4	0	3	0	0	0	0	1	0	0 =	8
Soc./mind-mod./relig.-mag.	10	14	23	4	1	0	0	2	0	0 =	54
Totals	114	101	53	12	2	41	7	19	14	7 =	370

for alcohol, tobacco, and some hallucinogens, with a wide variety of conditions of use.

The data in Table 11 may be summarized in five statements as follows: (1) The most frequent setting-intent for psychoactive drug use is the social one. Ninety per cent of all descriptions for all classes of drugs include a social-use component. By "social" we imply the enhancement or enrichment of interpersonal activities. (2) Slightly more than half (193/370) of all descriptions of setting-intent indicate that only a social component is present—that is, there are no implications of religious-magical rituals (including folk medical), of introspective private use, or of the escape use which implies psychological distress and its alleviation by drugs. (3) Multiple functions for drugs are very common—that is, psychoactive substances are frequently used under several different circumstances of setting and inferred intent. The implication is one of multiple social utility or psychological function for each class of drugs. (4) Drugs vary by class in the extent to which multiple functions are demonstrated. The stimulants show least variety and multiplicity of use, being limited to social and religious-magical functions. (5) Drugs vary by class in the predominance, cross-culturally, of one function (setting-intent) vs. another. Hallucinogens, for example, are rarely simply social and most often, proportionately, involve mind-modifying and religious components. Opium, in turn, is proportionately most often employed for psychological-escape functions.

Support for and restraint on drug use. We have sought to describe general attitudes toward drug use by rating support for and restrictions against drug use. One cannot be sure that an actual continuum exists from support to opposition, since within a culture these two views can exist side by side, whether in opposing subgroups or within persons whose judgment depends upon the circumstances of use. Rather than assume a continuum, we initially handled support and restraint as independent subscales—that is, positive value was rated independent of sanction, and kinds of restraints independent of both. Only after these independent ratings were complete was it apparent that such discrete analysis was unnecessary, sometimes because of lack of data, or perhaps because of a genuine continuum existing in nature, or because observers treated disapproval-approval as a continuum creating a spectrum in their observations. Table 12 presents the information on attitudinal supports and sanctions.

Table 12

Attitudes Toward Drug Use

	Alcohol	Tobacco	1-Halluc.	2-Halluc.	3-Halluc.
Positive value placed on the drug, support or approval (not exclusive of possible restraint on use)	42	20	22	1	0
Drug use sanctioned, no restrictions on use reported	68	70	3	2	0
Drug use sanctioned, but some restrictions on use exist that are other than religious	6	6	25	6	1
Use sanctioned, but religion constrains use	9	2	2	0	0
Use sanctioned, but religious *and* other restrictions limit use	15	8	27	6	1
Not sanctioned, disapproved:					
Restraints are legal (formal or codified, authority-enforced)	3	0	0	0	0
Restraints are social and/or religious	9	0	4	0	0
Restraints are legal and social and religious	2	1	1	0	0
Legal prohibitions imposed from the outside	16	0	9	1	0
No information on positive values (may be information on sanctions)	137	160	206	239	246
Conflicting information on values	1	0	0	0	0
No information on sanctions (may be information on support)	151	164	206	239	246
Conflicting information on sanctions	2	4	6	0	0

154

Table 12 (*continued*)

	1-Stim.	2-Stim.	Cannabis	Opium	Coca-Cocaine
Positive value placed on the drug, support or approval (not exclusive of possible restraint on use)	7	4	8	0	0
Drug use sanctioned, no restrictions on use reported	23	0	13	6	3
Drug use sanctioned, but some restrictions on use exist that are other than religious	4	4	3	1	0
Use sanctioned, but religion constrains use	1	0	0	0	0
Use sanctioned, but religious *and* other restrictions limit use	5	4	3	1	0
Not sanctioned, disapproved:					
Restraints are legal (formal or codified, authority-enforced)	0	0	0	4	0
Restraints are social and/or religious	3	0	1	1	0
Restraints are legal and social and religious	0	0	0	0	0
Legal prohibitions imposed from the outside	2	0	8	5	4
No information on positive values (may be information on sanctions)	215	243	231	236	243
Conflicting information on values	0	0	0	1	0
No information on sanctions (may be information on support)	216	243	230	234	244
Conflicting information on sanction	0	0	0	1	0

155

Inspection of the table suggests that positive values for drug
use with or without restrictions on use (lack of restrictions, of course,
may reflect indifference rather than approval) are the predominant
patterns for all of the drugs. Approval of use combined with restrictions occurs most often in the case of the hallucinogens. Outright (internal) opposition to use occurs proportionately more often in the case
of opium. Legal controls imposed on tribal societies by ruling nation-
states are found proportionately more often for coca-cocaine, opium,
and cannabis, in that order.

If one considers the information on positive values alone—
that is, on cultures approving rather than being indifferent to, or restrictive of, or opposed to use—one finds that the proportion of societies with positive values is greatest for tobacco and cannabis and
least for opium and some hallucinogens.

Sex differences among users. Table 13 presents data on sex
differences among drug users. There is no category for "females predominate" since no observation recorded that state of affairs for any
drug culture. As usual, there are the most information and the most
conflict among observers in regard to alcohol. One sees that in the majority of cultures it is males who predominate in the use of alcohol,
hallucinogens, cannabis, and coca-cocaine. Equality of the sexes in
drug use occurs most often among cultures for opium, stimulants, and
tobacco.

Status differences. Table 14 shows the distribution of drug-
use behavior differences as a function of status ranking (such as class
and caste). Few observers have recorded this. When reports are available, lower-status use is most prevalent for alcohol, cannabis, and
opium, while use by special-status groups (shamans, for example) is
most prevalent, proportionately, in the case of hallucinogens. Both
high- and low-status use is attributed to some stimulants. The small
number of entries leads us to stress the danger of attaching importance
to the proportions shown here.

Age differences. Given the limited observations, our categories are crude, contrasting cultures where children and adults may
use a drug to those where children (prepuberty) are not allowed to
use the drug. Table 15 shows that all-age use occurs more often for
alcohol, tobacco, stimulants, and opium (including, of course, folk
medical use), whereas children are prohibited, in most of the cultures
for which data are available, the use of hallucinogens and cannabis.

Table 13
SEX DIFFERENCES
(N = 247)

	Alcohol	Tobacco	1-Hallucinogen	2-Hallucinogen	3-Hallucinogen
No sex difference	35	30	8	0	0
Males predominate	48	30	19	7	1
No information	155	186	218	239	246
Conflicting information	9	1	2	1	0

	1-Stim.	2-Stim.	Cannabis	Opium	Coca-Cocaine
No sex difference	15	1	0	6	1
Males predominate	10	4	13	2	2
No information	222	242	233	239	244
Conflicting information	0	0	1	0	0

Table 14
Status Differences
(N = 247)

	Alcohol	Tobacco	1-Hallucinogen	2-Hallucinogen	3-Hallucinogen
Lower status only	3	1	0	0	0
Upper status only	2	1	0	0	0
Special-status groups	0	2	6	2	0
All classes use	1	3	0	0	0
No information	241	240	241	245	247
Conflicting information	0	0	0	0	0

	1-Stim.	2-Stim.	Cannabis	Opium	Coca-Cocaine
Lower status only	4	1	4	2	0
Upper status only	3	3	0	1	0
Special-status groups	1	0	1	0	0
All classes use	5	1	1	0	0
No information	234	242	241	244	247
Conflicting information	0	0	0	0	0

Table 15
AGE DIFFERENCES
(N = 247)

	Alcohol	Tobacco	1-Hallucinogen	2-Hallucinogen	3-Hallucinogen
All ages	31	18	5	1	0
No children, (adults only)	8	8	22	5	0
No information	205	221	219	240	247
Conflicting information	3	0	1	1	0

	1-Stim.	2-Stim.	Cannabis	Opium	Coca-Cocaine
All ages	14	1	2	4	1
No children, (adults only)	7	4	7	0	1
No information	226	242	238	242	244
Conflicting information	0	0	0	1	1

159

Resistance to use. Of special interest are those cases in which a nonliterate society is described as "resisting" use of one drug while, perhaps, at the same time heavily using or even abusing another. "Resistance" implies either the availability of the drug as an indigenous material or its availability to other groups geographically near by or with whom trading relations exist for other commodities. (On the other hand, from some of the reports one infers that what has been termed "reluctance to use" may simply be a matter of scarce supply.) Cultures with evidence of high availability and little or no use are the Navajo, Papago, and Tarahumara for datura, the Pawnee for alcohol, and the Amhara for tobacco. Cultures cited for inconsistent patterns—high use of one drug and resistance to another—are the Rundi with high use of alcohol and tobacco but resistance to cannabis; the Rwala, who use alcohol but resist tobacco; the Gond, using alcohol heavily but resisting opium and cannabis (see Carstairs [1954] for a related study); the Khasi, using alcohol heavily but resisting opium; the Yurok, Murdurucu, and Caingaing, using tobacco heavily but very little alcohol; the Tewa, using tobacco heavily but avoiding alcohol and hallucinogens; and the Tarahumara and Papago, using alcohol and tobacco heavily but resisting datura.

Drug use and other culture characteristics. In this section we list the significant (alpha = .05) and borderline (alpha = .10) associations between drug-use styles and culture characteristics that emerge from our analysis. The ordering of the data is by groups of related characteristics (such as child rearing, and environment) and within groups from characteristics most often associated with drug behavior to those least often associated with it.

1. Child Rearing and Childhood Experience

When pressure toward developing obedient behavior in the child is high, then:

ALCOHOL: Use rather than no use occurs, P < .05.

TOBACCO: Moderate rather than high or excessive use occurs, P < .10.

TOBACCO: Moderate or no use occurs rather than high or excessive use, P < .05.

HALLUCINOGEN: Use by adults rather than by all ages, P < .05.

STIMULANT: Moderate rather than high or excessive use occurs, $P < .10$.

STIMULANT: Male use predominates rather than use by both sexes, $P < .10$.

STIMULANT: Use by adults only rather than use by all ages, $P < .10$.

When early oral satisfaction is high, then:

ALCOHOL: Use is by both sexes rather than predominantly by males, $P < .05$.

TOBACCO: High or excessive use rather than moderate or no use occurs, $P < .10$.

STIMULANT: High or excessive use rather than moderate or no use occurs, $P < .10$.

STIMULANT: High or excessive use rather than moderate occurs, $P < .05$.

When positive pressure toward developing responsible behavior in the child is high, then:

ALCOHOL: Drug is plentiful rather than limited or scarce, $P < .05$.

TOBACCO: Moderate or no use rather than high or excessive use occurs, $P < .10$.

TOBACCO: Moderate use rather than high or excessive use occurs, $P < .05$.

TOBACCO: Drug is limited or scarce rather than plentiful, $P < .10$.

When pressure toward developing self-reliant behavior in the child is high, then:

ALCOHOL: Male use is predominant rather than by both sexes, $P < .10$.

STIMULANT: Use is by both sexes rather than by males predominantly, $P < .10$.

STIMULANT: Use is by all ages rather than by adults only, $P < .10$.

When indulgence of the child is high, then:

ALCOHOL: Drug is limited or scarce rather than plentiful, P < .05.

ALCOHOL: Use is by adults only rather than by all ages, P < .10.

When child's inferred anxiety over nonperformance of responsible behavior is high, then:

TOBACCO: Moderate use rather than high or excessive use occurs, P < .05.

TOBACCO: Moderate or no use rather than high or excessive use occurs, P < .10.

When pain inflicted on the infant by the nurturant agent is high, then:

TOBACCO: Use is by both sexes rather than predominant male use, P < .10.

2. Family and Kinship, including:

When the community is kin-homogeneous, then:

TOBACCO: Moderate rather than high or excessive use occurs, P < .05.

TOBACCO: Moderate or no use occurs rather than high or excessive use, P < .05.

TOBACCO: Drug is limited or scarce rather than plentiful, P < .05.

STIMULANT: Drug is limited or scarce rather than plentiful, P < .05.

STIMULANT: Drug use is by adults only rather than by all ages, P < .10.

OPIUM: No use rather than use occurs, P < .10.

OPIUM: Culture disapproves rather than approves of use, P < .05.

When the community is commonly exogamous rather than nonexogamous, then:

ALCOHOL: Moderate or no use occurs rather than high or excessive use, P < .05.

ALCOHOL: No use rather than use occurs, P < .10.

ALCOHOL: Moderate use rather than high or excessive use occurs, P < .10.

STIMULANT: Drug is limited or scarce rather than plentiful, P < .10.

STIMULANT: Male use is predominant rather than by both sexes, P < .10.

When kin group is exclusively patrilineal, then:

ALCOHOL: Use is by all ages rather than by adults only, P < .10.

STIMULANT: Drug is limited or scarce rather than plentiful, P < .05.

OPIUM: High or excessive use rather than moderate use occurs, P < .10.

When the community is a clan community, community-structured, segmented on a clan basis, then:

ALCOHOL: Moderate or no use occurs rather than high or excessive use, P < .10.

TOBACCO: Use is by both sexes rather than by males predominantly, P < .10.

When family is of an extended type rather than an independent type, then:

ALCOHOL: Use rather than no use occurs, P < .05.

OPIUM: Moderate or no use rather than high or excessive use occurs, P < .10.

When cousin terminology is of the Eskimo or Hawaiian type, then:

ALCOHOL: No use rather than use occurs, P < .10.

When kin group is patrilineal or double descent rather than matrilineal, then:

STIMULANT: Drug is limited or scarce rather than plentiful, P < .05.

When wives are obtained by relatively difficult means, then:

STIMULANT: Drug is limited or scarce rather than plentiful,
             $P < .05$.

*When commonly polygamous co-wives dwell together rather than sep-
arately, then:*

CANNABIS: Culture disapproves rather than approves use, $P <$
             $.05$.

3. Environment and Food-Production Settlement Pattern

When cereals are produced other than root foods, then:

ALCOHOL: Use rather than no use ocurs, $P < .05$.

ALCOHOL: High or excessive use rather than moderate or no
              use occurs, $P < .05$.

HALLUCINOGEN: Drug is limited or scarce rather than plentiful,
              $P < .05$.

STIMULANT: Use rather than no use occurs, $P < .10$.

STIMULANT: Excessive or high use occurs rather than moderate
              or no use, $P < .05$.

*When the natural environment is very harsh—desert, desert grasses,
tundra, steppe—then:*

ALCOHOL: Drug is limited or scarce rather than plentiful,
              $P < .05$.

TOBACCO: No use rather than use occurs, $P < .05$.

HALLUCINOGEN: Personal rather than group use occurs, $P < .05$.

STIMULANT: Moderate use rather than high or excessive use
              occurs, $P < .10$.

*When food production is by intensive rather than simple agriculture,
then:*

TOBACCO: Moderate or no use occurs rather than high or ex-
              cessive use, $P < .10$.

STIMULANT: High or excessive use rather than moderate or no
              use occurs, $P < .05$.

When food supply is secure and food shortages are rare or occasional, then:

> TOBACCO: High or excessive use rather than moderate use occurs, P < .05.

> TOBACCO: High or excessive use rather than moderate or no use occurs, P < .05.

When natural environment is very harsh—subtropical bush, temperate grassland—then:

> TOBACCO: No use rather than use occurs, P < .10.

> HALLUCINOGEN: Personal use rather than group use occurs, P < .10.

When settlements are fixed, then:

> STIMULANT: Drug is plentiful rather than limited or scarce, P < .10.

> STIMULANT: Extent of drug use does not increase, P < .10.

4. Social, Political, and Economic Organization

When class stratification based on wealth and/or occupational status is present, or based on occupation alone (two Textor descriptions combined), then:

> HALLUCINOGEN: Extent of drug use is not increased, P < .05 (occupation only).

> STIMULANT: High or excessive use rather than moderate use occurs, P < .05 (wealth *or* occupation), P < .10 (occupation only).

> STIMULANT: High or excessive use occurs rather than moderate or no use, P < .05 (wealth *or* occupation), P < .10 (occupation only).

> STIMULANT: Culture disapproves rather than approves use, P < .10 (wealth and/or occupation).

When political integration is the large state, the little state, or the minimal state, then:

> ALCOHOL: Use is by adults only rather than by all ages, P < .10.

> TOBACCO: Moderate or no use occurs rather than high or excessive use, P < .10.

TOBACCO: Use is by adults only rather than by all ages, P < .10.

When there is presence of hierarchy of jurisdiction, then:

ALCOHOL: Moderate use occurs rather than high or excessive use, P < .10.

HALLUCINOGEN: Group use occurs rather than personal use, P < .10.

CANNABIS: Moderate or no use occurs rather than high or excessive use, P < .10.

When the society works in metal, then:

ALCOHOL: Use rather than no use occurs, P < .05.

STIMULANT: Use rather than no use occurs, P < .10.

When headmen are hereditary, then:

ALCOHOL: Moderate use rather than high or excessive use occurs, P < .10.

CANNABIS: High or excessive use rather than moderate use occurs, P < .10.

When individual rights in real property and rules for inheritance are present, then:

TOBACCO: Use rather than no use occurs, P < .10.

TOBACCO: Culture disapproves rather than approves use, P < .10.

When class stratification is present, then:

HALLUCINOGEN: Drug use does not increase in extent, P < .05.

5. Interpersonal Themes; World View

When games are limited to games of skill only, then:

ALCOHOL: No use rather than use occurs, P < .05.

STIMULANT: Drug is plentiful rather than limited or scarce, P < .10.

STIMULANT: Drug use is by both sexes rather than male use predominantly, P < .10.

STIMULANT: Use is by all ages rather than by adults only, P < .10.

When dreams are used to control supernatural powers, then:

ALCOHOL: High or excessive use occurs rather than moderate use, P < .10.

TOBACCO: Drug is limited or scarce rather than plentiful, P < .05.

STIMULANT: High or excessive use rather than moderate use occurs, P < .10.

STIMULANT: High or excessive use rather than moderate or no use occurs, P < .10.

When games, if present, include games of strategy, then:

ALCOHOL: Use rather than no use occurs, P < .10.

ALCOHOL: Drug is plentiful rather than limited or scarce, P < .05.

STIMULANT: Drug is limited or scarce rather than plentiful, P < .05.

When military glory is strongly emphasized (or moderately), then:

ALCOHOL: Male use is predominant rather than use by both sexes, P < .05.

CANNABIS: Culture approves rather than disapproves use, P < .10.

When bellicosity is extreme, then:

ALCOHOL: Male use predominates rather than use by both sexes, P < .10.

HALLUCINOGEN: Culture approves rather than disapproves of use, P < .10.

When games, if present, include games of chance, then:

ALCOHOL: Use rather than no use occurs, P < .10.

ALCOHOL: Culture approves rather than disapproves use, P < .10.

When composite narcissism is high, then:

ALCOHOL: Male use predominates rather than use by both
sexes, $P < .05$.

ALCOHOL: Use rather than no use occurs, $P < .10$.

Forty out of the sixty-seven culture characteristics are shown to
have significant or borderline relationships to styles of use of one or
several mind-altering drugs. One sees that in all cases where three or
more associations occur between a culture characteristic and drug-use
styles, these apply to two or more different drugs. One also sees that
each type of drug is associated with cross-cultural characteristics, except for coca-cocaine. We tentatively conclude that culture characteristics will be found as correlates of the use of any class of mind-altering
drugs.

In terms of the number of significant or borderline associations
between drug-use styles and culture characteristics, these correspond,
with important exceptions, to the number of observations on the use
of the drug—that is, to the adequacy of the cross-cultural data. Alcohol, on which the largest number of observations are available, yields
thirty-two such associations. At the opposite extreme, coca-cocaine yields
none; observations on its use were available for only eight societies—
obviously an unfruitful N for contingency tests. The other drugs infrequently reported on (or infrequently employed, in fact) by observers
are opium and cannabis; for each of these only four associations are
significant—setting the alpha level at .10 for convenience of the present
discussion. A reversal of order occurs in the middle cases; twenty-four
associations significant beyond .10 occur, yet for the stimulants—observations of which exist for seventy-eight fewer cultures than tobacco
—thirty-two associations (alpha = .10) are noted. The hallucinogens,
on the other hand, observed in slightly more societies than stimulants,
yield only eight relationships significant when alpha is set at .10. Some
of these departures from a regular relationship between drug-data inadequacy and findings probably result from variations which occur in
available data on the culture characteristics themselves (see Textor,
1967). Some probably reflect real differences in the features of cultures
associated with the use of one drug versus another. One obvious conclusion is that the more adequate the descriptive data, the more likelihood there is of uncovering relationships between drug use and culture
characteristics. The possibility of a linear relationship is not excluded;

if that were the case, then one would expect careful observation to reveal a very considerable array of cross-cultural characteristics which would be predictive of drug-use styles. The alternative would hold also: knowledge of drug behavior would allow prediction of certain other culture characteristics.

We call attention to consistencies in the foregoing relationships which are based on the categorization of the discrete culture characterizations into sets of related variables.

1. *Child rearing* is related to the levels of use of several drugs and to their differential use within a culture (by age, sex, status). For example, trends toward moderation in use of alcohol, tobacco, and stimulants, as well as the unrestricted use of hallucinogens, stimulants, and tobacco, occur where there are childhood pressures toward obedience, where pressures toward responsible child behavior exist, and where anxiety over that responsibility exists.[2] Childhood self-reliance, child indulgence, narcissism, and pain infliction on the child all show relationships to what groups may use drugs.

2. *Kin and family relationships* appear related to levels of use of several drugs; kin-homogeneous communities show moderate tobacco use, little or disapproved opium use, and have a limited supply

[2] This study does not attempt to replicate that of Child et al. (1965). Comment is required on what may appear to be discrepancies between their findings and ours. Their study, focused on alcohol, pays special regard to the correlates of drunkenness and a factor analysis of drinking behavior; it used supplemental reading and direct inquiries to ethnographers to establish ratings; rating scales were 7 point continua, relationships were reported as correlations, and complex hypotheses linking several aspects of drinking behavior were explored. They used a sample of 139 societies, most of which were preliterate, 110 of which were known on the basis of the authors' earlier work, 57 of which were from Horton's sample.

In contrast, our study includes, but does not focus on, alcohol, did not seek to arrive at final judgments when two sources were contradictory, used fewer point-rating scales, and tested for association rather than using coefficients of correlation (although Child et al. do report significance of their correlations). We did not rate drunkenness per se or the same behavior factors used by them (for example, we combined "high" and "excessive" use and treated "abuse" as a general variable), and we did not test all of the culture characteristics tested by Child et al., nor did we test all of their drinking-behavior variables. Further and crucially, our sample contained 247 societies, 172 of which had alcohol use or nonuse specified. Even though our sample included the Child cultures, when their data on an item contradicted another source, we excluded that item from the analysis as unreliable.

We suggest that apparently discrepant findings as they exist are a function of conception method and sample.

of stimulants; exogamous communities are associated with from no-to-moderate alcohol use, scarcity of stimulants, and so on.

3. *Environment and food production* are related to levels of use of several drugs. Environmental harshness implies limited alcohol supply, absence of tobacco use, lower stimulant use, and personal rather than group hallucinogen use. Cereal rather than root production implies high alcohol and stimulant use, but low availability of hallucinogens; a secure food supply implies high tobacco use; intensive rather than simple agriculture implies greater use of tobacco and stimulants; a food-production society per se implies plentiful alcohol and, generally, when food supplies are plentiful, drug abuse is more common. Such an association, although intriguing, also demonstrates the need for caution in interpreting and generalizing. At the nation-state level, it appears that the poor rather than the wealthy are more in danger of drug abuse (such as alcoholism and opiate dependency), although use without abuse characterizes wealthier groups. Perhaps at the pre-industrial level, plant-production efforts are not devoted to nonnutritive substances until some level of abundance is achieved.

4. *The structure of social and economic organization* is also a drug-related feature. For example, political integration at the state level finds alcohol and tobacco use limited to adults; a hierarchy of jurisdiction implies moderate alcohol use, group rather than personal hallucinogen use, and low rather than high cannabis use. Also, wealth-and/or occupation-based class stratification implies high stimulant use and simultaneous disapproval of such use, no increase in hallucinogen use, and drug abuse as defined by outside observers. Hereditary chieftainships occur with moderate rather than high alcohol use but, conversely, with high rather than moderate cannabis use. Economic styles, other than agricultural, are also drug-behavior correlates. For example, the use of alcohol and stimulants is associated with metal-working societies; individual property rights are associated with tobacco use and disapproval of that use.

5. *Interpersonal themes* (to construct a loose category of valued behavior) appear related to the differential use of one drug versus another. For example, games of skill (but no other games) imply use of stimulants but nonuse of alcohol; military glory occurs in connection with cannabis approval; and bellicosity with hallucinogen approval. Magical-religious orientation is related to the level of use of several

drugs, for when dreams control supernatural powers, alcohol and stimulant use is high rather than moderate.

On the basis of these findings, we tentatively conclude that general relationships are likely to hold in nonliterate societies for styles of use of several drugs and for differential use of those drugs and specified culture variables. It appears that child-rearing practices are strongly implicated, as are kinship patterns and family practices, the nature of the natural environment and of agricultural practices, certain cultural themes or interests, magical-religious techniques, social structure, and economic styles.

The styles of drug use which are most often associated with culture characteristics are those of levels (amount) of use and the characteristics of persons using the drug (age, sex, status). We find no associations for most of the styles of use for which both original descriptive data and relationships were sought—for example, motivations, sanctions, attitudes, circumstances of use, sources, changes, and manner of introduction. Some relationships are demonstrated in connection with drug availability and abuse. We attribute this to the paucity of original observations, to the small frequency of observations in any one category in the more highly refined category schemes (for example, setting-motivation—see Table 11), and possibly to real differences, as well as to the likelihood that manner of introduction and present source of drug are less integral to cultural styles than is drug using per se.

We are limited to the conclusion that the extent of use of nearly all classes of mind-altering drugs, approval and disapproval of the use of at least some of these drugs, availability and selection of certain drugs over others, and the kinds of persons within a society who use particular drugs are all behaviors integrated with other features of (nonliterate) culture characteristics which are identifiable and appear in common on a cross-cultural basis. There is also some evidence suggesting that changes in extent of use (of hallucinogens) and that conditions of use—specifically as a group contrasted to individual phenomena—are related to particular characteristics of societies. These statements will come as no surprise to those familiar with alcohol studies, for such general relationships were demonstrated in earlier cross-cultural alcohol research.

Relationships among styles of drug use.   In this section are reported the significant (alpha = .05)´ and borderline (alpha = .10)´ associations (all two-tailed tests)´ among styles of drug use. An earlier model for interrelated styles is found in the 1965 study by Child *et al.* (for example, their study of the sex of drinkers in relationship to the presence of aboriginal drinking and to the presence or absence of integrated drinking within cultures)´.

ALCOHOL: The extent of use is high rather than low or moderate when observers indicate abuse is high rather than minimum, P < .05.
The drug is indigenous in origin when social reasons for its use are present, P < .05.

TOBACCO: Extent of use is low or moderate rather than high when magical-religious reasons for its use are present, P < .05.
The drug is indigenous in origin when religious-magical reasons for its use are present, P < .05.

STIMULANTS: The extent of use is high rather than low or moderate when the drug is plentiful rather than less plentiful, P < .05.
The extent of use is low or moderate rather than high when religious-magical reasons for its use are present, P < .05.[3]

CANNABIS: The extent of use is high, moderate, or low rather than no use when it is plentiful rather than less plentiful, P < .05.
The drug is indigenous in origin when religious-magical reasons for its use are present, P < .10.

The foregoing statements suggest that there are some interrelationships among styles of drug use for several classes of mind-altering drugs. The relationships between extent of use and availability are hardly remarkable; those between extent of use and religious-magical conditions of use—one of the conditions of "integrated" use—are of theoretical interest. What is most noteworthy is the paucity of significant interrelationships.

[3] Here again we note how contingent our associations are upon what observers have reported—observations very likely influenced by ethnographic fashions. What, for example, if our information on those drugs we find to be associated with religion-magic exists only because observers were interested in religion and magic, and so noted drug use in that context? It would mean that drug sampling was biased, so that any correlations would reflect sampling error rather than natural relationships; possibly, then, extensive use of these same substances outside of religious-magical contexts had been ignored.

Drug abuse in nonliterate cultures. In describing the extent of drug use, we have combined observer ratings of "high" or "excessive" use into one category (Table 1), which limits itself to the amount of the drug consumed. Judged abuse of drugs may or may not be related to amounts consumed, as Child *et al.* have shown, and we have used a separate rating scheme to report abuse, Table 8 showing the infrequency with which members of a culture describe (or are asked about!) it and Table 9 for abuse (or concern) described by the outside observer. We have seen that the extent of use of particular drugs —and to a lesser degree approval-disapproval (Table 12)—are associated with other features of societies. In this section we examine drug abuse per se, not limited in our analysis to a particular drug. Table 16, below, is a frequency count of the number of cultures in our sample abusing one or more drugs considerably, that abuse resting on an outside observer's judgment.

Table 16
FREQUENCY COUNT OF ABUSE

Number of different drugs considerably abused	0	1	2	3 or more
Number of cultures abusing	185	60	2	0

Reports of single- rather than multiple-drug abuse are the most common. Nonobservation on abuse predominates. Three quarters of the considerable abuse is for alcohol, again suggesting the inadequacy of data on other drugs. One asks whether any insights are gained by comparing cultures considerably abusing any drug—judged by outsiders—with those described as not abusing any (a contaminated procedure since abuse not noted does not assure its absence) or abusing them to a minor extent only. Below are listed those associations significant at the .05 and the borderline .10 levels.

Drug abuse occurs when the natural environment is very harsh, $P < .05$.
Drug abuse occurs when the food supply is plentiful, $P < .05$.
Drug abuse occurs when class stratification based on wealth and/or occupational status alone are present (a combined variable), $P < .10$.
Drug abuse occurs when military glory is strongly or moderately emphasized, $P < .05$.
Drug abuse occurs when bellicosity is extreme, $P < .05$.

There is only one association between drug abuse as described by persons within a culture and another culture characteristic; one finds, in remarkable contradiction to what outside observers report (see above)', that

Own-culture-perceived drug abuse does not occur when the food supply is secure and food shortages are rare or occasional, P < .10.

Drug abuse and the characteristics of nation-states. Earlier, we examined relationships between the variety of drug-use styles and the characteristics of nonliterate cultures. We now extend that analysis to nation-states, limiting the style of use to one feature—namely, drug abuse (excluding alcohol) as reported by governmental agencies in that nation. It will clearly be seen that the socioeconomic characteristics of the nation-states are not independent. The statistics applied to the ordered two-by-three contingency tables were the Wilcoxin two-sample test. All tests were two-tailed. *Relationships are as follows:*

Drug abuse is associated with population-growth rates of over 2 per cent per year, $z = 2.05$, P < .05.
Drug abuse is associated with an agricultural population of 34 per cent or more, $z = 2.99$, P < .05.
Drug abuse is associated with gross national product of less than $300 per person per year, $z = -3.63$, P < .05.
Drug abuse is associated with a gross national product of less than $600 per person per year, $z = -3.59$, P < .05.
Drug abuse is associated with low economic-development status (little prospect of attaining a self-sustained economic growth by the mid-1970's), $z = -3.17$, P < .05.
Drug abuse is associated with low rates of literacy (50 per cent or less), $z = -2.54$, P < .05.
Drug abuse is associated with low newspaper circulation (less than 100 per 1,000 population), $z = -3.72$, P < .05.
Drug abuse is associated with other than Christian religious affiliation by the majority of the population, $z = -4.33$, P < .05.
Drug abuse is associated with the absence of linguistic homogeneity among the population, $z = -3.44$, P < .05.
Drug abuse is associated with absent or only partial Westernization, $z = -3.12$, P < .05.
Drug abuse is associated with government instability, $z = -2.34$, P < .05.
Drug abuse is associated with limited or absent interest articulation

by institutional groups '(such as clergy, legislative blocs, and professional groups), z = 2.58, P <.05.
Drug abuse is associated with limited or absent interest articulation
by nonassociational groups (such as kin, ethnic, religious, regional,
status, and class), z = 4.02, P <.05.
Drug abuse is associated with infrequent interest articulation by
anomic groups (as in demonstrations and riots), z = 3.84, P < .05.
Drug abuse is associated with the absence of elitist political leadership (leadership is not confined to particular racial, social, or ideological strata), z = — 2.77, P < .05.

The following relationships were not found to be associated
(when alpha = .05):

Drug abuse and Muslim religious majorities in the population,
z = 1.09.
Drug abuse and religious homogeneity, z = — 1.79.
Drug abuse and Westernization through colonial status, z = — 1.55.
Drug abuse and former British colonial rulership vs. colonial ruler-
ship by others, z = 1.71.
Drug abuse and the freedom of group (political) opposition, z = .84.
Drug abuse and the extent of political enculturation (extremity and
extent of opposition, factionalism, disenfranchisement), z = — 1.20.

We conclude from the foregoing that drug abuse, defined by
national self-reporting, is associated with a variety of socioeconomic
characteristics; extensive own-nation-perceived drug abuse seems essentially to be a problem of the underdeveloped countries.

SUMMARY AND CONCLUSIONS

Observations on drug use in 247 nonliterate societies were
analyzed for descriptions of drug behavior. Various styles of drug use
were then tested for relationships to 67 culture characteristics. In addition, "narcotic" drug-abuse data from 102 nations were used in a
test for relationships to 21 nation-state socioeconomic characteristics.
The following major findings emerge.

Observers of nonliterate societies have tended not to report on
drug-use behavior in any detail; furthermore, observers are often in
conflict with one another, suggesting inadequate ethnographic methodology. A strong need exists, then, for interested ethnographers in
drug use and in training them to perform quantifiable and reliable
observations.

When data are available on nonliterate societies, the predominant use pattern which emerges is one of high use of alcohol, tobacco, opium, coca-cocaine, and some of the stimulants; hallucinogen and some stimulant use tends to be at low or moderate levels. As far as trends are concerned, increase rather than decrease in use is the pattern more often observed, with the exception of the stimulants and opium. High drug availability is common except for hallucinogens. Availability, in turn, may be a function of the observed tendency for drug production to become local, even if the original sources were not indigenous.

Problems of abuse are rarely noted, except for alcohol. It is rarer still for observers to inquire as to whether natives themselves conceive of their group as having an abuse problem; more often, the observer renders his own judgment. Both indigenous sources and outside observers, when their views are reported, cite considerable abuse of alcohol, cannabis, tobacco, and opium; outsiders, but not insiders, report the predominant picture for tobacco and cannabis is also abuse; neither outsiders nor insiders perceive many societies as abusing natural stimulants. It is important to keep in mind that abuse is seldom subject to careful definition and must be conceived as an expression of disapproval or concern.

Analysis of the settings and motives surrounding drug use indicates that social components are the most common and that the inferred enhancement, enrichment, or smoothing of interpersonal activities is a primary function for most classes of psychoactive drugs and is one component of action in all of them described here. It is also observed that multiple functions are common—that is, the same drug serves several functions within the same society. Drugs vary, by class, in their tendency to fulfill multiple functions and also in their predominant use for particular inferred functions. Stimulants, alcohol, and tobacco, for example, are very often simply social; hallucinogens, rarely social, are much more often religious-magical or mind-altering. Proportionately, opium is most often implicated in psychological-escape functions.

Positive values accompany the use of most drugs; in most cultures for which data are available, alcohol, tobacco, stimulants, cannabis, and coca-cocaine are used either with positive approval or without restraint. However, the number of societies disapproving and/or restraining alcohol use nearly matches those approving and not restraining it. Restraints, coexistent with positive values, predominate in the use of hallucinogens and some stimulants; outright opposition is the majority pattern for opium. Obviously, such opposition can occur simultaneously with high rates of use, suggesting cultural heterogeneity, individual (intrapsychic) conflict over use, or that strong interests in use generate counterreactions of control.

There are various distributions according to sex, age, and status. For no drug in any society reported here does female use surpass that of males. The predominant pattern for alcohol, hallucinogens, and cannabis is for primarily male use. Both-sex use is the majority pattern for opium, stimulants, and tobacco. Low-social-status use as opposed to high-status use occurs most often with alcohol, cannabis, and opium. Special groups (such as shamans) tend to use hallucinogens; high-status groups, the stimulants. The meagerness of data requires extra caution in viewing these drug uses and status findings. The use of culturally extant drugs by all ages is the characteristic pattern; on the other hand, children in most societies are prohibited the use of hallucinogens and cannabis.

A phenomenon of special interest is the resistance to the use of one drug by a society using other drugs and having access to the resisted substance. Certain resisting societies are identified. Further study of this behavior would be worth while.

In testing associations between drug behavior (and availability) and other characteristics of nonliterate societies, forty variables have been identified as possibly related to drug use. In view of the partial correspondence between the adequacy of observations and the frequency of significant findings, more intensive future work is likely to yield a considerable number of culture characteristics related to varying aspects of drug behavior. At present, our findings are limited primarily to associations with the amount of drug use and the characteristics of users.

The major expectation that behavior in regard to several classes of mind-altering drugs is related to social variables is borne out. When any cultural characteristic is found associated (alpha = .10, two-tailed test) with three or more drug-use styles, the association is with two or more different drugs; all drugs except coca-cocaine (on which the fewest observations are available) are so related. Generally, levels of drug use (high to low) are associated with child-rearing methods, the nature of the environment and food-production methods, kin relationships, and social structure. The choice of one drug as opposed to another appears related to social structure and to economic life styles. The particular associations which emerge here are best considered as sources of hypotheses, not as demonstrated relationships. The anticipated relations between other aspects of drug behavior and culture characteristics did not appear. Presumably, this is due to the insufficiency of original observations.

Certain relationships are also found between some kinds of drug behavior as, for example, availability and extent of use. These relationships among drug behaviors are few and unremarkable and suggest the need not only for more data but also for more explicit hypotheses and more refined approaches.

Comparing those nonliterate societies noted by observers for considerable abuse of any drug with societies viewed as not having abuse (even though it may occur and be unreported) yields but few relationships. Both the data and the comparison method are deficient, but the comparison does suggest that abuse is associated with environmental harshness, class stratification based on wealth and/or occupational status, military glory, and bellicosity. Since abuse as perceived by indigenous informants is limited to an association with an insecure food supply, even though observers also find abuse in association with plentiful food, it is evident that no conclusions are in order regarding the relationship between perceptions of drug abuse and the adequacy of food. These relationships certainly merit further inquiry.

The search for relationships between levels of drug abuse (excluding alcohol) as reported by nations and as revealed by the socioeconomic characteristics of those nations has been fruitful. Fifteen out of twenty-one variables are shown to be related; for example, abuse is least where populations are Christian, where there is political activity (articulation) by (nonassociational) interest groups, by anomic groups, and where newspaper circulation is high. Generally, the characteristics of nations with high self-reported rates of narcotic and other nonalcoholic drug abuse are those one associates with the underdeveloped non-Western nations. Were estimates of abuse to include alcohol and to be based on epidemiological rather than official case data, it is likely that more complex findings would emerge which would show that Christian and Western nations are not without serious drug-behavior problems.

It is our thesis that attention to patterns of drug use within cultures and across cultures is merited—those patterns to include the full range of mind-altering substances. Through such an approach, greater knowledge of correlates and determinants of drug behavior— including the problem behaviors and drug outcomes comprising abuse —will be gained. The present study suggests the complexity of drug behavior, but it also indicates, as has the work of many others, that one sector of the road to understanding lies in the study of childhood rearing and natural and social environments.

APPENDIX

List of Cultures* (N = 247)

Culture	Ethnographic Atlas No.	Date Information Source
Abipon	Sh 3	1880
Ainu	Ec 7	1900
Ajie	Ih 5	1860
Akha	Ej 7	1950
Alacaluf	Sg 5	1900
Aleut	Na 9	1830
Alorese	Ic 2	1940
Amhara	Ca 7	1950
Andamanese	Eh 1	1870
Aranda	Id 1	1900
Araucanians	Sg 2	1880
Ashanti	Af 3	1900
Aymara	Sf 2	1940
Azande	Ai 3	1920
Aztec	Nj 2	1520
Bacairi	Si 3	1940
Bali	Ib 3	1950
Baluba (Luba)	Ae 6	1930
Bambara	Ag 1	1920
Bari	Aj 8	1952
Batak	Ib 4	1930
Belu	Ic 3	1950
Bemba	Ac 3	1900
Bengali	Ef 2	1940
Bergdama	Aa 4	1920
Bhils	Ef 5	1900

* Alternate names of cultures are included in some instances.

APPENDIX

List of Cultures* (N = 247)

Culture	Ethnographic Atlas No.	Date Information Source
Boers	Cf 2	1850
Bororo	Si 1	1920
Botocudo	Sj 5	1880
Buka (Kurtatchi)	Ig 3	1930
Bunlap	Ih 3	1950
Burusho	Ee 2	1930
Buryat	Eb 6	1900
Bush Negro (Saramacca)	Sc 6	1920
Caddo (Hasinai)	Nf 8	1770
Caduveo	Sh 4	1940
Cagaba	Sb 2	1940
Cahita	Ni 7	1870
Caingang	Sn 3	1910
Callinago	Sb 1	1650
Caraja	Sj 1	1950
Carib	Sc 3	1930
Cayapa	Sf 3	1910
Chagga	Ad 3	1910
Chamacoco	Sh 6	1890
Cherokee	Ng 5	1750
Cheyenne	Ne 5	1860
Chibcha	Sf 6	1540
Chinantecs	Nj 1	1940
Chiricahua	Nh 1	1880
Chiriguano	Sh 7	1900
Choco	Sa 4	1960
Choroti	Sh 5	1910
Chukchee	Ec 3	1900
Cochiti (Queres)	Nh 7	1900
Comanche	Ne 3	1870
Coorg	Eg 5	1930
Cree	Na 7	1900
Creek	Ng 3	1750
Crow	Ne 4	1870
Cuna	Sa 1	1940

* Alternate names of cultures are included in some instances.

180

APPENDIX

List of Cultures* (N = 247)

Culture	Ethnographic Atlas No.	Date Information Source
Dagur	Eb 4	1940
Dard	Ee 5	1870
Delaware	Ng 6	1700
Dheglia (Omaha)	Nf 3	1850
Diegueno (Diguino)	Nc 6	1850
Dorobo	Aa 2	1920
Dusun	Ib 5	1920
Ellice	Ii 4	1890
Fang	Ae 3	1910
Fon	Af 1	1890
Fox	Nf 7	1830
Futajalonke	Ag 6	1890
Ganda	Ad 7	1880
Gilbertese	If 7	1940
Gilyaks	Ec 1	1920
Goajiro	Sb 6	1940
Gond	Eg 3	1930
Gros Ventre	Ne 1	1880
Guahibo	Sc 4	1950
Guato	Si 6	1900
Hasinai (Caddo)	Nf 8	1770
Hausa	Cb 9	1940
Havasupai	Nd 3	1880
Hawaiians	Ij 6	1880
Heroro	Ab 1	1900
Hukundika	Nd 5	1870
Huichol	Ni 3	1900
Iban	Ib 1	1950
Ifugao	Ia 3	1920
Ila	Ac 1	1920
Inca	Sf 1	1520
Ingalik	Na 8	1880
Irish, Rural	Cg 3	1930
Iroquois	Ng 10	1750

* Alternate names of cultures are included in some instances.

181

List of Cultures* (N = 247)

Culture	Ethnographic Atlas No.	Date Information Source
Java	Ib 2	1950
Jivaro	Se 3	1930
Kabyle	Cd 4	1890
Kachin	Ei 5	1940
Kalmyk	Ci 1	1920
Karen	Ei 7	1910
Katab	Ah 1	1930
Kazak	Eb 1	1910
Kerala	Eg 6	1880
Khasi	Ei 8	1900
Kikuyu	Ad 4	1930
Kiowa (Apache)	Ne 2	1870
Koryak	Ec 5	1900
Kung	Aa 1	1950
Kurtatchi (Buka)	Ig 3	1930
Kutenai	Nd 7	1880
Lango	Aj 4	1920
Lapps	Cg 4	1950
Lau	Ih 4	1920
Lepcha	Ee 3	1930
Lesu	Ig 4	1930
Lhota (Nagas)	Ei 2	1920
Lifu	Ih 7	1910
Lisu (Minchia)	Ed 8	1930
Lolo	Ed 2	1940
Lovedu	Ab 14	1930
Lozi	Ab 3	1890
Luo	Aj 6	1940
Malekula (Seniang)	Ih 2	1930
Manchu	Ed 3	1920
Mandan	Ne 6	1830
Manus	Ig 9	1920
Maori	Ij 2	1820
Margi	Ah 5	1930
Maricopa	Nh 5	1850

* Alternate names of cultures are included in some instances.

APPENDIX

List of Cultures* (N = 247)

Culture	Ethnographic Atlas No.	Date Information Source
Marquesans	Ij 3	1900
Marshallese	If 3	1940
Masai	Aj 2	1900
Mataco	Sh 1	1860
Maya	Sa 6	1520
Mazateco	Nj 5	1940
Mbuswe (Wambugwe)	Ad 5	1940
Mbundi	Ab 5	1930
Mbuti	Aa 5	1930
Mende	Af 5	1930
Miao	Ed 4	1940
Micmac	Na 41	1700
Minchia (Lisu)	Ed 8	1930
Min Chinese	Ed 6	1920
Miskito	Sa 9	1920
Miwok	Nc 5	1850
Mongo	Ae 4	1930
Mongol (Monguor)	Eb 2	1920
Montagnais	Na 32	1880
Mossi	Ag 2	1950
Mota	Ih 1	1890
Motilon	Sb 3	1940
Mundurucu	Sd 1	1950
Murngin	Id 2	1930
Nama	Aa 3	1850
Nambicuara	Si 4	1940
Nandi	Aj 7	1910
Naskapi	Na 5	1890
Natchez	Ng 7	1700
Navajo	Nh 3	1930
Ngoni	Ac 9	1940
Nicobarese	Eh 5	1890
Nootka	Nb 11	1880
Nuer	Aj 3	1930
Nupe	Af 8	1930
Nyakyusa	Ad 6	1930

* Alternate names of cultures are included in some instances.

APPENDIX

List of Cultures* (N = 247)

Culture	Ethnographic Atlas No.	Date Information Source
Nyaneka	Ab 7	1920
Nyoro	Ad 2	1950
Ojibwa	Nf 1	1940
Okinawa	Ed 7	1950
Omaha (Dheglia)	Nf 3	1850
Ona	Sg 3	1880
Orokaiva	Ie 9	1920
Paez	Sf 5	1900
Paiwan	Ia 6	1930
Papago	Ni 2	1930
Pawnee	Nf 6	1852
Ponapean	If 5	1910
Queres (Cochiti)	Nh 7	1900
Riffians	Cd 3	1920
Rotumans	Ih 6	1890
Rundi	Ae 8	1910
Rwala	Cj 2	1920
Samoans	Ii 1	1920
Samoyed	Ec 4	1900
Saramacca (Bush Negro)	Sc 6	1920
Sarsi	Ne 7	1880
Seminole	Ng 2	1940
Seniang (Malekula)	Ih 2	1930
Serbs	Ch 1	1950
Seri	Ni 4	1900
Shilluk	Ai 6	1900
Sindhi	Ea 1	1950
Sinhalese	Eh 6	1950
Siriono	Se 1	1940
Siuai	Ig 1	1940
Siwans	Cc 3	1920
Somali	Ca 2	1950
Sotho	Ab 8	1860
Swazi	Ab 2	1880

* Alternate names of cultures are included in some instances.

APPENDIX

List of Cultures* (N = 247)

Culture	Ethnographic Atlas No.	Date Information Source
Talamanca	Sa 5	1950
Tallensi	Ag 4	1930
Tamil	Eg 2	1880
Tanala	Eh 3	1930
Taos	Nh 6	1890
Tapirape	Sd 2	1930
Tarahumara	Ni 1	1930
Tehuelche	Sg 4	1870
Telugu	Eg 10	1880
Tenetehara	Sj 6	1930
Teton Dakota	Ne 8	1870
Tewa	Nh 11	1900
Thonga	Ab 4	1920
Tikopia	Ii 2	1930
Timbira	Sj 4	1930
Tiv	Ah 3	1920
Tiwi	Id 3	1920
Tlingit	Nb 22	1880
Toda	Eg 4	1900
Togalese	If 1	1820
Tokelau	Ii 6	1900
Trobriand	Ig 2	1910
Trukese	If 2	1940
Tuareg	Cc 5	1910
Tubalulabal	Nc 2	1850
Tucano	Se 5	1940
Tucuna	Se 2	1940
Tunebo	Sf 4	1950
Tupinamba	Sj 8	1600
Ukraine	Ch 7	1930
Ulawans	Ig 6	1900
Ute	Nd 2	1850
Vedda	Eh 4	1900
Venda	Ab 6	1900

* Alternate names of cultures are included in some instances.

185

List of Cultures* (N = 247)

Culture	Ethnographic Atlas No.	Date Information Source
Waica	Sd 4	1950
Wambugwe (Mbugwe)	Ad 5	1940
Washo	Nd 6	1850
Wichita	Nf 5	1860
Winnebago	Nf 2	1850
Witoto	Se 6	1910
Wogeo	Se 4	1930
Woleaians	If 4	1940
Wolof	Cb 2	1950
Wute	Ah 8	1910
Yahgan	Sg 1	1870
Yakut	Ec 2	1900
Yao	Ac 7	1920
Yap	If 6	1910
Yagua	Se 4	1940
Yaruro	Sc 2	1950
Yokuts	Nc 3	1850
Yoruba	Af 6	1950
Yukaghirs	Ec 6	1900
Yurok	Nb 4	1850
Zuni	Nh 4	1910

* Alternate names of cultures are included in some instances.

A Cultural Case Study: Temperate Achilles

Richard H. Blum
Eva M. Blum

IX

Our concern here is to examine the use of alcohol in three rural Greek communities, to suggest how its use is related to other aspects of rural Greek culture and personality, and to determine the extent of a specific health problem: alcoholism. In rural Greece there are illnesses that villagers say the doctors do not recognize; alcoholism is one that *no one* recognizes. This social fact is fundamental to understanding matters that range from the reporting of statistics to the handling of local inebriates.

Approximately three thousand years have passed since "blameless" Achilles, the epitome of Greek manhood, ravaged the army of the Trojans. Since the days of Homeric heroes the Greeks have seen their city states disintegrate and the centers of culture, wealth, and political power vanish. Yet, despite the changes of the centuries and the intermingling of racial stocks, much has remained of the ancient Greek spirit, of the Greek temperament. Tales and customs from antique times live on. Most important for the present study, the ideal of manly excellence, *arete,* has persisted practically unchanged. True, the modern Greek has a new word for it: *levendis*. To call someone *levendis* is high praise. The *levendis* is a joy to behold for his body is beautiful, his song deep and loud; with powerful leaps he leads the dancers, all full of grace and pride. Hospitable to the stranger is the *levendis* and a terror to whoever opposes him. He leaves no offense unavenged; he can drink more than anyone else at a festival, yet never falter in song or step. He is blameless—and blameless also was Achilles whose body had no flaw and whose courage in battle none dared to challenge. "To the *levendis*" is a toast given standing, drink raised high; it can bring tears of pride to the man so honored.

That was the hero of old and that is the Greek of today—at least, that is the portrait of himself which he would paint and maintain. Should an alien force intrude to disturb the flattering image, it must be erased, or suppressed, or at least verbally denied. No wonder, then, that no alcohol problem exists in Greece. For the individual to be a drunk is to be only "half a man," an animal, and so it is understandable that no villager will portray himself in this unfavorable light. What is true for the man is true for the nation. The national *philotimo,* or love of honor, demands there be no shameful blemish.

Many are the reasons offered to explain the land's good fortune in being free from alcoholic problems. The skeptical observer, knowing a bit about Greek pride and attendant Greek denial, may not be fully convinced. After all, even glorious Achilles had his weaker moments. Yet, when the observer sets out to inquire for himself, he may be surprised to learn that his Greek informants did not gloss over the facts as much as he had anticipated. And so it was with us. Social beliefs are social realities and, on occasion in human affairs, there is a substrate of empirical evidence to support them. Let us now examine the evidence and then the beliefs, reaching our conclusions as best we can from limited materials.

The findings reported here are the result of years of work, during which four study trips to Greece were undertaken, the last in 1962. The methods used were those of the social and clinical psychologist; they consisted in formal interview schedules with all families and healers in the area studied; observation and rating schedules included the Dodds Hygiene Scale originally used in Syrian villages. A third method was an action technique, whereby, in cooperation with the Ministry of Health, we introduced physicians into each community and conducted Greece's first morbidity survey and observed the villagers' reactions to medical care. Finally, we employed the informal observations derived from living with the village folk.

As a consequence, we became acquainted with each family in each village; with the local medical personnel—the doctors, pharmacists, and midwives; with the nonmedical healers—the priests, nuns, magicians, *practikoi,* and wise women; and with the village drunks and the village tavern keepers.

Three communities were studied in this formal manner. A fourth, in which we lived, provided informal observational data. The study communities were located in Attika:[1] Panorio with 126 peasant residents, ethnically homogeneous, and of Albanian-Doric stock; Dadhi with 200 people from Asia Minor who had come to mainland Greece in 1922; and the third, a community of eight families of Saracatzani shepherds, said to be descendants of ancient Greeks but today living scattered on the mountainside. None of the three communities has local authorities; they are all under the jurisdiction of the central community of Doxario, which boasts about a thousand inhabitants, and in which we lived. Our house contained a tiny coffee house-taverna and fronted a somewhat larger taverna. Thus, unobserved ourselves, we could watch the comings and goings of their habitués and study their behavior.

PATTERNS OF USE

In Doxario and the surrounding villages, it is relatively easy to distinguish those social settings in which, or occasions on which, alcoholic beverages are consumed. These are as follows:

> With meals, excluding the morning meal
> At the coffee house-taverna
> At family celebrations
> During the rites of hospitality
> At festivals
> During religious rites
> During efforts to heal the sick

Meal-time use. At the noon meal, at the evening meal, and during afternoon or evening "snacks," it is common for alcohol to be

---

[1] Names of places and people are fictitious to safeguard the identity of those who gave so generously of their time and of themselves. Case presentations have been altered so that none, as presented, describes an actual person.

consumed. It is usually taken in the form of *retsina,* a locally produced
white wine which has been flavored with resin from the local pine
trees and has an alcohol content between 12 and 14 per cent. After
dinner strong, sweet wines may be served, often diluted with water.

Coffee house-taverna. When they have leisure time, the men
gather at the coffee house. While there they may read the newspapers,
talk, play *tavli* (a game resembling checkers), sip coffee and water, or
consume alcohol. The most common alcoholic beverage ordered in the
coffee house is *ouzo,* an anise-flavored, distilled grape product containing about 46 per cent alcohol. It is usually taken mixed with a full glass
of water. Alcohol may be consumed any time during the day while at
the coffee house, but, more frequently, it is ordered during a show of
hospitality or friendship or in the evening. It is our impression that
evening consumption is increased on those occasions when musicians
are present or when a record player is playing.

Celebrations. We define "celebrations" here as festivities limited to family events or gatherings of family and friends. Celebrations
occur when a child is born, when there is a baptism, a wedding, or a
name day (equivalent to the American birthday celebration except
that it occurs on the day sacred to the saint whose name the celebrant
bears), when a house, an animal, or an enterprise is blessed by the
priest, or on "good days" when some happy event or good fortune be-
falls someone in the family. If the celebration involves all family members, it will take place at home. White wine, *retsina,* will be served. In
addition, depending upon income, social standing, individual preference, and the importance of the occasion, there may be *ouzo,* liqueur
(most often rose-flavored such as when *ouzo* is flavored with rose
water, but fruit liqueur may also be served), brandy (called "cognac"),
or, though rarely, *tsipouro* or *raki.*

A celebration may also occur at the coffee house-taverna, in
which case it will be limited to male friends. To mark a special occasion, beer may be served.

Hospitality rites. When a stranger[2] or visitor comes to call,
there are hospitality rites which occur regularly. A spoon sweet (*glyko*),
made of fruit preserves, is served with a glass of water. In addition,
among the peasants who can afford it, an honored guest—especially
in the case of men—may be offered *ouzo* or a rose or fruit liqueur.
Among the shepherds wine is the only drink which will be offered.

---

[2] The word *xenos* is the same for guest and stranger.

Community festivals—the panighiri.   We define "festivals" as community-wide events which may be celebrated by all of the village together. On these crowd occasions, the celebrants will be grouped either by family or by male friendship. Some community-wide occasions will be celebrated not en masse, but in the houses of each family. It is customary at these times for families to pay calls upon one another. Festivals include the name day of the local saint (the saint after whom the main church is named and who serves as the patron saint of the community), Easter, Carnival (preceding Lent), Harvest Festivals, the Day of the Cross (September 14), Beheading of St. John (August 29), the Sleeping of the Virgin (August 15), Epiphany (January 6), St. Basil's Day (New Year's), Christmas, and the Feast of St. Constantine and St. Helen. Which festivals are celebrated will depend upon the patron saint of the community, the region of Greece, the occupation of the folk, and the local traditions.

A church of St. Demetrius exists in one of our communities, and since his day, on October 26, coincides with the opening and the tasting of new wine, there is more than usual revelry on this occasion. For the shepherds St. Demetrius' Day marks the driving of the sheep down from the mountains to their folds on the plain. The feast of St. George on April 23 is also important for the shepherds, since it is on that day that the flocks are moved to the mountains. St. George, a warrior-saint like Saint Demetrius, is patron saint to the Saracatzani.

Festivals need not take place within the village, for there may be a pilgrimage to churches dedicated to saints nearby. For example, the Panorio and Dhadhi people go to Saint Marina by the ocean on her day to celebrate ritual, to frolic, and to bathe there. Drinking will be part of those festivities.

Religious rites.   As we can see, the festivals cited above are all religious occasions. They are characterized by a holiday spirit and the expectation that people will enjoy themselves while, at the same time, participating in a religious activity. We distinguish these fun-oriented occasions from the more solemn rites (although never deeply solemn in the North European sense of silence, serious-visaged piety, and ostentatious gravity that so often surround Protestant rituals) which accompany the Mass, Communion, funerals, and funeral feasts. A sweet red wine is usually served to communicants, although white wine can also be employed in church services. Funeral feasts occur after the burial of the dead, at memorial services forty days after interment and again three years later, and each year on All Souls Day.[3] At these meals white wine is served, but *ouzo,* brandy, or liqueur may also be consumed.

Healing. Various remedies may be employed to strengthen and to heal the ill. White wine, *ouzo,* brandy, sweet red wine, and beer are considered to have healing properties. In addition, *ouzo,* wine, *tsipouro,* and brandy may be applied externally as medicaments.

In the settings and occasions associated with the use of alcohol, one factor stands out: drinking occurs within a group context. It is done in the company of one's family or one's friends. It may be done in the presence of the whole community, or, at least, in the presence of a large number of one's neighbors, as at a fiesta or a sacred ritual in church. Its use in healing is an interpersonal event; the woman of the family who takes responsibility for nurturing and feeding will give the sick person his wine or brandy.

The people with whom one drinks are important people, persons with whom one is bound by ties of obligation, loyalty, emotion, and shared living. Except in the exercise of hospitality rites, one does not drink with strangers. When one does drink with a stranger, the host is usually in the company of his male friends or his family.

A second characteristic of drinking is that it is not a goal in itself or even the primary activity of the group. Its use in religious ritual is symbolic and secondary to the rites and intentions of the priest and congregation. Its use in healing is medicinal or magical, and again it is but one of many other on-going activities directed toward achieving or maintaining health. At mealtimes it is ingested as part of the meal— as another food thought to have its own nutritional or health-giving value, as well as providing appetite and good feeling, both of which in themselves are considered essential parts of the important family meal. At fiestas and celebrations its use is greater, but again drinking is only one of many on-going activities; it is one designed to bring pleasure, but in a facilitative fashion by enhancing one's ability to dance, sing, talk, be witty, or join in the festival mood. In the coffee house or taverna, its use is limited, and again is considered an adjunct to the social activities there. No one goes to a coffee house to get a drink; one goes to be with others and only incidentally does he have a drink.

[3] Strict observance requires the following funeral services: on the first, third, ninth, and fortieth day; then, every six months for three years and each year on All Souls Day.

Prescribed and proscribed foods and drinks. The choice of
food and drink on festival occasions is prescribed, within certain limits,
by custom. The use of alcohol is consistent with the larger prescriptions for diet and behavior at these times. Wine is an acceptable drink
on any festival or ritual occasion which involves eating or drinking,
whereas beverages with higher alcohol content are less often employed
and their use is, in a sense, less traditional. Certain foods are expected
to be served on certain occasions as, for example, lamb on the spit at
Easter, St. Basil's pie with a coin at New Year's, and *koliva* (boiled
wheat with almonds, sugar, parsley, raisins, fried flour and pomegranate seeds) for memorial feasts and offerings to the dead. Similarly
certain foods are proscribed on those occasions designated for fasting.
For example, on Clean Monday, which follows Carnival and begins
Lenten fasting, one takes unleavened bread and abstains from olive
oil, fish, and meat. Other fasting periods which are observed by the
communities in the Doxario area include the forty days before Easter,
the forty days before Christmas, every Wednesday and Friday, the first
fifteen days of August, and the Day of the Cross, September 14.

For each period certain designated foods may be taken, just
as certain ones must be avoided. Wine[4] is an acceptable beverage during fasting and no proscription is set forth against its use at these
times. The same holds for another cherished drink: coffee.

There are certain periods of fasting which are dictated by individual considerations rather than by the calendar. The bereaved family will abstain from elaborate foods before funeral rites and will observe such customs as not baking sweet things for one year following
a death. Pregnant women may also fast; we found some villagers voic-
ing the belief that wine was one of the substances to be avoided. By
no means, however, did all villagers subscribe to this proscription.

Some villagers say that the *lechona*—as a woman is called during the forty days after the birth of her child—must fast, but again
there is disagreement on whether or not she must avoid wine. Another
individual fasting period precedes taking Communion; at this time
people will also abstain from intercourse and will bathe as part of the
purification ritual. However, they need not refrain from drinking wine.

During all the community-wide fasting periods, women and
the older people are reportedly the two groups most likely to adhere

---

[4] Eating red grapes is not allowed on St. John's Day, August 29, in
memory of his beheading (Megas, 1958).

to the strict regimes of avoidance and other customary practices. Our
interviews showed a common core of agreement among all villagers
on what the fasting and feasting periods are and what foods and drinks
are appropriate to them; we did find lack of agreement on how stringently one should observe these customs. Some latitude apparently does
exist in the degree of adherence to culturally prescribed food and
drink regimes; nevertheless, tradition and immediate sanctions, as well
as availability and economics, determine much of what one will eat
or drink during any period or even on any single occasion. The latitude
allowed an individual or family in the choice of diet for fasting, festive
occasions, or daily regimes is not wide. The individual may decide
whether or not to avoid meat on Wednesday or Friday, but should
he fail to prepare *koliva* for the memorial service for the dead, or be
seen by his neighbor cooking meat on the Day of the Cross, reputations
would suffer. As a consequence, he prepares food with an eye to what
the neighbors might say. These informal sanctions operate as mighty
forces to determine conformity within a small community.

In addition, the individual has learned, as he grows up, to
follow the customary practices. He looks forward to St. Basil's pie and
lamb on the spit, he enjoys the *koliva,* and he takes pride in fasting,
knowing he is doing what is right and thus accumulating a kind of
credit for his soul—credits presumably tallied in a later life. Even if he
wished to deviate, few are the directions he might take. The local economy produces but a few products; everyone must eat what he raises
or, if he produces cash crops or animals, what he can buy locally. In
Doxario, small grocers provide a few items from elsewhere, but for the
people of Dhadhi and Panorio, and for the shepherds on the mountains, little or no choice exists—even presuming a person has the money
and does not demonstrate that local distrust for products grown in
unknown places or nourished by suspicious fertilizers that "spoil the
taste of food."

What is true for food is true for wine. For example, villagers
agree that the local wines are best: "The Athenians add yellow color
to their wines and dilute them; ours we know are good. Our grapes
produce wines with 14 per cent alcohol; elsewhere they have only 12
per cent." No store in the Doxario region stocks a single bottle of wine.
It is all in barrels, filled with the local produce. To drink a foreign
wine—that is, one from outside Doxario—might not be prohibited;
but it *is* impossible.

Food and wine are intimately linked in regard to beliefs about ingested substances (which we shall discuss later) and in the custom that wine is not ordinarily taken without something to eat along with it. There is no purpose to it in the sense of any conscious effort to retard intoxication; but it is a tradition and, as such, it is accepted usage —pleasurable and unquestioned. At the coffee house-taverna, alcohol is served with olives, a bit of fish, bread, or cheese. During heavier drinking at festivals or celebrations, wine is accompanied by loaves of bread on the table, and often by lamb chops or *kokoretsi* (intestines of sheep broiled on the spit). Eating and drinking occur together and are usages jointly governed by tradition.

LEARNING TO DRINK

Traditions do not govern in the abstract. They are learned and incorporated into the habits and opinions of individuals. In our three communities, learning about drinking begins in childhood. It is considered natural and proper that a child may taste wine and may have small amounts at meal times. There is some disagreement among villagers about when children should begin to have wine, just as there is some discrepancy between the age considered proper for starting to drink and the actual—but earlier—age when children first begin.

About a third of the villagers with whom we discussed this matter indicated that children should begin to drink wine in their early years (under ten), while the remainder agreed that it was proper to begin drinking wine sometime during adolescence. Since alcohol is rarely taken except in the form of wine, the age for tasting other beverages is difficult to ascertain; it is our impression that children may be allowed to taste *ouzo* when it is served and, indeed, may be given it for therapeutic purposes when they are ill.

Young boys visit the Doxario coffee house, where their manly antics earn them praise from the older men. Summertime brings several ten- to seventeen-year-old youngsters to the coffee house, where they sit all day, doing nothing, imitating their elders. From time to time, someone may treat them to a lemonade in return for an errand they are asked to run. The coffee-house sitting that the boys do results in their learning one of the most important functions of being a man: to take part in public life. The drinking is secondary, but it is in this context that the forms of public drinking will be learned.

No discernible difference emerges when proper drinking ages

for boys are compared with those for girls. Nevertheless, distinct differences between the sexes in drinking behavior emerge as individuals grow older. The villagers do not agree about what are the proper drinks for women to take. About half of them contend that a woman may drink anything a man may drink, that there are and should be no restrictions on beverages. The other half contend that it is improper for women to take the stronger drinks: *ouzo,* brandy, *raki,* or *tsipouro.* A very few would prevent women from having beer, but none would deny them wine. Nor would anyone deny them the sweet liqueurs, including rose water-*ouzo.*

In reviewing within-family drinking patterns, we find that there are abstainers in many families, but these are no more often women than men. The most frequent pattern is for all of the adults in a family to take wine with some—but by no means all—meals. It is also more common for all of the children to drink wine with meals than for none of them to take it. The most common reason for children's abstinence is that they are too young; for adults, either men or women, the reason for abstinence is that it is bad for their health or they do not like the taste. The notion of its being bad for health is expressed in the sense that it makes an individual sick, rather than indicating any belief that wine has general deleterious effects.

It is more common for villagers to remark that the women and children takes less wine with meals than the men do. It is in this difference of the amount consumed that one sees a consistent relationship between sex and drinking behavior. In other words, men drink more, and more often, than women. As we have said, the coffee house is a male institution. Women do not participate in its affairs. At festivals it is the men who may drink heavily; women are expected to conduct themselves with propriety and modesty—conduct forms which are not seen as compatible with any loss of control or exaggerated behavior.

That drinking can become a focus of family dispute in which the *underlying* issue is neither the expressed one of health nor one of morality (as is often the case in the United States) but, rather, one of "manliness" versus effeminacy, is reflected in the following observation at an Athenian family dinner:

> It was a pleasant gathering around a home-cooked meal at the usual late dinner hour (ten P.M.) presided over by the father. Grandfather and grandmother were present, as was the very sleepy only son, a nine-year-old. The mother was only intermittently to be

seen, since it fell upon her to prepare and to serve a complex party fare in honor of the visitors. It would have insulted the *philotimo* of our hosts had we insisted too much on helping her with her duties. Neither she nor her old mother-in-law drank anything, except a very small taste of the sweet, strong after-dinner wine. Upon those occasions when she joined us at the table, a tense discussion arose between her and her husband, one which seemed like a continuation of a long-standing argument between them. The mother was quite perturbed for she did not want her beloved boy, Tassos, to have any wine, alleging that it might harm his health, or if not his health, then at least his liver might be damaged. The father insisted the boy have his glass of wine; he turned to us for confirmation and support: "In the United States is it all right for boys to have some wine with dinner?" he enquired, adding, "You are psychologists, tell her (the mother) that to drink is good for a boy!"

Clearly, the real but unverbalized question was not "to drink or not to drink" but, rather, "Is it good for Tassos to act according to the feminine code and become a mama's boy, or should he be allowed to act in conformity to the male code and become a real man?" The drinking was merely a sign indicating the different roles which Tassos' parents visualized for him. For his father the principle was very simple: to drink is what a real man does and what a boy has to learn.[5]

VARIATIONS IN ALCOHOL USE

We have seen that, in learning to drink, age and sex emerge as associated variables. Young children drink less than older children; older children drink less than adults. Boys and girls begin to drink wine at the same age, but they will grow to adulthood having learned that men drink more than women and, to some extent, that women are less likely to be allowed to take high-alcohol-content beverages such as *raki* or *ouzo*.

Within age and sex groups not everyone drinks the same amount. While there is considerable uniformity in drinking behavior associated with settings and occasions, individual variation is also pres-

---

[5] The above example is atypical for rural Greece in certain respects; for the concern Tassos' mother voiced about the deleterious effects of wine on health in general was not heard in our villages. We believe it reflects the penetration of a Western orientation to hygiene into the thinking of educated Athenian Greeks. For another, conflict about male roles is not likely to arise in rural Greece, where the boys, at a very early age, are required to perform tasks traditionally assigned to the male sex and where they are initiated into the coffee house as soon as they can toddle there.

ent. We examine some additional variables that appear to be related to differential usage.

Among the villagers of Panorio and Dhadhi, no one abstains from alcohol because of his social position or because he would be threatened by loss of status should he drink excessively at festive times. On the other hand, in Doxario we found both local physicians expressing the belief that they had to be especially moderate in their behavior. Neither man "rubbed shoulders" with the hoi polloi and neither would jeopardize his position through excessive drinking, even on feast days. One of the priests, Father Manolios from Naxos, appeared to hold the same view: that he must be moderate and conduct himself so as to maintain dignity and circumspection. The other priest, Father Dimitri from a local family, voiced no such sentiments and was proud of his image as a *levendis*, a warrior at heart, a hale fellow who was no slouch at drinking.

These two factors, income and leisure, operate to determine what each person may drink and how much he may drink with consistency. Some families are so poor they cannot afford wine with any meal; some can have it only for celebrations. Many families cannot afford any beverage but wine; some can afford an occasional glass of *ouzo* or beer. Only a few can afford to purchase beer or *ouzo* at whim. In Panorio, we found it was a rare family which had anything but wine in the house. In Dhadhi, only a few families had a bottle of *ouzo* or liqueur on hand. Among the Saracatzani, none had anything but wine on hand and not all had that. In Doxario itself, with its larger population and wealthier citizens, the well-to-do farmers, merchants, and professionals were the families who could afford to stock several bottles of liqueur or to have brandy on hand.

Beer is more expensive than wine; consequently, it has more prestige, especially in the lower classes. In Athenian high society, many of the American ways have been adopted. Whiskey and gin are served for their snob value. Their high cost, however, has prevented these American imports from penetrating to the villages. Greeks consider beer (and whiskey) as innovations, although beer was introduced about three hundred years ago. Serious commercial manufacture started about a hundred years ago. When the villager serves beer as a sign of esteem for his guest, or on Sunday and festival days, he may say, "We'll even have beer"; in other words, it plays the role of champagne for him. Aside from the city, upward-mobile Greek, the average person contends that hard drinks such as whiskey are needed for "quick heat" in cold climates. Greece, they say, is warm and cheery; hence, such drinks are not needed.

Among the villagers of Dhadhi and Panorio and the Saracat-zani shepherds, leisure time is a rare commodity. Most of the days of the year are spent laboring in the fields or with the flocks or in maintaining property and possessions. We found that the coffee houses were empty except in the evenings, and by no means did every man have the energy or funds to join with his neighbors in socializing at night. People who rise with the sun retire with the sun, and few are the hours available for bending ears or elbows in conviviality. In Doxario, on the other hand, there were men whose wives had brought them a dowry or who had inherited good lands sufficient to enable them to survive with but little work. In some cases, survival was at a subsistence level—an income of no more than $30 or so a month, supplemented upon occasion by sending the wife to beg food from the landowner or richest farmer in the area. Nevertheless, these men could live with little work and their leisure was employed in the coffee house. Some we saw, almost every day, sitting there from morning until night. In the coffee houses of Doxario, a cadre of men were fixtures in the place, and the time—if not the inclination—to drink was theirs.

One of the Doxario town-council members, an able friendly man, explained his activities as consisting of doing as little as possible in his grocery store-taverna, so that he would have time to spend sitting in the shade. There he surveyed the unchanging scene in company with the habitués of his establishment, each drinking slowly from a glass of water and an aluminum cup of wine. He said, "If I wanted to work hard I could be a rich man. But why should I do that? I like the way I'm living. I want to have time. That is the best of all."

Some of the peasants of Dhadhi own vineyards which produce grapes for the local white wine.[6] None of them owns pine trees from which resin may be obtained but for a period of time in recent years some did contract with a landowner to tap a pine forest. A few families in Panorio also have vines and one family owns pine trees. Resin for

---

[6] Wine production in recent years has been reduced because of phylloxera which killed the vines. Not all growers elected to replace the vines with healthy stock, deciding instead to turn to growing vegetables for sale on the expanding commercial market. This decision was facilitated by the introduction of better roads and of trucks.

their wine is either obtained under arrangement with a landowner or by surreptitiously tapping trees without consent.[7] Grape growers may sell the grapes to a merchant or to a cooperative, take them to a government press some miles away for pressing and use or sale, or press and make the wine at home. Determining the machinery and extent of these practices was beyond the scope of our study. It does seem reasonable to expect that those peasants who produce grapes are more likely to have wine on hand than those who do not, especially in the case of poorer farmers whose cash is limited and whose barter agreements must support subsistence. If this is so—and we believe it is— ownership of vineyards is an additional factor associated with wine availability and, potentially, with differential consumption.

While statistical data on production and consumption for the whole of Greece must await another time, it would at least be useful to present statistics on production and consumption for the Doxario region. Unfortunately one cannot. The problem is that the present machinery for gathering information on production does not allow accurate estimates. There is also confusion over the nature of that machinery. According to one statement of the official system for alcohol taxation and production control, all vines are counted and estimates are made of grape production for purposes of tax control and statistical reporting. Informal statements by wine growers in the region indicate, however, that no such vine-by-vine monitoring occurs.

It is also said that official requirements call for the pressing of all grapes in government controlled facilities. Such controls are to provide for taxation and statistical reporting of production. Informal reports from the wine growers state that the only grapes to be pressed in the controlled facilities are those which are sold and which are used in the production of wine for bottling and for the distilled products made from residuals left after the pressing. These distilled spirits are processed and bottled in Athens rather than locally.

Wine which is intended for local use is not produced under government supervision, say these growers; nor is it bottled. It remains in barrels and is either sold or bartered in the region. We have men-

---

[7] Tapping is done destructively. A wide strip of bark is peeled off the tree; it may be two or three feet long and four to eight inches wide. An old tin can is cupped at the bottom of the swath. Each year a new strip is cut, going around the tree at eye level, so that within a few years the tree is killed. This uncontrolled tapping method leads to dangerous deforestation.

tioned that the only wine obtainable in the Doxario region is in barrels; no bottled wine is to be seen. Bottled liqueurs, *ouzo,* and brandy may be stocked on store shelves in Doxario. The bottles, though, are dusty and grimy, giving the impression that such products move but slowly in local commerce.

CULTURAL THEMES AND VALUES

Philotimo, or love of honor, influences drinking behavior among men. The way to attack a male, the way to express aggression, envy, or competitiveness toward him, is to attack his *philotimo.* This is accomplished through shaming him or ridiculing him by demonstrating how he lacks the necessary attributes of a man. Consequently, avoiding ridicule becomes a major concern, a primary defensive operation, among rural Greek males. He does this in part by prophylactic means: he controls his family with an iron hand, so that members will not become the instrument by which he is shamed. He also avoids situations which are potentially dangerous to the *philotimo.* Merely being manly, having *philotimo,* is no guarantee that others will not test one's mettle through probing attacks. In a culture shot through with envy and competitiveness, there will be an ever-present danger from others. Consequently, a man with *philotimo* must be prepared to respond to jeer, insinuation, or insult with a swift retort, an angry challenge, or, if need be, by the lightning thrust of his knife. *Philotimo* is enhanced if a man is physically sound, lithe, strong, and agile. It is enhanced if he can converse well, show his wit, and act in other ways that facilitate sociability and establish ascendancy. Generosity in ordering food and drink at a party is one method of adding to everyone's enjoyment while, at the same time, earning points of honor and prestige. Greek informants mention that drinking helps a man overcome his cautious hold on his purse strings and permits him to pay freely for new rounds of wine and snacks for his party companions. His friends will then praise him for his bounty, envy him for his increased ability to command respect and admiration, and will even emulate him so as not to be outshone by his generosity.

One aspect of *philotimo* can also be a spur to heavy drinking. A man with special characteristics becomes the *levendis,* our modern Achilles. But whoever aspires to the honor of achieving *levendis* status must drink competitively and win and, in doing so, not impair his abilities, at least, as a social warrior. Uncontrolled drunkenness poses dread dangers to *philotimo*. To be a "bloated wine-sack with dog's ears" was an insult in Homer's time and its equivalent is one now. Insofar as a man loses control over his body, over his speech, over his capacity to interact with others effectively, he is endangered by drink. Such a condition exposes him to ridicule and deprives him of the means to respond effectively to challenge; especially dangerous is the fact that he loses his wit and thus fails to hear the warning which would enable him to cut off the challenger verbally—short of the knife.

Philotimo can be enhanced at the expense of another. It has a see-saw characteristic; one's own goes up as another's declines. The Greek, in order to maintain and increase his sense of worth, must be prepared each moment to assert his superiority over friend and foe alike. It is an interpersonal combat fraught with anxiety, uncertainty, and aggressive potentials. As one proverb describes it, "When one Greek meets another, they immediately despise each other."

Strife was a theme important to Hesiod, and it remains important today. Then and now, it spurs to greater endeavor by testing one individual's capacities—strength, cunning, wit—against another's. These jousting matches are a feature of the convivial drinking gatherings in the coffee house. A party begun with a good meal, and sped on its way with the juice of the grape provides an excellent opportunity for men to show their worth. They ingest huge quantities of food, generously compete in ordering more food and wine, and demonstrate their self-control, no matter how often they may be challenged to show the "white of the glass bottom"—that is, "bottoms-up."

Let us illustrate:

Two young daughters of Athenian friends of ours were visiting us on a Sunday when our social workers had already left for their own homes in the city. Learning of our visitors, the Doxario dignitaries—imposing, white bearded Father Dimitri, two handsome, good-humored, charming policemen, the mayor, the teacher from Panorio (who had just purchased two live chickens for tomorrow's dinner and kept them tethered, squawking, under his chair), and our special friend, Panaiotis, a farmer—offered all of us the rites of hospitality. As the evening began, we met at the coffee house under a flowering Judas tree. The men outdid one another in providing the party. One challenge was particularly instructive. Father Dimitri was amusing himself by gently corrupting one of our Athenian guests. Slyly he filled her glass whenever she looked away, smilingly he teased her about not having finished her glass, happily he nodded approval as she, responsive to the interest of the handsome priest,

downed the white wine. He would then direct her attention elsewhere and proceed to repeat the cycle. It did not take too long before the poor girl was giggling outlandishly in her cups. Father
Dimitri's next play was to smoke a cigarette, casually offering the
young lady one, too. She refused, but soon he had persuaded her to
smoke one and then another. It was, of course, improper that a
girl should be seen drunk and smoking in public.

Father Dimitri had triumphed. We could imagine his
thoughts: "So those city girls will drink with the men, eh? Well,
I'll show her who is the master here." It was no accident that the
next song he chose to sing, a Klepht song, told of the priest's daugh-
ter, the spawn of the sperm of the devil.

Another moving challenge occurred that evening. Our other
Athenian visitor, a tall girl, flashing-eyed, arose dramatically. She
held her full glass out toward the handsome policeman. *"Aspro
pato"*[8] she exclaimed, flinging the gauntlet which summoned him
to a drinking duel. In one gulp she downed her wine (about six
ounces), a feat symbolic of female equality with the male. Her
opponent, a true gentleman, allowed her the pleasure, declining to
chug-a-lug his cup. She smiled triumphantly. She had vanquished
the man and with him some portion of her heritage of oppression
as a Greek woman at the hands of men. But the young man could
not quite bear it. When he believed himself unobserved, he quickly
downed his glass; polite to the end, he at least proved to himself
he was not to be bested.

The competition among men forces them to be inventive drinkers, or better said, inventive nondrinkers. As an evening progresses, one
or another will surreptitiously hide his glass as the brimming jug is
poured around. Casually he places his hand over the mouth of the
glass, implying it is full while it is, in fact, depleted. Busily he fills the
glasses of the others while pouring for himself a tiny splash. (On one
occasion when we saw that to hold our own we must compete and
win, we demonstrated an American brand of cunning and used our
own glasses as a pitcher from which we poured for others. The move
was taken with good humor, even though it deprived our hosts of the
pleasure of seeing their American guests under the table.)

Observers of Greek village life (Lee, 1953; Sanders, 1962)
have noted that father and son do not frequent the same coffee house.
Our experience supports this observation, although we did not find it
an absolute rule. For the most part, father and son will either be in
different coffee houses or will attend the same coffee house at different

[8] "Show the bottom of the glass."

times. We believe that this practice safeguards the father from the son, and, as a corollary, safeguards the family from the aggravation of potentially disruptive conflict. The competitive wit, comments, and drinking in the coffee house are not a seemly form of father-son interaction. Overt competition in any form must not take place between people of unequal status. Neither the realities of power nor the forms of respect will allow it. As a consequence, we suggest that in the coffee house peers or men less closely bound by emotional ties are the ones who may contain dangerous elements of revolt.

ENVIRONMENTAL SETTING

The coffee house and the home are the places where people drink. In the village, the taverna, or coffee house is a place in which everything from eggs, soda, and coffee to lamb on the spit may be served. In most of the smaller villages, the coffee house is, first of all, a general store. Whether small or large, the coffee house is the meeting place for men. There they may sit for hours without drinking anything more intoxicating than several glasses of water, play *tavli,* and watch time and the rest of the villagers pass by. If the occasion is more festive, a round of wine or *ouzo* may be ordered. A passing stranger, a cousin who lives in the next village, a representative of the agricultural bank, or a residing American, all of them provide an excellent reason for making the occasion a festive one.

In Doxario, the coffee houses are sometimes as spacious as 40 feet by 30 feet, with a patio outside for use in summer weather and tables set alongside the street where, on pleasant days, the habitués gather under open sky and leafy boughs. These coffee house-tavernas serve coffee, wine, the stronger *ouzo, raki, tsipouro,* and, with each alcoholic beverage, a glass of water and a bit of food, *mezes.* Meals may or may not be served, depending not only on the time and the day, but whether the pot from which the proprietor takes his dinner still has something in it.

There are in Doxario about eighteen coffee house-tavernas, ranging from the size of a postage-stamp bistro with only two or three tables to places capable of seating—at least outside—a hundred or so people. Estimating the adult male population of Doxario at about three hundred, one finds one coffee house for every seventeen males.

In Dhadhi, there is no splendor in the coffee houses, of which there are four serving the village. Three have patio areas bordering on the dirt road that runs through the town; all have a single inner room in which stand tables and chairs. They are simple places; gathering there does not depend upon atmosphere or aesthetics. The four coffee houses serve a population of about seventy adult males—in other words, there is one coffee house for each seventeen men.

Panorio has one main coffee house, although another villager has several tables and chairs located in her front room so that the men may gather there on a winter's evening. During our study a third villager was adding a room to his house with the apparent intention of opening an additional coffee house-grocery store (in Panorio the gathering place stocks the few staples which are available in the community). Considering the two available coffee houses, one finds, then, that there is one for every twenty-two men in the village.

While the number of men per coffee house in each of these two villages may suggest a rather considerable use of their facilities, observations indicate that such is not quite the case. Attendance is irregular and for many men a visit to the coffee house remains a pleasant but infrequent activity. Since each coffee-house owner in Panorio and Dhadhi operates the business only as a sideline—one usually requiring the joint effort of husband and wife—in addition to their ordinary farming activities, there need not be great profit from the enterprise for it to continue operating.

The Saracatzani, living as they do on the mountainsides, have no coffee houses at all. When the shepherd men wish to attend, they must walk or ride their donkeys into Doxario. The requirements of the sheep severely limit the number of such outings that can be made, especially in the summer season when the animals are on the mountain slopes.

The scope of our study did not allow us to gather detailed information on consumption of alcohol over time. Through observation and interrogation, we did derive information which allows us to make some estimates in regard to consumption.

At mealtime those families serving alcohol consume very moderate amounts. Women and children drink no more than 2 or 3 ounces of wine, men no more than 8. No alcohol is ordinarily served after the meal. If a man spends his evening in the coffee house, he ordinarily has one cup or, at the most, two cups of wine—normally 8 ounces— provided the evening is a quiet one without celebration, strife, or rites of hospitality. During rites of hospitality in the home, about an ounce or, at the most, 2 ounces of *ouzo*—usually diluted by at least a half and served in a glass of water—are offered to the men, and the male hosts match drink for drink.

If a male guest is being entertained in the coffee house, the occasion may become a festive one. This is especially likely on a Saturday evening, and on rare occasions the men may travel as far as Doxario— or the men of Panorio as far as Spathi—to listen to music and to dance, sing, and drink. On these occasions men may be expected to consume six, eight, or ten cups of wine (about 24, 32, 40, or more ounces). These amounts they may also be expected to consume, provided they can afford it, at community-wide festivals. Celebrations at home, in which all ages and sexes are present, are characterized by less consumption on the part of the men.

The amount consumed during religious rites is small. Communicants and participants in the Mass receive only a spoonful of wine. Those participating in memorial feasts to the dead take no more than a few ounces.

The villagers agree that people drink the most at festival days and family celebrations. They also agree that men drink more when together, as in the coffee house, than when they are with their families at home.

On certain rare occasions, a man may state his intention of drinking an extraordinary amount during the course of an evening, such as on a festive occasion at the coffee house or during a *panighiri* —a community-wide festival. He may say he wants to achieve *kefia,* a state of happy mood, and set about with determination to arrive there. Under such conditions he may order *raki, ouzo,* or *tsipouro* instead of the traditional resinated wine. However, we feel that such conscious efforts to seek an altered state of consciousness or mood are rare. At least, we did not observe them.

A few villagers told us, during discussions about the times when people drink the most, that life circumstance as well as social setting influences consumption. It was their belief—one by no means expressed by all villagers—that when troubles came upon certain individuals they would increase their rate of consumption. The intent in such cases is presumably to reduce felt distress or anxiety.

Families were asked to report their beverage consumption for the day prior to one interview. Table 17 below presents the results.

Obviously, water is the primary beverage consumed. Since the

Table 17

BEVERAGES CONSUMED DURING ONE DAY REPORTED BY A
SUBSAMPLE OF THIRTY-SEVEN FAMILIES INTERVIEWED
IN TWO COMMUNITIES

Beverage	Number Reporting Consumption
Water	37
(Amounts)	
Up to an *oka** per person	20
1 to 2 *okas* per person	9
2 to 3 *okas* per person	7
More than 3 *okas*	1
Coffee	11
Milk	11
Wine	6
Fruit juice	3
Cocoa	2
Soft drinks	1
Ouzo	1
No drink other than water	16

* An *oka* is roughly equivalent to 1 liter or almost 2 pints.

interviews were conducted in midsummer, when temperatures over 100°F. were reached, it is understandable why such large amounts might be taken. However, one must be cautious about accepting the accuracy of statements as to amounts.

Table 17 indicates that for a particular midweek day more families reported *no use* of wine than reported use of wine. We were not in a position to make observations of alcohol consumption for a sample of individuals over time, although that would have been desirable. It is our impression that a J curve best describes alcohol consumption behavior over time, with most individuals clustering in the low-consumption or no-consumption end of the continuum and decreasing numbers extending to the high-consumption end of the continuum. Among the individuals whom we knew well in the three communities, none was observed to be inebriated during the months of our study. Among persons known to us casually, several were inebriated upon occasion.

The villagers in Dhadhi did not agree as to whether anyone in their village should be described as generally drinking too much. However, about half did name individuals whom they considered to be excessive drinkers. Another quarter of the respondents were defensive in regard to this question, apparently hesitating to cast aspersions on their community or its citizens. Two men were named as the village's heavy drinkers. One was a lively old man in his late sixties who, though an effective member of the community, was widely known for his mastery of the art of cussing and his pleasures in the wine cup. During our months of study, we did not observe him to be inebriated as defined by any visible behavioral signs. The other Dhadhi villager named as an excessive drinker was a man in his mid-sixties who stood out because of his more-unshaven-than-most condition, but was never observed to be drunk by any of the investigators. His wife was firm in her belief that he drank too much. During the medical examinations to which she and her husband went jointly, she stood behind her husband gesturing to the physician with hands and tilted head to communicate tippling without her husband's seeing it.

The villagers of Panorio completely agreed that some men drank too much in the community. Three men were named, each in his mid-fifties. One person, who was said to be too often drunk, was spoken of as a man without adequate *philotimo*. This characterization marked him as a deviant and as a man who was not accorded full respect in Panorio. The second man mentioned was also considered to drink too much, but his children's accomplishments and his own bravery during the war were so well known that he was respected as well as criticized. Perhaps, these conflicting attitudes of villagers about him accounted for the awkwardness we observed in their mention of him, as well as for their apparent reluctance to discuss his behavior.

The third person mentioned as a heavy drinker was said to share this characteristic with all the men of his clan, only more so. Since all the men are admired for their ability to hold their liquor, the sentiments expressed about this man were more in the nature of admiration for his *levendis* characteristics than criticisms.

Among the shepherds, none was spoken of as heavy drinkers and, during our observations, we saw no one who was inebriated.

In Doxario, we found more extreme behavior. There, in a population of a thousand, two men were mentioned as drunks, one of them serving as the town fool and whipping boy. The latter we never observed to be sober; beginning in the early morning, he staggered about on his pathetic rounds. The other drunk we rarely saw, but occasionally he was pointed out to us. There seemed to be no question that these two were unable to function at work and that their behavior was symptomatic of chronic alcoholism.

EFFECTS OF ALCOHOL

We limit our discussion of alcohol effects to behavior which is observed as a function of social setting and emerges as idiosyncratic and, in a somewhat different category, to those conditions associated with physical condition. We begin with the latter.

Reviewing the physical findings presented in *Health and Healing in Rural Greece,* we find no diagnosis of alcoholism made, nor do we find diagnosis of conditions commonly associated with alcohol use, such as cirrhosis and peripheral neuritis. On the other hand, we do find the physician recommending that one resident of Dhadhi and another of Panorio should curtail their alcohol intake. The Panorio patient turned out to be one cited by the villagers as a heavy drinker and as a man lacking respect. He was described by the physician as melancholic, supersensitive, and pessimistic. The doctor attributed his poor mental condition to prior surgery and sickness; his diagnosis was chronic gastritis, aggravated by the use of alcohol. His recommendation of abstinence was for the treatment of gastritis. The Dhadhi patient also proved to be one cited by villagers—and his wife—as a heavy drinker. He was diagnosed as a nervous and overweight person with high blood pressure who should eat less food and drink less wine. We cannot be sure that such a recommendation was not in response to the dramatic gestures of the man's wife as she did a pantomime in the examining room.

Reviewing the clinical findings on the other villagers described by their neighbors as heavy drinkers, we find no physical evidence derived from the clinical examinations to indicate any serious physical disorder attributable to alcohol. It is worthy of note that the two men identified by a physician as having health problems associated with alcohol use were both described as having psychiatric problems. Since it is very rare for village physicians to describe psychiatric difficulties in their patients, we may take it that both of these men presented highly unusual personalities. In neither case were the psychiatric problems related by the physician to the use of alcohol. For our purpose here, we must suggest that there is some evidence for the existence of personality disorder—defined by Greek standards—in two out of the three non-*levendis,* heavy drinkers who were medically examined. This is not to make a claim for the accuracy of psychiatric diagnoses or to presume any causal relationship between personality deviation and heavy alcohol use. It does suggest, however, the need to attend to individual personality factors in studying the process which leads to villagers' characterizing a man as an unadmired heavy drinker.

As for the men identified by villagers as heavy drinkers—but not noted by physicians to have any problem associated with alcohol use—we find that only two out of three appeared for medical examination. The third man, the clever cusser from Dhadhi, along with his wife and soldier son (who was away on duty), failed to cooperate in this phase of our study. Of the two who did appear, both from Panorio, one was found to be without psychiatric or physical difficulties. The other was found healthy but overweight and in an exceptional characterization by the physician was termed "a joyful and teasing personality." Need we say this patient was our hearty *levendis?*

Doxario, with its thousand residents, might be expected to show a wider range of health problems and behavior than our tiny communities. We have already noted the presence in Doxario of two "confirmed" drunks. More serious health problems attributable to alcohol use were also found there. One physician reported that two of his patients had died either shortly before or during the study period as a result of cirrhosis of the liver. Both were elderly; one was a man and the other a woman. In addition, the pharmacist reported that one patient he knew had recently developed tuberculosis which he believed could be attributed to heavy drinking and poor nutrition.

It is worth noting at this point that one physician listed smoking, wine drinking, and eating heavy foods as partial evidence of a lack of "hygienic conscience" in the local residents. While he felt these were health threats, he said the local low morbidity rate was due to "good water and hard work."

When used at meals or hospitality rites or in the treatment of illness, wine is *not* expected by the villagers to change behavior. They consider it a facilitator of social or natural processes, just as it is at festivals and celebrations where larger amounts are consumed and where drinking is associated with a bon vivant spirit expressed in singing, dancing, flirtation, talking, and so forth. When this approved behavior occurs—and wine need not be taken for it to take place—no comment is made and the behavior is not necessarily attributed to the alcohol. In this context, the villagers observed that when drinking, people tend to be gay, to laugh, to joke, and to be happy.

On the other hand, behavior may occur which is notable in the sense that it is an exaggeration of ordinary actions or a deviation from them. In this framework, the villagers cited the following, in order of frequency, as effects of alcohol to be observed at or following heavy drinking occasions: (1) aggressive behavior including quarreling, cursing, beating wives and children, fighting, and killing; (2) overly talkative behavior, including shouting and being noisy; (3) boisterous behavior, as in breaking glasses or being capricious; (4) becoming sick, vomiting; (5) acting "crazy" and silly or showing irrational or unspecified deviant behavior—"going astray"; (6) sleeping or passing out; (7) amorous behavior—chasing girls, making love; (8) uncoordinated behavior, such as staggering; and, least often (9), being silent or crying.

If we may take frequency of being mentioned as evidence for the effects of alcohol on these special occasions, we see two common trends: the enhancement of sociable "fun"—dancing, singing, talking, and flirting—and the release or aggravation of aggressive-competitive impulses leading to quarrels and violence. The most bizarre behavior by local standards—and, by inference, very unusual—is being silent or crying.

There are no themes that our own observations can add to the villagers' descriptions of what they do when they drink a lot. We may select from our observations and their reports to illustrate what occurs.

> *At an all-day hospitality rite for visiting friends:* Everyone ate, danced, sang from one in the afternoon till eight in the evening. At eight, they sat down to a second major meal; chatting, drinking wine, singing. By midnight, the eleven-hour party was over. No one had become drunk; all had appeared to enjoy themselves immensely.
>
> *At an evening celebration in a coffee house-taverna:* Two neighbors began to quarrel. Old grievances were voiced. Insults were hurled. Both pulled knives. One was felled with an abdominal slash. He was taken to Athens but the police were not called.
>
> *At a festival on the name day of a saint:* Most of the village was present, sitting at tables which extended out into the street. Two bands played simultaneously and two singers vied to outshout one another. Three different dancing areas were occupied with changing groups of men and women, only men, only women, or

especially talented solitary or duo performers doing folk dances.
Wine and food were abundant; the noise level almost unbelievably
high by our standards. Everyone appeared joyous. No one appeared
to have lost control or to be unaware of the opinion of others.

On an ordinary evening: The town drunk of Doxario ordered food which he ate but then claimed he could not pay for.
The coffee-house owner—who had been drinking wine—picked him
up and threw him across the table. All the dishes were broken as
they crashed to the floor. The owner then accused the drunk of
having broken his good dishes and, with that, beat the man un-
mercifully for five minutes. The other habitués watched the proceedings without comment. Bruised and battered, the drunk was
eventually allowed to crawl away.

In the hut of the Saracatzani: As honored guests, we were
offered wine from a pottery jug. The host and his wife drank with
us; the children did not. The flies which had fallen in the jug, or
had fallen in the cups, were carefully plucked out of our cups by
the fingers of our host before they were handed to us. Quiet con-
versation and good humor occupied us for several hours, while no
more than two cups of wine were consumed.

At a harvest festival: The lord, owner of much land, invited
all his workers to the harvest festival. Abundant food, a special treat
of fruit, as much wine as one wanted, were available. Dancing and
talking were the main activities for five hours. No one behaved in
an idiosyncratic manner. There was keen competitiveness among
the male dancers and some sharp humorous exchanges occurred,
but in the presence of the great landowner, more than ordinary
decorum was exhibited.

At the Daphni wine festival: Hundreds of varieties of wine
could be obtained freely, in unlimited amounts and without payment. There may have been ten thousand people celebrating the
new wine the night we were present. Two men only had to be carried out, drunk. They were carried out tenderly, protectively; our
Greek hosts turned to us with a teasing smile, for the two men
wore the uniform of the American navy!

INTERPERSONAL CONTROLS

How a sober person acts toward one who has been drinking
heavily is shaped by their role relationship, by the setting, by general
attitudes, and by idiosyncratic factors. A prime consideration is whether
or not the drunken person has already been cast by community opinion
in the role of shameful deviate—that is—a man without *philotimo* or
a woman without modesty.

In the case of the confirmed drunk—one so defined by community opinion—there is common community rejection expressed by

isolation, ridicule, abuse, taunting, and physical brutality. The confirmed drunk, unable to defend himself physically because of his weakness and lack of coordination and because of his psychic surrender to the role of town fool and punching bag, may be treated aggressively with impunity. The aggression directed toward him may be taken as a direct expression of the disdain of the community for his complete loss of manly virtue. It also serves, for some individuals, as a means for amusement, as men or boys engage in drunk baiting, or for the release of more idiosyncratic, sadistic impulses on the part of those who attack the drunk physically.

No segment of the community of Doxario takes the side of the underdog. This is understandable among individuals who are more concerned with acquiring power than in equalizing its distribution. Police authorities do not intervene either to punish drunkenness or to protect the inebriate, unless homicidal weapons are brought into play. A beating may be interrupted if police are present in the town square at the time, but even this is problematical. As long as no great damage is done, the police will not interfere with the normal course of events.

In the same way, bystanders will not intrude should one or two set out to beat a drunk. His problem is not theirs; he is not family and his chronic alcoholism has made it unlikely for him to have built up among the residents any reserve of obligations which he might call upon by asking for assistance.

An individual designated as a heavy drinker but not one cast in the role of the town drunk is less vulnerable to assault. This is especially true if he functions effectively in the community in such a way as to have reciprocal obligations operating—ones which restrict the freedom of those who might like to deal with him harshly. In addition, the heavy drinker who is not cast in the deviant role still commands the loyalty of family—if not of kin—and the presence of his family members serves to deter any direct expression of aggression toward him. Nevertheless, if his drinking reduces his capacity to act "as a man," he will be the object of gossip, ridicule, and disdain. In our three small communities, one man in Panorio could be considered in such a position.

An individual who drinks heavily and perhaps frequently but who holds his liquor well is more respected than scorned. Other men will admire his capacity, and if his behavior includes the ability to dance, sing, talk, or fight well when he is drinking, he is a candidate for the role of a *levendis*. His sons will seek to emulate him and his peers will tell tales of his prowess.

The actions of family members toward the unmanly drunk are different from those of other residents. While others are free to scorn him, family members may not do so for they themselves are objects of scorn. The reputation of the father is applied to his wife and children. If he earns the disrespect of the community, they will all reap the fruits of his failure. The children will be ridiculed for their father's failings and the bad blood which they are assumed to have inherited. His daughters will find it harder to obtain a desirable husband, and his sons' blood will be questioned in the marriage negotiations. The wife may have the quiet sympathy of other women, for of all the groups in the community the ones tied by the gentlest bond are the women who know—and sometimes glory in—the suffering they share. Should the wife be beaten by her husband—and both the villagers and priest report that it is the sport of drunken husbands—she will deserve their sympathy. But she does have a final weapon: taking her dowry and going back home to her parents. In the case of the older woman, whose husband will be older and who is, according to our observations, more likely to be a heavy drinker, her parents may be either dead or living with her in her own house. In either case, she will have no other home to which to return.

We did not observe any wives being beaten. We knew wives whose husbands were reported to have beaten them. We also knew women with husbands who were reported to drink heavily, but who would hardly have dared to challenge their wives to any combat, verbal or physical. Seemingly, the Greek woman need not be submissive. Her response to her husband's drinking appears to be a function of personality and resourcefulness.

ATTITUDES AND BELIEFS

Attitudes and beliefs regarding alcohol are interwoven with cultural themes and life styles. Those that we consider most salient for health activities we set forth in *Health and Healing in Rural Greece*. We would present the following major areas for consideration here: the relationship between drinking and eating, the relationship between alcohol and other powerful or magical substances, concepts of moderation and their expression in regard to drinking, and orientation to altered states of consciousness. All of these play a role in regulating drinking behavior.

We have discussed the prescriptions and proscriptions which set forth the use of food and drink for feasting, fasting, and daily use. Insofar as one defines a food as an ingested substance taken for its presumed nutritive value, then wine taken at mealtimes is a food, for it is believed to be good for a person's health. Indeed, among all the liquids that the villagers listed as good for health, wine stood second to milk in value, while water ranked third, as reported during formal interviews. Among liquids considered to have special healing powers—as opposed to a mere good-for-you value—the various herb teas ranked first, milk second, and wine and *ouzo* third.

Just as foods can be dangerous to health, so too can wine. Among the foods, salted and fried foods and beans (*pulses*) were considered the most dangerous. Among the health-endangering liquids, alcohol *in excess* was nearly unanimously ranked first, followed by *ouzo,* milk, curative teas, and water. It can be seen from this that it is not feasible to set wine apart in some special category of substance; rather, some of the ways of viewing wine were closely linked to ways of looking at solid foods and nonalcoholic liquids. Among all of these classes of ingestible substances, certain items were considered good for health and certain ones bad for health, certain items had special healing qualities, and some had special dangers. Wine, interestingly enough —and to a certain extent *ouzo*—was listed as having all four effects.

There were certain similarities in the viewpoints that the villagers held toward water and wine. In rural Greece, water is no mere neutral substance taken when one is thirsty. It is more valued than that. The people pride themselves on being connoisseurs of water; long discussions ensue over the qualities of water from different springs or from different regions. In a land where it is scarce, water has come to be a focus of attention. While nearly everyone would agree that it is indispensable to health, some ascribe to it nutrient values, just as with food. Furthermore, it is commonly held, as with both food and wine, that water can also be dangerous. Too much water is bad, iced water can be harmful, dirty water can cause illness, and water taken on an empty stomach can cause the wandering navel.[9]

In *Health and Healing in Rural Greece,* we discussed the importance of food in Greece. We pointed out the emphasis placed on food as a substance which gives strength to ward off danger and how it is given to express love or to combat anxiety. Considerable anxiety

---

[9] A folk disease which physicians do not recognize nor understand. It is discussed in *Health and Healing in Rural Greece.*

results when an individual refuses food, shows loss of appetite, or is
too thin. In our communities, nearly everyone agreed that being too
thin was bad for health; while the same was said of being too fat, one
must remember that the standards of desirable weight differ from those
in the United States. What we might call "plumpness" is the villager's
standard for female beauty—a standard which can verge into what
Americans would call "fat" without any decrease in judged pulchri-
tude. Greek infants are, by American standards, overfed, just as they
are, by our standards, indulged. The heavy eater is much admired; we
recall the pride with which a man described his elderly father's vitality
in eating several pounds of bread at one sitting. The hostess forces
food upon her guests and is truly gratified when a guest responds by
asking for even more. In fact, the entire matter of food offering and
food intake is a subject of considerable interest and even preoccupation.

Given the importance of giving and receiving food, we tested
in one of our questions the notion of food's being used as a reward
for good behavior but not as a punishment for bad behavior among
children. The table below presents the definitive answers given by villagers of whom the question was asked.

Our observations were consistent with these reports. Parents are
more likely to indulge the young child than to punish him and more
likely to feed him more than he wants than to deprive him of food he
desires. We would suggest that a psychodynamic consequence of this
practice, certainly reinforced by prevailing attitudes, is that children
do not learn to associate being "bad" with food deprivation; as a result, they do not project onto foods associated elements of badness and
forbidden desirability. Foods, then, do not take on a simultaneous positive and negative valence, which might, in turn, make them objects
of approach-avoidance in the unconscious sphere related to the children's own feelings of badness and desire to taste the forbidden. Having ventured this far in speculation, we take the final leap to suggest
that wine is similarly free from projected conflictual elements and that
neither wine nor food will be as sought after as forbidden rewards
(either primitive or symbolic) by individuals who feel either neurotic
guilt or neurotic rebellion against punitive parental figures. We offer
this as a formulation for further testing.

In any event, we believe it useful to consider drinking as one
aspect of larger patterns of the ingestion of solids and liquids—all of
which are considered to have nutrient value and all of which are sub-

Table 18

USE OF FOOD FOR REWARD AND PUNISHMENT IN CHILD REARING

	N = 34	Per cent
Number reporting they use food as a reward	21	62
Number reporting they do not reward with food	13	38
	N = 31	Per cent
Number reporting they punish by depriving of food	5	16
Number reporting they do not punish by food deprivation	26	84

ject to similar definition of use in terms of cultural edicts and associated emotional response.

The earlier book discusses the importance of the notion of powers residing in deities, objects, and substances and the use of magic as a means for directing these natural forces to serve the intent of men. We feel there is evidence enough to argue for the belief that alcohol contains power which may be magically controlled, or that in itself it is a means by which other powers may be propitiated or warded off. We see this belief reflected in the use of wine in the Mass, in the employment of alcohol internally and externally in healing efforts, and in its use at Christmas time when it is poured on the hearth along with olive oil as an offering (Megas, 1958)—in ancient times the offering was to Hestia, goddess of the hearth. We see it in the Cretan Christmas custom according to which the priest offers a bottle of wine to strangers on Christmas day (in the belief that the dead return at Christmas and may appear in the form of strangers). We see it in Chios (Argenti and Rose, 1949) in the notion that the "wine sack" or drunkard becomes a *vrikolax* or revenant when he dies. We see it in the belief that red wine is good for the blood. In *Health and Healing in Rural Greece,* we have shown that a relationship of sympathetic magic exists between blood and wine.

While there is no evidence that the ordinary use of wine is circumscribed by taboo, its sympathetic association with blood in folk tales, its usage as a symbolic equivalent of blood, its usage at sacrifice, and its connection with becoming a revenant suggest that the rural folk are not unmindful of its potential magical dangers and applications. Given the belief that alcohol, especially wine, has magical properties, it follows that it is a substance which must be handled with more than usual caution. The wise man does not play with magical forces beyond his control; his approach to any substance which has power in itself is likely to be respectful.

While there is an empirical basis to the belief that wine may have both beneficial and deleterious effects on health, this double-edged conception is held regarding many powers within and outside of man which must be subject to magical, ritual control. Among the foods for example, beans are likewise believed by some to be both healing and dangerous. While the Pythagorean strictures against beans are well known, their association in earlier times with the cult of the dead is suggested by recent excavations conducted by Dakaris (*Archaeology*, 1962) at the Homeric nekromanteion near Ephyra. There was evidence at Ephyra of libation also ritually employed, quite possibly of wine.

Unquestionably, magical thinking plays a strong role in Greek rural life. One of the paramount features of forces magically manipulated is their capacity to work for the good or for the bad. Wine would seem to be one of these forces, and insofar as it is perceived as such, its use is subject to extraordinary caution. These same cautions may be inferred from institutionalized or ritual practices which are derived from antiquity. We surmise that man's early use and experience with alcohol was subject to considerably more magical practice than at present, but even in Homeric and classical times, it is possible to demonstrate that its use was highly formalized in association with its presumed efficacy as a means for propitiation of the supernatural, as well as in association with a belief about its "sympathy" with the blood—a belief, in turn, presumably related to the desire on the part of the dead to taste of it. These historical practices have led to institutional practices still extant, as seen in the Mass and possibly in the practice of adding resin to the wine.[10] Institutions define conduct and attitudes

[10] Adding resin to the wine—in the form of pitch—as is still the prac-

long after salient beliefs have passed; in their stead myths and rationalizations appear. The use of wine is still a part of institutional practice, a part of ritual, and these usages operate effectively both to define use and to engender attitudes commending restraint in drinking.

It is also true that some ancient practices emphasized the ecstatic use of wine, as in the Dionysian rites. Evidence of ecstatic use is not found in our communities, but Megas (1958) reports that in Thrace, where the worship of Dionysos was strong, the festivities on the first day of the vintage took place, until recently, "with such *frenzy* that a casual observer might have thought himself among the ancient Greeks worshipping Bacchus." It is also likely that the brotherhood of the Anastenarides in Thrace contains elements of Dionysian ritual. These practices, even though leading to ecstasy, are structured in a complex institutional framework which does not allow for any remarkable individual deviation. Both in restraint and in abandon we may deduce ritual operations designed to manipulate a natural power.

One informant described drinking practices in Doxario by saying, "They intersperse moderation with occasional orgies." We believe this to be a fair description; Greek life styles do present an oscillating rhythm which is expressed in drinking as in other conduct. Moderation is an ideal. Wherever moderation is emphasized among rural Greeks, one detects their awareness of their own potential for the extreme. The goal may be to live with one another in neighborly tranquility, but when asked what happens when people drink heavily, they describe the quarreling, the knife fights, and the brutality which follow. Moderation is more than a value—it is a plea, a direction toward which to turn for balance after the frenetic drama.

We believe that the villager wants to guide his drinking conduct according to the value of moderation. (Moderation, after all, is relative to practices and potentials in the Greek culture. When someone who has just consumed 2 *okas* of water says it is a moderate amount, he has in mind someone else who has just consumed 4 *okas*.) If the villager is not challenged by a situation or a threat that forces him to realize his extreme potential, his behavior will be consistent. Nevertheless, there are certain features of life which serve to trigger the Dio-

tice nowadays, did not stem from such practical considerations as waterproofing the jars, preserving the wine, or improving the taste, as has been suggested. Rather, it is our contention that the pitch was to keep the spirits of the dead from drinking the wine.

nysian mode: competitive strife, the warrior code, the occurrence of festivals where revelry and orgy are sanctioned, the postulated tenuousness of boundaries of the self which reduces control in the absence of others, a certain readiness to disregard the morrow in favor of the flaming moment, and, finally, a capacity to experience emotion without restraint—an openness to the full flow of feelings and a willingness to immerse oneself within that affective stream. This last characteristic we postulate as reflecting both a value in and a consequence of a culture which emphasizes propriety rather than sin and which directs emotional expression rather than suppresses it.

Alcohol may be employed as a means to achieve an altered state of consciousness—the latter conceived of as an end in itself. Dulling of monotony, a warm glow, forgetfulness, the freedom for ecstasy: these are illustrations. We may ask to what extent alcohol is employed in this fashion in rural Greece. It is subsumed under our broader inquiry into the use of intoxicants, hallucinogens, and stimulants.

Historically, there are legends about the sacred use of drugs to achieve altered states of consciousness. Best known is the Pythia at the oracle at Delphi, whose prophetic powers were associated with an ecstatic state supposedly induced either by vapors emitted from the earth or by chewing laurel leaves. While drugs may or may not have been employed at Delphi, some evidence indicates that opium was employed in Minoan-Mycenean times; there is no question about wine's being employed in Dionysian rituals to achieve an ecstatic state, as illustrated in the *Bacchae* by Euripides. Whether other drugs—for example, mushrooms among the hallucinogens—have been known in Greece remains an open question.

As we have previously indicated, alcohol is used primarily within a social context associated with food ingestion and with the facilitation of interpersonal activities. In the communities studied, it is not used now in sacred ways to achieve individual mystical experiences within a religious framework, although we have indicated that the rites of the Anastenarides in Thrace have such components (however, there is no evidence that alcohol is essential to the latter's ritual). An exception to prevalent interpersonal emphasis in alcohol use has been cited in reference to *kefia,* as when an individual states that he intends to drink in order to achieve a state of being "high." *Kefia* is usually said to enhance a pre-existing good mood rather than to reverse a mood or introduce a new state. Nevertheless, it is purposeful drinking in which a particular mental state is sought (we suspect only in conjunction with the usual sociability of the drinkers).

Perhaps closer to the conception of an altered state is that found in the expression *ta kopano,* meaning "to pound" or "to powder," as with a pestle in a mortar—in other words, "to get drunk." When an individual states his intention in this way, he indicates a desire to become "plastered" in the American sense. It represents the use of alcohol as a means of achieving a private state of altered consciousness. We must assume these intentions, so stated, are rare in the village. During our study we neither heard the expression in reference to any individual's stated purpose in drinking nor did we see any drinking behavior which appeared to reflect this intention. It would have been desirable, had we had the opportunity, to have learned the conditions under which one is likely to want "to pound" and to have seen what determines the response of others to the statement of intent and to its execution; and it would have been desirable to differentiate between those who drink to drink—that is, are addicted—and those who drink to attain an altered state—that is, use drinking to attain private goals.

We did not observe the use of any other drugs capable of producing altered states, nor were we in a position to extend our inquiries. While the use of hashish was denied, its use by foreigners, along with opium, was known to a number of our villagers. Whether the source of their knowledge came from information from the outside world or was derived from historical experience with Turks or others is not known. The use of the phrase "to powder" or "to pound" as an idiom for "getting drunk" is suggestive of drugs other than alcohol, and one wonders what the antecedents for this phraseology may be.[11]

On the basis of our present limited evidence, we must conclude that alcohol was not employed in our communities, except perhaps by deviant individuals, to achieve altered states of consciousness. Such states were not ordinarily sought by any means, whether by drugs or other devices (as, for example, through fasting or asceticism). When villagers were invited to discuss these individualistic forms of conduct, they were hard put to understand what we meant; when they did understand, they rejected such conduct as either improper or dangerous. The suggestion most often made was that only Athenians, not villagers, would seek out such experiences; rather than considering the mo-

---

[11] Another expression is suggestive: *pino ta skonakia mou*—"I drink my little powders"—to indicate a readiness to get high.

tives involved to be religious or mystical—as historical antecedents in Greece suggest—the villagers most often regarded idiosyncratic use of drugs as the result of personal stress, such as worry, poverty, or unrequited love. Possession by demons was also suggested as a reason. Only one villager among the few who undertood and discussed the issues considered that one might seek an altered state for pleasures residing in the state itself.

DISCUSSION

We have seen that drinking is an important activity in Greek life—one associated with four activities essential to that life: religious rituals, food ingestion, healing, and gregariousness. Its employment in these contexts is related to magical and nutritional efficacy and to its ability to enhance pleasurable social activities. We have seen that most, if not all, rural Greeks take wine. In terms of importance, wine is the primary alcoholic beverage. Its uses are well defined by setting and occasion and even heavy drinking occurs on those festive occasions where it is considered an integral part of community fun making. In spite of the considerable uniformity and acceptability of drinking practices, there are a few deviants. By local standards, only one or two individuals in Dhadhi and in Panorio drank too much, at the time of our visit. Both the individuals involved and their neighbors agreed on this characterization. While in one case the drinking was so excessive that it led to loss of respect, there was no instance in any of the three communities that we studied of an inability to work or to maintain ties with family and neighbors. On the other hand, in Doxario, a commercial town, there was evidence of more extreme behavior. By Western standards two persons were chronic alcoholics; two others, who have died since our visit, were characterized by their physician in a comparable way.

The medical conception of chronic alcoholism is foreign to the rural vocabulary. The villagers treat their alcoholics as unacceptable deviants and rush to scorn rather than to protect or rehabilitate. That "bloated winesacks with dogs' ears" exist is granted; that they might constitute, however, a social or medical problem in the American sense is unheard of. The winesack is a problem only to his family and to himself. The family carries the burden just as they would carry the burden of an idiot, a tubercular, a cripple, or a coward. The taint on reputation and the indication of hereditary weakness—both of which include all of the household—are the same. Because the unacceptable deviant is a family problem, we can understand the failure of the Greek to conceive of alcoholism as a social concern. Social concerns are limited to those rare matters which affect everyone in the village, and these are necessarily problems arising from natural disaster, political oppression, or other broad, immediately practical problems of survival.

We should not be surprised that the Greek does not share our Western definition of chronic alcoholism as a medical problem. In the first place, the newer Western conceptions of disease filter but slowly to the rural population, having to compete, as they do, with strongly held folk conceptions. In the second place, with the Greek emphasis on the concrete and the individual, there is little tendency to abstract from the case of the town winesack to the more general and less relevant class of chronic alcoholics or to the even less personal notion of alcoholic diseases.

We believe that conceptions are in part generated by the values, difficulties, and facilities of a given society. At the present time, Greece lacks the medical and social-welfare personnel who might, with their Western training, serve to identify individuals as alcoholics. Furthermore, such identification would be pointless until such time as facilities, trained personnel, and funds are available to handle identified cases, by some professional rather than traditional means. The pressures to assign responsibility for care of certain individuals will arise only when (1) it can be demonstrated that professional care can offer a more satisfactory solution—in terms of current cultural values—than traditional means or when (2) traditional means for the handling of the deviant or the disabled become strained. We posit that traditional means will become strained only when the society undergoes changes which reduce the resources of traditional institutions, or when change alters the values in regard to how the disabled should be treated, or when, without change in social institutions or values, natural or conceivably political events produce an increased number of disabled who by their number strain the resources of traditional institutions. We should note that a society defines as problems those social strains and personal pains which are most keenly felt in that society. Where strains and pains are many and resources few, a priority system in the defining of problems emerges. Those conditions which pose the greatest threat to community survival, community values, or the felt well-being of individuals will necessarily be most salient. Only as the resources of the society increase so that the more profound threats are discharged can we anticipate that the attention, even of individuals and families concerned, will be focused on the lesser distresses.

In considering the role of the disapproved heavy drinker in our Greek rural communities, we see no evidence of strain on any community institution or threat to any cherished value. Mild distress is reported by family members, mostly the women, and a certain uncomfortable awareness of being the subjects of opprobrium is reported by several of the drinkers themselves. Since these pose no problems for the community and since no other family or community institutions are strained, one would hardly expect any definition of a community difficulty to emerge. Furthermore, since the families themselves—at least in Dhadhi and Panorio—are maintaining themselves reasonably well within their own framework of expectation and relative to their economic and social positions as compared with those of their neighbors, the families themselves are not likely to define the heavy drinker as a high priority problem. Nor have they done so. The scope of our study did not allow us to investigate the reactions of the families in Doxario to their much-more-severe cases of what we call chronic alcoholism. Assuming now that one of these families did define its winesack father as a major source of distress and public humiliation, members were nevertheless expected to handle their problem head-of-household just as other families in the village handled their individual burdens of sorrow, pain, and shame. Given no alternative routes in Doxario for the handling of these cases, given approval for traditional conduct, given the absence of any community—as opposed to family—strain, threat, or shared concern, and given the absence, in fact, of any medical or social facility in the village or, indeed, in the whole of Greece[12] for alternate (professional) handling of the winesack, it is difficult to imagine that other than traditional responses and attitudes would operate.

Our findings support the observations of other social scientists who contend that in those cultures where drinking is integrated into religious rites (Glad, 1947; Skolnick, 1958; Snyder, 1955) and social customs (Field, 1962; Lolli, Serianni, Banissoni, Golder, Mariani, McCarthy, and Toner, 1952; Lolli, Serianni, Golder, Balboni, and Mariani, 1953; Mangin, 1957), where the place and manner of consumption are regulated by tradition (Netting, 1964; Platt, 1955; Ullman,

[12] One of the exceptions is the privately financed Alcoholic Movement in Greece, directed by Dr. Zoi Gaitanos. Dr. Thomas Katzakos is the president.

1958) and where, moreover, self-control, sociability, and "knowing how to hold one's liquor" (Lemert, 1958) are matters of manly pride (Madsen, in press), alcoholism problems are at a minimum, provided no other variables are overriding. On the other hand, in those cultures where alcohol has been but recently introduced and has not become a part of pre-existing institutions, where no prescribed patterns of behavior exist when "under the influence," where alcohol has been used by a dominant group the better to exploit a subject group (Bunzel, 1940), and where controls are new, legal, and prohibitionist, superseding traditional social regulation of an activity which previously has been accepted practice (El Mahi, 1962a, b), one finds deviant, unacceptable and asocial behavior, as well as chronic disabling alcoholism. In cultures where ambivalent attitudes toward drinking prevail (Simmons, 1962; Ullman, 1958), the incidence of alcoholism is also high. Heavy, but nevertheless regulated, drinking occurs generally where alcohol is associated with the warrior ethos (Carstairs, 1954). When this ethos, however, is superseded under the stress of acculturation by an invading, dominant group (as has occurred among the American Indians) or when the religious and traditional meaning of drinking has been lost under such an impact, drinking problems will be one of the consequences (Devreux, 1940; Washburne, 1961).

CONCLUSION

We introduced this chapter with the suggestion that our rural Achilles would be temperate. For the most part he is—as temperate as Achilles of yore; when he is less temperate, he joins his neighbors in an approved and usually very enjoyable orgy. Insofar as the villager has this evidence before him, he rightly says that no problem with alcoholism exists in Greece. Should our villager, by virtue of some sophisticated Western concern, turn his attention to the individual winesack, he may well state that a few of his neighbors drink too much and that one or two are disreputable "half-men"; but he will fit his judgments to the available scheme of things and since that scheme includes no culturally available definition of winesacks as chronic alcoholics or impersonal cases of disease, he will again conclude that Greece has no alcohol problem. And, finally, valuing wine as one of the most important elements in his life, as well as valuing himself and the honor of his country as blameless, he will be appalled at any suggestion that his nation could be afflicted with a disease—when it is so clear to him that it is, to the contrary, much blest by the grape.

A World View
of Drugs

Joel Fort

X

*I*n providing an international view of the complex of mind-altering drugs and their abuse, it is important to avoid the ethnocentrism, emotionalism, semantic confusion, and propaganda that can easily dominate such discussions. For example, one man's beverage is another man's drug, one country's drug is another country's medication, and one agency's subsidized crop is another bureau's focus for criminal law enforcement. Further confusion can arise when the word "use" (one-time, occasional, frequent, or daily) of a drug is confused with "abuse," "dependency," or "addiction." Even one-time use of a disapproved or legally prohibited drug is frequently equated by society with addiction, criminality, sexual deviation, and insanity, whereas even regular and excessive use of a drug (such as alcohol in most societies) that is permitted and encouraged by the scientific and political Establishment is equated with ordinary use. Unfortunately, subtleties such as the dose, purity, and mode of administration of a drug, as well as the elapsed time since taking it and the concurrent use of other drugs, are conveniently glossed over in the usual discussions of this subject.

Because we are not dealing here with all biologically active drugs or substances but only with those having direct effects on consciousness (the "mind"), it is necessary to make explicit that there are no uniform, consistent effects, and, thus, none of the mind-altering (psychoactive) drugs is inherently harmless, vicious, or magical in its properties. What we often attribute solely to the drug's physical or physiological properties and loosely refer to as the drug effect is a complex interaction among these varied factors: its pharmacological properties; the personality, character structure, expectations, and attitudes of the individual taking the drug; and the sociocultural setting or context, including not only the broader social values but the subcultural ones, as well as the immediate environment. Only with this conceptual background can there be a meaningful discussion of drug "abuse," whether national or international.

Certain general principles must be enunciated for assessing or evaluating drug abuse in a given country or region. What is "abuse"? When is a "problem" really a problem as opposed to being a statutory crime, a smokescreen, or a scapegoat? In general, I would define drug "abuse" or "misuse" as (regular, excessive) use of a drug to the extent that it is damaging to a person's social or vocational adjustment, or to his health, or is otherwise specifically detrimental to society. This seems a more meaningful and precise concept than the World Health Organization's term drug "dependency," which deals with the presumed medical and psychological effects of repeated administration of officially disapproved drugs and attempts to incorporate the old terms "habituation" (psychological dependency) and "addiction" (physical dependency). Distorting and dominating the scientific concept of drug abuse is the reality that in all countries any use or possession of some drugs is a criminal offense, thus making by statute any detected use an "abuse."

Obviously, if one hopes for more than the usual anecdotal or self-serving statements of government agencies or diplomats, as many independent and separate criteria as possible need to be used in estimating the extent and pattern of drug abuse in various countries. Even in a society where the use of a particular drug is fully sanctioned, one cannot measure drug abuse with the same accuracy achieved in a census of population—and, indeed, in many of the underdeveloped nations, even the latter is not adequately done. Add to this the notorious unreliability of crime statistics, of "addict" statistics, and generalizations from the minority who show pathology ("sick" or "criminal") and come to public attention, and we see a few of the major defects. Thus, this assessment can only attempt to approach the ideal. In outlining what this ideal might be, we perhaps are performing an equally important task. The background of this assessment includes the historical drugs, the current religious beliefs and practices, social and legal policies, and the degree and consistency with which they are implemented, along with subcultural (youth, caste minorities, and so on) attitudes, medical and quasi-medical uses, and other local or regional factors.

Specific determinations to be imbedded within this matrix should include the following:

(1.) The amount of production and distribution for "legitimate" drugs such as alcohol (except in most Moslem countries), sedatives, and stimulants (except cocaine), local manufacturers' annual production figures, prescription or over-the-counter sales, detected illicit traffic or production, advertising and marketing studies, and number of retail outlets and their sales; for "illegal" drugs such as cannabis, opium, and LSD, the estimated areas of cultivation, police seizures (generally thought to represent at best 10 per cent of the amount being smuggled), consumption, both gross and per capita for those over sixteen, and indigenous medical use. The world seizure figures for opiates is only 40 tons per year and for cannabis the figures (often listed in ounces to seem more impressive) are even less impressive. (2.) Surveys of users (and sometimes abusers)—drinking practices, drug use, college drug use, and similar studies. (3.) Estimates of use and abuse patterns made by users, distributors, police, government officials, public-health specialists, journalists, in-group members, and so forth. (4.) Clinic, hospital, and other medical records of intoxication, toxic reactions, addiction, suicide attempts, "bad trips," deaths, and other drug-associated reasons (direct and indirect) for professional attention, treatment, or rehabilitation. (5.) Arrest, jail, prison, and similar records involving drugs, both directly and indirectly. (6.) Draft, military, social security, license, census, and related types of data. (7.) Miscellaneous sources of information such as anthropological reports, intelligence information, botanical studies, accident and absenteeism figures, and social agency records.

In relating the above concepts, facts, and mind-altering drug groups to the world, we are—to leave the abstract—talking about some three and a half billion people of many highly diverse religions, races, languages, cultures, climates, and geographies. A majority of this world is immersed in a vicious cycle of disease, poverty, illiteracy, totalitarianism, and war, all of which may be conducive to drug use and all of which properly leads to drug abuse's receiving less attention and sensationalism than in the affluent or overdeveloped countries.

The most widely used and abused drug (excluding caffeine and nicotine) is alcohol. Cannabis is only a distant second in terms of use. Between a third and a half of the world's population probably use alcohol and probably in steadily increasing numbers and amounts, ranging up to 90 per cent of adults in some countries and including significant numbers of children in others. This pre-eminence of alcohol derives from its ancient history, cultural traditions, simple manufacture, enormous availability in a wide variety of forms and dosages with relative purity, generally low cost, and massive advertising equating its use with all forms of happiness. The overall number of cannabis users is much more difficult to estimate (although its history is probably as long) because of its official illegality and more restricted distribution, but it must be in the hundreds of millions, including indigenous medical use. In the Western world, nonmedical users of narcotics are in the millions; sedative, stimulant, and tranquilizer users in the tens of millions; cocaine users in the millions; and LSD-type drug users in the millions. How many of these are abusers in the scientific sense or even in the legal sense is much more difficult to estimate even crudely, but we will at least make the attempt, region by region, in order of population.

ASIA

In this land area of some seven million square miles with approximately two billion people, the major psychoactive drugs used are alcohol, cannabis, opium, and heroin. There is also considerable use of other indigenous substances, as well as of manufactured sedative and stimulant drugs. With the exception of Japan, the entire region is underdeveloped socioeconomically, so, not unexpectedly, the typical users of what the laws refer to as "narcotics" come from the lower class, are male, and range in age from twenty to fifty. Because the laws and governmental practice reflect American values imposed either directly or through the United Nations, all users of "narcotics" are referred to and handled as addicts, although many—and in some countries most—are occasional or intermittent users, or use such substances as cannabis which are not addicting (productive of physical dependency). In many of the countries and with many of the users in most of the countries, drug use is traditional and even in the recent past was culturally sanctioned, although present laws prohibit use, except for alcohol.

Although individual or social causes and effects of drug use or abuse are difficult to determine—and sometimes difficult to separate— certain major trends are apparent. The countries where drug abuse is considered a major problem include Hong Kong, Iran, Thailand, Japan, Singapore, and South Korea with narcotics; Ceylon, Japan, and India with alcohol. In India and Pakistan there is widespread use of opium and cannabis in oral forms, frequently through licensed shops as "quasi-medical" use or as a common ingredient of indigenous medical prescriptions for a variety of disorders. Most countries of the region fail to recognize the widespread and growing use and abuse of both manufactured and home-made alcoholic beverages; and several officially deny their obvious involvement in the production and distribution of opium and heroin.

There is increasing use of heroin in Asia. As compared with the users of the traditional opium, those who use heroin do so more frequently and are, more often than in the past, addicted; and most use is by the young adult (eighteen to thirty) compared with the older-age groups with whom opium was popular.

The abruptly imposed bans (after World War II) on the traditionally accepted use of opium has been a direct cause of more people's using more dangerous drugs in greater amounts, as well as of the development of a flourishing illicit traffic with extensive corruption and criminality. Placing, or misplacing, the major emphasis on police apprehension and punishment of the user has failed in Asia as it has in America, both now and in the 1920's. There is an almost total lack of attention to the underlying socioeconomic and psychological bases of drug use; no adequate programs of rehabilitation are in operation; and data-gathering procedures are nonexistent or primitive.

With its 700 million people, China has a history of opium use dating back to the ninth century A.D., which was later actively fostered by England, France, the United States, and Japan between the eighteenth and twentieth centuries. In the 1920's, it was estimated that 25 per cent of the adult population used opium with general public support or acceptance of its use. In the mid-1930's, some ten million were said to be opium users, and, since then, not even crude figures are available except for Hong Kong. The internal and external wars, the succession of totalitarian regimes (also a factor in the rest of Asia), and the breaking off of cultural and diplomatic contacts by the United States has made it impossible to make an adequate assessment of the current situation. The reports of the few Western scientists (none of them drug experts), journalists, refugees, and agencies in Hong Kong and other adjacent areas indicate that there has been a major decrease in opium use in China and that alcoholism is a minimal problem. Reduced cultivation, governmental and peer-group (commune) pressures, and full employment are some of the factors apparently responsible for the decline. Contrary to the propaganda periodically disseminated by the American Federal Bureau of Narcotics, the unanimous view of government officials, both local and American, in neighboring countries is that the People's Republic of China is not actively involved in the narcotics traffic. Most Asian opium is grown in a contiguous four-country area: Thailand, Burma, Laos, and the Yunnan Province of China. Their total production is estimated at 1,000 tons per year. The farmers growing it are isolated mountain tribesmen for whom the opium poppy is the sole or major cash crop. The opium or the refined morphine or heroin funnels through Thailand supervised and guarded by several thousand Chinese Nationalist (Republic of China) troops, who are reported to have received financial assistance from the American Central Intelligence Agency. Thus, complex local and international socioeconomic roots of drug abuse flourish while entire societies are diverted to the "menace of the addict." Alcoholism, however, is believed to be uncommon in China because of the traditional mores which frown upon excessive drinking, public drunkenness, or drinking apart from meals.

Cannabis use, as a medicament for several diseases and as a euphorient, has been known in China since 2730 B.C. and referred to (with much the same polarities of thought as exist today) as either "liberator of sin" or "giver of delight." Again, little is known of contemporary use patterns, although it does not seem to be considered a problem even in Sinkiang Province, where past use has been best documented.

The British Colony of Hong Kong with a population of about four million (99 per cent Chinese) has an estimated 300,000 illicit narcotic users—mostly heroin addicts who often mix it with barbiturates. The nearby Portuguese Colony of Macao has an estimated 6,000 users, mostly opium; and Taiwan (Republic of China) is said to have 40,000 users, mainly of heroin and morphine.

India and Pakistan, with a joint population of some 600 million people, have a history of opium use dating back to the ninth century A.D. It was consumed by eating, drinking, or smoking by all social classes and both sexes, children as well as adults. Around the fourteenth century, it was introduced into the Hindu Ayurvedic and Moslem Unani systems of medicine. An 1893 Royal Commission report stated that its use was moderate with no evidence of harmful physical or moral effects; that its use was due to the universal tendency of mankind to take some form of drug to comfort or distract themselves; that it would be impractical and unenforceable to prohibit use or limit it to medical purposes because of the ceremonial and social uses to which it was put and its general public acceptance; and that an increased consumption of alcohol would follow if opium were prohibited. India now legally produces about two thirds of the world's needs for medical opium.

Cannabis use has been known in India since 800 B.C. in the forms of bhang, ganja, and charas in beverage, confection, or pipe-smoking form. Since the seventh century, it has been used in Ayurvedic medicine and since the early nineteenth century in "Western" medicine for a range of complaints that include pain, insomnia, depression and other mental illness, and dysmenorrhea. The most detailed study that has yet been made of cannabis was the 1893 Report of the Indian Hemp Commission, which found no evidence of mental or moral injury or disease arising from moderate use and stated that such use produced the same effects as a moderate intake of whiskey. In contemporary India and Pakistan, there continues to be widespread indigenous medical, "quasi-medical," and illicit use of both opium and cannabis, probably more than a million users of each although the government estimate is around 200,000 each

Carstairs' (1954) study of daru (alcohol) and bhang (cannabis) use in an Indian village shows the strong partisan attitudes in two castes in favor of their intoxicant (and against the other drug). The psychological effects and associations and the different values and attitudes of the two groups are all shown to be involved in explaining the cleavage in choice.

The production and use of alcohol has a less precise but certainly a multicentury history that includes religious, dietary, medical, and entertainment uses. "Soma" was believed to have been one of the earliest fermented beverages. There are many millions of licit and illicit (since the Indian constitution properly considers alcohol in the same category as other undesirable drugs and several states [unsuccessfully] completely or partially prohibit its sale or use) consumers of alcohol. Despite religious—and sometimes legal—prohibition, alcohol is widely consumed in Pakistan. Considerable nonmedical use of barbiturates, chloral hydrate, and cocaine (500,000 users estimated in the 1930's) has also been reported.

Opium use in Iran dates back to 850 B.C., and by 1955 when it was prohibited, nearly 200 million people were estimated to be using it (mostly by smoking) for pleasure and treatment of various illnesses. There are now thought to be 500,000 opium users and 30,000 heroin users. Cannabis use appears to be minimal but alcohol is widespread despite the Moslem religious prohibition.

Thailand had a 200-year history of opium use prior to its banning in 1959. At present it has some 50,000 illicit narcotic users—mostly Thai but also Chinese and hill-tribes people—mostly of heroin in the cities (sometimes mixed with barbiturates) by inhalation. Cannabis, although illegal, is widely used without any apparent problems. Some amphetamine abuse and considerable alcoholism and drunk driving have become recognized in recent years. A plant (*Mitragyna speciosa*) known as "kratom" is also used but the exact pharmacological nature of its psychoactive effects is not yet known.

Japan has about 50,000 illegal narcotic users, mostly heroin (by injection) and 90 per cent Japanese (ten to fifteen years ago, 50 per cent were Korean and Chinese). Unlike the situation in the other Asian countries, this use seemed to be a new practice after the Second World War and, after widespread abuse of amphetamines, developed and receded. Barbiturate abuse is recognized as well as continued abuse of amphetamines and of a locally manufactured drug, Spa, which has mixed pharmacological effects. Alcoholism and drunk driving are major problems and are receiving increasing attention.

Opium was available in Ceylon through special shops until 1948 and there are now about 5,000 users, mostly Indian and Chinese. Cannabis use has a long history with about 200,000 users at present. Indigenous medical use includes use for relief of fatigue, improvement of appetite, aphrodisia, and treatment of insomnia. It is also sold as a powder which is smoked in a cigarette. As in India, alcohol use is taken seriously and, in fact, the most detailed alcohol statistics in Asia are kept in Ceylon. They show that alcohol is the most commonly used and abused mind-altering drug in the form of toddy (fermented palm-tree sap), arrack (distilled toddy), and "kasippu" (illegal arrack).

Burma has an estimated 100,000 narcotic users, mostly opium smokers in the Shan and Kachin states but also Chinese and Burmese in the cities. Cannabis is extensively used in the form of ganja, mainly by Indians but also by the Burmese. Beinsa (*Mitragyna speciosa*) leaves are chewed or used to make a syrup or powder which is eaten, smoked, or made into a "tea." Alcohol use is widespread and increasing.

Other Asian countries with recognized significant nonmedical use of narcotics (usually opium) include Singapore, Malaysia, Korea (heroin by injection), Laos, North and South Vietnam, and the Philippines. Indonesia, particularly in Sumatra, has extensive use of cannabis, and there are beginning problems with barbiturate, meprobamate, and amphetamine use and abuse. In Nepal there are also considerable use and production (some for export) of cannabis.

There is a theory of ethnic specificity which claims that Asians use opiates to satisfy their need for contemplation and passivity, that Africans use cannabis because of a need for fantasy and group experience, and that North Americans and Europeans use alcohol as a euphoriant because of their need for aggression, action, and extraversion.

Moving to the geographically ambiguous area of the Middle East, we find little factual information available despite the considerable involvement of several countries in the narcotics trade. Turkey is a major producer of illicit opium (as well as some for legal medical purposes) which is transported (raw or converted) through Syria to Lebanon, where underworld (Mafia) connections arrange its trans-shipment to Italy and France, on to the United States. Some use occurs in these countries but more widespread is the use of cannabis (usually in the concentrated form of hashish) and alcohol despite Moslem religious prohibitions and sometimes severe criminal penalties. In Saudi Arabia, Kuwait, and Yemen there is very extensive use of khat leaves, mostly grown in Ethiopia and containing an amphetamine-type stimulant. Concern has been expressed about the diversion of income and energy involved in this use.

AFRICA

In Africa there is much less diversity in terms of the pattern of drug use than in Asia. Again, the vast majority of the populations (except for the white South Africans) are in the low socioeconomic class, poor and uneducated. Both cannabis and alcohol are used widely in East, West, North, and South Africa under many different names, such as "kif" (Morocco) and "dagga" (South Africa) for cannabis. Several studies, some fairly extensive, have been published about various aspects of cannabis use in South Africa, Nigeria, Morocco, and Egypt. In general, they are designed to support the existing official government policy of prohibition of cannabis and are therefore highly selective and unscientific in their data and conclusions. To discuss two of the concepts used to indict cannabis (or other drugs officially disapproved by the establishments), its association with crime and with insanity, we see it in a context excluding alcohol, without control groups, without differentiation of substances (concentrated hashish or crude cannabis), and with a confusion of cause and effect. By labeling as "criminal" the use of a drug and arresting many of those who continue to use it, large and superficially impressive statistics can be compiled of "criminality" associated with the drug, but this is, of course, an entirely circular and statutory definition. Further, if most people are using the drug, it would follow that a large number of people arrested for actual crimes (against property or persons) would be users and their crime could be ascribed by the officials to the drug, particularly when those arrested are routinely asked (or it is suggested to them) whether they use cannabis. The second common association is with "insanity," so that any residents of the badly overcrowded and understaffed mental hospitals who give a history of cannabis use have their illness ascribed to this cause, even though in most, and perhaps all, instances they are schizophrenic or have an organic psychosis not causally related to the drug. Where actual problems exist, they appear to be caused by the sociolegal policies or by the underdeveloped socioeconomic conditions of the country. Alcohol consumption and production, legal and illegal, are heavy and growing throughout Africa, particularly in the large cities; it is associated with detribalization, loosening of family ties, industrialization, unemployment, and slums. There is a beginning awareness and documentation of abuses such as alcoholism, crime, drunk driving, job loss, liver damage, and so on. Only with the white South African has there been a special program established for alcoholism.

AUSTRALIA AND OCEANIA

In Australia and New Zealand, there is widespread consumption and advertising of alcohol with considerable tax revenue to the state (as is also true with nicotine [cigarettes] and is the case in the other geographical areas although less in the underdeveloped nations). Alcoholism is well recognized as a problem affecting directly about 3 per cent of the population and causing much personal and financial loss to families, agencies, and businesses. Drunk driving is also receiving attention. Small narcotic, sedative, and stimulant "problems" are said to exist in several large cities. Several Pacific island peoples use such mind-altering substances as kava (*Piper methysticum*) without apparent problems or abuse.

SOUTH AND CENTRAL AMERICA AND CARIBBEAN

Diverse patterns of drug use occur in this (primarily) Spanish-speaking area of the world. In the combined areas of Bolivia, Peru, Colombia, and Argentina, some five million people use cocaine, predominantly poor Indians living at high Andean altitudes who have a long cultural tradition of use to relieve hunger, fatigue, and cold. The coca leaf is widely available for local use and its value as a cash crop extends to its purchase by the Coca Cola Company as a flavoring agent. Some consider the Indian use as abuse and it seems likely that it impairs individual and social development; however, it is probably secondary to the poor socioeconomic conditions and the failure of those in authority to bring about basic social reforms.

Cannabis use is widespread in Brazil ("maconha"), the West Indian islands, and Mexico (marijuana) with some considering it a problem or abuse; adequate scientific evidence is lacking to say more than it possibly involves excessive diversion of income and certainly results in interference with the lives of those imprisoned for its use. Mexico is the major producer of the tons of illicit marijuana and opium (heroin) which are exported to California and involve collusion and corruption on the part of local farmers (economically dependent on it), police, and other government officials.

A variety of other substances, including "piptadenias," snuffs such as "vilca" and "epena," "ayahuasca," "caapi," "yagé," psilocybin (*Psilocybe-mexicana*), and peyote are used for mind-alteration by large groups in various parts of this geographical area.

In most of the major cities there is some degree of abuse of sedatives and stimulants.

Alcohol use is extremely widespread in a great variety of local forms derived from indigenous plants and grains. Alcoholism and, to a lesser degree, drunk driving are increasingly recognized as problems, although—as would be expected—conceptualized and handled in a very different manner from "drugs." Chile has been the most active in talking about alcoholism and has an estimated 2 to 3 per cent of its people with this problem ("illness"). Two villages studied by Bunzel (1940) showed quite different ways of using alcohol. One where there was little aggression or discipline had heavy drinking from childhood but without guilt; the other where there was repression of sexual and aggressive impulses showed occasional drinking binges followed by severe guilt.

EUROPE

By far, alcoholism is the most serious problem of drug abuse in Europe and the most extensively used drug is alcohol. This is true in the East and West, in communist, socialist, and capitalist countries, and in North and South Europe. France has the biggest problem with some 10 per cent of its population alcoholic, and drunk driving as an important problem. Several liters of wine daily compose the average adult consumption; drinking is throughout the day; much drinking is by children; and there is the belief that wine is associated with virility. A fourth to a third of the economy is dependent, in fact, on the alcoholic-beverage industry. Russia, Switzerland, Finland, Norway, Denmark, Sweden, the Netherlands, and West Germany are the other countries with well-recognized alcohol-abuse problems, both alcoholism and drunk driving. It is probable that the other countries also have significant and growing problems despite official blindness or reluctance to accept the facts. In both communist and capitalist countries, large revenues accrue to their governments from the sale of alcohol (and cigarettes).

Considerable use and abuse of a wide variety of manufactured drugs, sedatives, stimulants, and tranquilizers are known to occur in most of the large cities in Western Europe, particularly barbiturates, amphetamines, and phenmetrazine (Preludin)—particularly among young people. Marijuana use is not infrequent, following this same pattern, and is most noted in Denmark, Sweden, and England (associated with West Indian and African immigrants). The intellectual, artistic, nonconformist, and alienated groups of these relatively affluent societies seem to seek out these drugs, and more recently are beginning to use LSD-25, especially in West Germany and England. Heroin or other narcotic use is relatively infrequent, as is cocaine, but both have received much attention in the mass media in England, where drastic attempts are being made to modify the traditional medical approach to this problem.

NORTH AMERICA

The alcohol pattern here is quite similar to that of Europe, with both Canada and the United States (six million alcoholics) having 3 per cent alcoholic populations and major drunk-driving problems (half the deaths and injuries on the roads are associated with alcohol consumption). Although the few laws controlling drinking are scarcely enforced, there are widespread violations, including those of laws limiting sales to individuals over the age of twenty-one. About a half of those in prisons commit their crimes in association with alcohol use; in many large cities a half of the arrests are for drunkenness; and a large proportion of divorces, loss of jobs, welfare costs, and deaths (cirrhosis, homicide, suicide) are related to alcohol. Despite this record, alcohol remains relatively uncontrolled and is massively advertised ($300 million yearly) to associate its use with youthfulness, sex, beauty, and happiness.

Narcotic addiction receives far more attention than alcohol from politicians and police, although it has always been a relatively small proportion of the total drug-abuse problem and amounts to no more than 100,000 people in the United States (one half in New York City) and a similar proportion in Canada. Most illicit addicts are Negro, Mexican, or Puerto Rican Americans from large urban slums, culturally deprived backgrounds, broken homes, and with early exposure and encouragement to use heroin (or marijuana).

Millions regularly use (mostly by physicians' prescriptions) sedatives, stimulants, and tranquilizers; abuse, physical dependency, and suicidal attempts are very extensive with these drugs. Enough barbiturates, as an example, are manufactured each year in the United States to provide thirty to forty average doses for every man, woman, and child.

Marijuana use is very extensive and increasing not only among minority groups but more among intellectuals, artists, nonconformists, and high school and college students who are alienated, dissatisfied, and rebellious. The number of users is certainly in the hundreds of thousands and involves mostly the middle class, despite—or sometimes because of—the severe and irrational criminal penalties. Little abuse is observed and the main problem is making use a crime by law. Except for the minorities (though about 250,000 Indian members of the Native American Church use peyote regularly as part of their religious ceremonies), the same subcultural groups are using LSD-25 and, less often, D.M.T. (dimethyltryptamine), mescaline (peyote), morning-glory seeds, or psilocybin. Indiscriminate use and a wave of artificially created hysteria have created more use and led to the passage of the same types of harmful and unenforceable criminal laws; as a result, promising legitimate treatment and research have been discouraged. A small but significant number of adverse reactions (bad "trips") are occurring with overblown newspaper accounts.

Glue sniffing, gasoline or solvent inhalation, and the use of nutmeg (*Myristica fragrans*) and miscellaneous other substances have also become popular with generally small numbers of people, usually teen-agers.

CONCLUSIONS

The abuse of mind-altering drugs is an important social and health problem in all geographical areas of the world and most countries. Alcoholism and the destructive legal-punitive approach to most other forms of drug abuse remain the two biggest problems in this field. Despite extensive laws, agencies, and institutions which have been set up to control those aspects of drug abuse perceived as problems, individual countries have only the crudest facts at their disposal. Elementary scientific principles such as probability theory, deductive and inductive reasoning, use of control groups, sampling techniques, and precise definition of terms are noticeably absent. Thus, with pseudo solutions and oversimplifications, the real problems grow worse and nonproblems are increasingly defined as problems, such as cannabis (marijuana) use.

Drug use and abuse should be considered by the countries of the world as sociological and public-health matters. Criminal sanctions should be used very selectively for clearly antisocial behavior (which, for the most part, occurs without relationship to drugs and rarely as a direct effect of a drug such as alcohol) and for the distribution and selling of drugs proven harmful. All advertising and direct encouragement of mind-altering drug use in the mass media should be banned or heavily taxed and regulated as to content.

Massive rededication of individual societies will be necessary to correct the complex sociopsychological roots of drug use and abuse, but only such emphasis on the roots has any chance of success. In the meantime, there should be simultaneous (well-funded) efforts to reduce the availability of all of these drugs; provision of outpatient rehabilitation programs for those whose health or social functioning has been impaired by drug use; and the institution of general preventive public-health measures, such as education for youth and adults, the public and professionals.

The drug(ged) world serves as a barometer of human society —an indicator of underlying social illness and a warning of existing and approaching social storm. The storm is mounting.

Normal
Drug Use

Richard H. Blum

XI

C oncern over the abuse of psychoactive drugs implies a standard for normal or nonabusive drug use. Yet, with the exception of alcohol and tobacco, there have been no studies of the drug-using experiences of normal populations. Cisin and Cahalan's (1966) study of alcohol use is the most recent and extensive national study of what a representative sample of citizens does in regard to the use of one mind-altering drug. For most other drugs we do not know what normal use is; thus, we are not provided with a standard for comparison with individuals of interest, nor, on epidemiological grounds, can we see what national syndromes of use emerge or how such syndromes, once isolated, are associated with other factors which might play a role in producing different kinds of drug use, drug responses, or immunity to adverse reactions or styles of use.[1]

---

[1] Subsequent to the completion of this study, Cisin, Mellinger, Mannheimer, and their colleagues, working in cooperation with NIMH, have undertaken a national study of drug use and its correlates. Their study, with adequate samples and sophisticated inquiry methods, will be of great interest. Another

In 1964, we became interested in studying the drug experiences of a normal population. We wanted to know something about the life-time prevalence of use of various classes of psychoactive and self-modifying agents, to identify patterns of use, and to identify social and individual correlates of these patterns. We had hoped to under-take our work on a fairly large scale but lack of funds limited us to a pilot study. This paper presents some of the results of that work. In view of its exploratory nature, we have tried to keep our presentation relatively informal.

SAMPLE AND METHOD

A quota sample of 200 noninstitutionalized adults was drawn. The quota characteristics were defined by the most recent United States Census data. Because we were originally interested in a rough comparison of drug use in two cities within the larger San Francisco Bay area, we drew two separate subsamples of a hundred each, the quota of each defined by census data for the community. That initial interest in crude intercity comparisons soon faded and we combined the two samples for our pattern and correlate analyses. It cannot be assumed that either sample provided an accurate estimate of total-population drug behavior or that the combined samples are represen-tative of the larger metropolitan region. We do assume that the find-ings from the two subsamples and the larger combined sample reveal drug behavior not radically different from what occurs in the normal adult population, that hypotheses tested in the sample and found fruitful bear further testing in other populations, and that drug-use patterns as identified in the sample may be useful classifications or syndromes for others who undertake large-scale endeavors. The in-strument employed was a pretested questionnaire requiring about one and a half hours per respondent. The interviewers were a psychiatric social worker and three graduate students in psychology. Location of interviews was by assignment to neighborhoods of known socioeco-nomic level and racial composition. Within neighborhoods respondent selection was by quota requirements.

---

study, reported by Robins and Murphy in 1967, reports on drug use in a pop-ulation of Negro men in their thirties. Ten per cent of their sample admitted to heroin use, 50 per cent to illicit use of some drug. High school drop-outs were most prone to illicit experimentation; a drop-out with an absent father and a delinquency record was likely to use heroin.

AREAS OF INQUIRY

Difficulties arise from seeking to describe individual patterns of psychoactive drug use, for what constitutes a pattern? The focus may be on lifetime histories or only on a recent time period. One may wish to determine amounts ingested or simply use per se. One may wish to describe occasions of use by time or setting (social, private, institutional, medical, and so on) or to establish only average frequency rates (weekly, for example). One also has to decide whether dosage, or amounts, are to be inquired about, as well as manner of drug administration. The decision as to what classes of drugs are to be included as psychoactive is, of course, a critical one and once they are decided (inevitably with forebodings) the job is to find a way to ask people what they have taken so that they discuss at least something of what they know about their own drug behavior.

We decided to ask about the lifetime-use history of a number of subtances, some of which are not psychoactive in any conventional sense. For example, we wanted to know about such things as laxatives, aspirin, "health" and "appearance-enhancing" drugs, sexual-appetite changers, and even birth-control pills. Aside from simply being curious, we believed that a number of substances can play psychic functions, even though their pharmacological sites or modes of action are not of the kind that ordinarily and directly produce mind alterations. Such changes, if they occur, might be placebo responses, reactions to changed excitational or arousal (motivational) states, altered self- or role-conceptions, responses to physiological changes (pain reduction, contraception), and so forth. We did not have time to explore all possible "secondary" mind-altering substances (if they be that); therefore, our choice of substances for inquiry was limited to those cited by respondents during the pretests of the interview or to those we assumed to be widely known and employed.

In an inquiry about drugs used, one can ask in terms of common parlance, most of which are functional categories such as "stay-awake" pills or sleep aids, or one may inquire about more limited classes of drugs ranging in breadth from generic groups such as tranquilizers or sedatives to pharmaceutical families (barbiturates, amphetamines) or to specific agents (Demerol, heroin). Our assumption in approaching a normal population was that there would be a considerable variation in accuracy of reporting depending upon how we asked the question. Pretests of the questionnaire supported that fear. In consequence, we asked two different types of questions: one set based on the purposes for which drugs might be used ("Have you ever used any drug or drinks to help you stay awake, to make you more alert, less tired?") and the other set listing particular substances ("What has been your experience with such stimulants as amphetamine, benzedrine, dexadrine, dexamil, goof balls, or other pep pills?").[2]

We did not ask about dosage or routes of drug administration. We did ask about present use in terms of gross frequency (regular, occasional) and we inquired about the circumstances of initial use of each drug—who had suggested it and at what age the opportunity had arisen.

Childhood experience. One perspective from which we view drug use is based on the simple notion that people learn to use drugs from the same respected older people who teach them other things about living—primarily their parents but also physicians, teachers, older siblings, and so on. "Teach" is not meant formally; it refers to the transmission of knowledge, viewpoints, and habits—the whole culture which surrounds the growing child. Correspondence between what parents do and what children learn to do has already been shown in studies of two social drugs: alcohol (Knupfer, Rink, Clark, and Goffman, 1963) and tobacco (Salber and MacMahon, 1961). In addition, the role of prestigeful or dominant persons (husbands, employers, respected persons) in the initiation of less dominant persons into LSD has been shown (Blum and Associates, 1964). The role played by older persons as "immunizing" factors has also emerged in studies of heroin transmission (Stevenson, 1956; Chein, Gerard, Lee, and Rosenfeld, 1964).

We expected to find that parents also play a role in initiating their children into drug use not only through their social practices but through their "teaching" of medical care. By that we mean parental attention to illness, their use of prescription drugs and home remedies, and their transmission of views on the efficacy of pharmaceuticals as

    [2] One method which we would have employed—had we thought of it! —to facilitate drug identification is that now being used by Cisin, Mannheimer, Mellinger, *et al.* in their national study of drug use. Here the respondent is presented with pictures taken from the *Physician's Desk Reference.* Another method—to enhance accuracy of reporting for current behavior—which we are using in a subsample of our present study of student drug use requires the respondent to keep a daily diary of drugs ingested.

cures for ailments. We also expected to find a different kind of influence resulting from the way parents handle the emotions of their children. Making the assumption that parents who react adversely to emotionality in their child make him uncomfortable (conflict ridden) about his own emotions and that excessive, voluntary drug use represents an effort to alter felt emotionality, we expected that those children in our study who characteristically received adverse parental handling of emotionality would be in a higher-drug-using group. Although the memory-dependent data of this study prevented any final test of that latter expectation, we did make an initial test.

Orality: food habits. For the most part, drugs are taken orally. We expected that drug taking as one kind of oral behavior would be related to other kinds of oral behavior—specifically to food cravings, to intense food likes and dislikes, and to the presence of feeding problems in childhood or food aversions in adulthood. Since our expectation was that excessive or intensive drug experience (defined by its contrast to normal or common drug use as described later in this study) is likely to involve psychic conflicts centered about drug ingestion (such as cravings, dependency, and magic), we expected that people with other symptoms or intensive interest in the orality sphere would be in the high-drug-use group.

Relations with parents. We have already referred to parental handling of children's emotions as one factor we expected to be associated with drug use. Another factor, which is by no means independent, is how the adult recollects his view of his parents when he was young. We expected that persons who were hostile to their parents —or, at least, recollected as having been so—would be more troubled individuals who would express their general distress in excessive drug use.

The conventional psychodynamic thesis is that hostility to the father in particular is associated with rebellion against other kinds of authority; thus, the expectation is that persons engaging in illicit drug use will be particularly critical of their fathers. However, parent-directed expressions of hostility may be expected among the illicit drug-using group on other than simply psychodynamic grounds. Our preliminary observations of the hippie crowd suggest that the younger psychedelic set may find it fashionable to be critical of the Establishment—parents included, to exaggerate intergeneration conflict, and to present oneself in the pseudo-sophisticated psychological deterministic way as being the still-suffering child whose woes are attributable to inept parents. Consequently, subgroup fashions, as well as individual psychodynamics, may shape the expression of views of parents and thus contaminate efforts to measure hostility as such. Conceivably, the silent conservatives who abuse neither drugs nor the images of their parents may harbor strong resentments too. No conclusive test can be made by any interview method, but we inquired to sense the lay of the land.

Life satisfactions. We expected respondents' expressed satisfactions with themselves, their social relations, and their work to be least in the group with the greatest drug experience. A number of reasons underlay our thesis. The first was that the felt distress and conflict coloring views of parents might be one part of a more general outlook, a sour point of view which might reflect individual frustration, neuroticism, or despair but which, in any event, was an intrapsychic problem that might be associated with escapist or anxiety-suppressing drug use and with the search for new means to reduce unpleasant inner experiences. Another possible component in dissatisfaction might be sensitivity; the presumably idealistic person turning to inward experiences might do so because of disillusionment with the world as it is. Another component might be in the culture of the hippies and the New Left, which can elevate criticism into a cult of displeasure. Clearly, a diversity of possible reasons for expressed life dissatisfaction might be in order—a diversity which complicates and retards sound inference about the state of the inner man. Nevertheless, the essential expectation that dissatisfaction with self and others is a correlate of high drug use was, we felt, worthy of exploration.

Feelings and cathexis.[3] We asked respondents several questions about wanting things, craving things, disliking things, distrusting things, and fearing their own relationships to desired or suspect objects. Some of the questions centered on foods, cravings and aversions for which we have already discussed in terms of our notions of orality and drug use. But these same feelings, and related ones, may also be conceived in terms of cathexis, its intensity and polarity, and the conflicts, compulsions, and anxiety which center about that which is the

---

[3] Cathexis refers to the energy valence attached to objects (including persons) by a person. It includes both intensity and sign (negative or positive) and may include emotional, motivational-arousal, like-dislike, and other attitudinal components. As a psychoanalytic construct, it has potential utility in analyses of addictions and dependency.

object of such strong ties of emotion and desire or repulsion. We found it convenient to consider drug-dependency fears and suspicion about drug contents as part of a feelings-and-cathexis concept. One of our expectations, a straightforward one, was that those who used drugs least would be those with aversive responses—that is, the people who would most fear dependency and most suspect drug contents would be in the low-drug-use groups. That notion was predicated on a hidden assumption that we are, as a society, a drug-using culture, so that high drug use is normal and that those who use less than ordinary are reacting defensively against dominant influences. As our study shows, we were totally in error about the relationship of dependency fears to drug use. On the other hand, as our study will also show, there was reason to believe that the concept of cathexis intensity, measured by cravings and fears thereof, might indeed bear on drug-use patterns.

Other experiences. We were interested in aspects of drug use itself which we did not wish to include in our measures of use or in our pattern-identifying efforts. Are heavier drug users, for example, more sensitive to drug-induced mood changes in the social situations where psychoactive drugs are typically employed? We expected high drug users to be more responsive than low drug users to this social-facilitation effect. What about proselytizing and sensitivity to social criticism? Do heavier users admit to what others have observed (Blum and Associates, 1964), that they do have a missionary spirit and are sensitive to criticism? We thought they would be. If heavy drug users orient their life around drugs, as we believed they did, then wouldn't one find that they have used drugs in some uncommon way as tools or experiments? Might not these range from suicide attempts to religious experience? We tried to find out.

Background characteristics. Whatever explanations are offered for the differential patterns of experience in drug use or for the use of illicit-exotic drugs in particular, an identifiable pattern of drug use should be expected to be but one feature of a life style which has other distinguishing characteristics as well. In terms of the comparisons of groups differentiated by a pattern of drug use, certain constellations of background and behavior might be expected to be associated with the experienced drug users that do not characterize—or at least not so often—the less experienced, "lighter" users. Such expectations are based on the assumption that the personality and motives, social circumstances, learning opportunities, and even genetic predispositions possibly associated with drug-use patterns are but part of the larger fabric of life. By drug-use patterns we mean the patterns of medical care and prescription-drug use fully as much as social drinking or the more private use of heroin. Given these elementary expectations, we inquired about background features and then compared the status of the several drug-using groups. We expected to observe, for example, what others have already found: that exotic-drug use is primarily an activity of young males.

RESULTS

Our first task was to describe population subgroups based on lifetime drug use which would prove meaningful for identification and analysis. We first ranked classes of drugs—by name or function— by the number of persons in the combined ($N = 200$) sample[4] who reported one-time-or-more use in their lifetimes. Figure 1 presents those data. From Figure 1 we see that aspirin (and compounds containing it) is reported used by the largest number of persons and that any drug used to alter sexual appetites is least often reported.

The next step was to select cut-off points by which to divide our psychoactive (and self-modifying) drug spectrum into those classes of drugs most used, moderately used, and least used. Cut-off points were made at what appeared to be natural divisions in the kinds of use cited and, also, where relatively large step decreases in frequency of persons reporting experience with that class of drug could be seen. "Class of drug," of course, includes combined pharmaceutical, folk nomenclature, and functional (motivational) categories as a consequence of how we inquired about drug use and how it was reported back to us. The three cutting points can be seen in Figure 1. The first

---

[4] It may be of interest to see what similarity exists in drug use as reported by the two subsamples, one an N of 100 from the metropolitan center, the other an N of 100 from a wealthier suburban city. The greatest differences are in reported experience with anti-allergy substances; 21 per cent (city) vs. 35 per cent (suburb) for a spread of 14 per cent, and in sleep aids 37 per cent (city) vs. 49 per cent (suburb) for a 12 per cent spread. Most other figures are much closer, yielding an average difference in reported experience on twenty-two measures of only 5 per cent between the two samples. To what extent these differences reflect reality or sampling error cannot be said; it is of note that the metropolitan area more often yields the higher-use rates for illicit substances and social drugs. The relative similarity of the two samples allows us some comfort in believing that general patterns of use as described in the two surveys do not differ radically from the behavior of the populations from which the samples were drawn.

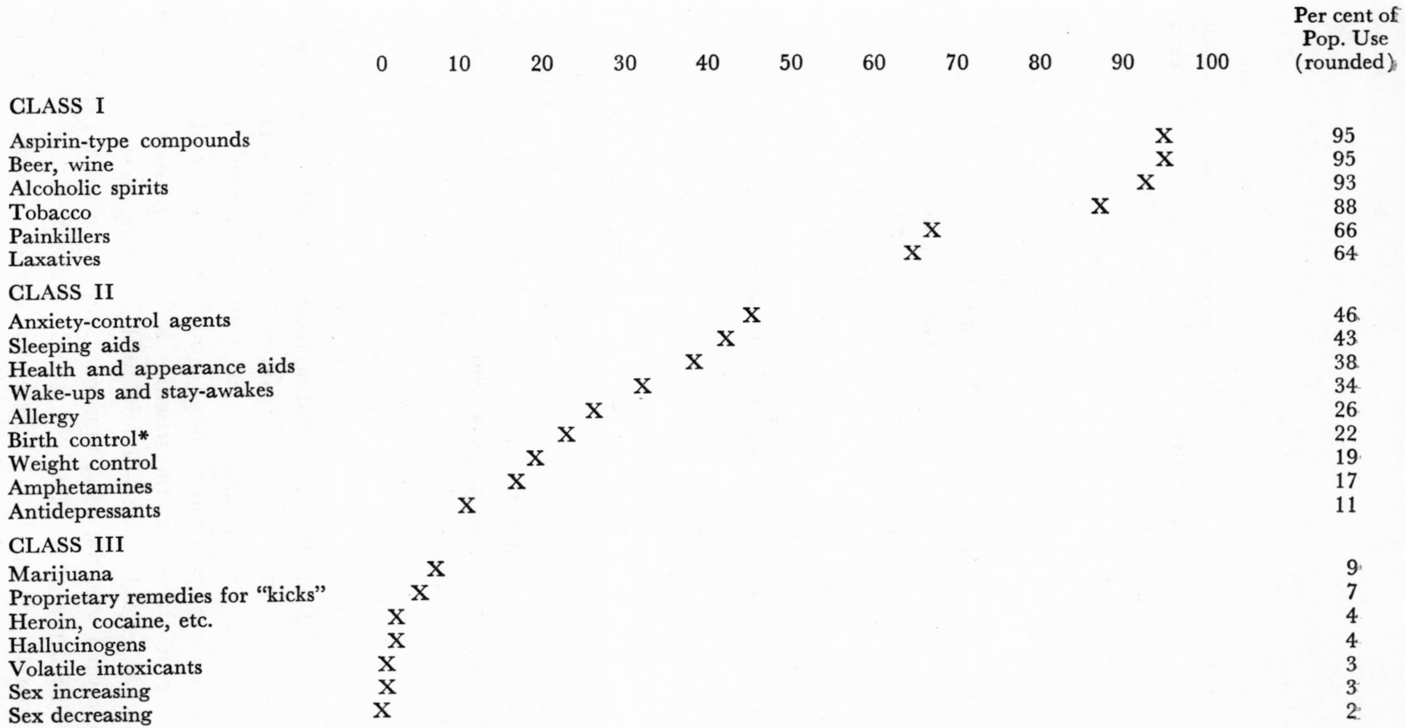
Per cent of Pop. Use (rounded)
0 10 20 30 40 50 60 70 80 90 100
CLASS I
Aspirin-type compounds 95
Beer, wine 95
Alcoholic spirits 93
Tobacco 88
Painkillers 66
Laxatives 64
CLASS II
Anxiety-control agents 46
Sleeping aids 43
Health and appearance aids 38
Wake-ups and stay-awakes 34
Allergy 26
Birth control* 22
Weight control 19
Amphetamines 17
Antidepressants 11
CLASS III
Marijuana 9
Proprietary remedies for "kicks" 7
Heroin, cocaine, etc. 4
Hallucinogens 4
Volatile intoxicants 3
Sex increasing 3
Sex decreasing 2

* Regarding proportion of female population only.

Figure 1. FREQUENCY OF REPORTED ONE-TIME OR GREATER USE OF PSYCHOACTIVE DRUGS.

group of substances are what we term "Class I," the most commonly employed drugs, and include the typical social drugs (alcohol and tobacco), the common home remedies (aspirin and laxatives) and the medical mainstays, and the painkillers (prescribed opiates, anesthesias). As we can see, all of these have been used by two thirds or more of our sample (save laxatives at 64 per cent). The second group, Class II, contains mostly drugs prescribed by physicians, although over-the-counter vitamins, sleeping aids, and weight-control preparations are included. The range is from a high 46 per cent for drugs to control anxiety to a low 10 per cent for antidepressant compounds. The third major division, Class III, consists entirely of exotic *and* illicit drugs except for one functional category, drugs used to alter sexual appetites (the drugs so used need not be exotic or illicit; alcohol was one). The range in Class III is from 9 per cent reporting marijuana experience to 2 per cent reporting having taken something to depress sexual desire.

Our next step was to set up four categories of persons based on their experience with the several drug classes. Members of Group I had no experience with any drug type or any drug-use function in our inquiry spectrum (N = 2). Group 2 (N = 28) were persons who had used one or more Class I drugs but had not used any drug in Class II or Class III. Group III (N = 135) included those subjects who had used one or more Class II drugs in addition to having used Class I drugs, but had not used any Class III drug. Group IV (N = 34) included those subjects who had used one or more drugs from Classes I and II and had also used a Class III drug. These groups, our "patterns" of lifetime drug experience, were derived from an inspection of the data. The progression (no temporal sequence implied) which defines an individual's group membership on the basis of experience with all preceding, but no following, drug classes is analogous to the cumulative property of Guttman scales (Guttman, 1944). This "scalogram" concept fits our data well, but certainly not all individuals in the population at large would fit into any of our four groups. We do think that the scheme—including, perhaps, work on coefficients of reproducibility—merits further investigation.

Group I was the most unusual group, since its two members had used no drugs of any kind. Statistically a dwarf, Group I is mentioned separately in our later analysis only because of our special interest in its members. Group I cases should be sought out for special study in larger numbers. Group II was also a small group, about an eighth of our sample; its drug experience was limited to common social drugs (alcohol, tobacco), common home remedies, and pain-killing drugs given on prescription or as anesthesia during surgery. Group III is the modal category consisting of persons who had only used social drugs and home remedies but who had also had consider-able experience using prescription psychoactives or over-the-counter preparations for control of a wider variety of psychic, somatic, and self-modifying functions. Group IV, about a sixth of our sample, had used social drugs, home remedies and proprietary mind-and-body alter-ing substances, psychoactive prescriptions, and also illicit drugs—and, in some cases, conventional drugs for exotic purposes, such as corti-sone to get "high," alcohol to suppress sex, and nonopiate cough syr-ups for "kicks." We would define Group IV as heavy users in terms of their variety of drug experiences.

Figure 2 shows the distribution of the variety of drug use by person, as opposed to reported frequencies of use by drug class (as in Figure 1). The distribution approximates a normal curve, and we feel safe in assuming such a distribution for drug experience in gen-eral. In our sample the modal frequency is seven varieties of reported drug experience. Only a few persons have had less than four of the different drug experiences on our spectrum and only a few have had fourteen or more.

Implicit in the scheme of classifications set forth in Figure 1 and in the notion of a normal distribution seen in Figure 2 are not only a search for constellations of drug use (or experience) but also a possible progression and prediction. Unfortunately, the present classi-fication scheme offers only a little help in these directions. For ex-ample, by knowing a person's drug group we know, for Groups I, II, and III, what kinds of drug experiences he has *not* had. At the upper end, Group IV, there is also some increased ability to estimate the drugs he has had, depending on the class of the drug. At one end, with aspirin, the best guess is that everyone except those in Group I has had it. At the other end of the spectrum are the hallucinogens. Only 4 per cent of our population have used such drugs, and all are in Group IV, one fifth of whom have had hallucinogens. In terms of the constellation of drug experience, no person reporting hallucinogen use has had less than twelve other drug experiences on the spectrum. For marijuana, the most common Class III drug, the average number

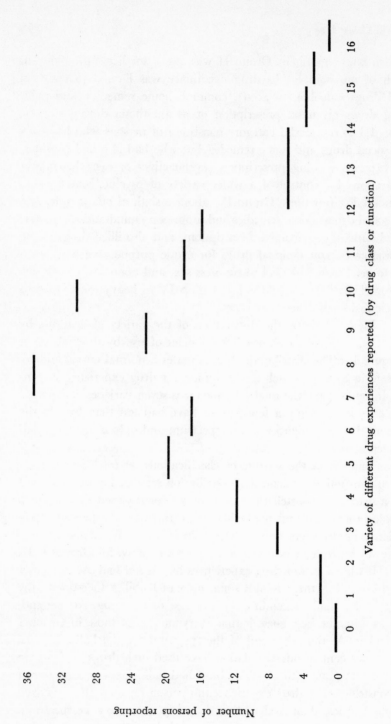

Figure 2. FREQUENCY OF DIFFERENT DRUG EXPERIENCES REPORTED BY PERSONS.

256

of other drug experiences for marijuana users is eleven although one person reported he had used only six other drugs. Figure 3 shows the minimal (not average) variety of other drug experiences among persons reporting the use of each of the drug classes in the spectrum.

Present use. We asked all respondents about their present use or nonuse of the various substances in the spectrum. *Regular* was defined as "often" or "periodic" use within the twelve months prior to the interview; *occasional* use was "rarely" or "sometimes" but "at least once" during the prior twelve months; *no present use* indicated no use of that drug within the last year. Table 19 shows that present-use practices closely approximate the lifetime experience for it and indicates the rank orders for frequency of lifetime use from Figure 1 as compared with frequency of present or occasional use from Table 19. Ranks are the same, or within two rank steps, for all but two major exceptions, the painkillers and heroin.[5] The great discrepancy is for painkillers, which were much more widely experienced than now used. That finding is consistent with the medical employment of these substances during acute injury or illness but not under normal care. Heroin (including cocaine and smoking opium) also has a greater lifetime-experience frequency than present-use frequency. (The implication is clear—if respondents were accurate—that past use of hard narcotics, either used medically or illicitly, is a transient phenomenon not necessarily leading to chronic use.) We conclude that the drug classes of lifetime-experience frequency of Figure 1 correspond well to the popularity of drugs as defined by their use within the last year.

Source for initial use. We asked all respondents who had first suggested they use the drugs about which we were inquiring. We find that although a variety of initiating sources do appear, there are, for each class of drug, one or two most common sources. Substances offered primarily by parents include aspirin, laxatives, and so-called health and appearance-enhancing drugs (such as vitamins). Parents also played an important role—although they are not the source most often mentioned—in introducing their children to beer, wine, and spirits. The latter substances were among the home remedies and ac-

---

[5] Another shift of interest—one not seen in Table 19 since ranks are not affected—is for tobacco. Of the sample, 37 per cent report past but not present use; only 52 per cent report present use. If not reflecting wish fulfillment among respondents, the drop may indicate some response to health warnings by the sample interviewed.

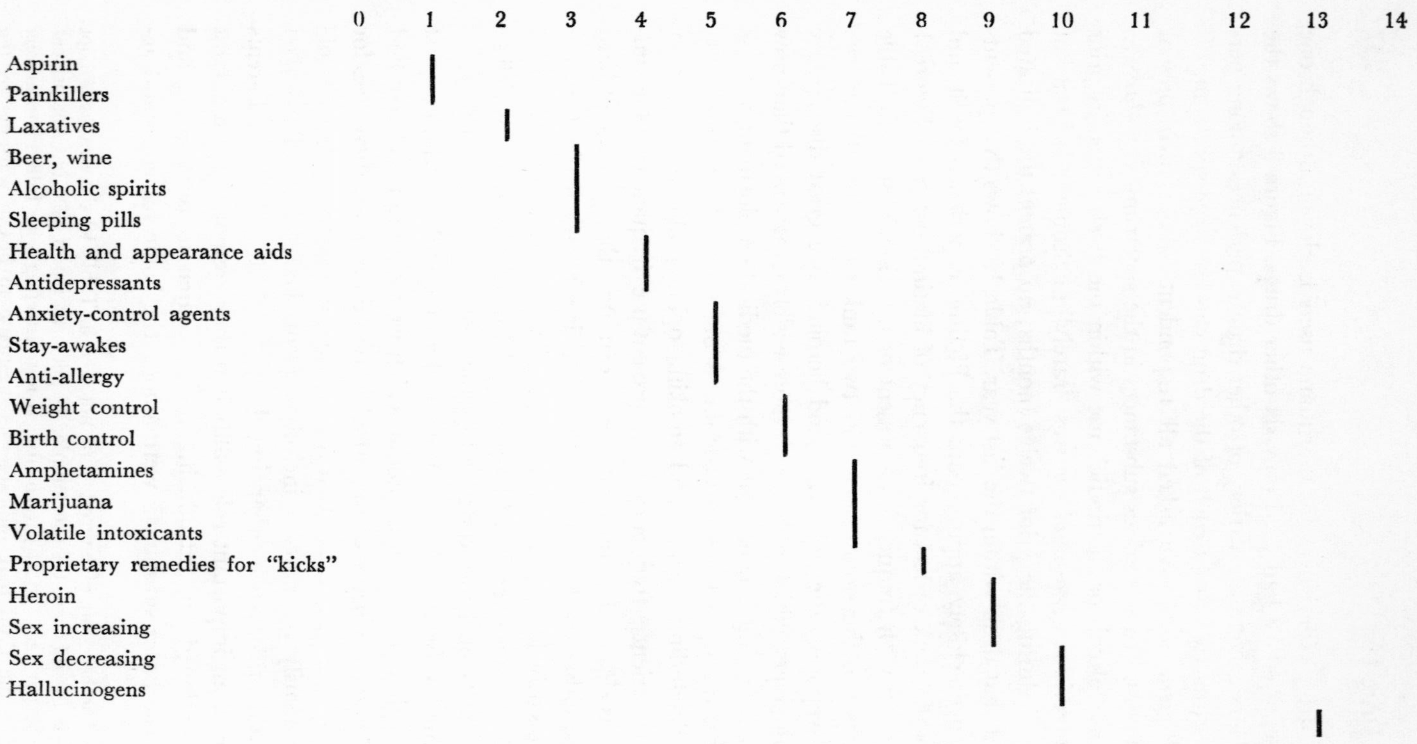

0   1   2   3   4   5   6   7   8   9   10   11   12   13   14

Aspirin
Painkillers
Laxatives
Beer, wine
Alcoholic spirits
Sleeping pills
Health and appearance aids
Antidepressants
Anxiety-control agents
Stay-awakes
Anti-allergy
Weight control
Birth control
Amphetamines
Marijuana
Volatile intoxicants
Proprietary remedies for "kicks"
Heroin
Sex increasing
Sex decreasing
Hallucinogens

Figure 3. MINIMAL NUMBER OF OTHER DRUG EXPERIENCES REPORTED BY PERSONS USING EACH DRUG ON THE INQUIRY SPECTRUM.

Table 19

LIFETIME PREVALENCE COMPARED WITH PRESENT USE
RANKED BY PERCENTAGE REPORTING EACH

	Lifetime prevalence rank	Present Use (regular or occasional) rank
Aspirin	1.5	1
Beer, wine	1.5	2
Alcoholic spirits	3	3
Tobacco	4	4
Painkillers	5	10
Laxatives	6	6.5
Anxiety-control agents	6	5
Sleeping aids	7	8
Health and appearance aids	8	6.5
Stay-awakes	9	9
Anti-allergy	10	10
Birth control	11	12.5
Weight control	12	14.5
Amphetamines	13	14.5
Antidepressants	14	12.5
Marijuana	15	16
Proprietary remedies for "kicks"	16	17
Heroin, cocaine, etc.	17	20.5
Hallucinogens	18	18.5
Volatile intoxicants	19	20.5
Sex increasing	20	18.5
Sex decreasing	21	20.5

ceptable social drugs offered early in life to most respondents. The ages of opportunity for taking these drugs as cited by respondents show modal frequencies for all but spirits during early childhood and the teens. Alcoholic spirits were not ordinarily offered until the mid-teens or later.

The physician is cited as a primary source for the following substances: painkillers (opiates), anxiety-reducing agents, sedatives, anti-allergy compounds, birth-control and weight-control prescriptions, antidepressants, and sex-decreasing drugs. The physician played an important role as source, but *not* as *the* major source, in initiating respondents into the use of laxatives, health and appearance-enhancing drugs, "stay-awakes" of all kinds (amphetamines specifically), sex-increasing substances, and, interestingly, remedies (such as cough syrups) which the patient might then use for "kicks." These drugs are, for most of our sample, medically employed substances, although it is also clear that many of these drugs may first be offered by non-medical sources.

Friends were the primary source of beer, wine, spirits, tobacco, "stay-awakes" in general and amphetamines specifically, marijuana, remedies used for "kicks," narcotics, hallucinogens, and volatile intoxicants (sniffed). It is worth while to note that some respondents differentiate between friends and acquaintances, the latter playing an important role in introducing respondents to narcotics, hallucinogens, and marijuana. Since the preceding drugs are all social drugs primarily diffused among peers, the role of casual acquaintances rather than friends in the distribution of illicit substances suggests a somewhat different (more casual, less intimate) social and transmission structure in association with them. The ages of opportunity for these peer-diffused drugs cluster in the teen years and the twenties. The generally acceptable (even if illicitly used) substances such as alcohol and tobacco become available earlier than do narcotics. In this sample, LSD and other hallucinogens make a later appearance than any other drug group. This means that in terms of age of initiation, interest groups, and diffusion routes the hallucinogens are to be differentiated from narcotics.

Only one other source remains to be mentioned; it is the drug user himself who on his own seeks a drug without an interpersonal recommendation or initiation. No drug in our sample appears to be predominantly self-introduced, although for aspirin, sleeping compounds, health and appearance substances, "stay-awakes," antidepressants, volatile intoxicants, and sex-increasing drugs, self-initiation is mentioned not infrequently. Such drugs must be available over-the-counter or in some other "nonsocial" way for self-initiation to occur.

Correlates of lifetime experience. There were a number of items of behavior and viewpoints about which we inquired and for which we expected differences among the several groups as defined by their reported lifetime drug experience. In order to present these findings as clearly as possible and with an economy of space, we will, for the most part, set them forth as a series of statements. The statements include proportion for low- versus high-drug-experience persons.[6] In many instances we have combined Groups I and II into a low-drug-experience group and Groups III and IV into a high-experience group when inspection reveals little difference between III and IV. We have selected the more detailed presentation of data for each group to show distributions of particular interest.

BEHAVIOR AND ATTITUDES

The first question we asked was whether the pattern which we selected as a criterion for constructing population groups—the reported variety of lifetime drug experience based on the classification of frequency of use of psychoactive and self-modifying drugs—had any relationship to other measures of drug use, for example, current use. The two persons constituting Group I report no drug use of any kind during the past year. Group II ($N = 28$) report an average use of 1.6 drugs and the occasional use of another 0.8 drugs. Group III ($N = 135$) report averaging 3.2 regularly and another 1.6 occasionally. Group IV ($N = 34$) report averaging 3.4 drugs regularly and another 2.2 occasionally. The trend is consistent in the expected direction. To express the relationship statistically, a correlation between current drug use (regular and occasional combined) and lifetime experience (each of three groups assigned equidistant values, Group I excluded) yields $r = .425$ significant beyond the .01 level. (For regular use only, the correlation between current and lifetime [by group] experience yields $r = .265$, significant beyond .01.)

Drugs kept at home. Another factor which we expected to vary with lifetime experience—assuming that experience reflects a propensity to take drugs—was the number of drugs kept on hand at home. (It is to be noted that many people, when asked this question, tend not to reply in terms of alcohol, tobacco, marijuana, or even home remedies; consequently, response may be biased toward prescription substances.) A count of drugs on hand reveals that the two people in Group I have no drugs in the home. Group II averages 1.6 drugs on hand at home, Group III averages 3.3, and Group IV averages 3.5. These quantities are consistently in the expected direction.

---

[6] With reference to the percentage reporting here, we caution the reader that the percentages represent those giving information-bearing replies and exclude the "no-answer" or "don't know" subjects. For most items the "no-answer" or "don't know" group is quite small.

A simple correlation between drugs at home and lifetime experience (Groups I, II, and III assigned equidistant values) yields $r = .262$, significant beyond .01. Whatever the trends, one must be impressed with the similarity between Groups III and IV in terms of their home supplies and the reported regularity of drug use. Both groups are frequent drug users compared with Groups I and II. What is suggested is that experience with illicit-exotic substances need not reflect itself in a fuller medicine chest or in a strikingly increased regularity of drug use.

Medication efficacy and practices. High drug users (Groups III and IV combined) more often than low drug users (Groups I and II combined) report that medicines have made a difference in how they feel (81 per cent vs. 60 per cent).

High drug users (III and IV) medicate themselves when feeling ill more than do low (I and II) drug users (33 per cent vs. 7 per cent).

High drug users (III and IV) more often than low (I and II) report giving medication to their children (22 per cent vs. 9 per cent).

High drug users keep proportionately more prescription drugs on hand compared with proprietary substances (1/3 vs. 1/22), whereas more low drug users keep special health foods and beverages on hand than do the high drug users (7 per cent vs. 2 per cent).

Health and medical care. High drug users report more frequent visits to the doctor in the prior year than do low drug users. Twenty-five per cent of Groups III and IV made four or more medical visits; 10 per cent of I and II made four or more visits. Most persons in all four groups consider themselves healthy. Ten per cent in Groups III and IV (combined) say they are ill, while 7 per cent in Groups I and II report present illness. Another 8 per cent of the high drug users say they have been neither sick nor well, while 10 per cent of the low drug users indicate an up-and-down health state. We take it that patterns of medical care differ between the high- and low-drug-use groups and that these differences may reflect other than health status per se.

As children, high drug users recall more serious illness than do low drug users (16 per cent vs. 7 per cent).

There is a general consistency in the amount of sickness reported by a respondent for himself as a child and for his present health status. Nevertheless, more shifts in health status between childhood and the present occur among high-drug-use groups than among low-drug-use groups (21 per cent shifts vs. 8 per cent).

As children, the high drug users recall more medicines in their childhood home than do low drug users (14 per cent of III and IV combined recall four or more different remedies; none in I and II recall that many medications on hand).

As children, more high than low drug users recall that they liked to be sick (17 per cent vs. 3 per cent).

More high than low users are able to recall advantages in addition to disadvantages to being ill as children. The figures by group are as follows: I, 0 per cent; II, 4 per cent; III, 25 per cent; and IV, 48 per cent.

Eating problems. High drug users report they had more childhood eating problems than do low drug users. The percentages are as follows: Group I, 0 per cent; II, 7 per cent; III, 28 per cent; and IV, 50 per cent.

High drug users report more eating problems as adults than do low drug users. The progression is Group I, 0 per cent; II, 4 per cent; III, 26 per cent, and IV, 41 per cent.

Parental handling of children's emotions.[7] High drug users more than low report that their parents responded with reactions which they rated as negative handling when they, *as children,* were excited or overexcited (0 per cent vs. 8 per cent). [Results are vitiated by the large "don't-know" response, which is greater among the low users (33 per cent) than highs (20 per cent).]

High drug users less than low recall negatively rated handling of their childhood anger by their parents (28 per cent vs. 53 per cent). [Differences are vitiated by the higher rate of not remembering among the high-drug-use group (20 per cent) than among the low (2 per cent).]

No differential trends are visible in ratings of parental handling

---

[7] The term "ego alien" employs some part of the person which is subject to unconscious conflict, something which does not fit and which may be rejected, dissociated, or otherwise handled in a stressful way. An emotion may be ego alien if the person does not admit it or express it integratively; the presumption is that a parent who disruptively rejects a child's emotion (perhaps because it is alien to the parent) is likely to create an ego-alien element. Parental responses to a child's feelings which are ones of guilt, hostility, denial, or rejection we consider to be negative. "Ego syntonic," on the other hand, indicates an integrated and harmonious situation which we presume develops out of positive parental handling of children's emotions.

of upsets and tears (low drug, 3 per cent negative handling; high drug, 5 per cent). Lows, more than highs, do not recall or don't answer (24 per cent vs. 15 per cent).

When respondents *as parents* describe their own methods of handling their children's emotions, high drug users (III and IV) are rated as more often responding with negative reactions to their children's anger than are the low drug users (27 per cent vs. 2 per cent).

As parents, low drug users more than high often describe reactions to their children's tears and upset which are rated as positive or ego syntonic (65 per cent vs. 50 per cent). There is a high "no-children" or "don't-know" reply rate (27 per cent for lows, 29 per cent for highs).

Response to a loving mood in their own children led to reactions rated as "ill-at-ease" or "unusual" (and potentially ego alien) only among the high-drug-use group (7 per cent of those with children replying vs. 0 per cent in Groups I and II).

High drug users report more negatively rated responses to their own children's excitement or exuberance than do low drug users (19 per cent vs. 0 per cent). (Low drug users more often can not describe their own reactions or deny overexcitement in their children, 26 per cent vs. 18 per cent).

Views of their parents. High drug users more often than low say they do not like their mothers (Group I, 0 per cent; II, 7 per cent; III, 15 per cent, and IV, 18 per cent).

The exotic-illicit drug users stand out as most often reporting dislike of their fathers (Group I, 0 per cent; II, 24 per cent; III, 16 per cent; and IV, 40 per cent).

High drug users more than low report disliking both their father and mother than do low users (Group I, 0 per cent; II, 0 per cent; III, 4 per cent; and IV, 12 per cent).

Varied dissatisfaction. With self: High drug users more often say they are dissatisfied with themselves than do low users (Group I and II, 0 per cent; III and IV, 15 per cent).

With social relations: High drug users more often than low say they are dissatisfied with how they get along with other people (Group I, 0 per cent; II, 0 per cent; III, 5 per cent; and IV, 15 per cent).

With work: High drug users more than low express dissatisfaction with their work (Group I, 0 per cent; II, 3 per cent; III, 11 per cent; and IV, 32 per cent).

Cathexis and dependency.[8] High drug users more than low say that they like certain things too much or that they overdo; eating, activities, and sex are most often cited as examples (Group I, 0 per cent; II, 9 per cent; III, 31 per cent; and IV, 38 per cent).

High drug users more than low report cravings, never getting enough of something (ungratifiable strivings). Most often cited are love and emotion (Never gratified in at least one area, Group I, 0 per cent; II, 12 per cent; III, 51 per cent; and IV, 63 per cent).

High drug users more than low report cravings for particular foods (Group I, 0 per cent; II, 7 per cent; III, 39 per cent, and IV, 50 per cent).

More high drug users than low report extreme or unreasonable dislikes. Most often cited are certain foods or activities (Group I, 0 per cent; II, 18 per cent; III, 40 per cent; and IV, 48 per cent).

High drug users more often express concern about becoming dependent on drugs than do low users[9] (Group I, 0 per cent; II, 3 per cent; III, 31 per cent; and IV, 56 per cent).

On a cross-analysis, persons expressing dependency fears tend to report food cravings. Using Chi Square, one finds that the association is significant beyond the .01 level (Chi Square = 11.92).

		DEPENDENCY FEARS	
		Yes	No
	Yes	34	39
FOOD CRAVINGS			
	No	28	99

On a cross-analysis, persons expressing dependency fears also tend to report unsatisfied strivings for things other than food. Using Chi

[8] We infer that overdoing may contain a compulsive component or involve stimulus-bound behavior.

[9] The reader will recall our hypothesis that low drug users, a culturally anomalous group in terms of the norms of use seen here (Group III as modal), would be the most fearful and suspicious of drugs. We saw their nondrug use as containing a defensive component. However, at the level of admitted feelings (we have no data on psychodynamics), this, we find, is not the case.

Square, one finds the association significant beyond the .01 level (Chi Square = 24.68).

		DEPENDENCY FEARS	
		Yes	No
	Yes	42	41
OTHER CRAVINGS			
	No	19	95

Dependency fears were compared among persons on the basis of the number of drugs they said they used regularly. Constructing four groups on this basis (not on the lifetime-experience patterns), one finds that those who use the most drugs regularly are those who most often express fears of becoming drug dependent. (Of those using zero–one drugs regularly, 0 per cent are fearful; two–three drugs, 31 per cent fearful; four–five drugs, 33 per cent fearful; and six-or-more drugs, 62 per cent are fearful of drug dependency.)

High drug users more than low say they are taking things they ought not to be taking[10] (Groups I and II, 0 per cent; III and IV, 16 per cent).

High drug users more than low are suspicious of the contents of drugs they have taken (Group I, 0 per cent; II, 4 per cent; III, 12 per cent; and IV, 35 per cent).

Drug experiences. High drug users more often than low say they have had accidental overdoses of drugs (Group I, 0 per cent; II, 0 per cent; III, 9 per cent; and IV, 15 per cent).

High drug users more often than low say that they ingest more when they are with people than when alone.[11] Smoking, drinking, foods are all included (Groups I and II, 13 per cent vs. III and IV, 53 per cent).

High drug users more than low report mood-changing and sociability-enhancing drug effects in social situations. Often cited are

---

[10] One may infer either fear or guilt from the affirmative replies.

[11] Our expectation, as the reader will recall, was in the opposite direction: that nonusers would be suspicious. The finding may reflect genuine bad experiences or that bad feelings as well as good ones are attributed to drugs, or that anxiety over drug use expresses itself in paranoid ideation.

stimulation and relaxation[12] (Groups I and II, 25 per cent; III and IV, 43 per cent).

High drug users more than low report having used a drug for religious purposes (Group I, 0 per cent; II, 4 per cent; III, 16 per cent; and IV, 30 per cent.

High drug users more than often than low report the use of drugs to reduce fear or induce courage (Groups I and II, 0 per cent; III and IV, 12 per cent).

High drug users more often than low report drug taking in response to being dared to by someone else (Group I, 0 per cent; II, 0 per cent; III, 14 per cent; and IV, 21 per cent).

High drug users more often than low report drug use as a matter of curiosity or experimentation (Group I, 0 per cent; II, 0 per cent; III, 32 per cent; and IV, 76 per cent).

High drug users more often than low report introspective, self-exploratory drug use (Group I, 0 per cent; II, 0 per cent; III, 2 per cent; IV, 21 per cent).

High drug users more than low seek to prolong any good moods they have; they may use drugs for this purpose (Groups I and II, 7 per cent seek to prolong good moods, but none uses drugs; III and IV, 22 per cent prolong good moods, and 5 per cent—of total—use drugs to do so).

High drug users more than low have "taken something" in suicide attempts (Group I, 0 per cent; II, 0 per cent; III, 4 per cent; and IV, 6 per cent).

Altered social relations. High drug users more than low report proselytizing for drugs, offering them and trying to persuade friends to try them (Group I, 0 per cent; II, 3 per cent; III, 31 per cent; and IV, 45 per cent).

More high drug users than low feel that persons taking drugs can fall under the (undesirable) control of another person[13] (Group I, 0 per cent; II, 7 per cent; III, 25 per cent; IV, 30 per cent).

[12] One may speculate that the high drug users are more suggestible and thus do as others do (more subject to social facilitation), that they "run" with a more oral crowd, which accounts for some part of their wider drug experience in the first place, or that individually they need a drug to enjoy their social relations.

[13] Here again, our findings run contrary to our expectations that the low-drug-use group would have the strongest distrust of drugs. Instead, as before, it is the more experienced drug users who worry the most about what drugs can do.

More high drug users than low feel others are critical of them for their drug use[14] (Group I, 0 per cent; II, 0 per cent; III, 20 per cent; and IV, 44 per cent).

High use of dependency-producing drugs. For a subsidiary analysis we identified those respondents who were regularly using the greatest number of those drugs which we deemed to have the greater dependency-producing potential. Our list—perhaps overly broad—included alcohol, tobacco, narcotics, remedies for "kicks," volatile intoxicants, "stay-awakes," weight-control products, sedatives, anxiety-controlling agents, marijuana, and the hallucinogens. We do not argue for any physiological addiction with most of these—only that they seem to be the drugs employed by persons who become identified as drug-dependent. In our sample 17.5 per cent say they use none of the foregoing regularly, 68 per cent say they use from one to three regularly, 11 per cent say they use four regularly, and 3.5 per cent say they use five or six. Prior to testing, we did not assume that the regular use of many drugs which are associated in some persons with dependency is any proof of dependency, nor did we assume that dependency occurs only with "multihabituation" (Cohen and Ditman, 1962) and not with single drug use. What we did assume was that—consistent with our focus on variety of drug use—persons regularly using many potentially dangerous substances are subject to greater risks. We expected the people in our sample to show the greatest amount of drug-associated worry. We also expected them to fall in our Group IV exotic-illicit category.

We were wrong on nearly all counts. Case analysis shows that six out of the seven multiple regular users are in the normal, high-drug-use Group III. Although five out of seven are worried about drug dependency, three limit their concern to conventional remarks about tobacco—"I ought to stop smoking"; two say they became dependent in the past on morphine but then withdrew themselves and now deny any present opiate use. Their expressed anxiety reflects their past, medically prescribed morphine experience, not any worry about present practices. With only one exception, none of these respondents expresses guilt or fear over his drug use, suspicion over drug contents, or fear of falling under the control of other drugs; nor have they suffered overdose effects or used drugs in suicide attempts. The one ex-

---

[14] One may infer a sensitivity to genuine disapproval or an expression of fear or guilt which is projected onto others.

ception, the most worried person (and not very worried at that!), is a Group IV user. It is clear that in our sample the multiple use of many drugs considered to have dependency-producing potentials can occur without any excursions into exotic-illicit drug use, can occur as part of a normal, high drug use as statistically defined and culture-compatible, and need not be associated with any expressions of unusual concern or distress about drug effects or drug use per se.

BACKGROUND CORRELATES

Age

Groups I and II: the majority are age forty or over
Group III: half are under forty; half over
Group IV: 70 per cent are aged thirty-nine or under

Religion

Groups I and II: the majority are Protestants; about a quarter are Catholic; 3 per cent nonaffiliated
Group III: half Protestant; a quarter Catholic; 2 per cent Jews (and only in this group); 15 per cent no answer or "don't know"; and 4 per cent agnostic
Total: 19 per cent nonaffiliated
Group IV: 35 per cent "don't know" or no answer; 9 per cent agnostic; almost a third Protestant; a quarter Catholic
Total: 44 per cent nonaffiliated
Church attendance within the last year:
Groups I and II: 82 per cent
Group III: 62 per cent
Group IV: 38 per cent

Education

Groups I and II: 18 per cent with some college education or more
Group III: 46 per cent with some college or more
Group IV: 59 per cent with some college or more

Family income

Groups I and II: 75 per cent with $10,000 or less; 7 per cent with $15,000 or more
Group III: 61 per cent with $10,000 or less; 13 per cent with $15,000 or more
Group IV: 72 per cent with $10,000 or less; 6 per cent with $15,000 or more

Sex

Groups I and II: two-thirds male
Group III: two-thirds female
Group IV: two-thirds male

Race

> Groups I and II: 72 per cent white; 11 per cent Negro; 18 per cent Oriental and other
>
> Group III: 91 per cent white; 7 per cent Negro; 2 per cent Oriental and other
>
> Group IV: 97 per cent white; 3 per cent Negro; no Oriental or other

Marital status

> Groups I and II: 14 per cent single; 69 per cent married; 14 per cent widowed; 3 per cent divorced
>
> Group III: 12 per cent single; 77 per cent married; 7 per cent widowed; 4 per cent divorced
>
> Group IV: 15 per cent single; 65 per cent married; 15 per cent divorced; 5 per cent widowed

Children

> Groups I and II: none, 23 per cent; one–two, 33 per cent; three plus, 43 per cent
>
> Groups III and IV: none, 29 per cent; one–two, 42 per cent; three plus, 29 per cent

Political preference

> Groups I and II: Democrat, 42 per cent; Republican, 34 per cent; Independent, 25 per cent
>
> Group III: Democrat, 45 per cent; Republican, 33 per cent; Independent, 19 per cent; other, 3 per cent
>
> Group IV: Democrat, 47 per cent; Republican, 18 per cent; Independent, 32 per cent; other, 3 per cent

YOUNG-AGE GROUP RECONSIDERED

Clearly, an association does exist between age and varieties of drug experience. In our sample the drug "conservatives" (Groups I and II) were older, the great middle group of high normal users (III) corresponded to the total population, and the illicit-exotic drug users (IV) were mostly under thirty-nine. No doubt, much of the variation in response to all the interview items can be considered as part of the constellation of background differences among these groups. Because of our special interest in youthful drug users, our focus was on all respondents age twenty-nine or under $(N = 57)$, distinguishing within that population the four subclasses of drug users. This method held age constant while observation was made of other background characteristics. The distribution of our young people was as follows: Group I, 0 per cent; Group II, 9 per cent; Group III, 72 per cent; and Group IV, 19 per cent. Only a minority of the young people in the sample, then, were in the exotic-drug-experience category, and they comprised only a third of the total exotic-drug-use group (N = 34).

Comparing these Group IV exotic-drug-experience respondents with the other (Groups I, II, III) respondents, age twenty-nine and under, we find the following:

Most (64 per cent) exotic users have *no* religious preference; most persons (80 per cent) in the other three drug groups *have* religious preferences.

Those with preferences and those with only nominal ties are Protestant in the majority—both in Group IV and in Groups I, II, and III combined.

Most exotic users have not attended church within the last year; most others (68 per cent) have attended.

Students comprise 36 per cent of the exotic-use group, while students comprise 24 per cent of the others; however, only 9 per cent of the exotic-use group have had graduate work; 26 per cent of the others have had graduate work.

Most young people in all groups are married.

The modal political preference for exotic users is Independent; for others it is Democrat.

The modal income category for exotic users is $5,000 or less; for the others it is $5,000 to $10,000.

The majority of exotic users are male; the others are divided about equally into male and female.

Exotic users are all whites; Negroes and Orientals are found in the other groups.

We see that when age is held constant, the same background features differentiate between the high- and low-drug-experience groups. We can conclude that the high-drug-use pattern is indeed part of a special constellation of sociocultural and psychological variables, not simply a phenomenon of being young alone.

SUMMARY AND CONCLUSIONS

An exploratory study of normal-population, psychoactive and self-modifying drug use was undertaken. Attention was directed to the identification of simple patterns of drug use and to the relationship between drug-use experience and social and personal factors. Two quota samples of a hundred each were drawn to be representative of noninstitutionalized adults in two communities within a larger metropolitan area. Reported drug use by the two samples was quite similar. Probable sampling error, limitations of inquiry method, and likely respondent-recall failures precluded exactness in estimating real population behavior from the samples.

Ranking classes of drugs used by frequency led to a threefold categorization. Class I drugs used by the majority included conventional social drugs (alcohol and tobacco), simple proprietary and home remedies, and the medical painkillers and anesthesias. Class II drugs were primarily prescribed psychoactive substances, but included over-the-counter remedies employed for particular purposes. Class III drugs were illicit and exotic; our definition of "exotic" included the use of a conventional drug for an unusual purpose.

From the grouping of persons according to their experience with the foregoing drug classes, our results show the following: the most unusual group (Group I, 1 per cent) is comprised of those who have had no experience in their lifetime with any psychoactive or self-modifying drug. Group II, about a seventh of the sample, has used only the most conventional social and proprietary drugs and the prescribed painkillers (Class I drugs). Group III, comprising two thirds of the population, has used both Class I and Class II drugs. The fact that the majority of the sample have had relatively wide experience with drugs indicates that normal drug use in a metropolitan area means a high rate of acceptance of drugs as ways for achieving a variety of personal, social, and medical purposes. Members of Group IV, comprising a sixth of our sample, have all taken Class I and II drugs, as well as Class III drugs; they are the heavy users as seen in terms of varieties of drug experience.

Exploring relationships between lifetime drug experience and other facets of drug use, we find that current drug use is greater the more the lifetime experience, $r = .425$, significant beyond .01. There is also a somewhat greater number of drugs reported currently on hand at home the greater the lifetime drug experience, $r = .262$ significant beyond .01.

We expected that the heavier users of drugs, defined in terms of our lifetime-experience categories, would differ from lesser users of drugs in a number of related areas. Our inferences were based on trend data, differences in proportions—these not subjected to statistical testing. Our data suggest the following:

Medical and sickness experience. Persons with the greater drug experience will have had more experience with medical care as such, will believe in the efficacy of medication more, and will both give drugs to others and self-medicate more; they will also have been more willing to be "ill" as children, having found advantages in taking the patient's role.

Orality. Persons with the greater drug experience will have had more psychological conflicts centered about orality, measured by reported eating problems, both as children and adults.

Parental handling of emotions. Vitiated by high rates of not recalling and by inconsistent directions of response, no clear-cut trends exist in reports of how respondent's parents reacted to their children's emotions. There is more consistency on the "turn-about" side, suggesting that high-drug-use respondents as parents may handle their own children's emotions more negatively. Our expectation that emotions would become ego-alien during the course of childhood development, so that adult emotionality would be handled by suppressive or dissociative drug use, remains, in the self and in children, at best unresolved.

Views of parents. The high drug users more than low express dislike of their fathers and mothers; important in terms of rebellion against authority, the greatest expression of dislike comes from illicit-exotic users and is directed toward the father.

Dissatisfaction. The high drug users are more dissatisfied with themselves, with their relations with others, and with their work.

Cathexis and dependency. The high drug users appear more subject to cravings, unsatisfied (insatiable?) desires, extreme likes and dislikes, possible compulsive activity, possible guilt over ingestion habits, evident suspicion of drug contents, and drug-dependency fears— all of which we infer to be related to more intense, polar cathexis, the latter reflecting psychodynamic conflict. On theoretical grounds we proposed a specific relationship between dependency concerns and cathexis intensity. Trends are in the predicted direction. Statistical tests of association between dependency fears and (1) food cravings and (2) unsatisfied desires reveal both to be significant beyond the .01 level. Dependency fears are also tied to drug use per se; the more drugs used regularly, the more likely that the respondent will report concern over becoming drug-dependent.

Social responsiveness.   The high drug users appear more subject to social facilitation as a spur to their oral-ingestion behavior in general and to drug taking in particular, for when they are with others, they say they take more food and drugs. They are also more responsive in the sense that, when young, they more often tried a drug on a "dare." Furthermore, they appear more subject to mood-enhancement or social potentiation of drug effects when in the presence of others.

Anxiety over social relations.   It is in the high-use group that drug proselytization, sensitivity to the criticism of others for drug use, and fear that a drug user can fall under the control of another (non-user) are most often expressed. We take these as indications of anxiety over social relations which are affected either by drug use per se or by the fact of membership in an "outside" group (Becker, 1963).

Drugs as tools.   The high users more often use drugs to achieve ends which were not part of our initial-inquiry spectrum. So it is that they report drug use for religious, courage-enhancing, introspective, or self-analytical purposes. Outstanding is the frequency with which the high users report drug use as a matter of curiosity or experimentation. We infer that a generalized notion of drug utility underlies such use, as does a qualified confidence in outcomes—"qualified" where there is conflict-ridden cathexis, anxiety over social relations, or experience with bad effects.

Bad effects.   More accidental overdoses are reported in the high-drug-use group.

Suicide.   Only in the high-drug-use groups does one find reports of the use of drugs in suicide attempts. The trend for Group IV is to report more (6 per cent) such drug attempts than Group III (4 per cent). We have no data on differential suicide-attempt rates by groups as such; the present findings suggest, for preventive work, which persons are liable to use drugs as suicide weapons.

Background differences.   In our study, considerable and consistent background differences separated the two least-drug-using groups (I and II) from the normal high users (III) and these, in turn, from the illicit-exotic Group IV. As one moves from least to most drug experience, one finds education, divorce, and the proportion that is white and youthful increasing. Conversely, as one moves from high to low drug experience, both church affiliation and church going increase as do age and Negro or Oriental ethnicity. Males predominate in the least- and most-drug-use groups, while females predominate in the high normal group. The high normals also have the highest average income and the least independence in political-party affiliation; the illicit-exotic group are the most often politically independents. We find no one word that aptly summarizes the background findings, especially since each group contains diverse elements. Perhaps "conservatives" comes close for the least-drug-experience people, "middle class" for the high normals, and "liberal disaffiliated" for the illicit-exotic people.

COMMENT

Given the limitations of this study, ranging from sampling errors through the overlapping drug classes reported and the inability to control for psychological sophistication as a source of differential-response bias among the groups, we do not contend that our observations constitute more than leads for more thorough work. It does appear that a measure of lifetime drug experience can be a useful one for approaching drug use and abuse, that "normal" drug use is considerable, and that individual differences are related to such factors as learning drug use in childhood, being socially responsive to others, being exposed to drug use by virtue of group membership (including institutional as well as peer-group affiliation), being disaffiliated with mainstream traditions, and, on a personal level, with psychodynamic factors possibly related to ingestion and orality, to cathexis intensity and polarity, to parental relations, and to satisfaction-dissatisfaction. By implication drug *abuse* must be considered as multidetermined, ranging from genetic and biochemical levels, not discussed here, through the individual psychological social and cultural levels touched upon in this study. It would appear that normal processes such as learning and social interaction must be considered in the development of use patterns—including abuse—along with pathological processes.

Drugs, Behavior, and Crime

Richard H. Blum

XII

*T*his chapter describes, in general terms, what is known about the relationship between the use of mind-altering (psychoactive) drugs and criminal behavior. Our definition of "crime" is broad, including dangerous as well as illicit conduct involved in accidents and suicide. Of necessity, we will also have to face the more general problem of the impact of drugs on behavior per se. It will be important, as well, to consider common misconceptions and to emphasize the limitations of our knowledge.

Psychopharmacologists, as well as scientists in other disciplines, have a great interest in learning what effects drugs have on human beings. Unfortunately, it is often difficult to establish what these effects are, since not only are the biochemical and neurophysiological processes involved both complex and difficult to isolate, but at the behavioral level, many determinants influence conduct aside from specific pharmacological effects. One example is the placebo effect, which is observed when a person is given an inert substance that he believes is chemically active. His response to the placebo can be remarkable—including rash, vomiting, and blood-pressure changes, on the one hand, or dramatic reductions in pain or disability, on the other. The placebo effect illustrates how other factors such as the subject's expectations and emotions, the doctor's or experimenter's instructions or expectations, and cues in the environment can all produce behavior changes which a naive observer might attribute to the pill itself. Even with quite powerful agents such as LSD or morphine, there can be strongly differing behavioral outcomes depending upon situational and personality factors. In addition, there are a number of drug factors, too— for example, the dosage of the drug, how it is administered, how often it is taken, the physiological state of the person at the time (nutrition, health, tolerance to drugs, possible physical dependency on drugs, and so on), and the presence of chemical antagonists or potentiating substances to counteract or enhance the specific effects. Even when attempts are made to control as many of these variables as possible, the choice of a measure for drug effects remains a challenging one. What kinds of behavior does one wish to observe over how long a period? How good are the instruments one has for making such a measure?

Given these problems in laboratory work, it is no surprise that attempts to assess the role of drugs in producing changes in behavior in real life are subject to serious limitations.

What *can* we say about the effects of mind-altering drugs on human beings? At the risk of error, we may offer the following statements. There are powerful agents which do affect the mind, mood, the biological cycles, the levels of energy, and the interpersonal behavior of humans. These agents are conventionally grouped into classes, those classifications representing what appear to be the most probable effects of the drugs. We can speak of intoxicants, sedatives, tranquilizers, stimulants, antidepressants, narcotics, and hallucinogens. These are already overlapping designations, since antidepressants are primarily stimulants, and tranquilizers may be classed as sedatives, as may narcotics. A particular drug such as alcohol may be classified, in addition, as a depressant or its effects may be rated as tranquilizing, sedating, or stimulating; it is also an intoxicant and its use can produce hallucinations (as in delirium tremens). Marijuana is considered by some to be an intoxicant, by others a hallucinogen; in large doses it can be a depressant or sedative, and under the law it is called a narcotic, although medically a narcotic is usually an opium-derived drug or a synthetic opiate analog. Sometimes, euphoriants are discussed as a drug class, meaning substances producing a sense of happiness or well-being. For some people opiates produce euphoria, but for the majority they do not. Drugs such as heroin, tobacco, alcohol, and LSD are called euphoriants, even though it is common for people to become quite ill or upset when they take these drugs; indeed, the same person may become ill one time, happy another, and experience relatively few effects on a third occasion of use. It is also common on the same drug-taking occasion for a variety of different effects to occur; for example, with alcohol an initial lift may be followed by sickness and then sedation. These diverse effects are important because so much discussion of drugs simply assumes a highly regular and specific effect when, in fact, drug-influenced behavior is best thought of in terms of probabilities; the accuracy of these estimates of probable outcomes increases as one knows more about the dosage and circumstances of drug taking and the person who is receiving the drug. Another point must be made. The higher the dose of most mind-altering drugs, the easier it is to make predictions, for behavior becomes less and less subject to variability as toxic effects are produced; by "toxic effects" we mean the typical bad results of stupor, coma, shock, psychoses, and ultimately death, which can accompany overdoses of so many of the mind-altering substances.

When considering drug effects, we must examine the intentions of those who give the drug (if it is administered by another or given socially) and of those who take it. In examining intentions, we must also look at typical settings for drug use; these may be institutionalized in a formal way as in religious rituals, festivals, family dining, medical care, or pharmacological experiments, or settings may be more informal, having fewer restraints and consequently leading to a greater likelihood of behavior variability. Intentions and settings are strong predictors of behavior. Most of the mind-altering drugs are used with a variety of intentions and in many different settings; typically, there is both institutional and informal use. As an example, opiates are used medically in the United States to a great extent, but they are also employed—to a much lesser extent—informally (and without approval) for "kicks" or in unsanctioned self-medication to reduce psychological distress or physical pain. There are probably as many other intentions in drug use as there are individuals with interests or hopes—individuals who as children of our technologically oriented, drug-using society have learned that drugs are tools to be employed in controlling states of mind. What this means is that the same drug can be used to produce—or to *try* to produce—quite different effects depending upon who is using it, how, and where.

The reasons a person has for taking a drug initially are often quite different from the reasons he has for continuing its use; further, the reasons for continuing use may be different from the reasons either for stopping drug use or for being unable to stop. For example, an adolescent slum boy may initially take heroin partly because he has been taught the use of other illicit drugs (tobacco, alcohol, marijuana) and so has become oriented toward drug use, partly because some experienced acquaintance has heroin available and induces him to try it (appealing to curiosity, "manhood," not being "chicken"), and partly because he is accustomed to delinquency and has no strong barriers of conscience or fear. After continuing this "social" use, the youngster may find himself feeling better, not just because of euphoria but because the drug dampens anxiety and "medicates" distress arising from his social-personal disorder. If addiction occurs—in this case physical and psychological dependency—use will continue even if the earlier happy mood has disappeared, even if increasing doses (tolerance-developing) will not produce euphoria; in fact, use now may be directed at maintaining an earlier level of adjustment or, possibly, at blotting out awareness. If use stops and painful withdrawal symptoms appear, the new motive is to continue use so as to prevent pain.

In another example, a college student may be introduced by the accident of association in a dormitory to LSD, marijuana, morning-glory seeds, and other illicit-exotic drugs, which constitute the pattern of multiple-drug interests of his "hippie" group. Originally curious, perhaps seeking religious experience or aesthetic revelations, he may continue because drug use dampens anxiety over his studies or career, helps him relax from pressure, or is symbolic of membership in a way of life that he finds pleasing. When he graduates and takes a job in the "square" world, there may be new pressures to make him conform which make him shift from the psychedelic crowd to conventional use of the social drugs alcohol and tobacco—a pattern he may continue without difficulty for the rest of his life.

A third illustration might be the working-class youngster whose Fundamentalist parents forbid use of social drugs. Personally maladjusted, he may associate in junior high with other troubled youths, from some of whom he learns to sniff gasoline, glue, paint thinner, and what-have-you. He graduates from these volatile intoxicants (if lucky, without liver damage) to the use of stimulants, such as "crystal" (methedrine) and perhaps barbiturates ("barbs") and cough syrups as well. At the same time, he is learning how to drink alcohol dangerously—that is, by consuming hard liquor in large amounts with his friends in secret. By the time he is thirty, he is socially misfit, on Skid Row or among its underworld neighbors, involved in petty crimes and dependent on alcohol. Since his drug use now centers on alcohol, he cannot abandon it without suffering serious physical and psychological distress; by continuing his alcoholism, he also guarantees continuing illness and a career of arrest for alcohol-related offenses (such as drunkenness and vagrancy).

In each of the foregoing cases, we can see a typical pattern of the use of a variety of mind-altering drugs in social and informal ways over time—a pattern which is shaped by associations, social circumstances, and personality. Motives and consequences vary and approved drug use is accompanied by illicit use. The use of illicit drugs or the illegal behavior associated with illegal drugs may be part of a long history of delinquency, personal maladjustment, and social disadvantage, or it may be, as in the college user's case, isolated and not associated with other visible criminality.

In the foregoing illustrations several different types of "crimes" involving drug use occur. There is underage use of the otherwise approved substances tobacco and alcohol. There is disapproved use (whether or not illegal) of otherwise available materials (gasoline, cough syrups, morning-glory seeds, and so on). There is the disapproved but legal use of disapproved and legally unavailable substances (LSD—its use is not a crime in many states), and there is the illegal use of illegal substances (marijuana, heroin). There is also the use of an approved drug in ways that are illegal (disorderly conduct associated with adult alcohol use).

Our examples above failed to cite other kinds of "criminal" behavior involving drugs—for example, tax violations (bootlegging), illicit sales (a bar selling alcohol to minors), illicit traffic (importing heroin), or pharmaceutical-industry violations of federal regulations governing drug experimentation, advertising, sales, and so on. Each act might be viewed as criminal, although the actual standards of enforcement are such that one surmises most violations of drug laws or administrative codes are never made visible by identification, arrest, or prosecution. It follows that illicit-drug behavior, like most other criminality, is in large part a "dark-number" phenomenon; like the bottom of an iceberg, the biggest part remains unknown.

One aspect, then, of crimes involving drugs is those crimes that are defined by drug use itself. Here, we are dealing with the major effort of federal, state, and local law-enforcement narcotic units in identifying persons who traffic in or acquire for personal use the substances listed under the narcotic statutes—opiates, marijuana, cocaine—or under provisions of dangerous-drug laws (medically available drugs illegal to sell, acquire, or use without certification or prescription, such as amphetamines, barbiturates, tranquilizers, anesthetics, and the like). With reference to heroin, estimates based on arrest figures for "addicts" (persons arrested for narcotic offenses) range between 100,000 and 200,000 persons.[1] There are no figures, and no reliable estimates, for the number of persons illicitly trafficking in or using dangerous drugs. The presumption, based on some pilot studies of population drug use and on high school and college studies, is that many millions of Americans have had at least one-time experience in the use of illicit drugs. (We are excluding the millions of young Americans who are underage drinkers and smokers.)

A number of assumptions can be made in the enactment of criminal laws seeking to control distribution and use of mind-altering drugs. One set of assumptions accepts use by adults and seeks only to raise revenues (although perhaps a hidden premise is that such use is a luxury or a minor vice). Codes requiring taxes on tobacco and cigarettes are an illustration. Another assumption holds that drugs are dangerous to those receiving them unless professional supervision is exercised. The explicit goal of the law is the protection of the health of the citizen. Such goals are apparent in some aspects of dangerous-drug laws requiring a physician's prescription, as well as in recent, related legislation constraining production and distribution of LSD without punishing acquisition of use per se. A third assumption is that drug use produces behavior dangerous to others, so that penalties are

[1] There are no bibliographical references in this article. The reader interested in more detailed discussion and in a bibliography is referred to the following: the President's Commission on Law Enforcement and the Administration of Justice, *Task Force Report: Drunkenness* and *Task Force Report: Narcotics and Drug Abuse* (Washington, D.C.: U.S. Government Printing Office, 1967).

justified not only in attempting to deter self-damaging use but also in preventing harm to others. Such an assumption has produced laws to prevent drunken driving, as well as a major emphasis in the argument for narcotic codes and dangerous-drug laws. Unlike the preceding "pragmatic" orientations, a fourth assumption, deeply rooted in Hebrew-Christian tradition, holds that certain acts are sinful regardless of consequences and that, specifically, drug use is an abuse of the flesh, an immoral act deserving of both prevention through threat of punishment and retribution should the act occur. Much of the effort against drug use, whether Prohibition efforts to prevent alcohol consumption, codes to protect the innocence of children by disallowing their drinking or smoking, or the punitive provisions of dangerous-drug and narcotic laws, may be viewed as enforcing these morals. Additional goals encountered elsewhere in the criminal law may also operate—for example, the desire to remove from public view those who act in ways offensive to public taste (drunk-and-disorderly laws), the belief in incarceration as an opportunity for penance or reflection after an offense, the catering to public demands for vengeance should morals be outraged, the possible need for recurring displays of prevailing codes which construct morality plays out of trials, and perhaps the trust that a law enacted stands as an educational lesson or that it serves as an ideal toward which citizens are encouraged to move. Underlying each of these beliefs, goals, or inferred functions is the general premise that the criminal law is a vehicle which shapes human behavior in the direction desired by the legislators and, as a corollary, that any untoward effects of the law on individuals or failures to shape behavior as desired are outweighted by the gains. A further premise is that the community has the right to intervene in what citizens do, even if what they do is a private act or one that takes place in a consenting or accepting group, which is the situation in most drug use.

We can readily see that each of these premises, explicit or implied, touches an area deeply involved in personal and social values. Turbulent emotion and strong attitudes exist regarding policies as diverse as how to raise and spend taxes, how to rear children, how to assess health, and how to view personal pleasure; they exist, too, in regard to whether one may or may not intrude in private behavior, what is the nature of sin, what should be the relation between criminal law and morality, and what are the effects of criminal laws. Given these issues, the fact of widespread and often increasing drug use (from alcohol to LSD), and the fact of widespread public concern about that drug use, it is no wonder that debates over drugs constitute a critical social issue.

There is no opportunity here to examine the premises of current or proposed laws or the social conflicts they reflect or generate. Two areas may be singled out for brief attention: one, the belief that drug use is harmful to drug users (whether these be one-time experimenters or chronic habitués) and the other, the belief that drug use leads a person to act in ways harmful to others.

Reasons for difficulty in assessing drug effects have already been discussed. Further examples illustrate problems in evaluating the damaging consequences of particular drugs. Cirrhosis of the liver is commonly associated with alcoholism. To what extent alcohol itself—in contrast to the life style which is the essence of being a down-and-out alcoholic—contributes to the disease is the question, for nutritional deficit, lack of hygiene, and other illness are also likely to play a pathogenic role for the liver. Another illustration focuses on drug dependency. Physical dependency (tolerance, withdrawal symptoms) does occur with continuing opiate use, yet medical patients are given opiates rather than have them suffer pain. Upon release from the hospital, nearly all medical patients are able to return to a morphine-free adjustment without notable difficulty. Heroin addicts, on the other hand, can suffer excruciatingly during withdrawal and yet will return to the habit in a short time, fully aware that the cycle of habituation and "laying up" will be repeated. The questions are, when is physical dependency a dire enough consequence to prohibit drug administration and how serious a matter is physical dependency per se? Another example focuses on amphetamines, which are the only major class of drugs consistently reported as enhancing the performance of normal human beings (for short periods mostly in muscle-using tasks). Although they are used by drivers to combat fatigue and are prescribed by physicians for overweight and depressed persons, increasing numbers of cases of paranoid-like psychoses are also attributed to the drug. Yet no one knows enough about what the probabilities of a psychotic outcome are for a given patient to guide decisions as to whether or not to give amphetamines.

Other policy problems arising out of probable drug effects are equally bedeviling. For example, marijuana is, as used in the United States, a relatively mild drug with very few verified ill effects; yet, when widely used by poor people, as in North Africa, its use is associated with apathy, stupor, and cannabis psychosis. What would happen in this country if it were legalized so that it could be used more frequently in heavier doses? LSD is widely claimed to be a drug which makes the user feel "more loving." Observers who do not use LSD report that users are not more loving, only more interpersonally dependent (as may occur with many toxic substances that interfere with normal brain function) and more self-centered. Whom is one to believe—the happy user or the disapproving observer?

In spite of the difficulties, a number of general statements, not fully accurate, can be made summarizing effects damaging to individuals. These are as follows:

Most users—one-time, periodic, or chronic—of most mind-altering drugs do not appear to suffer bad effects defined as damage to health or personal adjustment. Likelihood of damage probably increases as larger amounts of drugs are consumed over longer periods of time. There are notable exceptions in both directions—for example, those one-time users of LSD who suffer psychosis, as well as those individuals who take a one-time overdose of morphine, barbiturates, or other psychoactive substances and suffer death; on the other hand, those who in a lifetime make heavy use of alcohol may suffer no ill effects, as illustrated by the heavy-drinking businessman.

Damaging effects on physical and psychological health vary depending upon the condition of the individual. His condition, in turn, is a function of his social and medical history. The one group most likely to be identified as suffering the ill effects of heroin dependency and alcoholism are poor males dwelling in large cities. Other groups that appear to be in a high-risk category are those who have greater exposure to drugs, or the opportunity to use drugs in informal settings, such as physicians and nurses, who have access to opiates, bartenders who are surrounded by alcohol, and persons whose physicians overprescribe barbiturates and tranquilizers.

Damage also appears related to whether or not a person has learned to use drugs safely. For example, children taught alcohol use in the home are less likely to become alcoholics than those who learn drinking with peers. Patients taught to use morphine as charges in the hospital are less likely to develop a habit than slum adolescents taught by older peers. Proper teaching not only transmits information on dosage and dangers but also attitudes about propriety of use, functions, and the like.

Damage associated with chronic use is probably closely inter-related to the functions of use. Persons engaging in self-medication (unsupervised and unsanctioned) to escape, solve problems, reduce anxiety, and the like seem to run greater risk than those using drugs for social facilitation, religious rituals, and specific medical problems. These functions are intimately associated with the structure of situa-tions of use, formal versus informal.

Psychoactive agents, without known exception, pose potential dangers. The best epidemiological information on the extent of danger in social use is for alcohol and cigarettes; less adequate information is available about private users of "dangerous drugs." For example, about one out of every fourteen to twenty alcohol users becomes an alcoholic. One report shows 3 per cent of LSD users becoming psy-chotic (beyond the period of the "trip" itself). No one knows how many barbiturate users become disabled.

Dangers from these substances vary by substance and include dependency (physical and/or psychological), direct physiological ef-fects (from slowed reflexes or irritability, to shock, coma, and death), related pathological changes (for example, cancer, cirrhosis, and CNS pyramidal syndromes), direct psychological effects (toxic psychoses, confusion, anxiety, and depression), indirect sociopsychological effects (a life orientation toward drugs, self-centering, ethnocentrism), and suicide. The latter, suicide, may result deliberately from an overdose of barbiturates or from a self-destructive life style as indicated by a chronic use of alcohol or barbiturates; or suicide may be accidental as in the case of an LSD user who leaps out a window thinking he can fly.

No clear conclusion is possible in regard to the effectiveness of criminal laws in reducing health risks to drug users. Prohibition and current marijuana statutes illustrate the failure of laws to prevent large segments of the population from using a particular drug. The relative unavailability of opiates in illicit channels demonstrates an apparent success of the law in controlling distribution of these sub-stances. Similar laws attempting to control distribution of ampheta-mines and LSD do not seem remarkably effective, although no com-parative evidence shows what would happen without controls over "dangerous drugs."

Some citizens believe that drug fiends are responsible for most crime. A larger body of less-extreme opinion holds that drug use does play an important role in contributing some degree of menace to the community. The evidence is not as clear as one would wish, but for some drugs it is sufficient to warrant agreement with the less-extreme statement. The evidence is equally clear that the extreme opinion—no doubt, reflecting serious concern and aroused emotion—is erroneous.

"Crime" itself is such a broad term, describing so many acts committed with or without apprehension by so many citizens, as to be useless for most discussion purposes. Comment here will be limited to dangerous behavior as such, including accidents, personal violence, and, to a limited extent, offenses against property. The evidence linking drug use to dangerous behavior is inadequate. Nevertheless, many reports by public officials, both in testimony before legislative bodies or in the mass media, have linked crime to drug use. The consequence has been a pyramiding of conclusions based on unsupported opinion and fed by strong emotion, so that policy decisions have been made which cannot be defended on the basis of present knowledge. Illustrations of fact-free opinion include testimony to the effect that amphetamines play a significant role in auto accidents, that marijuana plays a causative role in crimes of violence, that marijuana is associated with unsafe driving, that heroin use leads to violence, that illicit drug use of any kind in adolescence creates or symbolizes disrespect for law and order as such or that it leads to criminal associations with subsequent induced criminality, that hallucinogens lead to violence, and so on.

Underlying many of the unsupported statements are not only a lack of data on the drug-use habits of offenders and nonoffenders but an appalling failure to consider the total life pattern of persons committing offenses and the role of drugs in their lives. There can also be a remarkable lack of scientific logic which allows conclusions to be drawn within benefit of knowledge of controlled studies or analogous observations providing comparisons of drug-influenced behavior with behavior uninfluenced by drug effects. There is also a consistent failure to note the contamination which occurs when several drugs may be in use simultaneously or in close sequence—a pattern frequently found among drug-interested persons.

However, a few statements appear to be sound on the basis of present evidence. "Sound" does not mean true, only that these statements are reasonable estimates of probable relationships—estimates very likely to be revised as better research becomes available or as population behavior changes either in regard to drug use or criminal acts. These are as follows:

There is a strong link between the use of one drug and the occurrence of auto accidents (both injuries and fatalities) and pedestrian-auto accidents. The drug is alcohol. The evidence is that driving is impaired by alcohol use, that drinking drivers account for more than their fair share of accidents—either to themselves or visited upon others—and that alcoholics in particular account for a disproportionate share of auto accidents.

There is no evidence that the use of other drugs is strongly associated with actual accident incidents, although experimental work shows how driving skill or driving-related skills can be reduced by depressant-type drugs and by marijuana-like drugs. Clinical evidence, on the other hand, can be adduced which shows improvement in performance as anxiety interfering with motor behavior is dampened by drugs—for example, tranquilizers.

There is evidence that drug use is often an integral part of life among persons described as having criminal careers. Work among Skid Row dwellers shows an important portion of these have had criminal careers prior to their becoming alcoholics and that after becoming alcoholics their arrest record changes in the direction of more drunk-related offenses and fewer types of other crimes. Similarly, persons identified as addicts (arrested for narcotic-law violations) tend to have records of delinquency prior to and following their initial narcotic apprehensions. Some evidence suggests that adolescents involved in the use of volatile intoxicants, amphetamine-barbiturate mixes and the like, are involved in other forms of maladapted and delinquent behavior. Marijuana occupies an ambiguous position; among slum adolescents with delinquent histories, its use is not uncommon; among college students and successful professionals, it is also used, but in the latter cases without evidence of any associated criminality.

Whether or not heroin use influences later criminality is not clear. Since prior to the initial heroin experience itself the user is already very likely to be a delinquent associating with other delinquents, heroin cannot be assumed to "cause" his crime. Some argue that the cost of maintaining a habit does lead to increasing theft by addicts; others argue that as a depressant heroin prevents crimes of violence among those who might otherwise have been violent. Significantly, no evidence shows that heroin users steal more or more successfully than their delinquent peers not using heroin.

Seemingly, the chronic use of any mind-altering drug by persons with delinquent histories is not associated with successful criminal careers. One may argue that chronic drug use impairs performance and prevents any complex crime planning or execution. It can also be argued that those who become chronic users were less likely to be candidates for success in any career, criminal or otherwise, due to social or personal deficiencies. There is also evidence that those who become drug-oriented may thereby sacrifice opportunities to be selected for successful criminal careers, since the user does not enjoy the prestige or confidence of more active delinquents or successful (professional or organized) criminals.

There is reason to believe that drugs may play a role in crimes of violence. The strongest evidence links alcohol to assault and homicide. However, these crimes are also linked to histories of violent behavior, so that one suspects an enduring pattern of both violence and drug use (as well as much other social and personal disorder) among those identified as violent. Case-history evidence of a sort suggests nonchronic drug use may also occasionally be linked to violence, as, for example, impulse release under marijuana, erratic conduct accompanying hallucinogen use, and irritability associated with amphetamine use. Such case-history data have little epidemiological value and do not prove any significant relationship between the incidence of such drug use and violence. A more prudent view would anticipate drug-facilitated violence primarily in persons with histories of personal difficulties, loss of control, impeded judgment, and the like—again, just those persons likely to be both delinquent and drug-using. It is highly unlikely that a well-adjusted citizen would become violent under any dosage of any mind-altering drugs. Rare exceptions might be anticipated in toxic psychotic reactions to amphetamines, cannabis, or hallucinogens.

No adequate data show the impact of present criminal laws in preventing dangerous behavior. Whether delinquent adolescents are deterred from drug experimentation by laws or whether offenders involved in drug use plus other crimes are likely to be restored to abstinence and honesty through any form of probation, imprisonment, or parole is much open to question. However, present methods of medical-psychological treatment, voluntary or otherwise, are equally unable to prove their worth in "curing" the chronic drug user and/or criminal, although modern methods hold forth some promise in the former. We assume that some drug use which might have untoward consequences is deterred or, at least, interrupted by direct penalties and by controls over drug distribution. We also assume that other drug use is untouched. It is also possible that present punitive methods either confirm or exaggerate the asocial or antisocial behavior of other users.

CONCLUSION

Drug use is widespread in the United States. Most of that use is approved and occurs without evidence of damage to the user or to the community. Much illicit use also occurs and is presumed to be unrecognized and nondamaging. No known drug, by itself, can be shown to "cause" crime, although when the use of a drug is illegal, the "crime" clearly rests upon the person's decision to acquire, possess, or use the drug illicitly. Drugs can cause damage to psychological and physical health, and although these effects are infrequent in terms of the proportion of citizens using drugs so affected, the actual numbers of persons suffering distress in association with drug use runs into the millions—for example, there are at least six million alcoholics in the United States.

A public concern which focuses on social drug dangers or drug abuse without also focusing on the drug user himself is misdirected. It is a person who employs a drug and a person who suffers harm himself or visits harm on others. It is what people do to themselves and to each other with or without drugs which justly arouses public concern or horror. It is, therefore, the person that must be attended to and the reasons for and consequences of his drug use that need to be established. Statistically, the persons most likely to harm or be harmed under circumstances in which drugs are implicated are most likely to be those who are already identified as suffering a variety of other deprivations, miseries, and deficiencies—primarily big-city, slum-dwelling males, with minority groups overrepresented. These groups are also overrepresented in the commission of crimes in the street. A useful perspective is one which sees drug use in the United States as common but drug abuse as uncommon—the latter to be taken as but one of many expressions of distress or disorder which are observable in the life of the user.

There is no question that drug use does occur in association with accidents and criminality. Strong doubts do exist about the role of drugs as being sufficient in "causing" crime; but it is likely that drug use influences the kinds of crimes committed. On the other hand, there is little question that drugs do play direct roles in accidents; alcohol is the acknowledged villain. Drugs also play a direct role in suicide, whether that act takes place outside of awareness or intentionally, and whether done suddenly or slowly.

Ideally, the hope is to prevent rather than to attempt to cure drug abuse and criminality. The evidence suggests that both honesty and safe drug use can be taught, but the apt pupil is already the one fortunate enough to be without severe social disadvantage or personal disorder. Consequently, the recommendation is for education and the prevention of poverty and misery—a prescription readily accepted by the "Great Society" but one which cannot yet be filled or administered to the many needy patients. In the meantime, it seems apparent that those who are untaught in safe drug use and who already have propensities for hurting themselves and others are well advised not to employ mind-altering drugs. Since these same people are unable to accept such easily given advice as to "shape up," "obey the law," "reform," or "keep healthy," it is ridiculous to assume they will be prudent in their use of drugs. Consequently, control over the distribution of drugs is in order.

Although it is one aim of narcotic and dangerous-drug laws to achieve that control, we lack evidence as how best to make laws which mold drug-use conduct.

Given that lack, we might suggest that the more extreme provisions of current drug laws are at least unkind and quite possibly destructive. If we accept the premise that the person abusing drugs is thereby giving signs of his own disorder, it would be well for those around him to take notice of that disorder—for the sake of their own safety as well as for his. If drug abuse is a sign of disorder, if it is a sign of distress, then we should ask whether it is effective to be so homeopathic in our approach—treating pain by giving pain? Without proof that it is effective, then both economy and kindness dictate that our attempts to control undesirable drug behavior emphasize features other than punishment. This is not to rule it out entirely—merely to suggest that flexibility and experimentation might better dictate our approaches until such time as we know more about how to influence drug-taking behavior or until such time that we conclude that we are quite unable, at least through policy decisions, to influence that behavior at all.

Legislators and
Drugs

Richard H. Blum

XIII

*T*here is scientific, practical, professional, and ideological importance in what legislators say and do. The behavior and opinions of lawmakers are in themselves fascinating areas for psychological inquiry. What they think of a profession and its practitioners affects the development and well-being of that profession and bears on legislative support for the institutions and endeavors in which such professionals are involved. And, ideologically, what legislators do matters. Their attempts to influence human conduct can have immense effects and those effects—as well as the intent of the acts—will be judged by moral and social standards. For these reasons we believe that psychologists will be interested in the results of interviews which we have had with key men in the California legislature. The subject of the interviews was legislation on mind-altering drugs and on drug users. The implications of the results extend, we believe, much beyond the interesting question of where legislators stand with respect to problems of drug use and abuse.

The value and feasibility of psychological studies of political

behavior are by now well known. Spranger (1928) and Lasswell (1930)
—if not Plutarch and Suetonius—led the way. Our own interest in
the views of legislators arose from some previous work on the use of
mind-altering drugs (Blum and Associates, 1964; Blum and Blum,
1963) and on personality and political and social outlook (Blum,
1958). It had become clear to us that the social issues surrounding
the use and abuse of drugs are important ones which illuminate a
number of social problems and value conflicts within our society. We
had also concluded that positions on drug issues are part of a larger
fabric of a person's outlook—one in which moral values, psychological
characteristics, and social and cultural surroundings play a determining role. We were not in a position to conduct any careful test of
hypotheses among legislators; they could not be expected to give us
the time necessary to participate in formal testing or experiments. On
the other hand, we would be able to assess their views on crucial questions and to relate these to the available data on political stance and
party affiliation.

In order to conduct the study, we approached the fifty-two
California legislators who in 1964 held appointments to one or more
committees which processed bills dealing with drugs or with the handling of drug users. These men had the greatest interest and knowledge
in and real power controlling drug legislation in the state. Fifty legislators (42 per cent of the 120 in the California legislature) were kind
enough to cooperate in the study. There were twelve senators and
thirty-eight assemblymen, thirty-three Democrats and seventeen Republicans in our sample. All were men; most were Protestant. More
than half, thirty-one, were lawyers; over a fifth, twelve, were businessmen. There were two high school teachers, one medical and one veter-
inary doctor, two ministers, a pharmacist, an economist, and a former
customs officer. The assemblymen had an average tenure of six years
in office; the senators, nine years.

THE INTERVIEWS

The interviews were conducted according to a schedule. The
core of each question on that schedule is presented in the following
sections in the order in which the questions were asked. Tangential
discussion was encouraged for as much time as the lawmaker had
available. Following the interviews, the respondents were rated as liberal, moderate, or conservative and as expressing views which we

classify as those of moral absolutists or of pragmatic men. We shall present the substance of the views of the sample in each inquiry area and will discuss the relationship of the several positions taken to political stance when the latter appears relevant.

Is drug abuse a serious social problem? We began by asking whether California is faced with a problem in the abuse of mind-altering drugs. Most of the legislators thought it is—88 per cent of the Republicans and 81 per cent of the Democrats answering in the affirmative. If we separate the "convinced" from the "perfunctory" affirmations, we find the political differences much more marked in the perception of a drug threat. Three quarters of the Republicans but only half of the Democrats seemed convinced that there is a clear and present menace to the social order arising from drug abuse. Although many were worried about drugs, what they were specifically worried about varied considerably. About a fifth spoke of their concern about crimes committed by narcotics users, mentioning murder and theft as examples. Fewer numbers spoke rather broadly of dangers to youth and of costs to the community and to users. A few legislators defined the problem in terms of the inhumanity of the present approach to the offender addict.

The discussions moved from what the problem is to what ought to be done about it. Two major positions and one minor one emerged, exclusive of that third of the lawmakers who volunteered no general solutions. One major position, representing the largest single group, emphasized punishment and control. This group of men wanted present laws more stringently enforced and/or wanted new laws imposing harsher penalties and tighter restrictions. The second position excluded coercive restraint or punishment; those proposing it called for new efforts at public education, the treatment of drug users, further research, and the alleviation of social conditions which are presumably at the root of the abuse. A minor position, never advocated as a sole approach, was taken by three lawmakers. They separated punishment from control—the latter in the form of the confinement or isolation of the offender for the purpose of reducing his dependency on drugs and preventing his contact with the community; they advocated nonpunitive restraint and isolation in combination with rehabilitation or with rehabilitation *and* punishment. A number of men called for diversified efforts; most often rehabilitation *and* punishment-control were recommended.

An examination of the distribution of these proposed solutions by party affiliation showed that the majority of those exclusively advocating more emphasis on punishment-control were Republicans (eight as compared with three Democrats). Six Democrats and three Republicans called for education-rehabilitation-research, while the suggestions for movement in several directions at once came from nine Democrats and four Republicans.

What does the voter want done? In our conversations with the legislators, we differentiated among three major classes of drugs: alcohol, the dangerous drugs (legally defined to include stimulants, sedatives, tranquilizers, and so on), and narcotic drugs (the legal definition of which in California includes the nonnarcotic and intoxicating marijuana and hallucinogen peyote). With reference to narcotics users, the most frequently expressed view of the legislators was that the public wants harsher penalties imposed as a means of controlling drug abuse and exacting retribution from wrongdoers. The public was said to prefer to see users of dangerous drugs handled just as if they were narcotics offenders (again more punitively than at present). The public was most often seen as having *no* interest in alcoholics. No legislator was of the opinion that the public desires a rehabilitative rather than a law-enforcement approach to narcotics addicts; but some did believe that the public would favor treatment rather than arrest (as is presently the case in public drunkenness) for alcoholics.

If the position of the legislators is compared in terms of their own proposals for what might be done to correct drug abuse with their views of what the public desires, the Republicans reflect a greater correspondence between the legislator's own position and his view of the will of the public. Only two Republicans saw any discrepancy between what they proposed and what the public wants, and in both cases what they proposed was harsh penalties and what they thought the public wants was even harsher penalties. Democrats, on the other hand, were much more likely to see a discrepancy between what they thought should be done and what the public wants; half of the Democrats espoused treatment but said the public still thinks in terms of punishment; a fourth of the Democrats said that there is *no* public opinion, that a variety of publics exist, each with a different viewpoint, and that, for the most part, people are apathetic and no public "opinion" as such exists on drug control.

It is clear that most legislators believed the public to be "out for blood" on the drug-control issue. It is also clear that there was a much greater perception of, and presumably tolerance for, difference among the Democrats between the legislator's own views and those he ascribed to the public.

What can laws accomplish? Fundamental to any proposals for legislation are beliefs about what laws can accomplish in influencing human conduct. In our discussion on these beliefs, the most frequent expectation voiced by lawmakers was that through the passing and enforcement of drug laws the amount of drug abuse could be reduced by limiting the supply of drugs—a matter of practical controls —and by placing a stigma on us—the stigma serving as a moral proclamation to deter citizens from drug experimentation and, at the same time, presenting drug abusers with the threat and fact of punishment. Men who held this view did not believe that any legal effort could eliminate drug abuse entirely. A smaller number of legislators said the laws functioned, presumably successfully, to protect society from the criminal menace posed by users and to provide morally necessary retribution, "an eye for an eye" for wrongdoing. A few legislators expressed the conviction that legislation could ameliorate the problems of society and the individual drug user by providing the user with treatment facilities. Three lawmakers saw no hope for any laws to control drug taking through any presently available methods, but they expressed the hope that laws which authorized research might lead to eventual solutions. Three Democrats and no Republicans expressed the latter view.

Of what use is social science research? About half of the lawmakers, in discussing the possible contribution to legislative planning of studies by social scientists, psychologists, and psychiatrists, took the position that social science is a good thing but that, at present, it has not developed enough information to be of much help. Some lawmakers nodded politely in the direction of research but discounted the importance of any findings, present or future. "I know it already" was the feeling or, as one man said, "The answers are so simple we don't need a psychiatrist to tell us." Over a fifth of the legislators rejected social-science research outright, their position being that it is useless, biased, dangerous, or otherwise nonsensical.

What would you expect from a social scientist? When the discussion shifted from the consideration of the value of research on human behavior to the more immediate question of what a social scientist or psychiatrist might tell legislators to aid them in drafting laws designed to influence human behavior, we were able to distinguish several different themes among the attitudes toward these professionals. That some lawmakers offered several different themes accounts for the fact that the percentages in the table below add up to more than 100 per cent. Table 20 presents the several views and illustrative quotations.

Obviously, the majority of legislators were critical of the knowledge, orientation, sense of responsibility, practical sense, honesty, or communication skill of social scientists and psychiatrists. Only a minority of lawmakers gave weight or priority to what these professionals might say and certainly few legislators, if any, would seek them out for information or advice. Even those lawmakers who were interested in what social scientists might tell them expected the scientist to take the initiative and come to them.[1]

Information needs for decisions on hypothetical drug legislation. In order to learn more about where legislators *would* get information on proposed drug legislation and to learn more about their stands on the punishment-isolation-rehabilitation continuum (for a continuum we believe it to be), we discussed with each man three hypothetical bills. One bill would make the hallucinogenic drug LSD more widely available by classifying it as a dangerous drug (it is now restricted to use in approved research only) and thus enable physicians to prescribe it. The second bill, following contemporary proposals in Great Britain, would make the use of marijuana legal, subject only to the same controls that govern alcohol sales. The third bill would remove public drunks from the concern of criminal law and would transfer the handling of alcoholics to public-health and medical authorities, who would be responsible for alcoholic-treatment programs. The police function would be limited to twenty-four-hour protective custody prior to mandatory medical disposition. In order to

---

[1] Along this line it is worth noting that a number of legislators seemed quite pleased that we had taken the initiative—as they saw it—in coming to see them. As a result of this step on our part, one offered to commission us to conduct research for his committee; another asked us to set up a conference between his committee and scholars in the university; another offered to introduce the hypothetical alcohol bill which we discussed with him, if we so desired. This response confirms the opinion that the social-science "Mahomet" had better be prepared to come to the legislative "hill" and also demonstrates that some lawmakers will be ready to offer warm and cooperative greetings.

Table 20

WHAT LEGISLATORS HAVE TO SAY ABOUT SOCIAL SCIENTISTS
AND THE INFORMATION THEY PROVIDE

Themes and Illustrative Remarks	N = 33 Dem.	N = 17 Rep.	Total per cent
Social scientists do not provide much information helpful to legislators because they are too vague, too impractical, or too much in disagreement with one another. The theme is that social scientists do not have hard facts at hand.	7	4	22

"They come up with broad speculations but no specific recommendations; hence, they are emasculated before a committee which wants a specific answer."

"By being unwilling to go out on a limb, they lose any influence they (might) have."

"If you have any opinion, you can get some social scientist or psychiatrist to support it."

Conflicts in orientation and value are so great between lawmakers and social scientists that the former are unwilling or unable to listen to what the latter have to say.[2]	3	5	16

"Psychiatrists pursue the philosophy that the individual is not responsible for his actions. I discount that sort of thinking."

"One believes either in environmental 'explanations' or that a man *is* responsible for what he does."

[2] Confirmation of the distance between the two groups attributable to points of view came from the observations of seven Democrats, none of whom was himself rejecting the academic or scientific position. Typical remarks were, "The average legislator isn't concerned with what the 'do-gooders' say but with what the D.A.'s and sheriffs say." "Because of my background—my wife is a social worker—I'm oriented to listening to social scientists, but the others up here aren't." "There is disdain for the book 'larned' by those who've made it the hard way."

Table 20—Cont.

Themes and Illustrative Remarks	N = 33 Dem.	N = 17 Rep.	Total per cent
"Psychiatry is phoney. Not five in a hundred know what they're doing."			
"Social scientists are self-serving. They justify their own operations."			
"Most of us have a history in law enforcement and we'd sooner listen to a police officer."			
"Older members have feelings against social scientists; they reject people who tend to be against the status quo."			
". . . ivory-tower educationalists are held in contempt."			
They may have information, but legislators don't have time to find out.	5	2	14
"The last thing a legislator can do is to *study* a problem!"			
"You listen so much that you learn how not to listen. . . ."			
"We have so much to cover . . . the best would be to get brief conclusions."			
A social scientist is just another interested party: there is nothing compelling about his views. His point of view is just one among many.	4	1	10
"Law enforcement has an opinion too."			
"Authority shouldn't be delegated to these 'social workers'; you risk infringing on individual liberties."			
They may have information but they don't offer it to legislators. They refuse to come forward.	4	0	8

Table 20—Cont.

Themes and Illustrative Remarks	N = 33 Dem.	N = 17 Rep.	Total per cent
"Professors haven't borne their responsibilities for getting into this arena."			
"University people are afraid to enter into debate . . . or to make statements . . . afraid of religious or ethical issues."			
"I've never received *any* unrequested information from any university or research faculty; I get only pressures from the police, and pamphlets from the Federal Narcotics Service."			
It depends upon the status and competence of the scientist himself.	2	3	10
"The social scientist or psychiatrist must be a man of authority (to be listened to with respect)."			
They may have information but they communicate it so poorly that it is lost or damaged in transmission.	3	1	8
"The researcher gets so involved in a subject that he forgets the lay reader."			
"The legislator will more readily listen to those he respects; the social scientist is not known, has no built-in rapport, and doesn't make any effort to build that rapport."			
Social scientists have much useful information to offer; university people can provide vital information to guide legislation.	6	2	16
"I believe in a close working relationship between universities and legislatures."			
"I resort (to their data) as often as I can."			

Table 20—Cont.

Themes and Illustrative Remarks	Dem. N = 33	N = 17 Rep.	Total per cent
They may have information, but it is not practical, may antagonize the electorate, or it may hinder legislative action by creating doubt without offering direction.	5	3	16

It . . . "doesn't have political 'milk.' "

"It's hard to sell scientific ideas to the electorate."

"Good laws may offend the people we represent."

"Their research may give you doubts, make you wish you could vote 'maybe' or 'if' on some bills."

decide on the LSD bill, two fifths of the legislators said they would need information dealing with the dangers of the drug to society should LSD be made more easily available. Their request presumes that society *is* endangered by any increased access to mind-altering drugs. A third of the lawmakers stressed the danger to individuals rather than to the community and said that they would want to know what the drug does to those who take it. These legislators would also want information on the benefits to be gained by LSD—the basic argument for changing the law—as well as information assuring them that any changes in the law would still provide careful controls and safeguards over access, and information on the motives and characteristics of those who propose that LSD be made more available. A fifth of the legislators said they had no need for any information, for their minds were already made up; to a man they would not make LSD more available and would maintain the present tight controls.

The sources that the legislators considered most reliable and trustworthy for those among them who would want information are shown in Table 21 below. Physicians—especially representatives of organized medicine—would most often receive a respectful hearing, while law-enforcement representatives were ranked second in order of mention as a source of reliable drug facts. Significantly, behavioral scientists were spontaneously mentioned as reliable information sources by only four legislators.

Table 21

TRUSTWORTHY SOURCES OF LSD INFORMATION

	N = 25 Dem.	N = 12 Rep.	Total Per cent
Medical people, particularly the representatives of the Calif. Med. Assn. or the American Med. Assn.	8	10	49
Public health people from state or federal health agencies	7	3	27
Professionals associated with private universities or research facilities, especially people from private medical schools "with no axes to grind"	8	2	27
Law enforcement: district attorney's associations, police and sheriff's associations, State Narcotics Bureau	6	3	24
Psychiatrists	3	4	19
Pharmacologists, drug manufacturers	6	3	24
The legislator's personal physician	2	2	11
Sociologists, psychologists	1	3	11
Other (criminologists, FDA bar association, scientific journals, persons who have taken LSD)	2	3	13

SPECIFICALLY EXCLUDED FROM CONSIDERATION
AS TRUSTWORTHY SOURCES

	N = 25 Dem.	N = 12 Rep.	Total Per cent
Law-enforcement people	3		08
Physicians, "wouldn't trust some doctors"	1		03
Psychiatrists		2	05
Sociologists		1	03

Asked what stand they would take on the LSD bill if they were to vote today, half said they did not know, that they could not decide without further information. More than a third did know how they would vote, but however they voted would be in the direction of

maintaining or increasing the present tight controls over LSD use.[3]
Six legislators (13 per cent of the forty-five discussing their stand)
would be willing to make LSD more available by making it a prescription drug, provided information gave them assurance of its
claimed benefits.

Making marijuana legal. Should a bill be introduced to make
marijuana use legal, what information would the legislators need in
order to decide how to vote? Half of them were not interested in further information; they already knew how they would vote—and that
would be against its legality. The reasons for that decisive opposition
varied; some were convinced the drug is evil or that it leads to evil.
Some, for example, said, "We've enough problems now, no use starting other evils," or "It makes people lose their moral responsibility by
promoting irrationality." Others were sure of the information they
already had, that marijuana is the first step toward hard drugs. Two
assemblymen gave statements that were politically wise, albeit cynical.
One said, "I'd make campaign speeches against it and be a hero";
the other said, "Because public opinion is definite, I'd vote against
marijuana."

The remainder of the legislators were nearly all interested in
learning what the effects of marijuana were, how it might be beneficial
or harmful. "Why is it desirable?" "Does it have clinical uses?" "Does
it really lead to addicting drugs?" "What are the consequences on
crime and traffic accidents?" Two legislators asked whether legislation
making marijuana legal was feasible in view of current public opinion.
"Can we remake our society so that people here view marijuana as
they do in Mexico?"

Only five legislators—their minds not yet made up—could
specify the preferred sources of information they would need; three
mentioned physicians, while two mentioned law-enforcement personnel. They also wanted to hear the views of interested parties, those for
and against such legislation. One legislator thought of university people as an information source.

In terms of a vote today, only five of the fifty lawmakers felt
unable to commit themselves. Two thirds would vote against the bill
out of conviction; another 8 per cent would vote against it because of
the political danger of voting for such an unpopular measure, even

[3] The following year, LSD possession was made a felony in California.
Lobbyists for the increased penalties included police and prosecutors.

though they themselves might favor it. Six legislators said that, realistically, the bill could never come to a vote for no one would be so courageous—or so foolish—as to introduce such legislation. "It would take twenty-five years of public education before anyone would dare."

Making alcoholism a rehabilitation rather than a police problem. In discussing a bill which would remove alcoholics who are public drunks from criminal prosecution, the legislators showed much greater willingness to consider a change from present practice and to be open to new information about proposals. Their decisions would be influenced by: *information about the mechanics of the program*—facilities, authority, needed changes in the law, and the protection of civil liberties in the commitment process (mentioned by a fourth); *information on the costs and sources of funds* for an alcoholic-treatment program (mentioned by a fifth of the legislators) ; *evidence for the advantages of a new program*—proof of benefits to be gained through treatment; *information about alcoholics themselves*—"What are they like?" "Is it really a disease?" "Is it really an addiction?" "Why is it a *health* problem?" "How many are public nuisances now?"; *data from other states or nations* where such programs are in effect showing how the legislation has worked, assurance that individuals who are drunk *and* commit other offenses would still be responsible for their criminal violations, and assurance that the public would accept the new approach (one legislator).

In discussing information sources, a number of legislators brought up an important point. To our inquiry as to where they would go for information, *they* replied that *they* would not go *anywhere,* that the people with information would come to them. Things would not be changed unless there was pressure for change. Such pressure occurs when individuals or groups come to the capitol to propose a bill. In presenting their proposals, interest groups are responsible for providing the evidence of need for new legislation and its benefits. When a legislator has listened to the interested parties and still needs more data, he relies on such standard procedures as interim-committee hearings and the reports of the research staff which committees employ. But if he is to seek something more, it will usually take the form of turning to an easily accessible source already known to him—for example, in drug controversies, to his own personal doctor, the familiar personnel of state health or law-enforcement agencies in the capitol, the ever hovering representatives of the state medical association, and so forth. Only a few legislators spontaneously think of specialists or experts in terms of professional disciplines or individual reputations. However, three lawmakers in our study did say they would turn to social scientists and psychiatrists for alcohol information, and one would ask the prohibitionists. This latter legislator had in mind one of the best-known lobbyists in the capitol, a fondly regarded minister who persistently advocated prohibition.

We asked what pressures from interest groups would be exerted should an alcoholism-treatment bill be proposed. Eleven legislators believed that some of the state's best-known police chiefs and district attorneys would oppose the bill because of their "lack of faith in rehabilitation." They also agreed that churches and temperance people would oppose it should there be any suggestion that the nonpunitive handling of alcoholics would "threaten to remove the stigma from drinking." The legislators' point was that the temperance people hold that drinking is evil and must be publicly stigmatized through arrest and conviction; if medical treatment were to imply acceptance of alcoholism as a disease rather than as an evil, temperance people would be afraid that drinking would be encouraged. In addition, they might argue that evil must be condemned and that rehabilitation is not condemnation.

Among other pressure groups interested in alcohol, the legislators mentioned the liquor industry—which would oppose a bill if its members had to pay any part of the costs of the new program or if it threatened sales. Taxpayers' organizations and civic organizations would also be interested—and opposed—if taxes were to be increased or if any menace to the community were perceived. Civil-liberties "extremists" would also be heard from should there be any danger of the alcoholic's being institutionalized against his will by health personnel without his having an opportunity for a trial or some other judicial review of his status. "Welfare bills may actually take people's rights away from them. It's better to be arrested as a drunk than as an alcoholic."

As for their present position on a bill to shift the burden of alcoholism to public health rather than law-enforcement people, a third of the legislators were uncertain, saying they would be favorably inclined if they were sure there would be no abuse of the law by the alcoholics themselves. Their fear was that alcoholics would be less motivated to recover if "indulged" through rehabilitation than if prodded by the knowledge of their being criminal offenders. "Punishment works to make us good; remove punishment and you remove the reasons for doing good." Another third of the lawmakers favored such a bill provided its administrative program could be worked out without increased taxes. The final third of the legislators said they would vote against the bill at the present time, although many of them offered reasons which suggested their opinions might change if convincing information were in their hands.

In reviewing the negative reactions on the bill, we think it curious that both liberals and conservatives were against it. The same liberals were critical of public-health proceedings and involuntary hospitalization because civil liberties were denied and the individual is socially harmed by being stigmatized as an "alcoholic" without due process of law to protect him from erroneous labeling. Some conservatives felt that "weak" as they are, alcoholics must be held responsible for their actions and punished if they "overindulge" themselves; furthermore, they felt that any transfer of social-control efforts from police to health personnel would threaten a breakdown in law enforcement and subsequent community safety. The latter position is not unrelated to that ascribed to temperance groups: evil exists and must be punished, while rehabilitation implies acceptance or neutrality and that is in itself amoral and conducive of immorality in others.

Voting in disagreement with constituents. "Under what circumstances would you go against your constituents' wishes in voting on any bill to control or change human behavior?" About a fourth of the lawmakers expressed clear unwillingness to vote contrary to the wishes of their constituents or—sometimes more specifically—their important supporters. Some of this group argued that such circumstances do not arise, that discrepancies can never be since they are so close in heart and mind to their constituents that they are as one with them on all matters. A larger group said they would be reluctant to oppose their constituents but would do so under certain circumstances—for example, on moral issues or if the electorate was uninformed. The remaining third stated that they would readily vote against their constituents, that their own special knowledge, judgment, and responsibility require that they act on behalf of, rather than merely under, the direction of the electorate. There were no major differences in the distribution of these three positions by party affiliation.

How to handle the drug offender. Early in our exchange with the legislators, we had encouraged them to offer solutions to the problem of drug abuse. About two thirds of the lawmakers volunteered suggestions; three positions and permutations of those positions emerged: punitive control, education-treatment, and isolation-confinement (nonpunitive). Later in the interview, we mentioned each of these three positions as a commonly advocated alternative and asked each legislator to express and elaborate his preferences. By providing a structured choice, as opposed to the earlier encouragement of spontaneous proposals, we found that all the lawmakers were willing to commit themselves to an approach. Table 22 below shows that more favored a combination of approaches than otherwise.

Table 22

PREFERRED HANDLING OF DRUG-DEPENDENT PERSONS

	N = 33 Dem.	N = 17 Rep.
Punishment-retribution alone	1	4
Isolation plus institutional treatment	16	4
Isolation plus institutional treatment plus punishment-retribution	4	9
Treatment only (no penalties, care, and, if need be, maintenance outside an institution)	12	0

That the majority stated their opposition to the treatment approach with no penalty is consistent with legislative history. Punishment, confinement, and within-institutional treatment is the legislative program for handling addicts in the state. Furthermore, some five years ago, a bill with provisions for no-penalty, noninstitutional treatment was proposed but was defeated. Among those opposing the bill were some leading police officials—an event in keeping with the comments of lawmakers to the effect that interest groups now opposing any "liberal" drug bills were law-enforcement people, conservative civic groups (PTA, mothers' clubs, fraternal societies), the liquor industry, and church and temperance groups. Legislators saw as supporters of the treatment-no-penalty approach the Friends (Quakers), American Civil Liberties Union, NAACP, California Democratic

Council, and the social-welfare people ("those do-gooders"). Wryly noting that "the addict has no friends," some observed that not only were the antitreatment forces much stronger than the protreatment ones but that the latter—for example, the civil-liberties groups—were themselves under fire for their "subversive" activities or were decried for their attempts to "break down law enforcement in the state."

Lest it rashly be thought that stated opinions are excellent predictors to positions on all related issues, we find it necessary to note that even the most punitive legislators approved of the Synanon[4] approach. They reasoned that Synanon forces the individual to take responsibility for his actions, that it does not coddle addicts but forces them to be withdrawn "cold turkey" from opiates, and that the entire effort is done without any cost to the taxpayer. Clearly, Synanon appeals to the economy-minded lawmaker and can be approved for its harshness to addicts by punitive legislators, while treatment-oriented men approve of its nonpenal rehabilitative aspects. We suspect that the legislator who observed that Synanon had a first-class, public-relations program in the capitol was by no means in error. The diverse appeal of Synanon should emphasize the possibility of obtaining agreement on the handling of drug-dependent people, even though stated positions would make it appear impossible that such agreement among lawmakers would ever be reached.

Opposing the lobbyists. Given the fact of powerful interests groups which lobby for and against pending drug bills, what happens to the legislator who decides to buck the pressure groups, voting against their persuasion and threats? Nothing much, according to the lawmakers, at least nothing disastrous as long as there are pressure groups on the other side, too. "No one is defeated [at the polls] on the basis of [his vote on] one issue." On the other hand, the legislator who opposes a powerful lobby will "have to explain things back home" and to accept the alienation of a few former supporters. Only one

---

[4] Synanon is a privately sponsored program for the rehabilitation of narcotic-dependent people. Users who have beaten the habit run the program and, in addition, to charismatic leadership, rely on communal living, strong discipline, and very frank and aggressive "interpretations" of addict ploys, weak points, defenses, con games, and alibis. Reportedly highly selective in its admission program, it is claimed to have had excellent results without the use of medical or mental-health professionals, without any government assistance, and often in the face of citizen opposition to Synanon houses in residential neighborhoods.

lawmaker saw potential catastrophe in opposing the strong antireha-
bilitation lobbies on drug bills. He explained that drug issues are particularly newsworthy, "Narcotics . . . have been made a political
football," he said. Another said, on this same point, "Some legislators
use rabble rousing [on drug issues] to gain votes," and a third com-
mented, "We are pushed and pressured . . . by overexaggeration.
Some people discuss it [drugs] as though every other person were addicted." In any event, it was foreseen that newspapers and law-enforcement people could whip up a storm over a vote for a lenient drug
measure, which could, in turn, arouse the electorate to reject the legislator.

Legislator's personal experience. Half of the legislators who
were willing to discuss their own personal experiences regarding the
abuse of drugs or alcohol indicated that they had had bad experiences;
most of these experiences had been with clients, employees, or relatives
who had been alcoholics. Half of those who had had bad experiences
denied that these had influenced their interests, thoughts, or convictions in any fashion. Among the remainder, several claimed they had
come, one way or another, to an understanding of alcoholism as a
disease. One legislator had himself given up drinking; another had
come to the conclusion that drug abuse was a psychological and social
problem; another had decided that penalties would have to be increased for drug peddlers. One legislator with an alcoholic kinsman
realized—in contrast, he said, to what he had believed before—that
an alcoholic might *not* be responsible (in the free-will and self-control
sense) for his continued drinking. Nevertheless, this same legislator
said he would shy away from legislation for the handling of drunks
as a civil rather than criminal problem because he would not want to
"dignify self-induced drunkenness." Furthermore, regardless of the
plight of the individual alcoholic, he felt his legislative obligation was
to protect the welfare of society. He believed he could best accomplish this through stigmatizing drunkenness and applying penalties as
a moral deterrent to others even if these would not help the alcoholics
themselves.

Political stance and attitudes on drug issues. We compared
the stance of legislators with reference to other social issues and the
views expressed during our interviews with them. First, we classified
each as liberal, moderate, or conservative based on his key voting record prepared by the California Democratic Council. That politically

liberal group scored votes they approved of with "plus" and ones they disapproved of with "minus." Typical pluses would be for a vote for a bill outlawing discrimination in housing, for a moratorium on the death penalty, for elimination of loyalty oaths, for withholding tax on wages, against exempting real-estate operations from antimonopoly laws, and so forth. There were seventeen CDC conservatives, nineteen CDC moderates, and fourteen CDC liberals in our sample.

After each interview we had rated each man as liberal, moderate, or conservative on the basis of his comments. This rating was done without knowledge of his voting record or the CDC score card. Ratings were done by one person, the interviewer, whose only prior information about the legislator was his party affiliation. Men who appeared open to new information, willing to change the status quo, and willing to consider a greater rehabilitative approach with a reduced punitive or controlling emphasis in handling drug-dependent persons were classed as liberals; moderates were those who showed less of each of the above qualifications; and conservatives were those who were least interested in new information to guide legislative decisions on new bills—that is, men who emphasized the need for retribution and deterrence in controlling the menace of drug abuse, as well as favoring the maintenance of the status quo. Comparing relative positions on these two measures, the CDC liberal-conservative continuum and our rating of drug liberality-conservatism, we obtained by using the Spearman rho a correlation of .91. Our conclusion was that a legislator's position on drug issues and his interest in new information and new ways to influence human conduct were predictable from his stands on other social issues. Drug views are part of the constellation of views which are generally spoken of as "liberal" or "conservative."

Being a conservative or a liberal on the basis of the CDC voting record was almost perfectly predictable from party affiliation: fifteen out of seventeen conservatives were Republicans; seventeen out of nineteen moderates were Democrats; and all fourteen liberals were Democrats. A similar trend held for those rated as liberals and conservatives on drug issues. Among sixteen conservatives on drug issues, twelve were Republicans; among fourteen moderates on drug issues, nine were Democrats and five were Republicans; and among the twenty liberals on drug issues, all were Democrats.

For all their differences, we suspected that the liberals and conservatives shared at least one thing in common, a commitment to a "harder" position on issues. The moderates, we thought, would be more willing to conform to what they saw to be the will of the electorate. We tested our expectation by comparing the degrees of stated willingness to "go it alone" among liberals and conservatives. Assigning scores of increasing value to the degrees of independence expressed and using the "t" test, we found that t = 5.98 (df = 30) which is significant beyond the .01 point. We concluded that the "extremists" were more "independent" in that they were more likely to state that they would oppose their own constituents on important issues.

PHILOSOPHICAL DIFFERENCES

From our earlier studies of issues involved in the use of mind-altering drugs, we have found it useful to be alert to two philosophical positions. One is a form of idealism and is moral absolutism; the other is relative and pragmatic. According to our definition, absolutists have a moral sense derived from faith in traditional values, which are based on authoritative sources. With reference to drugs, their views typically reflect the ascetic antipleasure sentiments of St. Paul and the spirit of wrathful vengeance found in the Old Testament. The absolutist position has much in common with that second stage of moral development described by Piaget (1948) in which laws are regarded as sacred and derived from unchallengeable sources. Suggestions for change in such laws are met with hostility, and the whole orientation involves a sense of (religious) respect for what is and what has been handed down as the proper order of things. In the absolutist view good and bad exist, and may be inherent in acts, without reference to the effects of those acts. Drug abuse, because it does involve—in the user *and* in the observer—strong feelings about pleasure, impulse control, spontaneity and constraint, and authority relations is one of the acts requiring moral evaluation and is, in that framework, sinful and wrong. The abuser, having made his responsible choice between good and evil, must be punished. Legislation which would fail to affirm the stigma of innate evil is in itself immoral regardless of *its* effects. Convinced of this much, the moral absolutist will approach the legislation of pleasure and pain with a very strong precommitment.

The pragmatist, by our definition, is very much an empirical and utilitarian man. In our society he is ordinarily also sustained by an idealism which has its roots in the same cultural traditions as the absolutist. But his moral position usually evolves through an evaluation of the effects of acts, and his criteria ordinarily are humanistic ones. Rejecting faith in traditional authority as a route to an ethical system, the pragmatist is not hostile to innovation and takes a relativistic position about good and bad.

Given these two philosophical positions (not to be found in this classical form, of course, in the real world of men), we undertook to rate the legislators for their adherence to or leaning toward one or another position. Ratings were made, in each case, by the interviewer and were based on the foregoing definitions applied to the interview remarks of the legislators. At the time these ratings were made immediately after the discussion, the interviewer was aware of party affiliation. We rated eighteen men as moral absolutists and twenty-six as pragmatists; six men were not rated because we felt unsure or felt they did not fit the typology. Expecting considerable overlap between these ratings and political stance, we found that fifteen absolutists were drug conservatives and three were drug moderates, while seventeen pragmatists were drug liberals, eight were moderates, and one was a conservative. A very similar distribution resulted for political stance as derived from the CDC scorecard. Here, again, we expected overlap between philosophical position and party affiliation as such, and found it. Twenty-three pragmatists were Democrats and three were Republican; eleven moral absolutists were Republicans and seven were Democrats.

As we have said, the overlap between political and philosophical positions was hardly surprising. In part, we were describing the same components but using different words and, in part, the ratings themselves were colored by uncertain reliability and more certain contamination. We grant all this readily and would not attempt to disprove it. But we do suggest that it remains useful to think in philosophical, as well as political or psychodynamic, terms when evaluating legislative, moral, or policy behavior and trying to understand why such a gulf exists between psychologists and lawmakers. We shall also try to illustrate that there can be predictive power derived from the identification of these positions as an aspect of personality.

Social science is pragmatic and social scientists are likely to be empirical, relativistic, and humanistic. As a result, a psychologist (or psychiatrist, pharmacologist, and so on) may confidently testify on the basis of available evidence that marijuana is not ordinarily harmful to the user and that the user does not become dangerous to those about him. Consequently, their testimony concludes that it is only reasonable that marijuana be removed from the list of illicit narcotic substances. In the same empirical vein, Chein, Gerard, Lee, and Rosenfeld (1964) state, "We started with the common belief that prolonged use of narcotic drugs is intrinsically devastating to the human being, physically and psychically, and it was not until we set to work . . . that it was brought home to us how completely without any scientific foundation and contrary to fact such a belief is" (p. 6). Or, again, ". . . by far the most horrible consequences [of opiate use], personally and socially, are directly traceable to its de facto illegality, . . . the incontinent use of opiates is far less dangerous . . . than that of alcohol" (p. 327).

The scientists' soul mate in the capitol, the pragmatic politician, is willing to listen and, if the evidence is persuasive, to agree. But to the moral absolutist the foregoing conclusions are blasphemy and apostasy. And because that is the case, the world view and morality of the social scientist are unacceptable to the absolutist. If he lacks an opportunity to learn how scientific findings might be of value or to find through acquaintance that pragmatists can also have an idealistic bent, the absolutist will reject social science and its practitioners outright.[5] Indeed, a frequent comment was that the social scientists' position was so different from that of many legislators that they were hearing-room outcasts.

If our speculations are correct, the moral absolutists will more

[5] We assume that the absolutist lawmaker perceives a philosophical difference which he cannot tolerate and which leads him to distrust and reject the social scientist. On the other hand, the scientist can also be disdainful of the absolutist and fail to respect the latter's idealism. When this happens, a vicious circle is established, which is a fair guarantee that the two views will remain polarized and that communication will be almost impossible. To assist the scientist in an appreciation of the moral absolutist's position, it may be well to remind the pragmatist that his own utilitarian ethic will be hard put to generate a hierarchy of values or to lend direction either to personal enhancement or social progress unless it is infused with some form of idealism. Without this, the pragmatist remains amoral and might well not only display but eulogize conduct which is conventionally considered to be unprincipled or corrupt. As long as that which works is good and that which does not harm others is not bad, elastic indeed is the standard of conduct. For example, the present emphasis on social adjustment as a mental-health goal is illustrative, for it serves to extol that which is "adaptive" but does do so only at the cost of sacrificing that maladjustment which is for the sake of principle. The administrator who protests against those who would "rock the boat" for any reason or who justifies "cutting corners" becomes Machiavellian.

often reject social scientists as information sources than will the pragmatic lawmakers. To test that premise and simultaneously to demonstrate that philosophical predilections once identified can be more powerful predictors than, for example, party affiliation, we returned to the interview data regarding "trustworthy and reliable" sources of information on the three hypothetical drug bills. On the basis of party affiliation, we found that expressed interest in the opinions of university people (including medical-school faculty), sociologists, psychologists, and psychiatrists was not predictable—that is, there was no significant relationship between reliance on social scientists as trustworthy information sources and the legislator's party label. On the other hand, there was an association (P is greater than .05) between philosophical bent and spontaneously mentioned interest in social-science and academic-information sources. Table 23 presents the distribution employed in the two χ^2 tests.

Table 23

READINESS TO CONSIDER SOCIAL SCIENTISTS AND ALLIED
PROFESSIONALS AS INFORMATION SOURCES

	N = 17 Rep.	N = 33 Dem.	N = 18 Moral absolutist	N = 26 Pragmatist
Cite social scientists as reliable information source	10	15	2	13
Fail to cite social scientists as reliable information source	7	18	16	13

The demonstration of a relationship between moral absolutism and the tendency to reject (or at best overlook) academic- and social-science information sources when considering drug bills must not lead to an oversimplification of the reasons for the low status of these pragmatists in the state's capitol. Remember that the *majority* of legislators in this sample—men in key posts in the legislature of the largest and most "progressive" state in the Union (defined by its welfare programs and government support for health, education, police service, consumer protection, and the like)—were reluctant to accept social-science, psychiatric, and university opinion. All of the reasons for this do not lie in the bosoms of the lawmakers. These professionals have not, as the lawmakers noted, put themselves forward. Their capitol contacts are usually limited to matters of direct interest to their professional organizations: certification and licensing, personnel posts, salaries, and so on. There have been no "unselfish" lobbies to further the scientific view of man or to assure the presence of these professions at hearings on bills designed to modify human behavior. Nor are they a visible group compared with the commercial or law-enforcement interests or the well-financed and smoothly run lobbies of organized medicine, labor, farmers, and the like. Furthermore, on those rare occasions when they do appear to testify, they do not wear well. The legislators spoke convincingly of the inability of some professionals to speak clearly and avoid jargon; they noted how the scientist, casting doubt or raising questions, may produce anxiety and discomfort in the listening lawmaker, who must vote "yes" or "no" regardless of the scientists' own uncertainty. It seems clear that the testifying experts have not realized the need to cast their knowledge in ways that can be useful to men who make laws, nor have they—unlike shrewder lobbyists—tried to guide legislators to the uses of the information that they present.

The fact that moderate and conservative legislators are unlikely to accept the value of scientific data about human behavior should not make us overlook what we nevertheless take to be the trend of the times, notwithstanding the recent upsurge of the reactionary right. The content of the interviews makes it clear that even the punishment-oriented, the most absolutist legislator cannot avoid some token acceptance of "liberal" ideas. A legislator can no longer safely be against "rehabilitation" or "humanitarian treatment" and still count on being re-elected. To give way to the impulse to "throw the key away," said one legislator, proves either that one is ignorant and unaware that "addiction is now a disease" or else that one is inhumane himself. Why—and to what extent—the punitive impulse is interwoven with the absolutist position—at least among the legislators we interviewed—remains an important question in political and religious psychodynamics. (In one study [Blum and Associates, 1964] of policemen working in narcotics, we found a product-moment correlation of only $r = .28$ between dogmatism and punitiveness.) In any event, the consequence of being an absolutist who is forced by the times to accept a more enlightened doctrine leads the legislator to be of two minds—that is, he compartmentalizes. "Of course we should try to rehabilitate but, after all, a man *is* responsible and should be punished for his irresponsibility." Or to use another illustration from a conservative trapped in a liberal net: "We should have (free) drug clinics for the user, but we should have the death penalty for the pusher." (In reality users and peddlers are often the same people.) One conservative put it this way: "I think psychology is the answer to all problems —one must use education and insight to reduce the abuse of dangerous drugs"; he went on to say that the solution to the use of narcotic drugs was to be found in heavy penalties and stricter law enforcement.

SUMMARY AND CONCLUSIONS

Drug abuse was considered to be a major social threat by the majority of California legislators in our sample. Holding key positions of knowledge and power on drug issues, they have reacted to this threat—as reflected in present law and practice—by trying to influence human conduct through punishment and confinement; such measures, of course, are thought to contain the problem rather than solve it. They have considered treatment, but, for the most part, it has been limited to within-institution programs. In our interviews many lawmakers felt that the present approach is inadequate, and a few thought it inhumane. Although many proposals for new legislation call for "more of the same"—that is, for harsher laws and stronger controls—a minority of those legislators interviewed were actively interested in new approaches. Their willingness to explore and innovate has not been reflected, according to the reports of all the legislators, in the opinions of the electorate. The public was generally said to be strongly in favor of punishment and confinement. In their own eyes, a good many legislators are more "liberal" than the people they represent.

Present positions on legislative alternatives in the handling of drugs and users varied according to the drug under discussion. About LSD, for example, many in our sample had no present convictions and were quite open to informed proposals. A hard core of a third of the legislators would stand by the present tight-control laws. With marijuana—a far milder drug than LSD but one about which public opinion is strong (and incorrect)—present punitive positions remained firm, and for reasons of conviction or political savvy, most legislators would oppose any effort to make its use legal. Their attitude toward alcohol was the reverse; they believed the public either to be willing to rehabilitate alcoholics or to be just uninterested in them. Concommitantly, most lawmakers were quite ready to remove the drunk from police purview, provided they were convinced that a treatment program would work and would not be too costly.

For those considering new approaches, the choice of sources for information was a matter of real importance. We found that in matters of drugs it was to the medical man—especially to organized medicine—and to the various law-enforcement associations and bureaus that the legislators would turn. Only a few spontaneously considered academic people: psychologists, sociologists, and psychiatrists. Nevertheless, about half of the legislators in our sample showed respect for the *potential* value of research in human behavior.

As for the relationships between these positions and other variables, we interested ourselves in our study in the conventional liberal-conservative continuum and in party affiliations. Men in our sample who were liberal on drug issues—seeking information, willing to change, and interested in rehabilitation as well as punishment—were also liberal when voting on other social issues; conservatives in the drug area were conservative in their other votes. Party affiliation and a legislator's stance as a liberal or conservative were related. Most of the conservatives were Republicans; all of the liberals were Democrats. While the conservatives and liberals had little in common politically, they did share that strength of conviction which makes them appear more willing than moderates to go it alone against the will of their own constituents.

Although both political stance and party label were consistent with approaches to drug issues, we found it useful to designate related philosophical positions: one, moral absolutism and the other, pragmatism. The assumptions implied in these two positions helped us to understand the extent of the differences between the poles of belief as to how to legislate so as to influence conduct. In addition, these philosophical positions, or personality predilections if one prefers, may prove to be useful variables in research. To illustrate, we learned from our sample that they bore a significant association with the willingness to entertain psychologists, psychiatrists, sociologists, and academic people in general as respected sources of information; absolutists tended to reject and pragmatists tended to accept what behavioral scientists might have to say.

From the practical standpoint of the profession of psychology, the candid views of these legislators provided a test of political reality against which to measure the profession's social importance, as well as its place in the capitol pecking order. The criticisms that they made about social scientists led us to the question of whether or not psychologists, as one of the professions criticized, should commit themselves to positions on social issues and enter the fray either as a pressure group or as a lobby—not in the way that a *conventional* lobby presses for bills affecting the welfare of the professional and vocational interests of its membership, but on behalf of the human beings whom the individual psychologists study and treat as the object of their vocations. In other words, should they do as some legislators recommend and lobby for the implementation of their findings as scientists or for the application of their reasoned inferences from their data in legislative programs? Or should they avoid a professional commitment to lobbying (for example, of the sort done by the scientific committees of the medical associations) and limit their political participation to their partisan, private-citizen domain, while keeping the professional self out of the rough and tumble of capitol cities? Certainly there is a potentially receptive audience for the information that psychologists might provide, but should the profession itself move in that direction, it would take a while for it to earn its spurs of respect in the hearing rooms and capitol offices.

We would raise one more issue. Because it is the general one which we asked the legislators to face, it would be less than fair to dodge it ourselves. It is substantive and ideological and is the issue of drug abuse. How is it to be viewed, how should society respond? The need for facts in order to reply is compelling enough, but the questions go beyond that to challenge us to consider our own personal views about what constitutes a social menace, what pleasure sources are part of individual freedom, and under what conditions and how society should intervene to influence drug use. It may be the nature of the scientist, derived from his work precautions, to wish to avoid a commitment until all the facts are in. But others will act while he waits and their actions will have effects—effects which must be judged according to some value hierarchy. Some of the most important actions that others will take will be to pass laws—laws to punish and laws to rehabilitate, laws to restrict drugs and laws to make them available, and laws to treat the symptoms and, much less often, laws to remove presumed causes. We ask our elected representatives to decide on these issues on our behalf, and they do. But is it right that professionals in the field of human behavior show less interest than their representatives in the effects of legislation, not only in regard to drug abuse but on other matters which affect human conduct and feelings and the course of our society? We think interest and involvement are to be preferred and, with it, an effort on the part of professionals to assist in the work of the legislature.

On the Presence
of Demons

Richard H. Blum

XIV

*T*he good pastor Cotton Mather, scholar and conservative church-man, was preoccupied with a variety of demons. His writings reflected, in the austere and heedful light of gallows hill, shapes tangible and intangible which infested certain New England women. These women, who were prayed over, occasionally given a clerical massage of breast and belly, or otherwise ardently beseeched to confess and repent, were sometimes hanged. That human form possessed by incubus, familiar, succubus, or other supernatural was no safe abode, no matter who was master or tenant. Suffice it to say, that once one chose or was chosen by the devil, the judges would do their duty and the hangman would do the rest. If, at the last moment, the gallows' crowd grew anxious over the wisdom of their law, Mather was there to reassure them that even if the condemned looked like an angel and wore the dignity of the cloth, there was no harm in hanging him, for it *was* the devil there.

Mather's demonology embraced powers that took another form, ones early alchemists had invoked in distillation, now our "spir-its" of alcohol. For Mather this supernatural was almost tangible, although, as with witches, a presence was inferred only from what people did. "Demon" rum Mather called the spirit, and not altogether figuratively by any means. This demon, too, took possession, but only by summons and without the difficult legal questions that surrounded the identification of which was witch, in the case of incubi. With those who were rum-bedeviled Mather was gentler, although many claim he was always a gentle man. No loop-noosed rope was needed when the demon was so familiar—after all, it is the stranger who is the more frightening—so the drunkard was simply taken off to jail. Lest, in spite of clemency, drunkards' ranks be increased, there were pleas for temperance, implying that one might, like kings eating arsenic, ingest demons in tolerable amounts.

Kai Erikson (1966) has written of the Puritans of Mather's time and earlier and in particular of the Quaker heretics then. He makes two observations noteworthy here. One is that from the period 1651 to 1680[1] there was stability in the recorded number of wrongdoers from year to year; the character of offenses brought to trial might fluctuate, the count of offenses itself might vary, the kind of punishments meted out might change, but wrongdoers stayed nearly constant in number. Thus, when the years were heavy with heresy and the gallows with martyred Quakers were hung, these added no new number to the offender count. What Erikson suggests is that the Puritans had a quota for deviants; in each period, come what may, a certain number of persons, as with the constant Athenian tribute to the Minotaur, were the objects—if not the victims—of the administration of justice. It is to be noted, as an aside, that in each period a certain number were convicted for disturbing the peace—drunkenness is assumed to be the major basis for such convictions—but this number, in Puritan times, was the smallest of the offense categories. Erikson's other point is that once a person had been defined as deviant—that is, had been arrested and convicted—more likely than not, a total characterological diagnosis had been made. Although most folk were foreordained for heaven, a few were meant for hell. These latter, the offenders, were permanently without the grace of God. Given an offense worthy of the wrath of God and man, the particulars of the crime did not matter; the man committing it had announced himself

---

[1] The hangings were in 1692, but court records used by Erikson did not extend that late.

outside the law. One need know nothing more about him; he had revealed himself and his relation to God and man. His character established—unless he were to give himself over to complete repentance,
which was deemed most unlikely—all the community could do was
to curb his permanent wickedness. It is Erikson's belief that our prison
system—and he gives no credit to modern rehabilitation-oriented penology—seeks to do only that. He cites penology's constant failure as
proof.

What of these Puritans? What do they matter to us? Even
though they are genealogical forefathers to only a few Americans,
their ideas may nevertheless be prototypes for much current belief
and practice with respect to drugs, illicit-drug users, and the treatment
accorded these persons. In the terminology of our times, there is no
place for demons frankly named or for witches and Dreadfuls, but
the conceptual basis exists. We have the doctrine of the choice of good
and evil, free will and responsibility under the law, and the implication that by certain significant acts a man commits himself irrevocably
to the "other" side. We can act as though a man, once caught bloody
handed in a stigmatizing horror, has moved so far away from outer
norms of inner complexity that we do no wrong in judging all of him,
his total character, by his one act, call him "criminal," "traitor,"
"hippie," "drunk," or "addict." Importantly, we conceive of power.
Outside of physics or politics that is rather vaguely defined, but generally we acknowledge forces beyond our control—and also beyond
our understanding—which move us mightily. Also importantly, we
conceive of intent and design. These imply that accident is not enough
and that mechanical determinism is insufficient; the powers and events
which affect us do so because of some relationship that we have to
them.

It is only a step from power and intent to magic. Magic flourishes where there are wish and fear, uncertainty and weakness, clever-
ness and the need to explain. It flourishes when something needs to be
done. Demons are one of the magical orders—a set of powers, on the
one hand, and a set of explanations, on the other, a constellation of
emotions and events along with the uncertainty necessary to nourish
the extraordinary. Demons are a convenience, for they can serve as
excuses for otherwise unacceptable actions and states of mind, as when
a person is "overcome," "beside himself," "possessed," or, in legal par-

lance, is "temporarily insane." Demons are convenient theater, too, not only richly dramatic but welcome relief, for were they absent, one might be forced to face, perhaps, his real troubles.

What does the above have to do with drugs? In 1967, we conducted a small-scale study which sampled citizens in a small California industrial and residential city. Aimed at finding facts and attitudes relevant for crime prevention, the study began with this initial question: "What types of crime do you think are the most serious menace to the community?" The actual crime facts in this city are that the most frequently reported major crimes are burglary, auto theft, and those against property. Among the more numerous minor crimes, traffic offenses rank first, followed by malicious mischief and petty larceny. Murder and other heinous offenses do occur, but rarely. In 1966, for example, there were ten rapes, eighteen armed robberies, thirteen aggravated assaults, but no murders.

The menacing crime most often mentioned by citizens was unrelated either to crimes against property or against person. Drug use was reported as the greatest menace.[2] The prominent place accorded to drugs as a crime menace to the community, when added to the finding of an earlier survey (Field Poll, 1966) showing that of *all* public problems crime and delinquency ranked highest (that was before Black Power, Vietnam, and student-protest demonstrations), does indicate that drug use stands out as a problem, as a threat, and as a preoccupation in the public mind. Political leaders are responsive to such concerns. When President Johnson delivered his State of the Union address (January 1968), his greatest applause reportedly came after proposals for suppressing crime and traffic in LSD. Given the available facts about drug use (see Chapters Eight and Nine), it appears that the menace unseen is greater than the presumed menace at hand—if by "menace at hand" we mean the incidence of self-damage due to mind-altering drugs or the incidence of crimes against persons and property shown to be attributable to the influences of drugs, with the exception of alcohol.

Mind-altering drugs have been invested by the public with qualities which are not directly linked to their visible or most probable

[2] The statistics for 1966 showed fourteen drug arrests, none for hard narcotics. During 1967, an increase in the rate of drug arrests was occurring; by the end of the year—several months after our interviews were completed—sixty-two persons had been arrested for marijuana and dangerous-drug offenses.

effects. They have been elevated to the status of a power deemed capable of tempting, possessing, corrupting, and destroying persons without regard to the prior conduct or condition of those persons—a power which has all-or-none effects. Gradations of results are not ordinarily considered as a function of the factors empirically shown to be responsible for them, such as dosage, purity, route of administration, frequency of use, nutritional states, the presence of biochemical antagonists or potentiators, social setting, subject's health, intentions and personality, and the like. The "power" in drugs is such that those identified as users are immediately reclassified socially—most likely as unregenerate outcasts. Such a power comes close to being demoniacal. Has Cotton Mather's demon in rum changed his residence? Have witches turned now to technology whereby they lurk in heroin, LSD, methamphetamine, and other materials?

Mather's demonology provided for exotic demons—some tawny colored, some Indian red, some black, but notably few white like a Puritan—who invested a person and turned him, or in those days more often her, into a witch. Once possessed by a devil, people themselves *became* devils capable of all manner of fiendish exploits. The witch embraced his possessor—that is, they incorporated one another, so that it was natural for the hangman to destroy both at once, the two being in league. There were exceptions: confession and repentance could save a person. The repentant witch was not hanged then, since she had presumably by that act returned to mortal ground and, in so doing, had evicted her dreadful tenant in ways not made explicit. On the other hand, the unrepentant witch, who claimed there was no demon inside her, no witchcraft abiding, or even denied the phenomenon of demons itself—that woman went a-carting to gallows hill.

Now consider the modern view. One group of Republican legislators responded negatively to the report of a Presidential Advisory Committee (Walsh, 1966) proposing hospitalization for drug offenders. They objected to what they saw as the modern principle that "the individual is not really responsible for his acts . . . as long as he has indulged himself into dependence on narcotic drugs (Walsh, p. 1726)." For these legislators, responsibility for self-indulgence in drugs must be punished. Others in and out of government, the police, and prosecuting-attorney associations sometimes speak of the abominable degradation of the addict who, paradoxically a victim of his habit, resists all efforts to correct him. These people deserve, so the lobbyists say, the harshest penalties. The drug "addict" (and it is impossible to set forth here all of the confusion surrounding this word) in their view has succumbed to temptation, has embraced the evil power in drugs, and refuses correction whether provided in hospital wards or prison cells. The only recourse is further punishment for his wickedness, his demon and himself now being one. Death itself is not ruled out as too high a price for scourging demons—and death is the penalty for drug sales under some statutes. On the other hand, the repentant junkie or acid head is the most welcome of guests. The prodigal returned to give testimony is, as are other extreme and reversible converts—for example, the girls of Salem and Andover who experienced witches—harshest on the unredeemed. Witness Synanon's corrective abuse (always with pride) or the descriptions and alarms of the professional "I was a drug addict" on the stage of the high school auditorium. This is not to argue that those who have known the plague should defend it; rather, it is to suggest that the Puritan parallels are striking. The demon and his possessed become one to frighten and repel the onlooker.

Recall the proposal that the fallen Puritan, so judged by one significant event or salient life style, revealed a total defect of character that made him a member of a different class neither likely to change nor be redeemed. In modern terms one thinks of prejudice and stereotypes, or of dominating-role characteristics. One also thinks of how difficult it is for an "ex-con" to get a job, for a nice girl to marry a criminal, for an addict to be conceived as personable or law-abiding in other ways, or for an acid head to be anything but totally irresponsible, amoral, and possibly crazy. Indeed, how easy it is to speak of drug users and to cast thereby into the pit, verbally and conceptually, the healthy student who has had a one-time casual experiment with marijuana. No problem exists for the "user" who is never officially charged, but for those who are brought before the bar, the casual experiment can be a lifetime stigma. There is no reason to exaggerate; even trial and conviction need not stigmatize in a day and age when citizens engage in civil disobedience, hold a jail sentence in respect, and when 40 per cent of our male children may expect to be arrested for nontraffic offenses (the President's Commission on Law Enforcement and the Administration of Justice, 1967). Yet to be a convicted drug user does carry social penalties which can be severe; these can include the character diagnosis of total undesirability.

The person who uses drugs illicitly but escapes without being caught is not condemned by the public even though his knowing friends may disapprove, or, if he advertises himself, like the hippies, he may suffer harrassment. Most users are, in fact, safe. Let us take the pilot-study data of Chapter Eleven, which reports that 18 per cent of the adult population have had one or more illicit-exotic drug-use experiences and that, for example, 5 per cent currently use marijuana and 6 per cent amphetamines, and then consider the 1967 drug-arrest figures for California (extrapolated from the semiannual report of the Bureau of Criminal Statistics), which indicate about 40,-000 such arrests. Is it not dramatically clear that more people use illicit-exotic drugs than are arrested for using them? Assume that metropolitan adults have an overall annual illicit-use (prevalence) rate of 6 per cent, which we believe is a conservative estimate: 40,000 arrests yield for the state as a whole (population over age eighteen $=$ 12,000,000) a rate of arrest of about 1/300. The proportion of illicit users in the adult population in any one year is at least 1/18, whereas arrests occur at the rate of 1/300, which means that the former exceeds the latter by a factor of 18.

If it is true that many people have used drugs illicitly but only a few have been singled out for punishment, how can we account for the fact? And how do we account for the remarkable fuss over those who have been caught in contrast to the presumably rare pillorying of those who are known to use illicit drugs but have not been publicly paraded? This is not to say that no concern exists over the "dark number," the unknowns. But it is a different kind of concern; the worry, it appears, is about their potential seduction, their potential castigation, not their present drug flirtation or even commitment. The case, of course, may be too strongly put, but what appears to occur is a sympathetic anxiety for the unidentified user or a fascinated interest if he is a hippie, contrasted to a public condemnation of the person who has been identified. It may not be incongruous, for it may simply reflect the value our culture places on discretion; the public is anxious for the undetected offender to remain discrete. Or it may simply be shared anxiety; each of us presumably has our darker side, our private log of our own offenses, and each of us as a "dark number" holds the hand of another, praying that he may not, as we may not, be caught.

The mechanics of the accounting for arrests for all offenses are easy enough. Police capabilities in narcotics and dangerous-drug con-

trol are established at the working level by those administrative decisions within law-enforcement agencies which set the number of officers working that form of vice. Whom these working officers arrest is,
in turn, decided by their ability to gather evidence meeting the standards for successful convictions; it is also a matter of the working officers' interest in "making" particular kinds of cases with particular
kinds of groups (Skolnik, 1966). Both administrative decisions and
investigational arrest practices on the street also reflect larger influences: political and mass-media pressures, discretionary and discrimi-
natory enforcement by class and race, available funds for law enforcement and the priorities for each departmental service, officer
expectations of prosecutor actions and judicial response, strategic needs
to protect informant offenders, and the like. These administrative and
individual factors do account for the upper limit of drug arrests possible in a city. They do not account for how it happens that an upper
limit is set far below the known prevalence of illicit-drug users in a
community. An explanation to the effect that the police cannot do
everything—that is, cannot identify and investigate all crime—is obviously correct. The explanation remains insufficient since it is not the
police but the community at large which establishes police budgets and
law-enforcement policies. It is to the community we must look.

At the community level several explanations are also forth-
coming. One would hold that drug "abuse" is so widespread that control is impossible. Most police would concur since, in spite of public
expectations to the contrary, police prevention and control of vice is
at best limited. But if control is impossible, if drug use is *that* widespread, how does the community account for the potential vehemence
of its response (defined by narcotics laws that provide punishments of
two, five, and ten years, for example, for marijuana use) to those few
offenders (the "quota" in Erikson's sense) who are convicted? The
facile replies of deterrence, community protection, or offender rehabilitation are also insufficient since obviously large numbers are not
deterred (although many more likely are); any actual menace requiring incarceration for community protection is negated by widespread
probation and parole, as well as by the fact of little demonstrable
menace existing among most nonalcoholic drug users and by the failure, so far, of rehabilitation programs.

Roche (1958) offers an interpretation of the system of justice
which may be relevant to the incongruity and to the quota itself.

Crimes involving violation of strong moral codes are dealt with by what is a religious ritual, for the trial is an edifying morality play. As a society's morals are publicly reaffirmed, the observing citizen has his own moral constraints reinforced and his criminal impulses consequently further subdued. Think of the prosecutor as super ego, the judge as ego, and the accused as id caught in the act. Just as in Greek drama, the outcome is predetermined—not that all are convicted, but the guilty must fall. Roche contends that the trial also serves as a theater for the repetition of the crime and its symbolic undoing—this within the onlooker as well as for the society. Within the onlooker there also occurs the internalized ritual of guilt fixing, condemnation, and expiation. Applying Roche's scheme, one would also anticipate that the public trial reaffirms individual confidence in the mythical omnipotence of the entire system of justice itself. In addition, it may also provide him with a vicarious enterprise, for the onlooker's own criminal saga—and it is assumed here that every onlooker has violated taboo if only in his mind—remains undetected. The onlooker, a master criminal, triumphs while watching another suffer for what he himself has done. Unlike the Christian parallel, the citizen may simply be delighted rather than provided salvation. In any event, the accused, whether the lamb or the scapegoat, relieves others of their pollution or, in modern terms, their culpability or sin.

Such dramatic interpretations obviously have little to do with the day-to-day business of administering justice, neither its origins, rationale, functions, or ordinary effects. Myriad forces influence who gets arrested and who gets convicted. One asks whether any part of the immense and rightfully inspiring structure of justice's works is built upon other than a rational appraisal of the evidence concerning the effects of drugs, the known characteristics and actions of drug users, the evidence of harm done to persons and property in consequence of such use, a clear knowledge of the consequences of intervention by the system of justice on these persons and on others, and, necessarily, a clear appraisal of our moral values so that those sanctions not of evident empirical value are strongly consonant with our ideals and ethical principles. The answer is before us. The structure is neither rational and consistent nor necessarily consonant with our moral and political ideals. This does not mean it is capricious or erroneous by design or unworthy of our greatest respect. But because it is a moral system in a complex and changing society, it represents many roots, many ends, and many compromises. It also represents in some ways a mythology about drugs.

It is discriminating demonology which posits more devil per drop in some preparations than in others. Aspirin, tobacco, barbiturates, and tranquilizers are of little concern, alcohol occupies a middle ground, the amphetamines, which once were of little importance, are now growing quite worrisome, but it is heroin, cannabis, LSD, and other hallucinogens which are deemed most devilish—that is, awesome, seductive, and menacing. Such a discrimination is a bit awkward on strictly pharmacological grounds, but if the characteristics of users and settings of use are considered, we see that the attribution of menace is linked closely to the degree to which the committed users of each drug advertise their escape from the fold. But whether they are black sheep or otherwise, the menacing drugs are those whose devotees have strayed and make a point of standing apart.

It is to their drugs—the hard narcotics (excluding, of course, all medical opiates about which there is no concern), cannabis, and LSD—that the great powers to tempt, to convert, and to destroy are attributed. This description shows us something more. It shows us that these are the *treacherous* drugs. It is not only that they have led their users away from ordinary social styles. They are also conceived of as deceitful; their allure leads to disaster not pleasure. This may simply be a dramatic allegory describing the conventional man's view of the social process whereby the committed users choose to become social outcasts. The drama of treachery is enshrined in the classic myth of the assassins whereby an initial taste of idyllic and sexual joy is followed by a bloody mind-killing enslavement. On the other hand, awareness of physical addiction as such and our cultural abhorrence of dependency in general is also involved, so that the drug is seen as betraying the hopes of the user, as well as separating him from society. No wonder that upon these drugs is placed a burden of public emotion: "disgust," "fear," "revulsion," "despair," and "anger" are the words narcotics officers in our earlier study used to describe public feelings.

Yet we would add another word, and that is "desire." "Temptation" and "seduction" as used to describe drug lures imply it. The term "pleasure-giving drug" acknowledges it, as do words like "high," "kicks," "joy-popping," and the like. The siren song is heard by all, and so it is upon these drugs, treacherous as they may be, that the burden of the public's great and unfulfilled desire is placed. There is the fancy of escape from pain and tedium, of gratifications in sex and gain, of perhaps—even as with the assassins and visions of "drug-crazed killers"—the license to harm, and perhaps of fraternal closeness, and, of course, of euphoria in all its forms. To these desires self-generated from the impulses in the inner man, add the songs of the prophets of the hippie scene, sweet melodies singing of love without obligation, of the vision of God beheld by those lacking either inner virtue or outer merit, of the joy of creativity without artistic skill, of aesthetic sensibilities without a sense of taste, of freedom without responsibility or consequence, of self-knowledge without self-criticism, of self-enchantment without increased complexity, of psychotherapy without doubts or anxiety, and, finally, of life itself without struggle. These are the siren songs. As with Faust, Satan promised a great deal for a very small down payment; out of that demonology Goethe constructed literature. For those who sing paeans of praise for the magic pills of pharmacology or their natural-growing cousins, the demonology is elaborated into a myth which constitutes a style of life. Those who embrace it call it good; those who fear its treachery call it bad. As with all supernaturals, the drug demon has a Janus head, is polarized, divisible into glory and evil. His disciplines and those potential disciples who, suspecting treachery, are his sworn antagonists will be among the battalions of extremists on drug issues.

It is not likely that such spiritual extremes account for a large portion of the beliefs of ordinary citizens in secular America. There are a number of other possible sources for errors in assessments of the drug menace. It is possible that, as we (Blum and Associates, 1964) discussed in *Utopiates,* the very notion of private pleasure is the kernel of the matter. To have pleasure in this once work- and discipline-oriented society—a society now moving into the automated leisure of wealth, as well as experiencing the traditional enforced leisure of poverty—remains a matter of distrust. Disapproved private enjoyments, beginning with masturbatory "self-abuse" and extending through other forms of sex and drug-induced altered states of consciousness, tempt and repel us along life's way. Satan, of course, is the pleasure prompter extraordinary in any Fundamentalist ethic; it is no surprise that his agents—rarely so delightful as Screwtape—may constitute an essence of the fantasied pleasure of pills, pot, heroin ("snow"), acid, and the rest. Not that all the users' pleasures are fantastic, although it is difficult enough to say what pleasure is in tough experimental terms. Nevertheless, the titillating anticipations of the disapproving public are likely to exceed by far the transient euphoria or chronic stupor of any heavy user.

Proposals have also been made—again in *Utopiates,* as well as elsewhere—that suspicion surrounds the mystic in Western culture. Strongly faithful that God is there, the church is nevertheless dubious when anyone sees Him too easily. Whether investigating miracles or one-man cosmologists, the conventional religionist, regardless of whether his God is learned through doctrine or felt sublimely, takes a dim view of visions. Yet most intoxicants can produce such states and visions if the user is in tune; witness Henry James on alcoholic joy. The visionary may sense a blessing but the skeptic wonders how often a genie-God is bidden to arise from a pill. The alternative interpretations are two: either the chemical mystic has produced his own gods—which is heresy and vanity at the least and, though not likely, madness as well—or the powers he has seen are real enough but bear the wrong credentials. Whether possessed by madness or by real devils, the drugged mystic is fair game for an explanatory demonology. Both the possessed and the possessors are demons of a sort.

A third proposal is that ecstasy and excess are what is wrong in a culture geared to moderation. The committed user is an extremist in a special way. Modlin and Montes (1964) describe physician addicts whom they have studied. "They desire euphoria . . . they . . . find this part-of-the-time feeling of complete gratification, satiation, wanting for nothing; this episodic tension-free frustration-free nirvana is worth to them whatever they have to pay (p. 360)." This is a Dionysian view, that short periods of total fulfillment or total release are far better than chronic, boring adjustment. Consider the orgiastic frenzies of some revelers, whether on pot, acid, or alcohol, and compare them with a Dionysian frenzy—the former, sexual and the latter, bloodily religious. Both are a Mardi Gras cycle of feast and fast (or, in the case of drugs, the piper is paid perhaps with psychosis, hangover, drug dependency, and physical illness), rather than the pursuit of Apollonian balance.

The Bacchantae were possessed in their time; the heavy drug users ("druggies") of our time deny a demon, but for simple observers whose psychology does not account for ecstasy and extremism, some external force is required. *"People* just don't act like that!" A drug as power suffices, but its essences as expressed in frenzy are maenadic enough to raise the lingering cultural ghosts. So it is that drug and magical essence of demon may blend.

At another level of frankness, even the ordinary man knows that people *are* like that, or could be if allowed. His example is himself—not the "real" man but the might-be man. Social life requires control; technology requires efficiency; respect and esteem require restraint and regard. It does not take a Freudian to know that these are not easily come by or ever perfectly maintained. Within ourselves disruption awaits, be it pique or passion. When disruption takes place, a normal response is to deny responsibility and to blame something or someone outside ourselves. Most cultures stock a variety of blameworthy objects and notions to account for unhappy events or the misbehavior of people. In our society these range from "bad luck" and "an act of God" through personal culpability—for example, ranging from "bad blood" or "constitutional psychopath" to unpopular groups such as Communists, the "military-industrial complex" and *"those* people." Drugs occupy an unusual place as one of the few material substances still animistically endowed. The anima in drugs is culpable. It lures, enslaves, and destroys. So it is that for any man aware of his own vulnerability to disruption—whether it be loss of control, giving up, or madness—the animistic principle in drugs stands as a constant threat, the menace of which the public speaks.

Pharmaceutical materials do not dispense themselves and the illicit drugs are rarely given away, let alone forced on people. Consequently, the menace lies within the person, for there would be no drug threat without a drug attraction. Psychoanalytic observations on alcoholics suggest the presence of simultaneous repulsion and attraction in compulsive ingestion. The amount of public interest in stories about druggies suggests the same drug attraction and repulsion in ordinary citizens. "Fascination" is the better term since it implies witchcraft and enchantment. People are fascinated by drugs—or rather by their own and the mass-media fantasies about drugs—because they are attracted to the states and conditions drugs are said to produce. That is another side to the fear of being disrupted; it is the desire for release, for escape, for magic, and for ecstatic joys. That is the derivation of the menace in drugs—their representation as keys to forbidden kingdoms inside ourselves. The Dreadful in the drug is the *dreadful* in ourselves.

There is yet another perspective. For those who are *already* disrupted, mentally disturbed, the anima in drugs provides an excuse, a relief, and a measure of control for, as Sylvester and Oremland (1968) observe, the person who is hallucinating and then takes hallucinogens can blame his disorder on the drugs. He can say the drug produces the voices. The pathological dissociation process is pushed one further step so that the drug becomes the doer. As long as he doesn't stop using drugs, the disturbed person can believe that he *could* stop hallucinating if he wanted to—that is, if only he stopped drug use. By making the drug responsible, he joins his explanation to the popular one. By adding his voice to the popular conception he also aids his social adjustment, for his accounting for himself then conforms to a "normal" explanation. This accounting also provides "evidence" in support of a popular theory of drug effects. The disturbed person becomes proof of what others believe and, much like a Salem girl confessing to what witchcraft she has done, he becomes a welcome and much-cited case.

Still another aspect may be considered. Mather's demon rum turned out to be a bore after long acquaintance. He is being defanged as polar practices of teetotaling or drunkenness are slowly being replaced by moderate drinking. Alcoholism is with us but, as with the cultural evolution of madness, no longer as possession but as illness or, in another set of formulations, as interpersonal behavior complexly determined. The public has not become so well acquainted with other forms of drug use that familiarity allows acceptance of medical or psychosocial theories about what is happening. The illicit-exotic drugs and their devotees are strangers to this public, and it is only in response to strangers and the strange that romance and fascination develop. How many Americans sense transport to the nether reaches of the archetypical racial unconscious when smoking a Chesterfield? How many learn to "love" when drinking a beer and watching a ball game? Do they discover inner beauty when taking an aspirin for a headache? It is no surprise that romance requires a stranger. If there is to be that fascination, there is also idealization. Ordinary romantic attraction or hatred in the service of sentiment prefers simple objects. Pure evil is a loftier enemy; Iago as interpreted at the high school level is what is needed. Against pure evil one marshals the choicest antagonist—the innocent purity of the child, just as the fairy stories have it.

For the confirmed drug user, the druggie, the same scheme

applies; only he reverses the field. He is the innocent and pure-born—corrupted only insofar as he has been soiled by his parents and other worldly folk. He is the flower child, free and loving. It is the rest of the world which stinks of evil, the evil of the city, of technology, of government—the overpowering evil of human beings living ordinary lives. The way both sides characterize themselves reeks, of course, of simplicity and sentimentality.

Sentimentality is a special notion. The Russells (1961) have considered it carefully and conclude that it is an elaborate deception based upon disgust, hostility, and projected feelings. It is linked, they say, to cruelty, addiction, and phobia. Its origins lie in parental hostility to the behavior or condition of the child—hostility which is introjected by the child, so that as he grows to manhood, the man too loathes that which his parents loathed. Let us say he is disgusted by dirt. Another person who is dirty arouses his hostility which, according to the formulation, becomes hostility perceived as coming from the dirty one. That unworthy must be punished. In so doing, the avenger relieves his own discomfort over his own hidden dirtiness. The punishment is visited in the name of virtue, cleanliness, crime fighting, protecting the innocent, and other sentimental appeals. The ideal, the sentimentally surrounded symbol, is the opposite to what one has, as a child, learned is repugnant inside himself.

In *Utopiates* we presented the thesis that dirtiness is associated with illicit-exotic drug use in the minds of many extremists pro and con. For hippies dirtiness is renamed and becomes spontaneity, freedom, or creativity. To link these reactions to toilet training and parent-child discipline problems requires no deep insight. Recall that "shit" is a term for marijuana and think of "pot" as something other than for cooking. More important, consider the street cant by which the heroin user is "dirty" and becomes "clean" only when off the drug. The hippie druggie has other sentimental symbols; he applauds love, flowers, beauty, peace, and goodness while ironically, as the work of Hensala, Epstein, and Blacker (1967) shows, harboring massive hostility, which he may release indirectly—not that hurting parents by running away from them is really indirect. This journey, like other "trips," is more likely away from, rather than toward, others.

Sentimentality may also surround the vision of things that druggies are thought to do or adore. Sexual orgies imputed to the drug crowd are an illustration. It is not that druggies eschew sex and do not engage in plain and fancy fornication, often polymorphous to be sure; yet, what is remarkable is the preoccupation with druggie sex life on the part of antidruggies. Even though a safe presumption is that chronic drug use in fact reduces sexual interest and potency (it may, however, also increase the duration of the male erection), the popular image of the hippie, main-lining prostitute, or other freak-out is one of frenzied copulation. In the lore that titillating notion is likely to be enhanced by racial fantasies which center on the proverbial animal Negro male violating the drugged blonde maiden while a hundred other Dreadful Marvels coil in sweaty embrace. Sentimentality converts desire to disgust, envy to hostility, and fear of retribution to flattery. What emerge are, as before, an evil *other,* a righteous self, and a set of simplistic mawkish symbols triggering insincere but intense reactions. The sentimentality on the druggie side shows him acting as a cultural complement, doing his/her best to live up to the advanced billing with exhibitionism, artfully erotic posters, party pads, nude dances, conspicuous interracial hand holding, and girls who wear no underwear.

The manifestations of demons? Does the false simplicity, polarity, deception, and emotionality of sentimentality convert themselves into a demonology? Yes, if one makes demons as the ancient Greeks did (Blum and Blum, 1968) out of unacceptable internal forces or of unachievable powers feared and flatteringly idealized. After all, the Eumenides, the "gracious ones," were in fact the avenging furies, the Erinyes. Whether it is necessary or not for us to admit druggie and antidruggie into an explicit demonology or simply to observe them respond to the sentimental appeals of a concealed demonology may not matter; the behavior is understandable by either scheme.

There is another aspect of drug use which relates to implicit or explicit demonologies. Mind-altering drugs are very likely to alter interpersonal relations. As we have reported elsewhere in this book, normal use is generally associated with enhanced social intercourse, although in unusual cases—whether of persons or whole cultures—the interference in social relations can be spectacular. In our study of narcotics officers as reported in *Utopiates,* one of their main complaints about pot heads was that they appear normal but behave in unpredictable ways. Such is not the case among drunks or junkies, for since they do not appear normal, those nearby are at least forewarned that the unusual will occur. What is implied in the officers' complaint about pot heads is their unresponsiveness or inappropriate responsiveness to ordinary social demands. This immediately brings to mind the charge that druggies are irresponsible and the counterdemand by hippies that every man should be left free to "do his own thing" regardless of conventions. In other words, the contention carried a step further implies that the druggie, whether intoxicated or not, is beyond the usual calls, manipulations, appeals, or predictions of the ordinary man using ordinary social devices. In a world requiring predictability not only for effective action but even for consistent self-definition, the presence of a group of erratic people who are not (yet) controlled by supervisorial institutions (jails, mental hospitals, the military) or enticed into consenting ones (families, schools, churches, jobs) is unnerving. One may focus on the junkie, LSD tripper, or alcoholic to find the same phenomena, the core of which is *self-induced* transport away from the world of ordinary signals and responses.

There are others in our society who are also unable to function according to ordinary expectations: madmen, the witless, or those with serious physical illness, or infirmity. In each case a protective explanation is available: they are victims of misfortune who would act conventionally if they could. They have not "willingly" opted out.

The acid head, pot head, meth freak, or what-have-you constitutes a different case. They are not victims of misfortune; insofar as they have enjoyed opportunities and benefits of the middle class, they cannot be excused on the popular deterministic grounds of cultural deprivation, poverty, and so forth. Junkies and many alcoholics, on the other hand, may be so excused and, because of this, one sees a kind of paternal sympathy for them. Even so, all of the druggies appear to have *chosen* their poison. They claim free will, a claim the public cannot dispute since our cultural ethos claims it too. So by their own free will, they are unresponsive to pleas made to them in the name of parental love, civil authority, educated argument, material reward, moral rectitude, medical wisdom, self-esteem, or public respect. Pray tell what else can a society devise to influence its youth?

By being unresponsive, by not acting normally in response to the usual interpersonal symbols, the druggies not only prevent the parent, cop, teacher, and doctor from enjoying the normal sequence of social behavior but, in a more general way, challenge the efficacy of all our devices. They do "opt out" and in such a way as to make others feel impotent about guiding interpersonal relations. They advertise that they are outsiders, as the Greeks would say. They are "exotica," supernaturals who hail from outside-of-here. Unlike the demon of rural Greece whose origins as well as actions are exotic, the druggie has once been one of us. He has been our child, our spouse, our parent, or coworker—a member of the inner circle. It is after *that* he leaves us of his own free will, as the doctrine of responsibility has it. It is a very special leave-taking because it is a betrayal. He has once accepted the conventional system, been sensitive to our words, enjoyed our benefits, and then has found it all wanting. That druggie challenges what most hold dear and true, renouncing the array of enticements displayed in our cultural bazaar. We ask what kind of a person would do this to us? We find it hard to say it is our own child. He is not himself, he is a changeling, he has been seduced and subverted by some evil force more powerful than his innocence or our affection. He has been enslaved and that is why he does not return. Once again, the ordinary man is thinking in terms of those possessed and how the possessed of their own free will, as the Christian dogma sets it forth, have embraced evil.

A further disconcerting feature of druggie irresponsibility is that he can evoke predictable responses in us even though it appears we cannot do so in him. He knows the system that binds us and can employ it at his pleasure. We are vulnerable to his manipulation whereas we feel we cannot, outside of coercion, manipulate him. Think of the cases where a drunken relative has captured an entire family by using his drug, himself, and the conventional signs and symbols to imprison its members. Think of the amusement of the more clever hippie child pressing the buttons marked "sore" in his parents' psyches. By remaining responsible, we can be victimized—or so it may feel—by outsiders. Again, we ask the primitive question: what manner of creature is it who is able, however disreputable he looks, to arouse our emotions and flay our sacred sentiments while we make no dents in him? Such a creature, free, powerful, and in the service of discontent, is a Miltonian Lucifer. And that Loathsome One is the stuff of demons.

If the speculations presented in this essay are pertinent to an accounting of how people think about drug use, the conclusion is warranted that a mythology pervades our approach to certain kinds of drugs and to certain groups of drug users. For the sake of classification that mythology is demoniacal. If it is a demonology, then its essence is that the fervent among druggies and antidruggies are both true believers.

Hippies: What the Scene Means

John H. Weakland

XV

*I*t is particularly apt that a cultural anthropologist should consider the nature and significance of student drug use and its most extreme development, the hippie scene. Such phenomena, whether transient or more lasting, constitute a social movement. Such movements are grist to the mill of modern anthropologists, whose work is now characterized by its concepts and approach rather than, as formerly, by a subject matter limited to remote and primitive peoples. Yet these earlier anthropological predilections are relevant to the present case. The hippies see themselves as a "subculture" outside of, apart from, our ordinary society which is the "straight" world. They see their way of living, especially its communal aspects and "tribes," as a return to simpler and more primitive social forms. Importantly, the straight world also tends to see the hippie scene as remote and strange—therefore, as interesting but curious, nonsensical but threatening, especially when the remote does not stay nicely and safely separate but impinges on the "normal," proper, everyday world by attracting interested inquirers and potential converts from among its young sons and daughters.

There is a further connection to anthropology. Among the hippies and other young drug experimenters, the experience of drugs, and other especially novel, interesting, or gratifying experiences is commonly referred to as "a trip." An anthropologist can hardly hear this word in such a connection without being reminded of those field trips that, although engaged in consciously and deliberately for purposes of research, become a central part of his personal life as well as of his professional career. There are very basic reasons for this response. As Gregory Bateson once said, "In the social sciences, when you put a probe into any human situation, the other end always sticks into you." A field trip, especially, means going out into the midst of a new and strange situation, not merely observing but necessarily becoming involved in a way of living and thinking that is unfamiliar, and being influenced by it. And that is not all. The anthropologist's return from the field to his normal haunts is equally important; it may be a comparably difficult adjustment or—as many Peace Corps workers have also found—even one more difficult. One is changed by the trip; this may be and often is felt by the anthropologist as broadening, as enlightenment. Yet, that does not remove, or even lessen, the problem of using this enlightenment in the old context or of achieving some integration.

The descriptions by drug users of their "trips" in both nature and functions correspond to this point for point, except that their trips are directed more toward an inner world than a different outer world —though this is largely a matter of explicit emphases and degree; certainly the hippies also explore a different social world, and anthropologists also encounter a new world of inner experience, as Bohannon (1954) describes so well, although they play this down in their usual professional discourse. We may well question whether the drug takers will achieve their stated goals, although their methods have many precedents in other cultures, but we can hardly question the stated aims of their trips—like those of the anthropologist—to explore a new world and to bring back from it new knowledge (or perhaps old knowledge rediscovered) which will be valuable for better living, for themselves or others.

An account focusing on those who take trips must except those who do not; thus, persons taking drugs outside the drug movement—

as, for example, those who seek "kicks" only—are tentatively classified as a different order of problem. Very possibly that group is of less
social significance despite the anxiety surrounding what they do. Even
so, we must remember that the search for kicks itself can be an aspect
or avenue in searching for the nature and meaning of life. As for the
question of whether drug trippers will ever return to the world from
which they have departed—have the hippies "gone native" to stay?—
its consideration will be deferred. For the moment, it is enough to
say that just as the spectrum of exploring travelers is wide, from tourists through anthropologists to various sorts of permanent expatriates,
so is the spectrum of drug travelers, and there, too, the ultimate expatriates certainly will be a small minority. The great majority, on
whom our practical social concern must focus, though not necessarily
our inquiry, probably are not even at the center of the scale, engaged
in field trips, but are only tourists despite common fears that even
these will somehow lose their way.

This chapter does not propose to focus mainly on whether the
drug users will succeed in their quest by such means. Since all life is
largely a search for the good life—yet, what is tried is always marked
by great variety from place to place and time to time—this question
ultimately seems unanswerable. At most, we may, in deference to the
anxieties this type of search has raised in our society, consider whether
it dooms its advocates generally, not just to a specific failure and dis-
appointment but to a foreclosure of chances for any other exploration.
The more major focus here, however, will be on a question which is
experientially, logically, and practically prior. What are the sources
of the remarkable current proliferation of people—especially the young
—who are taking this particular avenue of drugs? What is the attraction of psychedelic drug taking in general (or perhaps the repulsion
from something else that propels in this direction) and of the hippie
movement as its extreme form?

It has always been a fundamental part of the anthropologist's
job to produce some account of "strange native behavior" that would
make sense to those who never left home, with the additional hope
that such an account might seem accurate and acceptable even to
literate natives as well. This task is more difficult when the two cultures involved are mutually rather hostile, and especially so when they
are largely composed of parents on one side and their children on the
other. Nevertheless, this is still the aim here. Any answers proffered

to the above questions—or, more realistically, any interpretation of the drug movement—will be essentially anthropologically based (though nowadays this may include considerable psychological viewing), and this in two senses.

In the first place, the anthropological analogy of field trips and drug "trips" permeates much of this chapter as a general model for explanatory organization, though sometimes only in the background, and it will be pushed one step further specifically: it seems potentially enlightening to consider in a general way why anthropologists get involved in their own trips, as suggestive of possible motivations (and their interrelations) for taking trips out of the known into the unknown—or, better, the partially unknown, since both in anthropology and the drug movement considerable guidance and structuring from the more experienced members exist.

The other and larger part of this inquiry is an anthropological analysis of available data on the drug movement itself, in this case hippies and semihippies. These data were gathered from November 1966 to early 1968. The hippies represent the full flowering of the drug movement, and here, as elsewhere, the study of extremes or concentrated forms is likely to be especially illuminating about significant things to observe in more "everyday" examples, where they are less vivid and visible. As parallel examples, we may recall the value of studying psychopathology for psychology generally, and the value of studying ceremonies in anthropology as clues to everyday patterns of roles and ideas.

The data sources include, first, field-work sampling from a variety of settings and situations. One weekend was spent at a hippie camping area on the Big Sur coast. A number of visits were made to the major hippie colony in the Haight-Ashbury district in San Francisco, observing the public scene in the streets, shops, and hangouts and visiting with some of them in their pads. The movement, like other subcultures, has a ceremonial life, so several of the "be-ins" held in San Francisco and Palo Alto and Dr. Timothy Leary's public "Psychedelic Celebration" were attended. Music and art are usually closely related to ceremonies culturally, and the importance of posters and rock bands in the psychedelic scene is well known; accordingly, visits were made to the dances and light shows at the Fillmore and Avalon ballrooms (supplementing this with attention to records of music said to be especially pertinent or popular) and to exhibits of psychedelic art.

Considerable focused interview material was gathered (although drug users generally seem not very communicative verbally) in many settings, ranging from arranged interviews in an office setting, through group meetings with high school students as part of an official county inquiry into drug use, to talks with hippie hitchhikers while driving. In particular, these materials included a number of interviews with young drug users together with their parents in conjoint family therapy; of these about half the cases were my own, while the other half were tape recordings made available to me, with family permission, by James Sorrells. Information was also obtained from secondary but knowledgeable sources, including professional conferences, meetings with Haight-Ashbury observers, and so on.[1]

There was also much written material to be sampled. Highly relevant was the output of the movement itself, such as the San Francisco *Oracle,* the Berkeley *Barb,* and the Los Angeles *Free Press,* as well as Ashleigh Brilliant's *Haight-Ashbury Songbook* and hippie manifestos or notices. Of a different order were floods of journalistic reports about the drug scene. Although some of these were distinctly useful, the chief value of most such reports probably lies not in their "facts" but in their reflection of the attitudes of the straight social world about the drug movement. In addition, there have been many careful and reasonably accurate objective studies of drugs and their psychopharmacology, but, until now, much less examination of the drug movement or its wider context. Finally, there were fictional interpretations of aspects of this scene, ranging all the way from Stegner's (1967) *All the Little Live Things* to Welles' (1967) *Babyhip.*

It is plain that these data sources comprise a mixed bag, but this is common in anthropology—though even more so in real life. Anthropology aims to bring sense and order out of the chaos which results, mainly, from apparent strangeness, contradictions, and disjunctions in human affairs. The problem is primarily one of interpreting confusing data rather than one of lacking information—certainly so for the drug movement. The anthropological method for doing this interpretation really is not a matter of detailed recipes or techniques but consists in a general approach. This approach rests mostly on openness to new observations and ideas—a willingness to take the un-

---

[1] In addition to Sorrells, our sources here included Robert S. Spitzer; James Terrill; Paul Watzlawick; Jay Heley; G. H. Harrison of the LSD Rescue Service; and Al Rinker of the Haight-Ashbury Switchboard.

usual or supposedly trivial equally seriously with what is familiar and authoritative, to accept observable facts and relationships which ordinarily have been left out, ignored, suppressed, or denied. Somewhat more specifically, it attempts to make the strange more understandable by looking at it in relation to its own contexts and by pointing out connections or analogies to more familiar matters, to reduce or eliminate disjunctions by looking deliberately for new logical or phenomenal connections, and to make contradictions more intelligible by recognizing that in human affairs things can be *both* "yes and no" or "this yet that"—for example, taking drugs can be both "rational" and "irrational," depending on the context and viewpoint. However, since this is not a chapter on methodology, let us not labor further at describing the anthropological ways of proceeding from varied data toward a unified interpretation,[2] but let it show forth, hopefully, in an analysis of the motivations—and, to some extent, the probable consequences—of the student drug movement.

Earlier we said something about the nature of the field-trip experience for anthropologists, but our analogy must now be concerned with a different order of question: Why do anthropologists engage in this activity? After all, field trips involve experiences which are largely unpredictable; they can be, and often are, physically and psychically uncomfortable and may even be dangerous. What are the adequate reasons? Why not just stay home? No certain answers can be given even here.[3] Yet some information and speculations are available, and the picture that can be developed from these is useful for approaching the parallel questions about drug trips and the drug movement.

The main feature of anthropology, traditionally, is quite obvious. This profession has always involved leaving one's own culture. Field trips, in fact, are only the most extreme and specific form of this; even the library-armchair anthropologists of an older era were, in their minds, also voyagers to strange and far places. Yet this fundamental matter itself is full of contradictions, even paradoxes. Have anthropologists really been members of their culture to start with? Considering this question merely at a simple overt level, it has often been noted that

---

[2] This is discussed at more length in my article, "Method in Cultural Anthropology," *Philosophy of Science*, 1951, *18*, 55–69.

[3] This is not surprising, since little research has been done. Anthropologists, like other groups, have not inquired much into the motivations of their own characteristic behavior, even though this is their professed focus elsewhere.

a striking proportion of American anthropologists have been immigrants, Jews, or women—all in some sense only partial members of the American culture. Recently, perhaps, this overt disproportion has been less, but there is good reason to believe that, more covertly and psychologically, anthropologists still tend to be marginal members of their society even before they join the profession.

Once they begin to join the profession, however, further departure from the general culture is encouraged by the demands of this profession itself. That is, becoming an anthropologist, assuming attitudes of critical interest toward the variety of social arrangements observable in the world, and going on field trips are not purely a matter of individual interest and inclination, though these are important. Every anthropologist has a variety of personal interests for such work, ranging from curiosity about human living or desires to make life better to wishes for wider experience, and perhaps for personal challenges and proving himself. In that respect the difficulties and uncertainties of field work may be viewed *positively*. Beyond, or surrounding, such personal motivations, however, are professional motivations which are more clearly social. Field trips are important for the anthropologist not only for what he can learn by them—and this is great—but also as a ritual validating his status as a real anthropologist, a member of this socialized in-group, in contrast to other groups and American society as a whole. It is likely that this, too, is all the more true because the field trip, like drug experience and hippie living, is not all directly pleasant and positive in nature but includes important elements of ordeal.

Yet, despite all this, even as the anthropologist departs for the distant field of some strange society, he carries along much of his own native culture, often more than he recognizes. After all, how could our cultural valuation of scientific inquiry be more dramatically demonstrated and reinforced than by carrying it on at the ends of the earth among people who care nothing for it? Perhaps, thus, anthropologists in their own way of not "going native" even surpass those legendary Englishmen who dress for dinner in the jungle. The practical means of travel and exploration—for the anthropologist, largely physical—also reflect the inescapable society of origin; the field worker does not climb into a native dugout canoe until he has gone as far as he can by plane and steamship, and he carries along his professional tools—once simply notebooks and cameras, but now tape recorders and testing materials—to places where they never belonged before. Even if the ultimate and broadest aim of the anthropologist, on returning from the field, is to change and improve his own world, this aim, no matter how revolutionary, is defined in relation to and against the context of the society he has originally known.

The simple question "Why take trips?" leads first to considering the starting point. What is being departed from, and what is unsatisfactory about that place? Where is the traveler aiming to go, and what does he want to do there? What is the positive attraction of the goal? These questions should be in the plural form; the anthropological example already makes it plain that multiple functions are served by the trip. Also, we have seen the need for a further and more sophisticated question, "What does the traveler take along, perhaps unrecognized?" Necessarily, too, the general question "Why?" cannot be separated either from "What?" or from "How?" In the most obvious instance, on the basis of their means alone drug trips would usually be conceived and evaluated quite differently from anthropological field trips. This raises a further point, and one of considerable scope and complexity. In any attempt to explain behavior, the question "Why?" by itself is necessarily inherently biased in favor of maintaining a status quo assumed to be a normal and natural resting point. The question about the travelers must therefore be balanced by an inquiry of "Why not?" to clarify the attitudes of the stay-at-homes who have labeled the trips as a "problem." If this problem label is to be accepted as reason enough for an inquiry, it is only reasonable to examine its own background also. "Why not?" therefore is necessary to clarify what sort of a question the "Why?" is.

These several questions are basically a general explanatory structure, a set of labeled and interrelated, but empty, boxes. We must now begin to fill these boxes with content by looking at available data on the drug movement. In this effort three viewpoints need representation: that of the drug-using travelers, that of the straight stay-at-homes, and that of this observer and student. This last view draws on and brings in some factual data and observations from various sources, but progresses toward a general interpretation. Because of the limitations of data, space, and time, we shall not attempt here to fill out the explanatory schema completely. Rather, we shall focus first on what is either pervasive or prominent, what is emphasized about this movement by one party or another—and also on whatever may be conspicuous by its absence or avoidance, although the existence of opposing viewpoints already helps perform this function. This focus of attention on prominence will, however, be checked and balanced— that is, backstopped—by some systematic and persistent concern for considering: both the broad social scene and specific aspects within it; both observable behavior and verbalizations about it; both immediate activities and their presumed goals; and both social interaction and individual behavior and experience.

Since the drug movement is posed as a problem, we will begin by reviewing its nature and attempting to clarify its aims before approaching the more crucial matter of the contexts out of which it has arisen. Where are the young drug users traveling, anyway—both in the present sense, and in terms of their implicit and explicit goals? In the first place, although their evaluations of the two sides are poles apart, the straight and hippie worlds share a common belief that they stand opposed and distant from each other. By now this seems so obvious that it tends to be taken for granted; yet, as a central premise, it particularly needs careful examination. We will look first at the presumed opposition and separation, and later at what is common or interrelated.

Although particular aspects of the drug movement such as its philosophy of gentleness and nonviolence may be acknowledged as admirable if impractical ideals, in the eyes of the straight world this movement is viewed mainly as an *aberration,* in a fashion that is typical of our society's viewing of other behavior considered as aberrational, such as mental illness or extreme religious behavior. This basic conception is clearly implicit in typical statements which not only characterize the behavior of this movement's members as wrong, dangerous, and anxiety-provoking, but also label it as foolish and occurring without any good or understandable reasons, as in the common parental cry, "Why is my child doing all this when we've given him everything at home?" This conception, moreover, is not just a matter of negative attitudes and evaluation but a matter of negative *cognition* in the way the movement is labeled and described. That is, in general, the drug-using hippie world is characterized not directly but by contrast with what it *is not*—by how it differs from the straight world of normal American society. Such more direct and positive description of this world as there is focuses largely on the most specific and manifest features of the movement—drugs, costumes, music, and lights;

therefore, it does little to get at the inherent general nature of the movement, at what might be called its cultural systems and premises.

If there is to be any blame for this shortcoming, however, it must be substantially shared by those on the hippie side, because the movement in large measure carries on its tasks of self-definition in much the same way as the straight world—that is, in terms of opposition to and contrast with the values and activities of ordinary American society. For the movement broadly this is communicated quite clearly by both verbal and nonverbal means. The hippies explicitly state their belief in dropping-out of usual society and forming a different, opposing subculture—in the terms of Lou Gottlieb of the hippies' Morningstar Ranch, an "alternate society." Drug use in particular is often specifically promoted as a means for breaking out of the ideational mold of straight society. And the life style of the movement is not only different, and stated to be different, but it is inescapably and *observably* different. There have always been considerable numbers of young people (but also quite a few older ones) who did not buy all the standard middle-class American beliefs and practices, but in the past most of them went their different ways more privately and *sub rosa,* individually or in small groups. Today, even the drug use of students is more of a group affair and less concealed from the adult world, while the hippie extreme makes one thing very clear: although the movement's aim may be stated as each person "doing his thing" as an individual, the doing occurs mainly on a group scale and whatever it is, it is *pointedly* different from usual American behavior— even before the sensation-minded mass media point this out further.

The same business of behaviorally insisting on difference and separateness from the straight world appears repeatedly in many more specific ways in the drug movement, whether or not this is claimed or denied as a conscious aim of these behaviors. The use of drugs by properly raised middle-class young people for purposes either of enlightenment or pleasure (although this must receive more analysis later) is only the central example. The practice of unashamed begging or other forms of dependence is clearly parallel to the unashamed use of drugs. The dress of the hippies, though sometimes also practical in terms of cheapness, obviously makes the same point about difference. Identification with the American Indians, just as with Eastern mystical experience and wisdom, equally involves a clear rejection of the culture of origin in favor of foreign models—regardless of whether these are really understood or not. The "love ethic" is strongly claimed not only to be at an opposite pole from an American culture viewed as competitive, hostile, and violent but, specifically, at the sexual level to contrast with middle-class precepts, if not always practices, enough so that many of the parents concerned are shocked. This list could be extended almost indefinitely—for example, "free stores" versus commercial enterprise may be mentioned as another polarity—but the pervasive emphasis on difference, opposition, and separation is already amply evident. That is, this is *itself* a central and fundamental principle of the movement, not just part of the straight world's jaundiced view.

This principle alone, however, is not enough to characterize the essential premises and basic nature of the movement. To make this characterization it is also necessary to see how the same general principle of distance and separateness or noninvolvement operates even within the movement itself, to view some of its secondary correlates or subprinciples, and to relate such broad orientations to the level of individual attitudes and behavior. This may now be approached by considering some of the movement's major social and individual goals. The drug movement has repeatedly been attacked as having no social goals: "OK, so you drop out to look after your own soul. But what about all the other problems in the world today? You're just escaping from them." But this is not quite the whole story; the movement does offer one social "answer," which also is alluded to in Leary's famous slogan, "Tune in—turn on—drop out." One should not only get with this scene himself, he should join with others, and they should then endeavor to turn on equally even the squares of the world. The significant point here is not whether this is possible or what problems would remain if it happened. Rather, it is the conception, partially but not wholly implicit, that the gap between the two opposed worlds can only be dealt with effectively by a process of conversion of the members of the establishment, so that they become fundamentally like-minded with the hip. The often-emphasized "communication gap" seems to be viewed as unbridgeable, at least by any ordinary verbal means such as confrontation of differences. What is still more striking, however, is that this "similarity principle"—essentially, that one can make real contact and get along only with those like oneself in values and attitudes, and not with those who are different—appears strongly even within the movement. Despite all the emphasized belief in freedom and doing one's thing, the hippie world (and, significantly, also the peer group of student drug users) is very marked by its own kinds of conformity. This is perhaps most evident in terms of dress and drug use, but the hippie world also has its own moral standards and fixed conceptions of proper social behavior—in fact, quite rigid ones.

At the center of these is the "love ethic," especially as it applies to social relationships generally. The movement is, of course, much concerned with social relationships and even with ideas of building a new society—one of its main differences from the old beatnik movement—but its conception of this is very special and, in an important sense, very limited. First, "love" is seen as the sole valid basis for any positive human interaction. Any behavior which might influence or order human relationships by any other means—that is, any deliberate means, or even any influence from spontaneous expression of emotions such as anger—are conceived both as evil and doomed to ultimate failure. Obviously, this view is closely connected with the idea that positive social intercourse is limited to similar people, that little useful contact and communication is possible with those who are different. Acting on this view, one would have to abandon not only government but even psychotherapy—except that new schools of therapy oriented around similar conceptions are now springing up.

Second, the conception of "love" involved here is also a very special one. Although often spoken of, the hippie idea of love is vague and hard to clarify. It is evident, however, that this "love" is centered in the individual, connected with one's personal achievement of self-knowledge and realization of harmony with the entire universe—"consciousness expansion" by drugs, meditation, or otherwise—and harmonious social relationships are seen as mainly a natural resultant of the achievement of this similarly by many individuals, in parallel yet essentially separately. Or, as the Beatles' guru put it in a recent interview, " 'I've been going around the world with my message of inner peace for the individual, and thereby attempting to create a natural state of world peace for all men.' He explained that through meditation . . . the body relaxes and the mind expands and tensions and frustrations float away. And it is individual tensions and frustrations, he said, that collectively lead to war."[4]

---

[4] Jerry Buck, "Beatles' Guru Offers Prescription for World Peace," *Palo Alto Times,* January 22, 1968.

In other words, the main focus is on the individual and his relation to the world, globally, rather than on the specifics of one person's relationship to another or others. This basically individual-internal focus is characteristic of many aspects of the movement. Most notably, of course, it accords with the dominant role of drug use, for whether drugs are used for enlightenment or for "kicks," the focus is on inner experience. The same orientation exists in the movement's interest in inwardly-focused Eastern philosophies and religions, and in the often espoused aim of life as "self-actualization." That inward focus ties back logically and behaviorally to the major theme of separateness. Aside from getting "high," the state that is claimed most desirable is "keeping one's cool"—the "hang-loose" ethic that is perhaps much more widespread among young people today than the drug movement specifically. It almost seems that the only alternative envisioned, if this noninvolvement is lost, is becoming "uptight." That is, not only is manipulation seen as necessarily bad—except influencing another by "love"—but there is also little conception that commitment and intense feelings, especially toward another person, might be positive or desirable. And, indeed, personal relationships among the hippies, though pleasant and easy-going, often appear as cool and thin, as essentially transient—not necessarily brief, but never necessarily lasting. This even appears true of "love" in the specifically sexual sense, although the amount of free sexual activity (even this may be overestimated) makes it hard for the straight world, hung up on a mixture of moral disapproval and secret envy, to see that the amount of personal involvement is limited. The same impression is produced by a visit to the Avalon or the Fillmore Ballroom; in these large halls, crowded with dancers and listeners, there is amazingly little contact, physical or verbal.

Much of the above was summed up in a more concrete and personal form in the course of an interview with two sisters who were hitchhiking from Big Sur to Carmel. One asked me what I thought was the main aim in life. My answer was "To handle my relationships with other people well," meaning this to include both the pleasant and the difficult relationships that anyone must encounter. The elder sister demurred and stated her own aim as "self-actualization." I raised some question how this could be done without effective dealings with others, which, in turn, led to her view that often such dealings are impossible—in particular with her own parents. I inquired about them; there was little doubt from her description that they were very difficult people. But when I made the suggestion, based on a considerable experience with families in conjoint therapy together, that there were several possible ways she could deal with them better—not by submission but by being more active and exerting more influence on them—she would not entertain this idea at all. Her one view was that the only answer for her lay in as complete separation from them as possible; she persisted in this view even when I suggested that one has to get together with people to a certain extent even to get away from them.

In attempting to bring out some central aspects of the drug movement and put them together in a new way, the preceding account has been one-sided and unfair in not viewing this movement in relation to the straight society which it opposes and from which, after all, it derives. It will take some time to balance out the picture by giving an account of some features the two worlds share despite their opposition, and then of the social contexts of the movement. Until this can be done, it should be stated explicitly that most of the features of the movement pointed out rather critically here also have important positive value in emphasizing things neglected in our society or in opposing things overdone. Moreover, even where the movement's own emphases appear excessive or misdirected, these "irrationalities" are themselves usually rooted in the social situations from which the hippies began their journeys.

What are the drug users taking along on their journey from their starting points in middle-class America? Any detailed answer would require some close examination of the point of departure, which is yet to come; here we intend only to present a few examples and some general principles about change and continuity, to suggest that continuity and similarity are much more prevalent than is apparent on the surface. Indeed, although both the straight world and that of the drug movement make such a point of their difference and distance, basic similarities have appeared already. For instance, the hippies' insistence that the parental world of the supposed Establishment can contact them only by "turning on" themselves is the exact counterpart of what the young people recurrently complain of bitterly, with considerable justification—that they can only get together with their parents if they behave according to the parents' terms and standards.

The standards and evaluations are in opposition, but underlying both positions is the common premise that contact depends on likeness.

The observer comparing two social positions or sets of practices should not expect all-or-none identities. Thus, upon finding, as in the foregoing, an overt difference with covert similarity, we must not stop there. We must also ask whether there are overt similarities and covert differences. The quality of life and personal relations, for example, is thin in the middle-class and in the hippie group, but quite possibly for very different reasons. It is also well to examine apparent opposites most closely for, as in mirror images, these may be complementary. Denial, for instance, suggests the probability of a connection with what is denied.

The matter of extremism is especially interesting because the hippie culture appears to be typified by extremes. On the one hand, there are the numerous apparent extremes of rejection of prominent features of ordinary American life—commercialism, material comforts, and alcohol, to mention only a few. On the other, and less noticed, side, many central features of the hippie culture represent extremes of acceptance of old, established American traits or values—such as taking seriously beliefs in love, individual freedom, equality, and social harmony. Even the importance attached to drug use in the movement is largely visible as an extreme acceptance of ordinary American valuation of drugs, plus certain shifts of focus that we discuss later. In addition, a further point of connection is recognizable. On an outside viewing, American culture itself appears as extremist in many important respects, such as its emphasis on success, on material comfort, and on social conformity rather than individuality; it could even be said that middle-class America is extremist about moderation and rationality. To sum up, if one is comparing these two worlds not to isolate and attack one side or the other, but rather to understand and move toward some resolution of conflict, he must be wary of the illusion of alternatives; apparent opposites may in fact be closely related and fundamentally similar. To return to a familiar but central example, the view that there is a basic gap between similarity and contact on the one hand, and difference and distance on the other is largely shared, though in opposing specific manifestation, by the drug and straight worlds. Both of their versions, however, are very different from the third view that human relationships always necessarily involve some mixture of differences and similarities, distance and contact, with communication as a complex but versatile tool to be used for making connections.

Moving on, one asks what are the means of travel involved in going to or with the drug scene and in taking trips within it? How are the means related to the goals, and to the points of departure? The strikingly evident features of the movement's life style, such as its argot, hair styles, styles of dress which are really costumes, the intense noise level of the music, the manner of housing and being together, and the business of food and self-care, have multiple significance. They may be seen as characteristic values of the hippies which then become goals of those joining the scene; their adoption becomes the means for becoming a hippie or, for semihippies, expressing a predilection. Further, they are the devices which establish, maintain, and dramatize the difference and the distance between the straight world and the hippie world. These aspects are extreme, appear extreme, and yet in contextual analysis function much like the professional attitudes and practices which characterize the anthropologist's initiation and early career.

Just as the anthropologist may go only to a local ethnic community, perhaps farther to the Indians of the American Southwest, or still farther to the interior of New Guinea, the journey of participation in the society of the drug movement is also a matter of degrees and stages. A large number of youth never travel beyond occasional use of marijuana (and, in fewer numbers, LSD), rather quietly and inconspicuously in their own peer groups and within their local communities. Some go on with more drug use and greater display of other aspects of the related life style to become hangers-on or week-end hippies, and fewer still—though certainly enough to be very visible and disturbing to the straight world—become full-time hippies. Yet, as the field worker in interior New Guinea still maintains some contact with his home base, even this last group not only takes along aspects of the straight world but maintains some contact with it. Some otherwise thorough-going hippies receive financial support from the families they have left—remindful of the old English custom of the family black sheep's becoming a remittance man. Even the most detached and independent members of the movement still live within the physical and social boundaries of American society and, therefore, cannot be completely detached from it. One may even question seriously whether they really want to be—some contact is necessary to make a point of being separate and distant.

The use of psychedelic drugs is the chief means of entry into the movement, the chief means of "trips" within it, and a chief means of characterizing the drug world and differentiating it from the straight world. Accordingly, the use of drugs is also central for the evaluations made of the movement, from both sides. It is probable that drug users overrate the value of drugs and that their opponents overrate their dangers. Also—and in line with our society's tendency to be more concerned with the special, spectacular, or sensational than with what is important simply because it is ordinary and pervasive—both sides may focus on the matter of drugs so strongly as to neglect broader and even more basic aspects of the movement. Nevertheless, drug use exists as a central emphasis, and it is correspondingly important now to look at its nature and social context.

American society is very much a drug-using society. That observation solves one problem, but it makes two others more acute. The American reliance on drugs in conjunction with easy availability of psychedelic agents obviously gives such drugs a head start as a means for the movement's purposes. But, on the other hand, why should a movement centering around opposition to the straight world adopt one of its favorite agents? And when drugs are adopted, why should the straight society object so violently? The answer to both questions lies in the fact that while drugs as such are culturally accepted, the kind of usage promoted by the movement is opposite to what is culturally approved. In American culture drugs are acceptable and approved essentially when used to relieve some kind of pain, illness, or disability or, more generally, to help bring a person from some negative state toward or up to a condition seen as "normal." The disabilities countered by drugs usually are medical or psychiatric, although they may be social as well. For instance, it may be more or less all right for a student to take stimulants to meet the specially rigorous demands of examination week or for a tense hostess to have a pick-me-up to help her greet guests properly. In general, however, for drug use to be acceptable in cases of disability, the disability should be involuntary—that is, "not the person's own fault." Also, although the principles are the same, the rules are applied with more leeway in the case of drugs which are not culturally defined as drugs—tobacco and alcohol being the prime examples. Consequently, the latter drugs may be used to enhance "normal" social behavior or to provide or even justify the release of "normal" but ordinarily "unacceptable" impulses such as aggression, sex, or tenderness.

In the drug movement, on the contrary, the drugs used are "real drugs" and their use is clearly and explicitly stated to be for the purpose of going beyond the normal, to get "high," whether this high is viewed as "consciousness expansion" or just "kicks." This statement may not be altogether accurate, and it would be interesting to speculate on the public reaction if the members of the movement said they were just trying to get back to normal with these drugs after being made miserable and sickened by social forces—but they have defined the situation otherwise, as one for which drug use is not tolerated in our particular society.

It appears, however, that the proscription of drug use in our society is about as indirect as the prescription, and both are justified on much the same grounds, which are almost exclusively an anxious concern about someone's physical or mental health. In the case of the psychedelics, this dominant orientation seems to account for the extreme extent to which parental and social interest in the movement is focused on the possible hazards of drug use—the only other comparable focus is on young people's behaving too independently, especially leaving home on their own—and on the accompanying conviction and insistence that these hazards *must* be serious. The drug users themselves find it easier to attribute these "over-thirty" attitudes to hypocrisy, stupidity, or ill-will rather than to acknowledge that everyone's views are culturally determined or that parents may be genuinely quite worried.

We do not mean to imply that there are no realistic hazards from drug use. In some cases these are clear and considerable. Equally clearly, however, fear of drug use often goes beyond realism. Indeed, the basic attitude that the use of drugs for positive enhancement of experience *must* be bad is so strong that the suggestion may be made quite seriously that if any drug exists or is found which delivers such results with *no* direct ill effects—no damage, no hang-ups, and no hang-overs—it would still be attacked, and quite possibly even more strongly, by denial of the facts or the invention of new grounds for objection, if necessary. Such may already be the case for marijuana, which is probably the safest drug, yet is the most savagely attacked of the psychedelics.

The view that concern about the possible specific hazards of drugs is partly nonrational, perhaps even a screen or substitute for other concerns, is also supported by two more concrete lines of observation. In the first place, there is much more concern about drug hazards than about a similar degree of hazard involving other means. As Lettvin (1967), no advocate of drugs, puts it, "The chances of going mad or getting permanent brain damage are certainly there, but then what adventure is not accompanied by danger? A fair number of scuba divers, mountain climbers, and astronauts are killed off by what they do, and nobody makes much fuss (p. 15)." Second, there is plainly an attitude of insistence that such drug use must be seriously injurious, no matter what the available evidence is. If limited scientific tests indicate, inconclusively, a possibility of chromosomal damage by LSD, this is at once generally interpreted in a conclusive and maximal way, while any findings of absence of harmful effects are seen as indicating nothing reassuring, but only as a need for further and more intensive work to uncover the deleterious consequences that somehow are *known* to be lurking somewhere.

However, these drugs have one undeniably real and fearsome influence. Whatever their physiological effects, their use, as a means and as a symbol, plays an important part in young people's rejection of and moving apart from their parental homes and society. But before the drugs as such are given too much credit and blame for this—that is, taken as a cause—one must look both more closely and more broadly at what is being left. This act of rejection, like the act of violence in a murder mystery, requires a motive, an opportunity, and a weapon. Drugs may provide an opportunity, and even, in parental eyes, a weapon, but for the motive we must look also at the social contexts to which the movement is a reaction.

What are the young drug users getting away from? This question must be less simple than it seems, because we now have considerable *information* available on this without having made much apparent progress toward any *answer* that seems both sensible and satisfying. There is much evidence that the young members of the drug movement come very largely from middle-class families, and there is some indication that they generally are intelligent kids rather than the

reverse—even parental and official anguish and complaint to the effect: "How could they do these *stupid,* irrational things?" testifies in
this direction. There is much talk of "lack of communication" between
parents and children as underlying the similar lack between the straight
and hip worlds, and that the "generation gap" is wider than ever before. Yet these attempts at explanation seem not to provide much enlightenment but, rather, to leave a similar question: "Why is there such
a lack of communication?" Nor is the matter resolved by the usual
references to the wider social context and its urgent, disturbing problems, such as the Vietnam war, civil-rights struggles, and widespread
student dissatisfaction with the nature of the educational system.
Though all these factors obviously are somehow relevant, this "somehow" remains vague—the pieces have not yet been put together.

Perhaps a fresh and closer look at some of these factors which
aims more toward *what* they are like and *how* they are related will
enable the "why" of the situation to emerge more naturally, less forced.
We may begin with the wider social context and then move toward
the family situation as the concrete locus of communications and interaction between parents and children. At the same time, this examination will also be proceeding from the more overt and factual levels
toward the more covert and psychological levels. This re-examination,
with one exception, is not new in data, but in varying ways is new in
point of view—some views will include aspects previously not interrelated, some will invert usual viewing, and some will attempt to bring
opposites together.

For the broad middle-class scene, in spite of our ideals of individual freedom, equality, and tolerance, it appears that American
views about social organization and social behavior have traditionally
been rather simple, dualistic, and extreme. In the sphere of evaluation
and attitudes, it is not only on TV shows that our world is antitheti-
cally divided into, individually, good guys versus bad guys, and, socially,
"the American way of life" versus "un-American" views and actions.
Such dualisms have been pervasive and have been paralleled by a related dualism in our traditional cultural ways of handling the inescapable and persistent problem of conflict between social group norms
and the differing orientations of individuals or subgroups; the dominant formula over a long period has been "Take it or leave it" or "If
you don't like the way it is here, go elsewhere." In other words, in
relation to the problems of social order and conflict, freedom has con-

sisted largely in freedom to join the established order by adaptation and conformity—very strikingly illustrated by the acculturation to American ways of millions of immigrants—in combination with the freedom to leave this established order and behave differently elsewhere—exemplified variously in the earlier behavior of these same immigrants, in the "frontier" movements, and in the pronounced American pattern of leaving the parental home, and often locality, at maturity. One observer, Saul Bellow (as quoted in the *Stanford Daily,* 1968), puts it this way:

> Americans have a way of seceding when conditions displease them. . . . When they do not secede publicly they do it internally, subjectively. The early settlers were separatists, and separatism is still an important American phenomenon. Under certain pressures, when people feel that they are being conned, snowed, put on or bamboozled (the very abundance of terms for this is itself a sign of great sensitivity to the phenomenon), they abstract or remove themselves. They light out for the territory ahead, like Huck Finn, or become sages at Walden (a rare reaction today) or take pot or LSD.

Today, however, this set of social devices appears increasingly less workable, at least in the traditional forms of simple adaptation or simple departure. With increasing size and power of all kinds of social organizations—governmental, economic, and educational—more pervasive communication, and population growth, both the social and physical worlds are becoming vastly more encompassing in extent, as well as in the degree to which they control even formerly "private" areas of behavior. There is both less chance to take one's leave, since anywhere is much the same now, and greatly increased general demands for conformity, even if many specific social and moral norms have been replaced or abandoned. And all this applies not only to the adults enmeshed in government controls and company standards, but also to their children, who are now not only faced with greatly increased pressures for performance in school, but outside school with the Little League instead of spontaneous games and city specifications even for tree houses. Moreover, the more standardized, pervasive, and publicized the dominant social goals become, the more strained the situation grows for those to whom these goals are not rewarding, or to whom their access is denied—at the same time that these goals are built up as the only things worth living for, with no viable options available.

There appear to be three major lines of response to this situation. The most constructive focuses on actively working for a change of social organization and relationships in one's own social system, large or small. This involves a combination of the two traditional poles of departure and adaptation. The idea that everyone should have some real voice in shaping the social contexts in which he must live has been a major aspect of the woman's suffrage movement early in the century and continuing struggles for equality of the sexes, of the labor movement, of the minorities' struggles for civil rights, of the current student movement for more voice in the direction of higher education, and even in the rise of family therapy as a means of resolving conflicts within this small but fundamental social system. In all these instances—although there have been many failures and often the creation of new constricting systems—it is plain that established authority and procedures have been challenged by the formerly weak, disadvantaged, and passive adapters, with the aim of achieving some generally positive reorganization of the system.

The other two lines of response, however, are much more germane to the question of the drug movement. The main and obvious line, of course, is the majority position of further adaptation and conformity to things as they are, the established order, perhaps modified by a partial and compartmentalized escape in one's leisure time—to the extent that this itself has not yet been encompassed within the going system.

The less obvious line of response is the course of separation, to whatever extent it is still possible. "Dropping-out" in this sense is the legitimate successor to the old pattern of taking one's leave for greener —or at least different—pastures. This line of response leads, in today's circumstances, to such manifestations as the setting up of "Free Universities" by students on their own as against reformist attempts to gain influence in university administration, to the Black Power position in the Negro-White conflict, and to the drug involvement and the hippie movement on the youth versus age front.

These phenomena, of course, are all extreme manifestations along this line. Ordinarily, both acceptance and rejection are engaged in more minimally or even apathetically; then, the two are much less distinguishable. There are, however, as suggested earlier, important sociocultural bases for such extremism itself. As already mentioned, there is an American tendency toward polarization between a majority view of proper social behavior and minority views, with little provision for working out changes or mutual adjustment of differing positions. Objectively, in the middle-class world today, considerable order, comfort, and security exist, but along with these there are also much dull routine and regimentation, frantic competition, and lack of deeper meaning and satisfaction. Outside of this middle-class America, there is some evidence of historical progress but obvious problems of war, poverty, and oppression of minorities. But when middle-class majority attitudes and values are seriously questioned, apathy gives way mainly not to discourse but to active self-righteous defense and counterattack. Naturally, this reaction is reciprocated, with the result of increasing polarization, so that the parental world ("over thirty") comes to see itself almost exclusively as good and the world of the separatist young as bad. To use currently fashionable terminology, there is a lack of communication built into our system, which is obscured by the fact that a considerable degree of "free speech" exists. Communication, however, also requires "free hearing." To speak but not be heard and replied to plainly is common today, and this is probably more frustrating and confusing than to know one must be discreetly silent.

One aspect of this situation especially contributes to the extremism of the drug and hippie movements, though it has largely been overlooked. Precisely because the established order today is so pervasive and encompassing—yet also amorphous, impersonal, and even flexible and tolerant at certain levels—it is not only directly powerful but also enormously absorptive and hard to confront. It takes extreme behavior and attitudes to establish and make stick any difference from and opposition to such a system. There seems to be no effective way to be moderately different and independent. For this reason, beyond and in addition to any other values and functions, the characteristic features of the drug-movement's life style—not only long hair and odd costumes but especially the open use of drugs—must not only be different from the ordinary but blatantly so. High visibility of the withdrawal from straight society is essential for the movement's existence.

Yet, given the relevance and importance of these broad social factors as a background for the existence of the movement, further explanation is obviously required. After all, despite all the furor, the movement clearly represents only the behavior of a minority, for the full-fledged hippies are a very small portion of America's young people. Nevertheless, this minority is significant. All social movements begin as minorities, and even if, like most, this one never proceeds further, there remains the question "Why do the particular young people in the drug movement become involved?"

This question cannot be answered definitively here, but important leads can be found by viewing their social background. This, of course, has already been a main focus of interest and concern, and from at least three different sources. One is the parents, worried or angry, or both, with their recurrent cry, "Why are our children doing this?"—often, implicitly or explicitly, "to us"—"when we've given them so much?" Another source is the children who speak strongly but not clearly of the intolerable pressures and emptiness of life, and of no understanding from their parents. Still another source is all the observers and students of the scene who are concerned about "lack of communication" and the "generation gap." Yet, with all this expressed concern, not much understanding of the family's relevance to youthful unrest and the drug movement has been reached, mainly because all of these viewings are oversimplified and lacking in perspective.

In the first place, factors of real importance, such as parental authority, value differences between the generations, and communication are commonly viewed separately and absolutely rather than in terms of combinations, contradictions, and the complex interrelations of individual behavior and family contexts. The use of drugs especially is usually viewed in a simple-minded, absolute, and isolated way, not as behavior in a context of family relationships, whether this use is being condemned by parents as inherently evil, or being upheld by their children as the magic key to a more abundant life (although the young appear more flexible in this area than their parents). Given this sort of isolation, either the drug use or the parental objections must appear inexplicable and senseless. Let us illustrate how drug use can better be seen as more complexly involved—yet more simply understandable—in connection with the large issues of family authority, independence, and communication. At a meeting of high school students, one girl described how her mother had enjoined her to be careful and rational about drugs, not just to get caught up in drug taking because other students might be taking them, but to be aware of the dangers. As a result, the girl went to the library and did rather extensive reading in the literature on drug use; she then reported back to her mother that there was little evidence of harmful effects from smoking marijuana, although she had not yet tried it herself. Her mother's response was to hit the ceiling and to say she knew otherwise—on the basis of a couple of popular-magazine and newspaper stories she had seen. In reporting this episode, the girl made it clear that it was not simply her mother's position and authority she was complaining about, but the bind into which she had been put. This bind was real and complex and is widely relevant. The story, in fact, suggests that in today's society many parents may abdicate their real and inevitable responsibility to lead their children by presenting them with incongruent combinations of directions—a very different matter from simplistic ideas about conflict between parental authority and youthful pressures for independence. The parents may be "permissive" but with hidden strings or reservations. Thus, one mother of a pot-smoking boy seen in therapy was clearly much too willing, in response to his complaints, to do things she really saw as wrong (such as helping him get a transfer to a school in a different district and letting him live away from home) in order to "help" him, when he could not but be aware that she did not really approve of these moves. Or parents may recite to children their advantages of education and position, exhorting them to work hard, utilize their knowledge, and be responsible, and then try to halt them as soon as they try to carry out any independent action that the parents do not like. Anthropological study of many widely differing cultures has shown that children can and usually do learn to behave as their parents expect them to if only the set of expectations and prescriptions are fairly consistent. Response to incongruent instructions, however, is a different matter.

Another major aspect of the family context has also been neglected. Even when some attempt has been made to consider interaction, this has often been only in terms of *parents* versus children, as if the mother and the father were one and the same. "Parents" is a unity only as a category; in any real family this means two individuals who may differ greatly from each other and have conflicts and communication problems. From data derived from psychiatric study and treatment of whole families, one is led to expect that family structure and problems would be highly relevant to the drug scene. Some available specific data are in agreement with this general expectation, although no systematic studies have yet been made along these lines.

We may consider Stegner's (1967) novel, *All the Little Live Things,* for a starter, since essential patterns are often more clearly portrayed in works of art than in actual life, even if such evidence is less conclusive. Stegner's narrator Joe, a straight but intelligent middle-aged man, makes it quite plain that his antihippie attitude is closely related to past experience with his own wastrel son, Curtis; it is equally clear not only that the parents were at odds over the handling of their son but that the mother was overprotective of him in relation to her own usual standards—much like the mother of the pot-smoking boy discussed above. Here, Joe asks

> What should one do? If Ruth had any better luck with him [Curtis] I would have thought that he simply had to attach himself to antifatherly gods until he proved himself a man in his own terms. Ruth was infallibly gentle with him, though tartness is more her natural style. She didn't push him, she followed him clear to the bottom of his burrow, trying to understand, she forgave him incessantly, she was the pacifying force when he and I clashed. And he went out of his way to treat her with even greater impatience and contempt than he treated me . . . . Sometimes I wonder if he didn't abuse her because she tended to take his side—he wanted no mediator between us (pp. 177–178).

Although Joe sees the difficulty with his son, characteristically, only as a conflict of value systems, a psychological connection between the unresolved and often-covert parental conflict and the son's delinquency is visible to the reader. The whole pattern is played out again when Ruth, through repeated subtle maneuvers that Joe does not face up to, pressures him against his wishes into letting Jim Peck, the hippie, camp on their land. Despite their many subsequent conflicts, Joe sometimes wishes to communicate with Jim, to meet him halfway, but he always rejects these tendencies, and the breach widens—perhaps he has nothing left after going so far to meet his wife's way.

Babyhip is a very different work from *All the Little Live Things*. Sarah, the teenybopper, is immersed in her own world (a strange mixture of realism and wild fantasy in which she sees herself as an individual *because* she's "classless, stateless, homeless, establishmentless, schoolless, moneyless") and remote from her parents' world (strangely fantastic in its determined everydayness and to Sarah occupied not by individuals but only by classes of people who make up her "Idiot List" and other derogatory lists). Nevertheless, as in Stegner's book, we get clear glimpses of persistent parental conflict, with her indulgent father undercutting her mother, and of conflicting messages from each parent individually.

An examination of the communication and interaction patterns of real families with a problem about drug use provides confirmation of literary insights. In interviews these families repeatedly exhibit parental conflict—conflict that, whether covert or open, is focused on side issues. The "problem" child figures importantly as a buffer in these parental conflicts. He is used as the focus for indirect conflict and as a means for avoiding direct between-parent battles. Parents get together in attacking his "bad" behavior, yet disagree on what to do about it. Even while they jointly disapprove of long hair or smoking marijuana, they may argue about how one or the other handles the child instead of how they treat each other. The child's "wrong" behavior thus plays a positive role in maintaining the going family system of relationships, though this fact and that the child may be encouraged to be "bad" are unrecognized by all the participants. The child's "difficult" behavior serving such functions may, like long hair, be more pervasive but less extreme than using drugs or leaving home—although even these extremes often may unite the parents through mutual anger or mutual concern.

For example, in one such family, in addition to other problems, the son wanted a motorcycle. The father opposed it, while the mother covertly encouraged her son—for example, by pointing out motorcycle ads to him—but backed down and denied her encouragement when explicitly asked whether she thought the boy should have a cycle. The father's objections, typically, were strongly moralistic but yet amorphous; although he said the boy would first have to show enough stability and self-control to justify a driver's license, he would not establish any explicit standards for judging either. Meanwhile, the boy on the surface struggled noisily to defend himself, while actually, at bottom, protecting his parents at his own expense. He made no comment on how his mother left him in the lurch over the motorcycle ads, and although at times he would begin to point out the vagueness and impossibility of his father's standards, at the crucial point he would always become vague himself and get excited in a way that his father could use against him and thus escape. The incidents that his father used as evidence for his son's getting "upset over trifles" were ones in which the boy was involved in protecting his mother's interests instead of his own against his father's power, but no one, including his mother, took note of this fact.

Such patterns, while often markedly clear in families with a drug-use problem, are too broad to be claimed as specific causes;

rather similar patterns occur, for instance, in families with schizophrenic children. Until there is further study of the more specific factors involved in choosing one line of symptomatic behavior rather than another, it is only possible to offer tentative suggestions about the determinants of becoming involved in drug-oriented groups. In conjunction with the drug movement's promises of individual escape, new experience, and group support, easy access to the drug movement as a way of life seems of prime importance. This is not just a matter of easily available drugs and drug-using social scenes; a more crucial factor is that, despite its emphasis on individuality and opposition to the straight world, the drug movement, steeped in conformity to in-group codes, is not really such a big jump from the restrictive world of family pressures to conform.

In conclusion, some words of clarification and judgment—part apology and part criticism—are necessary in fairness to the drug movement and its relationship to American society. This movement has been looked at here in a rather special and unusual way. In contrast—almost in opposition—to most commentaries on the hippie scene, this chapter has paid little attention to the stated hippie ideals, claims, and criticisms of the straight world; instead, emphasis here has been on relating characteristic features of the movement and of the straight world and on inquiring especially about the family as well as other social contexts pressing young people toward drug use.

Lest this be seen as indicating general hostility to the drug movement, a denial of its aims and ideals, or because of references to "symptomatic behavior," as offering the view that the drug movement is just "sick," let us clearly state that such is not our intention. In line with a growing orientation in family psychiatry today, "symptomatic behavior" is not construed as "sick" in any absolute sense, but as an instance of human behavior that is special only in being socially identified and focused on as a problem. Correspondingly, an "identified patient" in a family is not to be considered as any more "sick" than the other members. Indeed, some sympathy with the position of the young should arise from the analysis and the examples we have presented. As for a conclusion, it must be that in a family "they're all in it together," regardless of apparent separation and obvious difficulties in communication. We are, in fact, all of us in it together as members of our society.

We can also *agree* that much of the movement's criticisms of middle-class society *are* apt and many of its ideals are desirable, although questions must be raised about the extent to which these views are seriously held in the movement at large. Hippie goals and especially the means by which they are supposed to be realized—not just drug use but the whole life style of the movement—are not to be taken at face value, any more than are middle-class claims about the good life. In this area, the really important focus is not on where the hippies themselves say they are going but on the actual consequences of the movement. The probable outcomes appear quite different both from the utopian claims and expectations of the drug users and the dire predictions of the middle-class world.

The essential point is that both parties deny that they are all in it together. That is their basic communality. Parents of drug users will, for example, claim that they have nothing to do with drug use, that it is the child's own choice and conduct. Drug users, on the other hand, claim they can resolve their "hang-ups" by themselves and without improved relations to parents or community. The drug users present their concentration on self as a glorious and universal solution to the problems of social living. They do not look upon what they do as a desperate reaction to particular pressures. Nevertheless, observers who see a shift in the drugs of choice—as, for example, the shift from marijuana and LSD to methamphetamine and opiates, or from occasional to chronic use—may well infer that drug users are finding that their initial drug choices are not solving their troubles. The observer, but not the hippie, will also predict that the escalated use of drugs will not provide the solutions either.

As far as real solutions are concerned, the theme presented here is that what happens among and between people is as important in accounting for behavior and feelings as anything psychodynamically idiosyncratic or pharmacologically induced, and ultimately is inescapable. Accordingly, the challenge facing youth is not how to make a break for a getaway but how to "get more with" their own families, how to get to see the situation as it is, and thus to make possible a limited but genuine freedom. A spurious and temporary escape into what seems a radically different situation but is genotypically quite similar can hardly be conceived as successful progression.

There can be no question that the drug movement, with its hippies, parahippies, and interested followers is having and will have an appreciable effect on the participants, their families, and the community, but these consequences will reflect neither the hopes of the hippies nor the fears of the straight world. As in every generation, some of the young will be lost, and some will find a new and different life, but these will be few. The majority will rejoin society, changed and matured a bit, but, for the most part, only older. Their families and the larger society will have changed a little, too; one already sees the popularization of psychedelic art and music, of hippie language, even of hippie costuming. How can a separatist movement survive absorption through superficial emulation and more profound vitiation? It cannot. The changes it brings will be less than those worked upon it.

Paradoxically, the real problem of the drug movement is not that it is too extreme. The problem is that it does not go far enough in genuinely new and integrative directions. It is not that most of the young drug experimenters will never return to the straight world but that when they do return, they will be too little changed in happier ways, and what is new and different that they do bring home will make too little difference in their own lives and in society. Too much will be absorbed, too much ignored, too much forgotten. Sad, yes, but remember that others who take trips also return home with much that might have been learned or transmitted brushed aside or but briefly practiced. The anthropologists themselves, though professional travelers, have not yet made a brave new world either.

Bibliography

ABERLE, D. F. *The Peyote Religion among the Navajo.* Chicago: Aldine, 1966.

ABOTT, A. in Walton, R. P. *Marihuana, America's New Drug Problem.* Philadelphia: Lippincott, 1938.

ADAMS, R. M. *The Evolution of Urban Society: Early Mesopotamia and Prehistoric Mexico.* Chicago: Aldine, 1966.

ALLEN, N. *The Opium Trade: Including a Sketch of Its History, Effects, Etc. as Carried on in India and China.* Lowell, Mass.: Walker, 1850.

ANATI, E. "The Bagnolo Stele: A New Approach to Prehistoric Religion." *Archaeology,* 1964, *17* (3), 154–161.

"Ancient Tobacco Smokers." *Science,* 1960, *132,* 1021.

ARGENTI, P. P., and ROSE, H. J. *The Folklore of Chios.* London: Cambridge University Press, 1949.

ASUNI, T. "Socio-psychiatric Problems of Cannabis in Nigeria." *Bulletin on Narcotics,* 1964, *16,* 17–28.

AUSUBEL, D. P. *Drug Addiction: Physiological, Psychological, and Sociological Aspects.* New York: Random House, 1958.

BACON, M. K., BARRY, H., and CHILD, I. L. "A Cross-Cultural Study of Drinking." *Quarterly Journal of Studies on Alcohol,* 1965, Supplement No. 3.

BALES, R. F. "Cultural Differences in Rates of Alcoholism." *Quarterly Journal of Studies on Alcohol,* 1946, *6,* 480–499.

BANERJEE, R. D. "Prevalence of Habit Forming Drugs and Smoking among the College Students—A Survey." *Indian Medical Journal,* 1963, *57* (8), 193–196.

BANKS, A. S., and TEXTOR, R. *A Cross-Polity Survey*. Cambridge: Massachusetts Institute of Technology Press, 1963.

BARBER, B. "A Socio-Cultural Interpretation of the Peyote Cult." *American Anthropologist*, 1941, *43*, 673–675.

BATTUTA, I. *Travels* A.D. *1325–1354*. Works issued by the Hakluyt Society, second series, #117, Vol. 2. London: Cambridge University Press, 1959.

BAY, C. "American Dilemmas: A Historical Survey of Forces that Shape Attitudes toward Alcoholic Beverages," in Sanford, N. (Ed.) *Alcohol Problems and Public Policy*. New York: Oxford, in press.

BEARD, C. A., and BEARD, M. *The Rise of American Civilization*. New York: Macmillan, 1947.

BECKER, H. S. *The Outsiders: Studies in the Sociology of Deviance*. New York: Free Press, 1963.

BECKETT, S. J. *The Fjords and Folk of Norway*. London: Methuen, 1915.

BEECHER, H. K. *Measurement of Subjective Responses: Quantitative Effects of Drugs*. New York: Oxford, 1959.

BEJARANO, J. "Present State of Coca-Leaf Habit in Colombia." *Bulletin on Narcotics*, 1961, *13*, 1–6.

BEJEROT, N. "An Epidemic of Phenmetrazine Dependence—Epidemiological and Clinical Aspects." Paper given at the Symposium on the Pharmacological and Epidemiological Aspects of Adolescent Drug Dependence, London Hospital Medical College, September 1–2, 1966.

BELLOW, S. "Is America Losing its 'Sanity of Power'?" *Stanford Daily Magazine* (January 19, 1968), *2*, No. 10.

BENABUD, A. "Psychopathological Aspects of Cannabis Use in Morocco: Statistics for the year, 1956." *Bulletin on Narcotics*, 1957, *9*, 1–8.

BENEDICT, R. *Patterns of Culture*. New York: Mentor Books, 1950.

BERAN, T. "Excavations at Bogazkoy: Report on Recent Archaeological Research in Turkey." *Journal of the British Institute of Archaeology at Ankara*, 1962, *12*, 23.

BEVERLY, R. *The History and Present State of Virginia*. Written in 1705. Republished by the Institute of Early American History and Culture, Williamsburg, Virginia. Chapel Hill: University of North Carolina Press, 1947.

BEWLEY, T. "Heroin Addiction in the United Kingdom (1954–1964)." *British Medical Journal*, 1965, *2*, 1284–1286.

BEWLEY, T. "Recent Changes in the Pattern of Drug Abuse in the United Kingdom." *Bulletin on Narcotics*, 1966, *18*, 1–13.

BIBBY, G. *The Testimony of the Spade*. New York: Knopf, 1956.

BINKLEY, O. T. "Attitudes of the Churches," in McCarthy, R. G. (Ed.) *Drinking and Intoxication: Selected Readings in Social Attitudes and Controls*. New Haven: College and University Press, 1959.

BLAKESLEE, A. F., AVERY, A. G., SATINA, S., and RIETSEMA, J. *The Genus Datura*. New York: Ronald, 1959.

BLANKE, F. "La reformation contre l'alcoolisme." *Societé de l'histoire du Protestantisme Française*, 1953, *99*, 171–185.

BLUM, E. M., and BLUM, R. H. *Alcoholism: Modern Psychological Approaches to Treatment*. San Francisco: Jossey-Bass, 1967.

BLUM, R. H. "The Choice of American Heroes and Its Relationship to Personality Structure in an Elite." *Journal of Social Psychology*, 1958, *48*, 235–246.

BLUM, R. H. *The Management of the Doctor-Patient Relationship.* New York: McGraw-Hill, 1960.

BLUM, R. H. "Drugs, Dangerous Behavior and Social Policy," in *Task Force Report: Narcotics and Drug Abuse.* Report to the President's Commission on Law Enforcement and the Administration of Justice. Washington, D.C.: U.S. Government Printing Office, 1967. (a)

BLUM, R. H. "Mind Altering Drugs and Dangerous Behavior: Alcohol," in *Task Force Report: Drunkenness.* Report to the President's Commission on Law Enforcement and the Administration of Justice. Washington, D.C.: U.S. Government Printing Office, 1967. (b)

BLUM, R. H. "Mind Altering Drugs and Dangerous Behavior: Dangerous Drugs," in *Task Force Report: Narcotics and Drug Abuse.* Report to the President's Commission on Law Enforcement and the Administration of Justice. Washington, D.C.: U.S. Government Printing Office, 1967. (c)

BLUM, R. H. "Normal Drug Use: An Exploratory Study of Patterns and Correlates." *Proceedings of American College of Neuropsychopharmacology,* in press. (d)

BLUM, R. H. "Social and Epidemiological Aspects of Psychopharmacology," in Joyce, C. R. B. (Ed.) *Psychopharmacology: Dimensions and Perspectives.* London: Tavistock, 1967. (e)

BLUM, R. H. Unpublished study of a small industrial city, 1967. (f)

BLUM, R. H., and Associates. *Utopiates: A Study of the Use and Users of LSD-25.* New York: Atherton, 1964.

BLUM, R. H., and Associates. *Students and Drugs.* San Francisco: Jossey-Bass, 1969.

BLUM, R. H., and BLUM, E. M. "Temperate Achilles: A Study of Practices and Beliefs Associated with Alcohol in Rural Greece." Monograph for the Cooperative Commission on the Study of Alcoholism. Stanford: Institute for the Study of Human Problems, 1963.

BLUM, R. H., and BLUM, E. M. "Drinking Practices and Controls in Rural Greece." *The British Journal of the Addictions,* 1964, *60,* 93–108.

BLUM, R. H., and BLUM, E. M. *Health and Healing in Rural Greece: A Study of Three Communities.* Stanford: Stanford University Press, 1965.

BLUM, R. H., and BLUM, E. M. Personal Observations, 1965 and 1967.

BLUM, R. H., and BLUM, E. M. *The Dangerous Hour: A Sociopsychological Study of the Lore of Crisis and Mystery in Rural Greece.* London: Chatto and Windus, 1969.

BLUM, R. H., and FUNKHOUSER-BALBAKY, M. L. "Legislators on Social Scientists and a Social Issue: A Report and Commentary on Some Discussion with Lawmakers about Drug Abuse." *Journal of Applied Behavioral Science,* 1965, *1,* 84–112.

BLUMER, H. "The World of Youthful Drug Use." Addiction Center Project Final Report. Berkeley: School of Criminology, University of California, 1967. (Mimeograph.)

BOGORAS, W. "The Chuckchee. Report of the Jessup Expedition, 1900–1901." Vol. 8 of *Memoirs of the American Museum of Natural History.* New York, 1909.

BOHANNAN, L. (Elenore Smith Bowen, pseudo.) *Return to Laughter.* New York: Harper, 1954.

BRETSCHNEIDER, E. "Botanical Investigations into the Materia Medica of the

Ancient Chinese." Part III of *Botanicum Sinicum*. Shanghai, Hong Kong, Yokohama, and Singapore: Kelly and Walsh, 1895.

BROMBERG, W. "Marihuana Intoxication." *American Journal of Psychiatry*, 1934, *91*, 303–330.

BROOKE, E. M., and GLATT, M. M. "More and More Barbiturates." *Medicine, Science, and the Law*, 1964 (October), 277–282.

BROWN, L. B. "Enforcement of the Tennessee Anti-narcotics Law," in O'Donnell, J. A. and Ball, J. C. (Eds.) *Narcotic Addiction*. New York: Harper, 1966.

BROWN, T. T. *The Enigma of Drug Addiction*. Springfield, Ill.: Thomas, 1963.

BUNZEL, R. "The Role of Alcoholism in Two Central American Cultures." *Psychiatry*, 1940, *3*, 361–387.

BUNZEL, R. "Chichicastenango and Chamula," in McCarthy, R. G. (Ed.) *Drinking and Intoxication: Selected Readings in Social Attitudes and Controls*. New Haven: College and University Press, 1959.

BURNEY, C. A. "Anatolian Studies: A First Season of Excavations at the Urartian Citadel of Kayalidere." *Journal of the British Institute of Archaeology at Ankara*, 1966, *16*, 55–112.

BURROUGHS, W. "The Naked Lunch," in Ebin, D. (Ed.) *The Drug Experience*. New York: Grove, 1961.

BURTON, R. *The Lake Regions of Central Africa*. New York: Horizon, 1961. (First published in 1859.)

CARLSON, J. R. *Cairo to Damascus*. New York: Knopf, 1951.

CARSTAIRS, G. M. "Daru and Bhang: Cultural Factors in the Choice of Intoxicants." *Quarterly Journal of Studies on Alcohol*, 1954, *15*, 220–237.

CHAPPLE, P. A. L. "The Changing Character of Narcotic Addiction in Great Britain." Abstract of a paper presented to the Royal Medico-psychological Association, July 9, 1964.

CHAPPLE, P. A. L. Personal communication, February 9, 1965.

CHEIN, I. "Narcotic Use among Juveniles." *Social Work*, 1956, *1* (2), 50–60.

CHEIN, I., GERARD, D. L., LEE, R. S., and ROSENFELD, E. *The Road to H: Narcotics, Delinquency, and Social Policy*. New York: Basic Books, 1964.

CHILDE, V. G. *New Light on the Most Ancient East*. New York: Grove, n.d.; (London, 1952).

CHILDE, V. G. *Piecing Together the Past: The Interpretation of Archaeological Data*. New York: Praeger, 1956.

CHILDE, V. G. *The Dawn of European Civilization*. New York: Vintage Books, 1964.

CHOPRA, P. N. "Culture and Society During the Mughal Age, 1526–1707." Doctoral dissertation. Agra, India: Shiva Lal Agerwala, 1955.

CHOPRA, R. N. "The Morphine Habit in India." *The Indian Medical Gazette*, 1933 (July), 368–370.

CHOPRA, R. N. "Drug Addiction in India and Its Treatment." *The Indian Medical Gazette*, 1935, *60*, 121–131.

CHOPRA, R. N., with CHOPRA, G. S. "Administration of Opium to Infants in India." *The Indian Medical Gazette*, 1934 (September), 489–494.

CHOPRA, R. N., and CHOPRA, G. S. "The Present Position of Hemp Drug Addiction in India." *Indian Medical Research Memoirs*, 1939, *31*, 1–119.

CHOPRA, R. N., CHOPRA, G. S., and CHOPRA, I. C. "*Cannabis sativa* in Relation to

Mental Diseases and Crime in India." *Indian Journal of Medical Research*, 1942, *30* (1), 155–171.

CHOPRA, R. N., and CHOPRA, I. C. *Drug Addiction with Special Reference to India*. New Delhi: Council of Scientific and Industrial Research, 1965.

CISIN, I. H., and CAHALAN, D. "American Drinking Practices." Social Research Project, George Washington University. Presented at the Symposium on The Drug Takers at the University of California at Los Angeles, June 12, 1966.

City of New York, Mayor's Committee on Marijuana. "The Problem of Marijuana in the City of New York." Report made to the Mayor in 1940. (Usually referred to as *The La Guardia Report*.)

CLARK, J. G. D. "Archaeological Theories and Interpretation: Old World," in Kroeber, A. L. *Anthropology Today*. Chicago: University of Chicago Press, 1953.

CLAUSEN, J. A. "Social and Psychological Factors in Narcotics Addiction." *Law and Contemporary Problems*, 1957, *22*, 34–51.

COCTEAU, J. *Opium: The Diary of a Cure*. Trans. by Margaret Crosland and S. Road. New York: Grove, 1957.

COFER, C. N., and APPLEY, M. H. *Motivation: Theory and Research*. New York: Wiley, 1964.

COHEN, S., and DITMAN, K. S. "Complications Associated with Lysergic Acid Diethylamide (LSD-25)." *Journal of American Medical Association*, 1962, *181*, 161–162.

COMBER, E. "A Police Administrator Comments on the Drug Movement," in Blum, R. H., and Associates *Utopiates: The Use and Users of LSD-25*. New York: Atherton, 1964.

Committee on Public Health of the New York Academy of Medicine. "Misuse of Valuable Therapeutic Agents: Barbiturates, Tranquilizers, and Amphetamines." *Bulletin of the New York Academy of Medicine*, 1964, *40* (2), 972–979.

"Congress: A New Option for Addicts, a Look at LSD." *Science*, 1966, *152*, 1726.

CONLON, M. F. "Addiction to Chlorodyne." *British Medical Journal*, 1963, *5366*, 1177–1178.

CONNELL, K. H. "Ether Drinking in Ulster." *Quarterly Journal of Studies on Alcohol*, 1965, *26*, 629–653.

COON, C. S. *The Origin of Races*. New York: Knopf, 1962.

CORTI, C. *A History of Smoking*. New York: Harcourt, 1932.

CROTHERS, T. D. "Inebriety in Ancient Egypt and Chaldea." *Quarterly Journal of Inebriety*, 1903, *25*, 142–150.

DAVIDSON, B. *Lost Cities of Africa*. Boston: Little, Brown, 1959.

DAWSON, W. R. *Magician and Leech: A Study of the Beginnings of Medicine with Special Reference to Ancient Egypt*. London: Methuen, 1929.

de CIEZA, P. de L. *The Incas*. Trans. by Harriet de Onis from the chronicle first printed in 1553. Norman: University of Oklahoma Press, 1959.

DEL POZO, E. C. "Empiricism and Magic in Aztec Pharmacology," in Efron, D. H., Holmstedt, B., and Kline, N. S. (Eds.) *Ethnopharmacologic Search for Psychoactive Drugs*. Public Health Service Publication #1645. Washington, D.C.: U.S. Department of Health, Education and Welfare, 1967.

de MONFRIED, H. *Pearls, Arms, and Hashish*. New York: Coward, 1930.

de MONFRIED, H. *La Poursuit du Käipan.* Paris: B. Grasset, 1934. Published in London, 1935, under the title *Hashish.*

de ROPP, R. S. *Drugs and the Mind.* New York: Grove, 1957.

DEVREUX, G. "The Function of Alcohol in Mohave Society." *Quarterly Journal of Studies on Alcohol,* 1940, *9,* 207–251.

DOOLITTLE, J. *Social Life of the Chinese: With Some Account of Their Religious, Governmental, Educational, and Business Customs and Opinions, with Special but not Exclusive Reference to Fuhchau.* New York: Harper, 1867.

DUBOS, R. *Mirage of Health.* New York: Harper, 1959.

DWARAKANATH, S. C. "Use of Opium and Cannabis in the Traditional Systems of Medicine in India." *Bulletin on Narcotics,* 1965, *17* (1), 15–19.

EBIN, D. (Ed.) *The Drug Experience.* New York: Grove, 1961.

EFRON, D. H., HOLMSTEDT, B., and KLINE, N. S. (Eds.) *Ethnopharmacologic Search for Psychoactive Drugs.* Public Health Service Publication #1645. Washington, D.C.: U.S. Department of Health, Education and Welfare, 1967.

EFRON, V. "The Tavern and the Saloon in Russia: An Analysis of I. G. Pryshov's Historical Sketch." *Quarterly Journal of Studies on Alcohol,* 1955, *16,* 484–503.

EISENBERG, L. "A Psychopharmacological Experiment in a Training School for Delinquent Boys." *American Journal of Orthopsychiatry,* 1963, *33,* 431–437.

EL MAHI, T. "A Preliminary Study on Khat together with the Institutional History of Coffee as a Beverage in Relation to Khat." World Health Organization, Regional Office for the Eastern Mediterranean, March 1962. (a)

EL MAHI, T. "The Use and Abuse of Drugs." World Health Organization, Regional Office for the Eastern Mediterranean, August 1962. (b)

Encyclopaedia Britannica. 1962 and 1965 editions.

ERIKSON, K. *Wayward Puritans.* New York: Wiley, 1966.

EVANS, I. *Among the Primitive Peoples in Borneo.* Philadelphia: Lippincott, 1922.

FABING, H. D. "Toads, Mushrooms, and Schizophrenics." *Harper's,* 1957 (May), 50–55.

FIELD, P. B. "A New Cross-Cultural Study of Drunkenness," in Pittman, D. J., and Snyder, C. R. (Eds.) *Society, Culture and Drinking Patterns.* New York: Wiley, 1962.

FINCH, B. *Passport to Paradise. . . .?* New York: Philosophical Library, 1959.

FINESTONE, H. "Cars, Kicks, and Color," in Stein, M. R., and White, M. (Eds.) *Identity and Anxiety.* New York: Free Press, 1960.

FLANNERY, K. V. "The Ecology of Early Food Production in Mesopotamia." *Science,* 1965, *147* (3663), 1247–1256.

FORD, C. S. "Ethnographical Aspects of Kava," in Efron, D. H., Holmstedt, B., and Kline, N. S. (Eds.) *Ethnopharmacologic Search for Psychoactive Drugs.* Public Health Service Publication #1645. Washington, D.C.: U.S. Department of Health, Education and Welfare, 1967.

FORT, J. "Narcotics: The International Picture." *Quarterly of California Youth Authority,* 1961, *14,* 2.

FORT, J. "The Use and Abuse of Alcohol and Narcotics Around the World," in

Proceedings of the Third World Congress of Psychiatry. Toronto: University of Toronto Press, 1962.

FORT, J. Personal communication, 1964. (a)

FORT, J. "The Problem of Barbiturates in the United States of America." *Bulletin on Narcotics,* 1964, *16* (1), 17–35. (b)

FORT, J. "Social and Legal Response to Pleasure-Giving Drugs," in Blum, R. H. and Associates *Utopiates: The Use and Users of LSD-25.* New York: Atherton, 1964. (c)

FORT, J. "Giver of Delight or Liberator of Sin: Drug Use and 'Addiction' in Asia." *Bulletin of Narcotics,* 1965, *17* (3), 1–11. (a)

FORT, J. "Giver of Delight or Liberator of Sin: Drug Use and 'Addiction' in Asia." *Bulletin on Narcotics,* 1965, *17* (4), 13–19. (b)

FORT, J. "Recommended Future International Action Against Abuses of Alcohol and Other Drugs." *The British Journal of the Addictions,* 1966, *62.*

FREEDMAN, A. M. "Public Health Aspects of Narcotic Addiction." *New York State Journal of Medicine,* 1963, *63,* 1656–1665.

FRIEDL, E. "Trager medialer Begabung im Hindukusch und Karakorum." *Acta Ethnologica et Linguistica,* Österreichische Ethnologische Gesellschaft. No. 8. Institut für Völkerkunde der Universität, Vienna, 1965.

GAGER, F. L., Jr. "Ancient Tobacco Smokers." *Science,* 1960, *132,* 1021.

GAGER, F. L., Jr. "Letters to the Editor." *Science,* 1961, *133,* 1021.

GAJDUSEK, C. "Recent Observations on the Use of Kava in the New Hebrides," in Efron, D. H., Holmstedt, B., and Kline, N. S. (Eds.) *Ethnopharmacologic Search for Psychoactive Drugs.* Public Health Service Publication #1645. Washington, D.C.: Department of Health, Education and Welfare, 1967.

GEORGE, M. D. *London Life in the 18th Century.* New York: Harper, 1965.

GLAD, D. D. "Attitudes and Experiences of American-Jewish and American-Irish Male Youths as Related to Differences in Adult Rates of Inebriety." *Quarterly Journal of Studies on Alcohol,* 1947, *8,* 406–472.

GOLDSMITH, O. "Letters from a Citizen of the World to His Friends in the East," in *The Collected Works of Oliver Goldsmith.* Vol. 4. New York and London: Putnam, Knickerbocker, 1908.

GORDON, B. L. *Medicine Through Antiquity.* Philadelphia: Davis, 1949.

GRANIER-DOYEUX, M. "Some Sociological Aspects of the Problem of Cocaism." *Bulletin on Narcotics,* 1962, *14* (4), 1–16.

GREMEK, M. D. "Intoxicating Beverages and Poisons of the Ancient Illyrians." *Farm. Glasn., Zagreb,* 1950, *6,* 33–38.

GRENFEL, B., and HUNT, A. S. *The Oxyrhyncus Papyri.* London, 1899.

GRIMLUND, K. "Phenacetin and Renal Damage at a Swedish Factory." *Acta Medical Scandinavia Supplement,* 1963, *405,* 1–26.

GUNTHER, R. T. *The Greek Herbal of Dioscorides.* New York: Hafner, 1959.

GUTTMAN, L. "A Basis for Scaling Qualitative Data." *American Sociological Review,* 1944, *9,* 139–150.

HAGGARD, H. W. *Devils, Drugs, and Doctors.* New York: Harper, 1929.

HALBACH, H. "Possibilities of Prevention of Drug Addiction." *The British Journal of the Addictions,* 1959, *56,* 27–44.

HARPER, R. F. *The Code of Hammurabi, King of Babylon.* London: Luzac, 1904.

HELBAEK, H. "How Farming Began in the Old World." *Archaeology,* 1959, *12* (3), 183–189.

HELBAEK, H. "Studying the Diet of Ancient Man." *Archaeology,* 1961, *14* (2), 95–101.

HELBAEK, H. Personal communication, 1965.

HENSALA, J. D., EPSTEIN, L., and BLACKER, K. H. "LSD in Psychiatric In-Patients." *Archives of General Psychiatry,* 1967, *16* (5), 554–560.

"Heroin and Cocaine." *British Medical Journal,* 1964, *5420,* 1280–1281.

HESS, A. G. *Chasing the Dragon.* New York: Free Press, 1965.

HILLS, K. L. "Dubosia in Australia—A New Source of Hyoscine and Hyoscyamine." *Journal of the New York Botanical Garden,* 1948, *49,* 185–188.

HODGSON, M. G. S. *The Order of the Assassins: The Struggle of the Early Nizari Isma'ili Against the Islamic World.* 's-Gravenhage: Mouton, 1955.

HOFFMAN, M. *5000 Years of Beer.* Frankfurt: Metzner, 1956.

HOLE, F. "Investigating the Origins of Mesopotamian Civilization." *Science,* 1966, *153* (3736), 605–611.

HOLMES, L. D. "The Function of Kava in Modern Samoan Culture," in Efron, D. H., Holmstedt, B., and Kline, N. S. (Eds.) *Ethnopharmacologic Search for Psychoactive Drugs.* Public Health Service Publication #1645. Washington, D.C.: U.S. Department of Health, Education and Welfare, 1967.

HORN, D. "Test May Help Smokers Quit." Associated Press report, September 12, 1967.

HORTON, D. "The Functions of Alcohol in Primitive Societies: A Cross-Cultural Study." *Quarterly Journal of Studies on Alcohol,* 1943, *4,* 199–220.

HORTON, D. "Primitive Societies," in McCarthy, R. G. (Ed.) *Drinking and Intoxication: Selected Readings in Social Attitudes and Controls.* New Haven: College and University Press, 1959.

Indian Hemp Commission Report, 1893–1894.

INGALLS, D. H. G. Personal communication, 1967.

ISBELL, H. "Historical Development of Attitudes toward Opiate Addiction in the United States," in Farber, S. M., and Wilson, R. L. (Eds.) *Conflict and Creativity.* New York: McGraw-Hill, 1963.

JAMES, E. O. *Prehistoric Religion.* New York: Praeger, 1957.

JAMES, W. *The Varieties of Religious Experience.* New York: Modern Library, 1902.

JELLINEK, E. M. "Old Russian Church Views on Inebriety." *Quarterly Journal of Studies on Alcohol,* 1943, *3,* 663–667.

JELLINEK, E. M. *The Disease Concept of Alcoholism.* New Haven: Hillhouse, 1960.

JOCHELSON, W. "The Koryak. Report of the Jessup Expedition, 1900–1901," Vol. 10, Part 2 of *Memoirs of the American Museum of Natural History.* New York, 1909.

JOHNSON, H. T., and CLELAND, J. B. "The History of the Aboriginal Narcotic, Pituri." *Oceania,* 1933, *4,* 201–223.

JOHNSON, J. B. "Elements of Mazatec Witchcraft." *Ethnologiska Studier,* 1939, *9,* 128–149.

JOHNSON, B. Series of articles for the *Arizona Daily Star,* based on the work of anthropologist Earl Morris, 1967.

JONES, E. *The Life and Work of Sigmund Freud.* Vol. I. New York: Basic Books, 1953.

JOYCE, C. R. B. Personal communications, 1964, 1965, 1967.

KALANT, O. J. *The Amphetamines: Toxicity and Addiction.* Springfield, Ill.: Thomas, 1966.

KELLER, M. "Early Medical and Official Views of Spirits in the Army and Navy of the United States." *Quarterly Journal of Studies on Alcohol,* 1944, *4,* 606–634.

KELLER, M. "Alcohol in Health and Disease: Some Historical Perspectives." *Annals of the New York Academy of Science,* 1966, *133,* 280–287.

KENNON, G. *Tent Life in Siberia: Adventures among the Koryaks and Other Tribes in Kamchatka and Northern Asia.* New York: Putnam, 1870.

KERVINGANT, D. "The Consumption of Khat in French Somaliland." *Bulletin on Narcotics,* 1959, *11* (2), 42.

KEYS, A., and BROZEK, B. *Studies in Hunger.* Minneapolis: University of Minnesota Press, 1950.

KILOH, L. G., and BRANDON, S. "Habituation and Addiction to Amphetamines." *British Medical Journal,* 1962, *2,* 40–43.

KIRKBRIDE, D. "Beidha, An Early Neolithic Village in Jordan." *Archaeology,* 1966, *19* (3), 199–207.

KLUVER, H. *Mescal: The Divine Plant and Its Psychological Effects.* London: Kegan Paul, 1928.

KNUPFER, G., FINK, R., CLARK, W. D., and GOFFMAN, A. S. "Factors Related to Amount of Drinking in an Urban Community," in *The California Drinking Practices Study, Report #6.* Berkeley: State of California Department of Health, 1963.

KNUPFER, G., and ROOM, R. "Age, Sex, and Social Class as Factors in Amount of Drinking in a Metropolitan Community." *Social Problems,* 1964, *12,* 225–240.

KOLB, L. *Drug Addiction: A Medical Problem.* Springfield, Ill.: Thomas, 1962.

KRAMER, S. N., and LEVY, M. "First Pharmacopeia in Man's Recorded History." *American Journal of Pharmacy,* 1954, *126,* 76–84.

KRIEG, M. B. *Green Medicine.* New York: Rand McNally, 1964.

KRITIKOS, P. G., and PAPADAKI, S. N. *The History of the Poppy and of Opium and Their Expansion in Antiquity in the Eastern Mediterranean Area.* Athens: Anatypon ek tes Archeologikes Ephemeridas, 1963. See also under the same title in *Bulletin on Narcotics,* 1967, *19* (3), 17–38 (Part I), and *19* (4), 5–10 (Part II).

KROEBER, A. L. *Anthropology Today.* Chicago: University of Chicago Press, 1953. (a)

KROEBER, A. L. *Handbook of the Indians of California.* Berkeley: California Books, 1953. (b)

KWANG-CHIH-CHANG. *The Archaeology of Ancient China.* New Haven: Yale University Press, 1963.

LA BARRE, W. "The Aymara Indians of the Lake Titicaca Plateau, Bolivia." *American Anthropological Association Memoir No. 68,* pp. 3–250.

LA BARRE, W. "Twenty Years of Peyote Studies." *Current Anthropology,* 1960, *1,* 45–60.

LA BARRE, W. *The Peyote Cult.* Hamden, Conn.: Shoestring, 1964.

LAMB, H. *Babur the Tiger: First of the Great Moguls.* New York: Bantam Books, 1961.

LAMBO, T. A. "Medical and Social Problems of Drug Addiction in West Africa." *Bulletin on Narcotics,* 1965, *17* (1), 3–13.

LANSDELL, H. *Through Siberia*. London: Simpson, Low, 1883.

LASWELL, H. D. *Psychopathology and Politics*. Chicago: University of Chicago Press, 1930.

LAUFER, B. "Introduction of Tobacco into Europe." Field Museum of Natural History Pamphlet No. 19. Chicago, 1924. (a)

LAUFER, B. "Tobacco and Its Use in Asia." Field Museum of Natural History Pamphlet No. 18. Chicago, 1924. (b)

LAUFER, B., HAMBLY, W. D., and LINTON, R. "Tobacco and Its Use in Africa." Field Museum of Natural History Anthropology Leaflet No. 29. Chicago, 1930.

LA WALL, C. H. *Four Thousand Years of Pharmacy*. Garden City, N.Y.: Garden City Press, 1926.

LA WALL, C. H. *The Curious Lore of Drugs and Medicines*. Garden City, N.Y.: Garden City Press, 1927.

LEAKE, C. D., and SILVERMAN, M. *Alcoholic Beverages in Clinical Medicine*. Chicago: Year Book Medical Press, 1966.

LEE, D. "Greece," in Mead, M. (Ed.) *Cultural Patterns and Technical Change*. Paris: UNESCO, 1953.

LEMERT, E. M. "The Use of Alcohol in Three Salish Indian Tribes." *Quarterly Journal of Studies on Alcohol*, 1958, *18*, 90–108.

LESTER, R. H. "Kava Drinking in Vitilevu, Fiji." *Oceania*, 1941, *12* (December), 97–121 (Part I) and 1942, *12* (March), 226–254 (Part II).

LETTVIN, J. "You Can't Even Step in the Same River Once." *Natural History*, 1967, *76* (8), 6–19.

LEWIN, L. *Phantastica: Narcotic and Stimulating Drugs*. Berlin: Stilke, 1924. Reissued, New York: Dutton, 1964.

LINDESMITH, A. R. *The Addict and the Law*. Bloomington: Indiana University Press, 1965.

LINTON, R. *The Tree of Culture*. New York: Knopf, 1955.

LIVINGSTON, R. B. (Ed.) *Narcotic and Drug Addiction Problems*. Proceedings of the Symposium on the History of Narcotic Drug Addiction Problems at Bethesda, Maryland. Publication #1050. Washington, D.C.: U.S. Department of Health, Education, and Welfare, 1958.

LOEB, E. M. "Primitive Intoxicants." *Quarterly Journal of Studies on Alcohol*, 1943, *4*, 387–398.

LOLLI, G. "On Therapeutic Success in Alcoholism," in Podalsky, E. (Ed.) *Management of Addictions*. New York: Philosophical Library, 1955.

LOLLI, G. *Alcohol in Italian Culture*. Glencoe, Ill.: Free Press, 1958.

LOLLI, G., SERIANNI, E., BANISSONI, F., GOLDER, G. M., MARIANI, A., MCCARTHY, R. G., and TONER, M. "The Use of Wine and Other Alcoholic Beverages by a Group of Italians and Americans of Italian Extraction." *Quarterly Journal of Studies on Alcohol*, 1952, *13*, 27–48.

LOLLI, G., SERIANNI, E., GOLDER, G. M., BALBONI, C., and MARIANI, A. "Further Observations on the Use of Wine and Other Alcoholic Beverages by Italians and Americans of Italian Extraction." *Quarterly Journal of Studies on Alcohol*, 1953, *14*, 395–405.

LOLLI, G., SERIANNI, E., GOLDER, G. M., and LUZZATO-FEGIZ, P. *Alcohol in Italian Culture*. New Haven: Yale Center of Alcohol Studies Publications, 1958, and Glencoe, Ill.: Free Press, 1958.

LUCIA, S. P. (Ed.) *Alcohol and Civilization*. New York: McGraw-Hill, 1963. (a)

LUCIA, S. P. *History of Wine as Therapy.* Philadelphia: Lippincott, 1963. (b)

LUCIA, S. P. "The Antiquity of Diet and Medicine," in Lucia, S. P. (Ed.) *Alcohol and Civilization.* New York: McGraw-Hill, 1963. (c)

LUZZATO-FEGIZ, P., and LOLLI, G. "The Use of Milk and Wine in Italy." *Quarterly Journal of Studies on Alcohol,* 1957, *18,* 355–381.

LYLE, D. "The Logistics of Junk." *Esquire,* 1966, *65* (3), 61–67.

MACGREGOR, H. G. "Alcohol and Alcoholism." *Journal of the Royal Institute of Public Health and Hygiene,* 1948, *11,* 266–283.

"Mad Mushrooms." *San Francisco Chronicle,* August 11, 1965, p. 15.

MADSEN, W. *Alcoholics Anonymous as a Subculture.* In press.

MADSEN, W. *Health and Society in the Lower Rio Grande Valley.* Austin: University of Texas, Hogg Foundation of Mental Health Publication.

MALLETS, M. *Northern Antiquities.* Trans. by Bishop Percy. London: Bell, 1902.

MANDEL, J. "Hashish, Assassins, and the Love of God." *Issues in Criminology,* 1966, *2* (2), 149–156.

MANGIN, W. "Drinking among Andean Indians." *Quarterly Journal of Studies on Alcohol,* 1957, *18,* 55–65.

MARSHALL, O. "The Opium Habit in Michigan," in O'Donnell, J. A., and Ball, J. C. (Eds.) *Narcotic Addiction.* New York: Harper, 1966.

MASAKI, T. "The Amphetamine Problem in Japan." Sixth Report of the Expert Committee on Drugs Liable to Produce Addiction, in *World Health Organization Technical Report Series,* 1956, *102,* 14–21.

MCARTHUR, C., WALDRON, E., and DICKINSON, J. "The Psychology of Smoking." *Journal of Abnormal Social Psychology,* 1958, *56,* 267–275.

MCCARTHY, R. G. (Ed.) *Drinking and Intoxication: Selected Readings in Social Attitudes and Controls.* New Haven: College and University Press, 1959.

MCCARTHY, R. G., and DOUGLASS, E. M. "Prohibition and Repeal," in McCarthy, R. G. (Ed.) *Drinking and Intoxication: Selected Readings in Social Attitudes and Controls.* New Haven: College and University Press, 1959. (a)

MCCARTHY, R. G., and DOUGLASS, E. M. "Systems of Legal Control," in McCarthy, R. G. (Ed.) *Drinking and Intoxication: Selected Readings in Social Attitudes and Controls.* New Haven: College and University Press, 1959. (b)

MCGLOTHLIN, W. H., and COHEN, S. "The Use of Hallucinogenic Drugs among College Students." *American Journal of Psychiatry,* 1965, *122,* 572–574.

MCGLOTHLIN, W. H., COHEN, S., and MCGLOTHLIN, M. "Personality and Attitude Changes in Volunteer Subjects Following Repeated Administration of LSD." Paper presented before the Fifth International Congress, Collegium Neuropsychopharmacologicum, March 1966.

MCKINLAY, A. P. "Ancient Experience with Intoxicating Drinks: Non-Attic Greek States." *Quarterly Journal of Studies on Alcohol,* 1949, *10,* 298–315.

MCKINLAY, A. P. "New Light on the Question of Homeric Temperance." *Quarterly Journal of Studies on Alcohol,* 1953, *14* (1), 78–93.

MCKINLAY, A. P. "Attic Temperance," in McCarthy, R. G. (Ed.) *Drinking and Intoxication: Selected Readings in Social Attitudes and Controls.* New Haven: College and University Press, 1959. (a)

MCKINLAY, A. P. "Early Roman Sobriety," in McCarthy, R. G. (Ed.) *Drinking and Intoxication: Selected Readings in Social Attitudes and Controls.* New Haven: College and University Press, 1959. (b)

MCKINLAY, A. P. "Non-Attic States," in McCarthy, R. G. (Ed.) *Drinking and Intoxication: Selected Readings in Social Attitudes and Controls*. New Haven: College and University Press, 1959. (c)

MCKINLAY, A. P. "Non-Classical Peoples," in McCarthy, R. G. (Ed.) *Drinking and Intoxication: Selected Readings in Social Attitudes and Controls*. New Haven: College and University Press, 1959. (d)

MCKINLAY, A. P. "Roman Attitude toward Women's Drinking," in McCarthy, R. G. (Ed.) *Drinking and Intoxication: Selected Readings in Social Attitudes and Controls*. New Haven: College and University Press, 1959. (e)

MCKINLAY, A. P. "Roman Sobriety in the Later Republic," in McCarthy, R. G. (Ed.) *Drinking and Intoxication: Selected Readings in Social Attitudes and Controls*. New Haven: College and University Press, 1959. (f)

MCMULLEN, J. "The Business of Heroin." A CBS documentary television broadcast, January 22, 1964.

MCPEEK, F. W. "The Role of Religious Bodies in the Treatment of Inebriety in the United States." Lecture #26 in *Alcohol, Science and Society*. New Brunswick: Quarterly Journal of Studies on Alcohol, 1945.

MELLAART, J. "Early Cultures of the South Anatolian Plateau, II." *Anatolian Studies*, 1963, *13*, 226.

MELLAART, J. *Catal Hüyük, A Neolithic Town in Anatolia*. New York: McGraw-Hill, 1967.

MERRILLEES, R. S. "The Opium Trade in the Bronze Age Levant." *Antiquity*, 1962, *36*, 287–292.

MERRILLEES, R. S. "Reflections on the Bronze Age of Cyprus." Mimeograph, 1963.

Ministry of Health and Welfare, Japan. "Brief Account on the Situation of the Control of the Dangerous Drugs in Japan." Pamphlet, December 1964.

MOBERG, C. A. "Spread of Agriculture in the North European Periphery." *Science*, 1966, *152* (3720), 315–319.

MODLIN, H. C., and MONTES, A. "Narcotics Addiction in Physicians." *American Journal of Psychiatry*, 1964, *121*, 358–365.

MOORE, M. "Chinese Wine Drinking," in McCarthy, R. G. (Ed.) *Drinking and Intoxication: Selected Readings in Social Attitudes and Controls*. New Haven: College and University Press, 1959.

MOREAU, J. de T. *Du Hachisch et de l'Alienation Mentale. Etudes Psychologiques*. Paris: Librairie de Fortin, Masson, 1845.

MORTIMER, W. G. *History of Coca: The "Divine Plant" of the Incas*. New York: Vail, 1901.

MURPHY, H. B. M. "Le cannabisme, revue de la litterature psychiatrique recente." *Bulletin on Narcotics*, 1963, *15* (1), 15–23.

NETTING, R. M. "Beer as a Locus of Value among the West African Kofyar." *American Anthropologist*, 1964, *66*, 375–384.

NORRIS, K. *Jamaica: The Search for an Identity*. Institute of Race Relations Publication. New York: Oxford, 1962.

O'DONNELL, J. A., and BALL, J. C. (Eds.) *Narcotic Addiction*. New York: Harper, 1966.

OMAN, J. C. *Mystics, Ascetics, and Saints of India*. London: Fisher, 1903.

OWEN, D. E. *British Opium Policy in China and India*. New Haven: Yale University Press, 1934.

OZGUC, P. "Kultepe-Kanis: Report on Recent Archaeological Research in Turkey." *Journal of the British Institute of Archaeology at Ankara*, 1963,*13*, 22.

PASAMANICK, B. "Anti-Convulsant Drug Therapy of Behavior Problem Children with Abnormal EEG." *Archives of Neurology and Psychology*, 1951, *65*, 752.

PETRULLO, V. *The Diabolic Root: A Study of Peyotism and the New Indian Religion among the Delaware*. Philadelphia: University of Pennsylvania Press, 1934.

"Peyote." *Bulletin on Narcotics*, 1959, *11* (May–November), whole issue.

PHILLIPSON, R. "Alcoholism." *Royal Health Society Journal*, 1964, *84–85*, 267–271.

PIAGET, J. *The Moral Development of the Child*. New York: Free Press, 1948.

PITTMAN, D. J., and SNYDER, C. R. (Eds.) *Society, Culture, and Drinking Patterns*. New York: Wiley, 1962.

PIGGOTT, S. *Ancient Europe from the Beginnings of Agriculture to Classical Antiquity*. Chicago: Aldine, 1965.

PLATT, B. S. "Some Traditional Alcoholic Beverages and Their Importance in Indigenous African Communities." *Proceedings of the Nutrition Society of England and Scotland*, 1955, *14*, 115–124.

PLAUT, T. F. A. *Alcohol Problems: A Report to the Nation*. Prepared for the Cooperative Commission on the Study of Alcoholism. New York: Oxford, 1967.

POZNANSKI, A. "Our Drinking Heritage," in McCarthy, R. G. (Ed.) *Drinking and Intoxication: Selected Readings in Social Attitudes and Controls*. New Haven: College and University Press, 1959.

PRIBRAM, K. H. "The New Neurology and the Biology of Emotion: Structural Approach." *American Psychologist*, 1967, *22*, 830–837.

PUHARICK, A. *The Sacred Mushroom*. New York: Doubleday, 1959.

QUINN, V. *Seeds: Their Place in Life and Legend*. New York: Stokes, 1936.

RADJI, A. M. "Opium Control in Iran: A New Regime." *Bulletin on Narcotics*, 1959, *11*, 1–3.

REDFIELD, R. *The Little Community*. Chicago: University of Chicago Press, 1960.

REININGER, W. "Historical Notes," in Solomon, D. (Ed.) *The Marihuana Papers*. New York: Bobbs-Merrill, 1966.

REININGER, W. "Remnants from Prehistoric Times," in Andrews, G. (Ed.) *The Book of Grass*. New York: Grove, 1967.

RICE, T. T. *The Scythians*. New York: Praeger, 1957.

RIVERS, H., and RIVERS, E. "The Habits, Customs, and Ceremonies of East-Central Australia," in *Report of the Fifth Meeting, Australian Association for the Advancement of Science*. Adelaide, September 1893.

ROBINS, L. N., and MURPHY, G. E. "Drug Use in a Normal Population of Young Negro Men." *American Journal of Public Health*, 1967, *57* (9), 1580–1596.

ROCHE, P. Q. *The Criminal Mind*. New York: Farrar, Straus, 1958.

ROLLESTON, J. D. "Alcoholism in Classical Antiquity." *British Journal of Inebriety*, 1927, *24*, 101–120.

ROSEVEAR, J. *Pot: A Handbook of Marijuana*. New Hyde Park, N.Y.: University Books, 1967.

ROUECHÉ, B. "Alcohol in Human Culture," in Lucia, S. P. (Ed.) *Alcohol and Civilization*. New York: McGraw-Hill, 1963.

ROUECHÉ, B. *The Neutral Spirit.* Boston: Little, Brown, 1960.

RUDENKO, S. I. *Kulturnoe naselenie gorovo Altaya v Skifskoe vremia.* Moscow: U.S.S.R. Academy of Science, 1953.

RUSSELL, C., and RUSSELL, W. M. S. *Human Behavior.* Boston: Little, Brown, 1961.

SADOUN, R., LOLLI, G., and SILVERMAN, M. *Drinking in French Culture.* New Brunswick: Rutgers Center of Alcohol Studies, 1965.

SAFFORD, W. E. "Cactaceae of Northeastern and Central Mexico," in *Smithsonian Institution Report,* Washington, 1908.

SAFFORD, W. E. "An Aztec Narcotic." *Journal of Heredity,* 1915, *6,* 291–311.

SAFFORD, W. E. "The Identity of Cohoba: Snuff of Haiti." *Journal of the Washington Academy of Science,* 1916, *6,* 547–562.

SAFFORD, W. E. "Peyote, the Narcotic Mescal Button of the Indians." *Journal of the American Medical Association,* 1921, *77,* 1278–1279.

SALBER, E. J., and MACMAHON, B. "Cigarette Smoking among High School Students Related to Social Class and Parental Smoking Habits." *American Journal of Public Health,* 1961, *51,* 1780–1789.

SALBER, E. J., MACMAHON, B., and HARRISON, S. V. "Influence of Siblings on Student Smoking Patterns." *Pediatrics,* 1963, *31* (4), 569–572.

SALBER, E. J., REED, R. R., HARRISON, S. V., and GREEN, J. "Smoking Behavior, Recreational Activities, and Attitudes toward Smoking among Newton Secondary School Children." *Pediatrics,* 1963, *32* (5), 911–918.

SALBER, E. J., and ROCHMAN, J. E. "Personality Differences between Smokers and Non-Smokers." *Archives of Environmental Health,* 1964, *8,* 459–465.

SANDERS, I. *Rainbow in the Rock: The People of Rural Greece.* Cambridge: Harvard University Press, 1962.

SASSOON, J., and YELLEN, J. "Pipe Smoking, African Habit Centuries Old." Associated Press Report, Dar-es-Salaam, Tanzania, 1966.

SCHMIDT, E. F. "Anatolia through the Ages: Discoveries at the Alishar Mound 1927–29," in Publication No. 11, p. 78, of *Publications of the Oriental Institute of the University of Chicago.* Chicago: University of Chicago Press, 1931.

SCHULTES, R. E. "The Aboriginal Therapeutic Uses of *Lophophora Williamsii.*" *Cactus and Succulent Journal,* 1940, *12,* 177–181. (a)

SCHULTES, R. E. "Teonanactl: Narcotic Mushrooms of the Aztecs." *American Anthropologist,* 1940, *42,* 429–443. (b)

SCHULTES, R. E. "Botanical Sources of the New World Narcotics." *Psychedelic Review,* 1963, *1* (2), 145–166. (a)

SCHULTES, R. E. "Hallucinogenic Fungi of Mexico." *Psychedelic Review,* 1963, *1* (2), 166–176. (b)

SCHULTES, R. E. "The Botanical Origins of South American Snuffs," in Efron, D. H., Holmstedt, B., and Kline, N. S. (Eds.) *Ethnopharmacologic Search for Psychoactive Drugs.* Public Health Service Publication #1645. Washington, D.C.: U.S. Department of Health, Education, and Welfare, 1967. (a)

SCHULTES, R. E. "The Place of Ethnobotany in the Ethnopharmacologic Search for Psychomimetic Drugs," in Efron, D. H., Holmstedt, B., and Kline, N. S. (Eds.) *Ethnopharmacologic Search for Psychoactive Drugs.* Public Health Service Publication #1645. Washington, D.C.: U.S. Department of Health, Education, and Welfare, 1967. (b)

SCHUR, E. M. *Narcotic Addiction in Britain and America.* Bloomington: Indiana University Press, 1962.

SCOTT, P. D., and WILCOX, D. R. C. "Delinquency and Amphetamines." *British Journal of Psychiatry,* 1965, *3,* 865–875.

SCOTT, W. "Abstract of the Eyrbyggja-Saga: Being the Early Annals of That District of Iceland Lying Around the Promontory Called Snaefells," in Bishop Percy's translation of Mallet, M. *Northern Antiquities.* London: George Bell, 1902.

SHARMA, P. B. Personal communication, 1967.

SIGG, B. W. *Le Cannabisme chronique: Fruit du sous développement et du capitalisme.* Marrakesch, 1960; Algiers, 1963.

SILER, J. F., SHEEP, W. L., BATES, L. D., CLARK, G. F., COOK, G. W., and SMITH, W. A. S. "Marijuana Smoking in Panama." *The Military Surgeon,* 1933, *73,* 269–280.

SIMMONS, O. G. "Ambivalence and the Learning of Drinking Behavior in a Peruvian Community," in Pittman, D. J., and Snyder, C. R. (Eds.) *Society, Culture and Drinking Patterns.* New York: Wiley, 1962.

SIMPSON, G. E. "The Ras Tafari Movement in Jamaica." *Social Forces,* 1955, *34,* 167–171.

SKOLNICK, J. H. "Religious Affiliation and Drinking Behavior." *Quarterly Journal of Studies on Alcohol,* 1958, *19,* 452–470.

SKOLNICK, J. H. *Justice Without Trial: Law Enforcement in a Democratic Society.* New York: Wiley, 1966.

SLOTKIN, J. S. "Peyotism, 1521–1891." *American Anthropologist,* 1955, *57* (2), 202–230.

SLOTKIN, J. S. *The Peyote Religion.* New York: Free Press, 1956.

SMARTT, C. G. F. "Mental Adjustment in East Africa." *Journal of Mental Science,* 1956, *102* (428), 441–466.

SMITH, E. "A Negro Peyote Cult." *Journal of the Washington Academy of Science,* 1934, *24,* 448–453.

SMITH, M. G., AUGIER, R., and NETTLEFORD, R. *The Ras Tafari Movement in Kingston, Jamaica.* Kingston: University College of the West Indies, Institute of Social and Economic Research, 1960.

SMITH, W. H., and HELWIG, F. C. *Liquor, the Servant of Man.* Boston: Little, Brown, 1940.

"Smoking and the Public Interest." Mount Vernon, N.Y.: Consumer's Union, 1963. (Pamphlet.)

SMYTH, R. B. *Aborigines of Victoria.* Melbourne: Government of Australia, 1878. (Document.)

SMYTHIES, J. "A Logical and Cultural Analysis of Hallucinatory Sense Experience." *Journal of Mental Science,* 1956, *102,* 336–342.

SNYDER, C. R. "Studies of Drinking in the Jewish Culture: Culture and Sobriety." *Quarterly Journal of Studies on Alcohol,* 1955, *16,* 700–742.

SOLOMON, D. (Ed.) *LSD: The Consciousness Expanding Drug.* New York: Putnam, 1964.

SOLOMON, D. (Ed.) *The Marihuana Papers.* New York: Bobbs-Merrill, 1966.

SONNEDECKER, G. "Emergence and Concept of the Addiction Problem," in Livingston, R. B. (Ed.) *Narcotics and Drug Addiction Problems.* Proceedings of the Symposium on the History of Narcotic Drug Addiction Problems, Bethesda, Maryland, March 27 and 28, 1958. Public Health Service

Publication #1050. Washington, D.C.: U.S. Department of Health, Education, and Welfare, 1958.

SOTIROFF, S. Personal communication on narcotic drugs, 1965. (a)

SOTIROFF, S. Personal communication on cannabis use in Africa, 1965. (b)

SPELLMAN, R. Personal communication, 1967.

SPINDLER, R. "Personality and Peyotism in Menomini Indian Acculturation." *Psychiatry,* 1952, *15,* 151–159.

SPINDLER, G. *Sociocultural and Psychological Processes in Menomini Acculturation.* University of California Publications in Culture and Society, vol. 5. Berkeley: University of California Press, 1955.

SPRANGER, E. *Types of Men: The Psychology of Ethics and Personality.* New York: Steckert, 1928.

STANLEY, H. M. *Through the Dark Continent.* London: Sampson, Low, 1890.

STARKEY, M. L. *The Devil in Massachusetts.* New York: Knopf, 1950.

State of California, Bureau of Statistics. "California Field Poll." Sacramento, 1966. (Mimeograph.)

State of California, Department of Justice, Bureau of Criminal Statistics. "Drug Arrests in California—1967 Mid-Year Preliminary Survey." Sacramento, 1967. (Mimeograph.)

STELLE, C. C. "American Trade in Opium to China Prior to 1820." *Pacific Historical Review,* 1940, *9,* 425–444.

STEVENSON, G. H. "Drug Addiction in British Columbia." Vancouver: University of British Columbia, 1956. (Mimeograph.)

STEWARD, J. H. "Evolution and Process," in Kroeber, A. L. (Ed.) *Anthropology Today.* Chicago: University of Chicago Press, 1953.

STRONG, W. D. "Historical Approach in Anthropology," in Kroeber, A. L. (Ed.) *Anthropology Today.* Chicago: University of Chicago Press, 1953.

SULLIVAN, M. Personal communication, 1967.

SYLVESTER, E., and OREMLAND, J. Personal communication, 1968.

TAYLOR, B. *Library of Travel, Exploration, and Adventure: Central Asia, Travels in Cashmire, Little Tibet, and Central Asia.* New York: Scribner, 1874.

TAYLOR, N. *Narcotics: Nature's Dangerous Gifts.* Rev. ed. New York: Delta, 1963.

TAYLOR, N. "The Pleasant Assassin: The Story of Marihuana," in Solomon, D. (Ed.) *The Marihuana Papers.* New York: Bobbs-Merrill, 1966.

TE-DUC-LUAT. *Physique de l'opium.* Paris: Editions du Monde Moderne, 1925.

TERRY, C. E., and PELLENS, M. *The Opium Problem.* New York: Committee on Drug Addictions and the Bureau of Social Hygiene, 1928.

"Test May Help Smokers Quit." Associated Press report in *Palo Alto Times,* California, September 12, 1967.

TEXTOR, R. B. *A Cross-Cultural Summary.* New Haven: Human Relations Area Files Press, 1967.

THOMPSON, C. J. S. *The Mystic Mandrake.* London: Rider, 1934.

THORWALD, J. *Science and Secrets of Early Medicine.* New York: Harcourt, 1963.

UKERS, W. H. "Tea," in *Encyclopaedia Britannica,* 1965 edition.

ULLMAN, A. D. "Sociocultural Backgrounds of Alcoholism." *Annals of the American Academy of Political and Social Science,* 1958, *351,* 48–54.

ULLMANN, W. *The Individual and Society in the Middle Ages.* Baltimore: Johns Hopkins University Press, 1966.

United Nations Committee on Narcotic Drugs. *The Frequency of Addiction.* Document E/CN.7/439. New York, February 20, 1963.

United Nations Economic and Social Council. *The Question of Cannabis: Cannabis Bibliography.* Twentieth Session of the Commission on Narcotic Drugs, Geneva, September 1965. (Mimeograph.)

United States, Philippines Commission. *Report of the Committee to Investigate the Use of Opium in the Far East.* 59th Congress, 1st Session, 1905. Government Document #265. Washington, D.C.: Government Printing Office, 1905.

von MUELLER, F. "Pituri," in "Letters to the Editor," *Australian Medical Journal,* 1877 (February), 60–61.

von SNOY, P. "Darden-Nordwestpakistan-Gilgitbezirk Schamanistischer Tanz," in Wolf, G. (Ed.) *Encyclopedia Cinematographica.* Gottingen, 1960.

von WISSMAN, H., WOLF, L., FRANCOIS, C., and von MUELLER, H. *Im inneren Afrikas, Ein Erforschung des Kassai Wahrend der Jahre 1883–84 und 85.* Leipzig: Brockhaus, 1891.

WAKEFIELD, DAN (Ed.) *The Addict.* Greenwich, Conn.: Fawcett, 1964.

WALEY, A. *The Book of Songs.* London: Allen and Unwin, 1954.

WALEY, A. *The Opium War Through Chinese Eyes.* London: Allen and Unwin, 1958.

WALKER, D. E. *The Modern Smuggler.* London: Secher and Warburg, 1960.

WALSH, J. *Congress: A New Option for Addicts; A Look at LSD. Science,* 1966, *152* (3727), 1726–1729.

WALTON, R. P. *Marihuana, America's New Drug Problem.* Philadelphia: Lippincott, 1938.

WASHBURNE, C. *Primitive Drinking.* New York and New Haven: College and University Press, 1961.

WASSÉN, S. H. "The Use of Some Specific Kinds of South American Snuff and Related Paraphernalia," in *Ethnologiska Studier,* #28. Goteborg: Etnografiska Museet, 1965.

WASSÉN, S. H. "Anthropological Survey of the Use of South American Snuffs," in Efron, D. H., Holmstedt, B., and Kline, N. S. (Eds.) *Ethnopharmacologic Search for Psychoactive Drugs.* Public Health Service Publication #1645. Washington, D.C.: U.S. Department of Health, Education, and Welfare, 1967.

WASSÉN, S. H., and HOLMSTEDT, B. "The Use of Parica: An Ethnological and Pharmacological Review." *Ethnos,* 1963, *1,* 5–45.

WASSON, R. G. "Seeking the Magic Mushroom." *Life* (May 13, 1957), 100.

WASSON, R. G. "Hallucinogenic Mushrooms of Mexico." *Transactions of the New York Academy of Sciences,* 1958, *21,* 325–339.

WASSON, R. G. "The Hallucinogenic Fungi of Mexico." *Psychedelic Review,* 1963, *1* (1), 27–42.

WASSON, R. G. "Fly Agaric and Man," in Efron, D. H., Holmstedt, C., and Kline, N. S. (Eds.) *Ethnopharmacologic Search for Psychoactive Drugs.* Public Health Service Publication #1645. Washington, D.C.: U.S. Department of Health, Education, and Welfare, 1967.

WASSON, V., and WASSON, R. G. *Mushrooms, Russia, and History.* New York: Pantheon, 1957.

WAY, E. L. "Control and Treatment of Drug Addiction in Hong Kong." Paper read at Narcotics Conference, University of California at Los Angeles, 1963. (Mimeograph.)

WEAKLAND, J. Personal communication, 1968.

WELLS, F. H. "The Habits, Customs, and Ceremonies of the Aboriginals on the Diamentina," in *Report of the Fifth Meeting, Australian Association for the Advancement of Science*. Adelaide, September 1893.

WESTERMARCK, E. *The Origin and Development of the Moral Ideas*. 2nd Ed. London: Macmillan, 1912, 1917.

WHEELER, M. *Civilizaton of the Indus Valley and Beyond*. London: Thames and Hudson, 1966.

WILLEY, G. *North and Middle America*, vol. I in *An Introduction to American Archaeology*. Englewood Cliffs, N.J.: Prentice-Hall, 1966.

WILLIAMS, E. T. *China, Yesterday and Today*. New York: Crowell, 1923.

WILSON, J. A. *The Culture of Ancient Egypt*. Chicago: University of Chicago Press, 1951.

WILSON, R. C. *Drugs and Pharmacy in the Life of Georgia*. Atlanta: Foote and Davies, 1959.

WILSON, T. C. "Coffee," in *Encyclopaedia Britannica*, 1965 edition.

WINICK, C. "Maturing Out of Narcotic Addiction." *Bulletin on Narcotics*, 1962, *14* (1), 1–7.

YAMAMURO, B. "Japan," in McCarthy, R. G. (Ed.) *Drinking and Intoxication: Selected Readings in Social Attitudes and Controls*. New Haven: College and University Press, 1959.

YOUNG, T. C., Jr., and SMITH, P. E. L. "Research in the Prehistory of Central Western Iran." *Science*, 1966, *153* (3734), 386–391.

YOUNGKEN, H. W., sr. "Rauwolfia Serpentina." *The Herbarist*, 1957, *23*, 35–43.

ZEUNER, F. E. *Dating the Past*. Rev. ed. London: Methuen, 1950.

ZILBOORG, G. *The Medical Man and the Witch During the Renaissance*. Baltimore: Johns Hopkins University Press, 1935.

ZINGG, R. M. *The Huicols: Primitive Artists*. New York: Stechert, 1938.

Name Index

Subject Index